CRITICAL PEDAGOGY
in the new dark ages

Studies in the
Postmodern Theory of Education

Shirley R. Steinberg
General Editor

Vol. 422

The Counterpoints series is part of the Peter Lang Education list.
Every volume is peer reviewed and meets
the highest quality standards for content and production.

PETER LANG
New York • Washington, D.C./Baltimore • Bern
Frankfurt • Berlin • Brussels • Vienna • Oxford

CRITICAL PEDAGOGY
in the new dark ages
challenges and possibilities

EDITED BY Maria Nikolakaki

FOREWORD BY HENRY GIROUX
AFTERWORD BY ANA- MARIA FREIRE

PETER LANG
New York • Washington, D.C./Baltimore • Bern
Frankfurt • Berlin • Brussels • Vienna • Oxford

Library of Congress Cataloging-in-Publication Data

Critical pedagogy in the new dark ages:
challenges and possibilities / edited by Maria Nikolakaki.
p. cm. — (Counterpoints: studies in the postmodern theory of education; vol. 422)
Includes bibliographical references.
1. Critical pedagogy. 2. Neoliberalism.
I. Nikolakaki, Maria.
LC196.C7566   370.11′5—dc23   2011028783
ISBN 978-1-4331-1428-1 (hardcover)
ISBN 978-1-4331-1427-4 (paperback)
ISBN 978-1-4539-0147-2 (e-book)
ISSN 1058-1634

Bibliographic information published by **Die Deutsche Nationalbibliothek**.
Die Deutsche Nationalbibliothek lists this publication in the "Deutsche
Nationalbibliografie"; detailed bibliographic data is available
on the Internet at http://dnb.d-nb.de/.

The paper in this book meets the guidelines for permanence and durability
of the Committee on Production Guidelines for Book Longevity
of the Council of Library Resources.

© 2012 Peter Lang Publishing, Inc., New York
29 Broadway, 18th floor, New York, NY 10006
www.peterlang.com

Printed in the United States of America

To Paulo Freire and Joe Kincheloe,
pioneers of Critical Pedagogy,
who are no longer with us

CONTENTS

Acknowledgments

If a creation of a book can be presented as a birth of new ideas, the father of this book is Donaldo Macedo, whom I appreciate and respect enormously and to whom I am eternally grateful. The idea of this book was created through an international critical pedagogy conference that I organized in 2007 at the University of Thessaly, Greece, with the theme "democracy, education and culture." There, too, Macedo was the inspiration, and the support that we had through the whole event was beyond words. He is one of the most generous people I know.

I am deeply grateful to Henry Giroux for both his foreword and his kind words for the book and his contribution to it with his chapter. He is one of the most celebrated critical pedagogues in the world, and I deeply believe Paulo Freire would be proud of both of these continuers of his work and legacy.

Special thanks are owed to Shirley Steinberg. She is a sister and a comrade to everyone and a true critical pedagogue, combining her theory and praxis in life. I owe the final push to publish this book to her, and I am profoundly grateful.

My friend—and a role model to all humans—Nita Freire has enormously contributed to this book, and I am deeply grateful to her. Her friendship is an honor to me.

Special appreciation and deep respect are owed to Noam Chomsky. His willingness to visit Greece and support the Greek community in a time of crisis shows the extent to which his theory matches his praxis and that it is not a coincidence he is one of the greatest intellectuals of our time.

I am deeply grateful to Slavoj Žižek for his immediate response to my request that he contribute to this volume and to Zoe Castoriadis for the permission of the publication of her late husband's chapter, which has been translated.

And finally special appreciation and gratitude are owed to all the contributors of this book who have trusted me with their work. I feel the high responsiblity and honor of editing the work of the most celebrated intellectuals on education in the world.

Preface

Maria Nikolakaki

Critical pedagogy was originally influenced by the works of Paulo Freire, argu-ably the best known and celebrated critical educator. In *Pedagogy of the Op-pressed,* one of the greatest works in educational theory, Freire challenges students' ability to think critically about their education situation; this way of thinking allows them to "recognize connections between their individual problems and experiences and the social contexts in which they are embedded." This influenced many others, who as followers and creators got involved in the field that was later to be called critical pedagogy.

Although critical pedagogy has its roots in the critical theory of the Frank-furt School, as a dynamic field, it has no static definition, since the term has undergone many transformations through the last 30 years of its presence, by educators who have been exploring and using new strategies to confront changing social and historical contexts. Critical pedagogy refers to educational theory and teaching and learning practices that are aimed to raise learners' critical conscious-ness regarding oppressive social conditions. Critical pedagogy not only focuses on personal liberation through the development of critical consciousness, but has a strong political component in that critical consciousness is positioned as the nec-essary first step of a larger collective political struggle to challenge and transform oppressive social conditions and to create a more egalitarian society. For critical pedagogues, social transformation is the product of praxis at the collective level.

But critical pedagogy is more than just a theory. It is a way to be in this world. As Shor (1992) describes, critical pedagogy is:

> Habits of thought, reading, writing, and speaking which go beneath surface meaning, first impressions, dominant myths, official pronouncements, traditional clichés, received wisdom, and mere opinions, to understand the deep meaning, root causes, social context, ideology, and personal consequences of any action, event, object, process, organization, experience, text, subject matter, policy, mass media, or discourse. (p. 129)

As one can see in this book, many scholars define themselves as critical pedagogues and offer their work to be used to disrupt the effects of oppressive regimes of power both in the classroom and in the larger society. At the same time, there are scholars who are defined as critical pedagogues by others. So in this book one can see Freire, Giroux, McLaren, Macedo, Steinberg, Aronowitz, and others but also Chomsky, Žižek, Cornelius Castoriades and Howard Zinn as intellectuals who offer their thoughts to the conscientization and liberation of education and society.

This book comes as a necessary step at this stage to illuminate clouds and misconceptions that have grown recently, and to underline the importance of critical pedagogy as an educational theory at a time of withdrawal of human rights and accomplishments. Under the neoliberal attack, education is regarded as a space to be shrunk. Education is more or less surrendered to the markets and has been used to insidiously make society embrace the neotelology of "market driven society." This means that *paideia* is an enemy of the system, which will provide only restricted, system-safe knowledge and expertise incapable of seeing the larger picture, criticizing and revolting against the dehumanization in progress. This consists of one of the larger threats to society, since without critical thinking and conscientization—as Freire supports—and resistance, there would be no basis for a reversal of this situation. Markets know that; but is society fully aware of the danger?

Education has always served society's needs; now it is called to serve the markets' needs, a conglomerate of greedy, ruthless people playing "gods" on the backs of millions of people around the world who suffer. Education is the foundation stone of society, and the alteration of its basic mission from the first awakening of mankind through thousands of years of history for the first time is frightening. Critical pedagogy as the only radical sphere in education has a historical duty to play, awakening society through critical education of the people. Because, as Freire so convincingly said, education is influenced by all sectors of society, but it is the only sector that can influence all sectors of society. And educators around the world need to understand their mission under these horrifying circumstances.

Notes

1. Shor, I. (1992). *Empowering education*. University of Chicago Press.
2. It is of great importance that Donaldo Macedo has edited books with both Chomsky and Zinn on education.

Rethinking the Promise
of Critical Pedagogy

A Foreword

Henry A. Giroux

While it is very much in fashion to write or edit books on critical pedagogy, with rare exceptions, the authors of these books fail, on the one hand, to capture the historical moment that gave rise to what is now called critical pedagogy in the United States and, on the other hand, because of a lack of a thorough understanding of history, many of these authors often reduce critical pedagogy to a methodology to be implemented or, for that matter, a slavish attachment to knowledge that can only be quantified. On the contrary, critical pedagogy emerged as a contestation of the increasing imposition of the dominant narrative in society, in general, and in schools, in particular. It emerged along with critical writings in other fields by authors such as Noam Chomsky, Howard Zinn, bell hooks, Nancy Fraser, Linda Brodkey, and Stanley Aronowitz, among others. The brilliance of Maria Nikolakaki's edited volume *Critical Pedagogy in the New Dark Ages: Challenges and Possibilities* lies in her deep understanding of Paulo Freire, who believed that pedagogy was a political and performative act organized around the "instructive ambivalence of disrupted borders,"[1] a practice of bafflement, interruption, understanding, and intervention that is the result of ongoing historical, social, and economic struggles which take place in multiple spheres. Hence, Freire is central to the emergence of critical pedagogy, and his legacy informs and shapes a multitude of pedagogical interventions that link the details of everyday life and the connections the latter had to a much broader, global world. He consistently reminded us that political struggles are won and lost in those specific yet hybridized spaces that link narratives of everyday experience with the social gravity and material force of institutional power. Hence, we cannot understand critical pedagogy without the centrality and the contribution of Freire, one of the most important critical educators of the twentieth century. [2]

I first met Paulo in the early 1980s, just after I had been denied tenure by John Silber, then the notorious right-wing president of Boston University. Paulo was giving a talk at the University of Massachusetts, and he came to my house in Boston for dinner. His humility was completely at odds with his reputation, and I remember being greeted with such warmth and sincerity that I felt completely at ease with him. We talked for a long time that night—about his exile, my firing, what it meant to be a working-class intellectual, the risk one had to take to make a difference—and when the night was over a friendship was forged that lasted until his death 15 years later. I was in a very bad place after being denied tenure and had no idea what my future would hold for me. I am convinced that if it had not been for Freire and Donaldo Macedo, also a friend who became Freire's trusted translator and coauthor, I am not sure I would have stayed in the field of education. But Freire's passion for education and Macedo's friendship convinced me that education was not merely important but a crucial site of struggle.

Unlike so many intellectuals I have met in academia, Paulo was always so generous, eager to publish the work of younger intellectuals, write letters of support, and give as much as possible of himself in the service of others. The early '80s were exciting years in education in the U.S., and Paulo was at the center of it. Together we started a critical education and culture series at Bergin and Garvey that could be considered the launching pad for the development of critical pedagogy in the United States. In 1985, our series published Freire's book *The Politics of Education: Culture, Power, and Liberation,* which was translated by Macedo—a book that was considered at the time his most significant after *Pedagogy of the Oppressed.* The publication of *The Politics of Education* was followed in 1987 by *Literacies: Reading the Word and Reading the World,* coauthored with Macedo and which became one of the best-selling books published by Bergin and Garvey. In essence, Bergin and Garvey became a critical space where a second wave of critical pedagogues such as Peter McLaren, among more than 100 young authors, were published, many of whom went on to have a significant influence in the academy. Jim Bergin became Paulo's patron as his American publisher, Donaldo became his translator and a coauthor, and we all took our best shots in translating, publishing, and distributing Paulo's work, always with the hope of inviting him back to the U.S. so we could meet, talk, drink good wine, and recharge the struggles that all marked us in different ways. Of course, it is difficult to write simply about Paulo as a person because who he was and how he entered one's space and the world could never be separated from his politics. Hence, I want to try to provide a broader context for my own understanding of him as well as those ideas that consistently shaped our relationship and his relationship with others in the early years of critical pedagogy.

Occupying the often difficult space between existing politics and the as-yet-impossible, Paulo spent most of his life working with the belief that the radical elements of democracy are worth struggling for, that critical education is a basic element of social change, and that how we think about politics is inseparable from how we come to understand the world, power, and the moral life we aspire to lead. In many ways, Paulo embodied the important but often problematic relationship between the personal and the political. His own life was a testimony not only to his belief in democracy but also to the notion that one's life had to come as close as possible to modeling the social relations and experiences that spoke to a more humane and democratic future. At the same time, Paulo never moralized about politics, never employed the discourse of shame, or collapsed the political into the personal when talking about social issues. For him, private problems had to be understood in relation to larger public issues. Everything about him suggested that the first order of politics was humility, compassion, and a willingness to fight against human injustices.

Freire's belief in democracy as well as his deep and abiding faith in the ability of people to resist the weight of oppressive institutions and ideologies were forged in a spirit of struggle tempered by both the grim realities of his own imprisonment and exile, mediated by both a fierce sense of outrage and the belief that education and hope are the conditions of both agency and politics. Acutely aware that many contemporary versions of hope occupied their own corner in Disneyland, Freire fought against such appropriations and was passionate about recovering and rearticulating hope through, in his words, an "understanding of history as opportunity and not determinism."[3] Hope for Freire was a practice of witnessing, an act of moral imagination that enabled progressive educators and others to think otherwise in order to act otherwise. Hope demanded an anchoring in transformative practices, and one of the tasks of the progressive educator was to "unveil opportunities for hope, no matter what the obstacles may be."[4] Underlying Freire's politics of hope was a view of radical pedagogy that located itself on the dividing lines where the relations between domination and oppression, power and powerlessness continued to be produced and reproduced. For Freire, hope as a defining element of politics and pedagogy always meant listening to and working with the poor and other subordinate groups so that they might speak and act in order to alter dominant relations of power. Whenever we talked, he never allowed himself to become cynical. He was always full of life, taking great delight in eating a good meal, listening to music, opening himself up to new experiences, and engaging in dialogue with a passion that both embodied his own politics and confirmed the lived presence of others.

Although Freire was a theoretician of radical contextualism, he also acknowledged the importance of understanding the particular and the local in relation to larger, global and cross-national forces. For Freire, literacy as a way of reading and changing the world had to be reconceived within a broader understanding of citizenship, democracy, and justice that was global and transnational. Making the pedagogical more political in this case meant moving beyond the celebration of tribal mentalities and developing a praxis that foregrounded "power, history, memory, relational analysis, justice (not just representation), and ethics as the issues central to transnational democratic struggles."[5]

But Freire's insistence that education was about the making and changing of contexts did more than seize upon the political and pedagogic potentialities to be found across a spectrum of social sites and practices in society, which, of course, included but were not limited to the school. He also challenged the separation of culture from politics by calling attention to how diverse technologies of power work pedagogically within institutions to produce, regulate, and legitimate particular forms of knowing, belonging, feeling, and desiring. But Freire did not make the mistake of many of his contemporaries by conflating culture with the politics of recognition. Politics was more than a gesture of translation, representation, and dialogue; it was also about creating the conditions for people to govern rather than be merely governed, capable of mobilizing social movements against the oppressive economic, racial, and sexist practices put into place by colonization, global capitalism, and other oppressive structures of power.[6]

Freire left behind a corpus of work that emerged out of a lifetime of struggle and commitment. Refusing the comfort of master narratives, Freire's work was always unsettled and unsettling, restless yet engaging. Unlike so much of the politically arid and morally vacuous academic and public prose that characterizes contemporary intellectual discourse, Freire's work was consistently fuelled by a healthy moral rage over the needless oppression and suffering he witnessed throughout his life as he traveled all over the globe.

It is within this spirit of healthy moral rage coupled with hope that the authors who are included in this important edited volume give testimony to what it means to struggle for a democracy that is always threatened by a powerful military-industrial complex and the increased power of the warfare state. But Freire also recognized the pedagogical force of a corporate and militarized culture that eroded the moral and civic capacities of citizens to think beyond the common sense of official power and its legitimating ideologies. He never lost sight of Robert Hass's claim that the political job of education "is to refresh the idea of justice going dead in us all the time."[7] At a time when education has become one of the official sites of conformity, disempowerment, and uncompromising modes of punishment, the legacy of Paulo Freire's work in critical pedagogy is more important than ever before.

Notes

1. Bhabha, H. (1995). The enchantment of art. In C. Becker and A. Wiens (Eds.), *The artist in society: Rights, roles, and responsibilities* (pp. 24–34). Chicago, IL: Chicago New Art Association, New Art Examiner Press.

2. One of the best sources on the life and work of Paulo Freire is Peter Mayo, who wrote *Liberating Praxis: Freire's Legacy for Radical Education and Politics* (New York, NY: Praeger, 2004). Two of the best translators of Freire's work to the American context are Donaldo Macedo, who wrote *Literacies of Power* (Boulder, CO: Westview, 1994), and Ira Shor, who wrote *Freire for the Classroom* (Portsmouth, NH: Boynton/Cook, 1987).

3. Freire, P. (1994). *Pedagogy of hope.* New York, NY: Continuum Press.

4. Freire, P. (1994). *Pedagogy of hope.* New York, NY: Continuum Press.

5. Alexander, J. M., & Mohanty, C. T. (1997). Introduction: Genealogies, legacies, movements. In J. Alexander and C. Mohanty (Eds.), *Feminist genealogies, colonial legacies, democratic futures* (p. xix). New York, NY: Routledge.

6. Surely, Freire would have agreed wholeheartedly with Stuart Hall's insight that "It is only through the way in which we represent and imagine ourselves that we come to know how we are constituted and who we are. There is no escape from the politics of representation." Hall, S. (1992). What is this 'black' in popular culture? In G. Dent (Ed.), *Black popular culture* (pp. 30). Seattle, WA: Bay Press.

7. Pollock, S. (1992). Robert Hass. *Mother Jones, 17(2),* 22.

On Education and Neoliberalism

ONE

Critical Pedagogy in the New Dark Ages

Challenges and Possibilities: An Introduction

Maria Nikolakaki

Without consideration, without pity, without shame
They built great and high walls around me.
And now I sit here and despair.
I think of nothing else: this fate gnaws at my mind;
for I had many things to do outside.
Ah why did I not pay attention when they were
building the walls.
But I never heard any noise or sound of builders.
Imperceptibly they shut me from the outside world.

—*The Walls*, by Constantine P. Cavafy (1896)

Introduction

Although Cavafy's wall metaphor was written in 1896, it poignantly captures the paradox facing Western-style democracies under the neoliberal regime and the inglorious role played by policy makers as well as intellectuals in reproducing the type of antidemocratic practices that create a world order where "War Is Peace; Freedom Is Slavery; Ignorance Is Strength" (Orwell, 1949, p. 17). And while the fall of the Berlin Wall was celebrated with great fanfare by the Western media, other walls were being erected with the complicity of all those who conveniently preferred not to see or hear "any noise or sounds of builders." I am referring to the astutely hidden neoliberal ideology that has, in the past few decades, walled the imagination of most politicians and intellectuals in Western democracies, while "walling," restricting or even cutting off human rights along with freedom and dignity. The insidiousness of the neoliberal ideology lies in its ability, according to Paulo Freire and Donaldo Macedo, "to kill ideology ideologically" (Freire & Macedo, 2002). In other words, the fall of the Berlin Wall, we were told, not only meant an end of communism, but we were also coerced into accepting the neoliberal discourse that proclaimed the death of ideology and the death of history while falsely arguing that the problems of the world would be best solved by market forces free from cumbersome government regulations—a doctrine that according to Freire, "is [an] obfuscating fatalistic ideology contained in the neoliberal discourse. It is an ideology that seeks the demise of ideology itself and the death of history, the vanishing of utopia, the annihilation of dreams" (Freire, 2008, p. 102).

Karl Marx's leading ideas are always relevant, and his penetrating analysis of capitalism as the unceasing movement of profit-making is so evident today. It is so clear that if there is no profit to be made, there can be no capitalism and that it matters little that capitalism depends on exploitation and oppression. At the same time, the death of ideology as proposed by the discourse of neoliberalism discourages us from knowing that capitalism is the first social regime that produces an ideology according to which this very regime is "rational," fosters "prosperity," and is nonideological. In fact, it equates prosperity with economic measures, resulting in "economic rationality" (Castoriadis, 2007, p. 13)—a rationality that imprisons society by relentlessly attacking democracy. The challenge that we now face is to find ways to imagine possibilities to escape the fatalistic and restrictive force on us, while accepting that "there is [a] duty, for example, to never, under any circumstances, accept or encourage fatalist positions" (Freire, 2004, p. 37). On the contrary, we need to reject aggressively the erosion of humanity under way, which is leading to a form of subhumanity known only in the Dark Ages. Concurrent with the promotion of fatalistic views of the world is the promulgation of a "type of education for domestication, which borders on stupidification [that] provides no pedagogical spaces for students . . . [to] question the received knowledge and want to know the reasons behind the facts" (Macedo, 2006, p. 18).

The aim of this introductory chapter is to help readers unveil the neoliberal ideology characterized by "some sort of 'dark cloud' [that is] enveloping present history that currently affects the different generations" (Freire, 2004, p. 102) and that sentences billions of people to a subhuman existence. Then I will highlight the consensus that emerge in the chapters included in this volume that challenge us to think outside the box and imagine a world where substantive democracy is an everyday practice rather than a ritual periodically exercised in the voting booths. Finally, I will join hands with the contributing authors by arguing that critical pedagogy offers a language of possibility that announces our "presence in history and in the world and filled with hope . . . [and that we should] fight for the dream, for the utopia, for the hope itself, in a critical perspective. And that is not a vain struggle" (Freire, 2004, p. 102).

Neoliberalism: Society under Siege in the New Dark Ages

One can trace the emergence of a global public discourse in the early 1970s, designed to legitimize a regime change in worldwide capitalism. Under the rubric "neoliberalism," this new economic and political doctrine is based on a set of global economics developed by Milton Friedman (the University of Chicago) and Friedrich von Hayek and was proposed as an academic counterdiscourse, replacing Keynesianism with its social welfare impact in the postwar period promulgated by the capitalist order as an alternative to the perceived spread of communism and socialism. It was to become the dominant ideological force of economic and social policy under Ronald Reagan and Margaret Thatcher, and its tenets have since achieved wide consensus as the only "natural" and "rational" way of managing the new technologically, demographically, and environmentally changing world (Harvey, 2003). Neoliberalism successfully articulated neoclassical economic theories and became singularly effective, as Pierre Bourdieu (1998) argued, at "making itself true and empirically verifiable" and as a "strong discourse" dominated by the liberal individualist conception of political freedom. Noam Chomsky's chapter in this volume succinctly demonstrates that "as the doctrinal system has narrowed under the assault of private power, particularly in the past few decades, the fundamental libertarian values and principles now sound exotic and extreme, perhaps even antiAmerican, to borrow one of the terms of contemporary totalitarian thought in the West."

The central focus of the neoliberalist discourse is the deregulation and privatization of public systems (including public schools) and the dismantling of trade and tax barriers in order to maximize the global mobility of capital. Despite its efforts to legitimize itself through appeals to "progress" and "democracy," the consequence was that the rich got richer at the expense of the poor getting poorer—a process facilitated by the ruling elites in periphery countries who act as functionaries of the economic-center countries and which has led to the successful globalized poverty and social exclusion as correctly documented by Roy (cited in Macedo, 2006):

> The whole purpose [of neoliberalism and globalization] is to institutionalize inequity. Why else would it be that the United States taxes a garment made by a Bangladeshi manufacturer twenty times more than a garment made in Britain? Why else would it be that countries that grow cocoa beans, like Ivory Coast and Ghana, are taxed out of the market if they turn to (produce) chocolate? Why else would it be that countries that grow 90 percent of the world's cocoa beans produce only 5 percent of the world's chocolate? Why else would it be that rich

countries that spend over a billion dollars a day on subsidies to farmers demand
that poor countries like India withdraw all agricultural subsidies, including subsidized electricity? Why else would it be that after having been plundered by
colonizing regimes for more than half a century, former colonies are steeped in
debt to those regimes and repay them some $382 billion a year? (p. 206)

Given the neocolonialism imposed by neoliberalism, it is not surprising that 80%
of the global population remain poor, with 53 percent living on less than $2 a
day (Ronaldi, 2008, p. 37), while the countries from the "triad"—namely, North
America, Europe, and Japan—with only 12% of the global population, pocket
two-thirds of the global income. The GDP (gross domestic product) of the 41
Heavily Indebted Poor Countries (567 million people) is less than the wealth of
the world's seven richest people combined (Fotopoulos, 2008, p. 42). At the same
time, local governments are taking measures to facilitate the greed for profit of
the few at the expense of the majority. In Germany, for example, business profits
increased by 90% since 1980, while the wages of its workers increased only by
6% (Apostolopoulos, 2008, p. 49). In the same country, taxation for the workers
was doubled, whereas for the corporations it was cut to half . The combination
of deregulation and privatization of public systems, along with free international
mobility of capitals, defines the basic neoliberal cocktail, a sure recipe for stagnation and crisis.

Neoliberalism imposes a specific form of social and economic regulation
based on the prominence of finance, an international elite coalition of financial
interests (lead industrialists, traders and exporters, media barons, big landowners,
local political chieftains, the top echelons of the civil service and the military,
and their intellectual and political proxies across the world), the subordination of
the poor in every country, and universal compliance with U.S. interests, mainly
corporate banks that have received more than $1 trillion dollars in bailout money
in the current economic crisis caused by the very architects of neoliberalism. This
leads to the alliance between the U.S. ruling class and local dominant capitalist
institutions in the periphery countries, which constitute the ruling elite of the
world. The ambitious power project centered on neoliberalism in the U.S. and
the current imperial globalism abroad are implemented by social and economic
political alliances in each country involved,[1] but the interests of local finances and
the ruling elite, itself dominated by finance, are hegemonic.

The most distinctive feature of neoliberalism is the systematic use of state
power, which is used in a variety of antidemocratic policies and practices in order
to impose (financial) market imperatives in a domestic process that is replicated
internationally by "globalization"—a process that is hidden by the neoliberal public discourse that argues for less government regulation, in order to promote the
interests of the ruling elites—interests that are strongly promoted; IMFs (Inter-

national Monetary Fund), and other related multilateral institutions such as the WTO (World Trade Organization) or the OECD (Organisation for Economic Co-operation and Development) have acted as vehicles of neoliberal global capitalism. That does not mean that the "globalized" world is more than ever a world of nation states. Rather, it means it is a world of globalized states, i.e., states serving the interests of global capital rather than those of their nations, as Wood (1995, p. 208–213) claims. It is important to understand that the ruling elite is religionless, stateless, and nationless (many of the decisions made were contradictory to nation-state's interests) as well as ruthless and greedy. Siemens the electric company, for example, was charged in October 2008 with cooperating to buy out governments and opposition parties in 38 countries, in order to promote corporate interests. It goes without saying that these governments were corrupt and willing to make decisions against their own countries' interests. The local political elite serves the interests of international capital, even at the expense of its constituents, whom it should nominally serve through what the World Bank has called "macroeconomic management . . . by an insulated technocratic elite" (The World Bank Group, 2001).

Neoliberalism has been beneficial to few and detrimental to many. The insulation of economic affairs from political authority does not necessarily mean that neoliberalism wants the state to be "weak." On the contrary, it requires a strong state that can ensure the primacy of private property, preserve the dominance of markets over social control, and thus limit the operation of democratic power. The shrinking of the state at the service of the masses was mandated by the necessity to protect corporations instead. In essence, neoliberalist states guarantee "free" markets for the poor, government protection for the rich, with devastating results. The poor are at the mercy of the greed of the rich and are led to further impoverishment and ultimately to enslavement.

As I have been demonstrating, governments in states operate in ways that serve the elite's interests—not in ways that foster social justice. So they are not defined by the state serving the nation but the global elite. For example, under the privatization plan, many states have given away all their public properties—gas, water, electricity, and telecommunications, to mention just a few—to the hands of the local elite. Then the international elite takes over the local, thus leading to the concentration of global wealth to the conglomerate that plays humanity's future and prosperity in its hands. The underlying assumption that capitalists will operate competitively in order to reduce the prices has been proven to be a sham. As public space is increasingly commodified and the state becomes more closely aligned with the capital, politics are largely defined by their policing operations rather than their role as an agency for peace and social reform. At the same time, the state abandons its social investments in health, education, and public welfare.

The challenge in all of this is how to turn the resistance of society to the market's domination into the practical democratic operation of the institutions.

A New Dark Age?

Inherent in the current neoliberal doctrine is a regression in human history that is comparable with the Dark Ages, which had once characterized our historical past. As Gounari (2010) accurately captures:

> We live in dark times where the rhetoric of fear, terror, and evil has reached a new level. From apocalyptic talk, Messianic calls for salvation, and eschatological cries for the doomsday of our planet by religious ultra-right and fundamentalist Christians, to the War on Terror, the Axis of Evil, the neoconservatives of the Bush administration aided by the Christian right and a docile media have carefully crafted a reactionary capitalist neoconservative administration centered around a rising authoritarianism and militarism. (p.180)

Unfortunately, the Obama administration was not successful in changing the "lifeworld" as Habermas would say. Bosses, bureaucrats and experts are going the way of kings, priests and landlords (Stavrianos, 1976, p. 165). Under the guise of a culture of fear, in which a false dilemma is constructed—that between safety and terror—and within the turmoil of the financial crisis which has also been an excellent excuse to suffocate society, depriving it from the little rights remaining, there is a clear mark of insidious neoliberal measures, from the point of "inevitability" in this era, in which we evidenced a withdrawal of working rights and accomplishments, societal connections and individual happiness. All this is happening at a time of great technological achievements. For, as Stavrianos (1976) observed, a striking difference between the new and the old Dark Ages is the presence of technology: "The Roman empire was hobbled by technological stagnation, but the problem facing the world today is the exact opposite, how to make rational and humane use of a powerful and proliferating technology" (p. 165). At the same time, "there is a remarkable similarity between these necrophilic historical epochs: a) economic imperialism, b) ecological degradation, c) bureaucratic ossification, and d) a flight from reason" (Stavrianos, 1976, p.165). The Dark Ages were characterized by the brutality of the age. It was a time of constant warfare, despotic chiefs and minor kings, migrations of whole nations of people over many hundreds or thousands of miles, the complete eradication of whole cities of people, plagued by violence, lust, greed and barbarism. The New Dark Ages are, in turn, characterized by a ruling elite—mostly unknown to the majority—hegemonical ideologies, fundamentalisms, a steady denial of human rights and democratic working conditions (including salaries and benefits), a conservative if not reactionary aspect of culture, a miseducation or an education of ignorance, and all these conditions unfold under the guise of a determinism (a kind of superstition, so frequent in the Dark Ages) that, in turn, leads to feelings of helplessness, alienation, and surrender. It is worth mentioning that any ideology that opposes current neoliberal "sophistication" is demonized. For example, the war on terrorism includes the workers who protest for their rights, and EU has many times tried to pass legislation that would sentence communism to illegality. There should be no opposition, no alternative, no hope, just massification, passification, and surrender.

It is important that we understand the neoliberal reductionism in the equation of free markets with democracy to the extent that capitalism is predicated on the accumulation of wealth. By influencing interest rates and inflations through central banks, it can generally regulate the value of money, thus influencing the living standards of peoples around the world. Money accumulation is based on debt; this self-generating debt leads ultimately to enslavement of all forms. Capitalism typically generates crises in order to expand. When capitalism reaches a deadlock, a crisis is often constructed by the ruling economic elites, so that its further development is ensured. Many crises have occurred at various times (see, for example, the economic crisis in 1873, the Depression in 1929, and the current implosion of the world economy) and have been dealt with in ways which are by no means beneficial for the people, as the current bailout of major banks and other corporations demonstrate. According to neoliberal global capitalism propaganda, economic crises or problems are blamed on governmental intervention in the economy. Thus there is the call for less government even though the capitalist order cannot function without government subsidies, bailouts, or regulations designed to protect the business community, which is usually promoted under the banner of "economic liberty." In other words, according to capitalism's fundamental principle, the economy must be "free" from restraints in order to operate. It, therefore, views protective policies such as social programs and regulations as impediments (in fact in GATT [General Agreement on Tariffs and Trade], they were called "barriers to the free flow of trade and capital"), and so theruling elite fostered the elimination of social security programs, government housing programs, minimum wage laws, environmental protection laws, labor-protecting legislation, import taxes, price controls, and subsidies when they are applied by developing nations.

As a result, conditions for dehumanization are set in a new form of enslavement in which workers have no rights, work as much as possible (the last "deal" allows companies to occupy workers for as much as 70 hours per week) and are paid hardly a living wage (wages are dramatically declining, creating in the context of the European Union, what is called the 700–euro monthly generation; in Greece particularly it has been reduced to 590 euros). In other words, workers are increasingly more vulnerable to exploitation and oppressive working conditions as unions are being slowly destroyed. Of course, all these are imposed under the threat of unemployment (also enhanced by technological development), which indeed is not a side effect of capitalism, but a structural characteristic used to manipulate people and keep wages low. In line with the Orwellian reality ushered by the neoliberal policies, new terms are introduced, such as "flexicurity" and "employability," aimed at subverting existing laws that were the result of centuries of social struggle for the protection of the workers. Even work is a long lost and forgotten word because it is associated with the concept of rights. The term "peoples" have been replaced by "citizens," a concept promoting the individualistic approach to citizenship that undermines prior communal concepts. Another distorted term is "reform." The term ceased to be associated with land redistribution or income redistribution and is now synonymous in the neoliberal discourse with the "opening up" of the economy and the "liberation" of the market from political control or regulation which consist, in reality, in the basement bargain sale of public wealth to the ruling elite. At this juncture, the commodified language becomes both the tool and the end of neoliberal ideologies that operate so as order to "guarantee" and legitimize their aggressive and often inhumane practices (Macedo & Gounari, 2006, p. 13).

By using convenient and manipulative concepts such as of "trickle down," neoliberals have managed to convince a large segment of the world that the resulting increase in economic growth will benefit all, giving the lower classes the illusion that their interests are linked, side by side, with those of the upper classes. The social classes were led to believe that they could become richer with the growth of the economy. This delusion was ephemeral. The temporary rise of wealth among the lower and middle classes—social imaginary significations—was supported mainly by plastic money which translated into huge debts and have not only shrunk the middle class, but have doomed both the lower and middle classes to impoverishment and enslavement.

However, the enormous success of the neoliberal ideology in the current economic hegemony and the coming of these New Dark Ages could not have been achieved without a compliant media and an education that domesticates and is designed to debase democratic practices and aspirations as Macedo (2006) so convincingly argues:

> The public's role was, once, again reduced to the process of rectifying through elections, the politicians whose fates are practically controlled by the business and corporate interests. It is important to highlight that the emergence of fascist features [through the neoliberal doctrine] in American democracy [as well as other Western democracies] is taking place with the approval of the majority of citizens, albeit manipulated by the corporate media and other institutions whose interests lie with the business class and against the general public. (p. 201)

Given the antidemocratic neoliberal educational policies designed to debase democracy under the pretext of privatization, accountability, and "scientific" approaches to education, it behooves educators to embrace Henry Giroux's call for a democratic education (in this volume), not only as a countermeasure to the current assault on any and all things public, but also as a means to participate more fully in the practice of democracy.

Rethinking Democracy Beyond Ritualistic Practices

Since the principal goal of neoliberalism is to maximize the profits of private enterprise, it dedicates itself to the privatization, liberalization, or deregularization of the economy, while carrying out the so-called stabilization programs, with enhanced exploitation of the people in new forms of dehumanization. It is a regression, a rehashing of the old formula of exploitation, a "new imperialism," a global rape and pillage of human and natural resources so essential to the most primitive form of capitalism. According to Castoriadis (2007), this regression is not limited to the field of the economy. It also takes place in the field of political theory—the unquestionable character of "representative" democracy, while it is simultaneously being demoted in the conscience of the people.

Representative democracy is democracy made safe for capitalism. "Democracy" here is restricted to "free" competition among leaders for votes, participation by citizens in selecting leaders in periodic elections, and expression of views to the elected leaders between elections. The preservation of this "democratic" system can be assured by restricting mass participation to the minimum activity necessary for the functioning of the electoral machinery. This form of representative but nonparticipative democracy has been the rule in the modern world. But the fact is those who enter the political system to run for office have already been "approved" by the system, and received donations from it too. At the same time, running for office is an expensive sport, so from the beginning those who run for office are not working class. These two issues remain unexamined. Once politicians are elected, no one really knows what they are up to, while they really conform, in so many ways, to the power exemplified to them by the ruling elite—their donors or beneficiaries.

Eventually, representative "democracy" is oligarchy, i.e., as in the Aristotelian tradition, domination by the rich. In the classical Athenian meaning, democracy was the sovereignty of "demos," the people,[2] in the sense of the direct exercise of power by all citizens capable of governing and being governed. So its real meaning involves people participating in societal decisions which affect their lives; it was "government by the people," the idea that the people can collectively manage their societies. Representative "democracy" has functioned as the political complement of the system of market economy and has institutionalised a formal separation of society from polity, as the necessary complement of the separation of society from economy established by the system of market economy (Fotopoulos, 2008).

According to Castoriadis (1993, p. 211), "representation," in theory and in practice, is the alienation of power, that is, the transfer of power from the "represented" to the "representatives." Representation creates a division of the political structure, a division between the rulers and the ruled, between the leaders and the led, which is also realized through the elections in a heteronomous society (Castoriadis, 1993). Oikonomou (2005) says:

> The predominant idea today that there are political "specialists," or "specialists" of the universal and technicians of the whole, "makes a mockery of the very idea of democracy." Moreover, real power does not belong to the 300 or 400 elected members of the parliament, the so-called representatives of the public will, but to the parties and especially to the one which wins the elections and thus becomes the chief holder of power. Behind the parties are the real holders of power, huge economic interests, "inter-related" interests in the current jargon, supra-national organizations and the logic of the economic marketplace, the owners of the extremely powerful mass media and information technology. The politicians selected by the ruling elite secretly promote shadowy agendas that are against the interests of most citizens, and often openly defy the wishes of the majority, while paying lip service to being servants of the people. Democracy has been subverted by voteocracy, where the only right and freedom a citizen enjoys is the right to vote, and where the supreme power is vested in the state and exercised by the state.

As Aristotle notes, the ancient Greeks considered elections characteristic of aristocracy and oligarchy and the drawing by lot a characteristic of democracy. The politicians work with a circumscribed and neutralized notion of democracy, in which "democracy" is neither of the people, by the people, nor for the people, but rather, only in the supposed name of the people. "The moment a people gives itself representatives, it is no longer free," proclaimed Rousseau (1762) in *The Social Contract*. At the most basic level, representation demands that we give our freedom away to somebody else; it assumes, in essence, that some should have power and many others shouldn't. Without power equally distributed to all, we renounce our very capacity to join with everyone else in meaningfully shaping our society. We renounce our ability to determine ourselves, and thus to claim our liberty. Therefore, no matter how enlightened leaders may be, they are governing as tyrants nonetheless, since we—"the people"—are servile to their decisions. In a truly Orwellian twist, people have mistaken the freedom to select tyrants and become absolute slaves to the will to them for real freedom and democracy. In fact, with voting and elections, the supreme power is wrested from individuals, and invested in representatives. These representatives can then ignore the will of individuals and groups, both majority and minority, and cater for the special interest groups that they really represent. Voting and elections are a ruse to steal power from the individual, to rob democracy of any real meaning, keeping the outward form, but lacking the inner essence.

Castoriadis's answer is that the solutions which lead to "alienating political structures"—in other words to "representations,"—must be rejected. We must seek out solutions that

> give the best possible power to communities whose dimensions permit direct self-government or solutions which maximize the participation of citizens in decisions and their control over what happens in the units, whose dimensions (or on subjects whose nature) does not permit direct self-government.

As Zinn and Macedo argue (in this book), "The one thing that you were social-ized in was to believe in the importance of elections and to pour all of your civic energy into elections."

What we are witnessing is the breakdown in the social contract, upon which parliamentary democracy by universal suffrage was based, and that contract now needs to be renegotiated on a basis that shares power much more widely. As Stavri-anos (1976) explains:

> The functioning of the Western democracies and the reactions of their citizens indicate that the source of political malaise is not too much democracy but too little. The need is not to restrict mass participation, as some argue, but rather to facilitate it and broaden its scope

Polanyi (1957) pointed out that the domination or

> control of the economic system by the markets is of overwhelming consequence to the whole organization of society: it means no less than the running of society as an adjunct to the market. Instead of economy being embedded in social rela-tions, social relations are embedded in the economic system. (p.14–15)

The separation of the economic sphere from the political sphere in capitalist soci-ety has far-reaching implications. According to Wood (1995):

> For one thing, it has made possible the legal equality of all citizens regardless of race, gender, class or other social characteristics. This formal levelling individu-alizes citizens and detaches citizenship from any social or communal identity. That is what is "democratic" about it. But at the same time, it also disempowers citizens from any real control over their economic fate and the ability of capital to appropriate surplus value from their labor as workers. In this way, democracy is limited via the separation of the political and economic spheres. Capitalism, then, made it possible to conceive of "formal democracy," a form of civic equal-ity which could coexist with social inequality and leave economic relations . . . in place. (p. 208)

In other words, neoliberalism presents itself as an economic doctrine that professes free markets, deregulation, and freedom from government restrictions and trade controls, disguised under a positivistic economist discourse of "naturalness" and "inevitability." At the same time it neglects to talk about the effects of this economic theory on real people or the social costs of implementing such an economic order" (Gounari, 2006).

Neoliberalism has transformed our lives since society is transformed in the image of the market and the state itself is now "marketized." Citizens are regarded as consumers. It follows that neoliberals privilege the market mechanisms, as the most "efficient" and "rational" tool to construct human agency, by promoting individualism, and by assuming social and political determination. As Polanyi (1957, p.14–15) has persuasively shown, the establishment of the market economy implied sweeping aside traditional cultures and values and replacing the values of solidarity, altruism, sharing and cooperation (which usually marked community life) with the values of individualism and competition as the dominant values. New modes of subjectivity and citizenship are forged through a social mandate to provide for one's survival solely through individual "choice," leading to, according to Habermas (1986), an "instrumentalism of existence" (p. 31). As a result, people are brought together in competition rather than in cooperation in finding a living. The prevailing motto derived from neoliberal global capitalism is consume, compete, and win at any cost.

All the major communication institutions of a modern society—including the media and education, facilitate the replacement of democratic values by market values. As Beder (2008) writes, "the market values of competition, salesmanship and deception have replaced the democratic ideals of truth and justice," and

> the conflict between democratic values and corporate values is even more evident at a personal level, given that in the new global culture—where people are rewarded for their greed—increasingly there is little room for the expression of higher human values and qualities such as generosity, compassion, selflessness, willingness to seek out and expose the truth, courage to fight for justice.

Furthermore, Stoppard (personal communication, Oct. 26, 2008) illustrates that society within a capitalist context tends to corrupt the best instincts of people. Instead the lower instincts prevail, leading to a subhumanity of the mankind.

Very useful for this analysis is Castoriadis's conception of heteronomous and autonomous societies (see in the following chapter). Since the establishment of the market economy about 200 years ago, the world has been transformed from autonomous communities into heteronomous world markets, that is, from self-determining societies to societies where all the decisions that refer to it are taken from centers outside of it. As a consequence, we have oppression, manipulation, exploitation and human misery. According to Castoriadis (2003), there cannot be an autonomous individual without an autonomous society:

> . . .in the contemporary West, the free, sovereign, autarchic, substantial "individual" is hardly anything more, in the great majority of cases, than a marionette spasmodically performing the gestures the social-historical field imposes upon it: that is to say, making money, consuming, and "enjoying" (if that happens to occur). Supposedly "free" to give to his life the meaning [*sens*] he "wants," in the overwhelming majority of cases this individual gives to his life only that "meaning: that has currency, that is to say, the non-sense of indefinite increases in the level of consumption. (p. 80)

This individual's "autonomy" is in reality heteronomy again, since s/he succumbs to a generalized conformism. In other words, there can be no individual "autonomy" without collective autonomy, and no individual "creation of meaning" outside of the framework of a collective creation of significations.

The growing realization of global contradictions raises up local initiatives setting out the process of change. An inclusive democracy would result from dialectic between institutional and human change. According to Fotopoulos, under these circumstances

> the problem for emancipatory politics today is how all the social groups which potentially form the basis of a new liberatory subject would be united by a common worldview, a common paradigm, which sees the ultimate cause of the present multidimensional crisis in the existing structures that secure the concentration of power at all levels, as well as the corresponding value systems.

Largely relying on Karl Polanyi, Fotopoulos stresses that the reintegration of society with the economy is a necessity if an autonomous society is to be built. Any talk about democracy, which does not also refer to the question of economic power, is "hollow." According to Fotopoulos (2008), "To talk about the equal sharing of political power, without conditioning it on the equal sharing of economic power, is at best meaningless and at worse deceptive" (p. 206). And as he supports, "in the last instance, it is *paideia* that may effectively condition democratic practice." (Fotopoulos, 2008, p. 196).

A new inclusive education will intend to shape new citizens in a democratic society. As Zinn and Macedo show in this book, a miseducation has been always a device for conformity. "Those who are the victims of the educational system are considered to be disposable bodies, which were never supposed to be educated in the first place." This has to be stopped. There are no simple solutions. Hence it becomes crucial for educators at all levels of schooling to provide alternative democratic conceptions of the meaning and purpose of both politics and education.

In what follows, I want to argue that one of the primary tasks facing educators, students, community activists, and others in the 21st century should center around developing political projects that can challenge the ascendancy of cynicism and antidemocratic tendencies in the United States (and not only) by defending the institutions and mechanisms that provide the pedagogical conditions for critical and engaged citizenship.

Critical Pedagogy as Democratic Practice in the New Dark Ages

The neoliberal agenda has had profound implications on education, and childhood in general, across the world. Statistics are very revealing about the consequences of the neoliberal agenda in education: Nearly a billion people entered the 21st century unable to read a book or sign their names. Less than 1% of what the world spent every year on weapons would have been enough to put every child through school by the year 2000, and yet this never happened. One billion children live in poverty (1 in 2 children in the world). Six hundred forty million live without proper shelter, 400 million have no access to safe water, 270 million have no access to health services. In 2003, 10.6 million died before they reached the age of five (or roughly 29,000 children per day). The fact is that the available wealth of humanity, if properly distributed, could be used to eliminate poverty and suffering all around the world. The questions that have to be asked then are: How can people turn their backs to this reality? How can anyone feel like a proper human being, when all these terrible things are happening in various corners of this planet? Momentary sympathy, of course, is not enough. At the turn of the 21st century, in a time of unprecedented crisis as described above, where dehumanization has set in on a regression and where successes achieved through centuries of social struggle have been rolled back, where we are experiencing a New Dark Age for humanity, critical pedagogy, as one of the few radical transformative pedagogies, has a historic role to play. As Darder and Mirón (2006) remark:

> It is in this "new" time of national uncertainty, along with the everyday uncertainties of old, that we look for critical pedagogy to provide us with direction and inspiration to struggle against the growing inequalities and difficulties that our children are facing in schools and society. (p. 7)

This is the time to break the culture of silence, to demystify the social imaginary significations; it is the time to promote humanization again. As Steinberg (2007) claims, "Critical pedagogy has the right to be angry, and to express anger, anger at the uses of power and at injustices through the violations of human rights."

Education under the Neoliberal Regime

Under neoliberalism education faces a dual trauma. On the one hand, there is a continuation and intensification of teaching as indoctrination, in order for future citizens to have no critical consciousness and to passively accept the neoliberal dogma. The teaching of indifferent, useless and out-of-context knowledge has been used as a means to this end. On the other hand, education in neoliberalism has been given over to marketization, with devastating consequences.

As Castoriadis (1988, p.19) describes, the student is considered a passive vessel to which the teacher pours in a certain amount of knowledge. The student is considered a simple executor in a process whose aim is the student him/herself as a fixed product of a certain type and quality of education. In all this procedure s/he has no initiative—s/he just has to learn what s/he is told and that is that. This training or miseducation will continue to exist if teachers, as John Dewey (1954) had already described, continue to teach (and preach)

> certain collections of fixed, immutable subject matter that they were taught which they in turn transmit to students under them. The educational regime thus consists of authorities at the upper end handing down to the receivers at the lower end what they must accept. This is not education but indoctrination, propaganda. It is a type of "education" fit for the foundations of a totalitarian society and, for the same reasons, fit to subvert, pervert and destroy the foundations of a democratic society.

Paulo Freire (1970) described this as the "banking concept," and according to that, "it is the people themselves who are filed away through the lack of creativity, transformation and knowledge in this (at best) misguided system. For, if disassociated from inquiry, from the praxis, individuals cannot be truly human" (p. 53). Freire (1970) insightfully describes that "implicit in the banking concept is the assumption of a dichotomy between human beings and the world: a person is merely *in* the world, not *with* the world or with others; the individual is a spectator, not re-creator" (p. 56).

Castoriadis (1988) remarks that:

> If someone really thinks about it, away from his superstitions, school is a monstrous institution. The child goes into an artificial world for X hours, immobilized at a desk, amongst four walls, forced to learn things which are, for the most part, strange, useless, and indifferent. S/he is forced to be passive against someone who stuffs him/her with knowledge. S/he suffers a complete separation of his/her physical and mental development, a fragmentation in which the curriculum inserts some ridiculous beautifying aspects, like 1 hour of gymnastics or 1 hour of art, etc. The result is that when s/he leaves school s/he is a disabled person, who shouldn't—if the educational system had had its way—have either body or mind. If s/he has still a body or mind it is because of his/her resistance to the system. (my own translation) (p.35)

The values of education have been eroded during the last 30 years. Under this neoliberal dominance, schooling takes the form of miseducation, an apaideia; it becomes a domain for the promotion of ignorance. The student in this school has to be filled with useless knowledge and must be mentally and psychologically amputated. S/he must be rendered unable for critical analysis and for linking knowledge with his/her own reality, personal or political. In a world of blurred and shifting boundaries under the neoliberal regime, the purpose of education has certainly shifted from that of a public good to a commodity, while meanings of education have become reconstituted, as have the roles of educators and students. As Castoriadis (2003) explains and is worth quoting at length:

> Not so very long ago, school was, for parents, a venerated place, for children an almost complete universe, for teachers more or less a vocation. At present, it is for teachers and pupils an instrumental form of forced labor, a site for present or future bread-winning (or an incomprehensible and rejected form of coercion), and, for parents, a source of anxiety: "Will my child get into the right schools [*l'enfant, sera-t-il ou non admis à la filière menant au Bac C*]" . . . It is only apparently a paradox. Economic value having become the only value, educational overconsumption and anxiety on the part of the parents of all social categories concerning the scholarly success of their children are uniquely related to the piece of paper their children will or will not obtain. This factor has become ever weightierthese past few years. For, with the rise in unemployment, this piece of paper no longer automatically opens up the possibility of a job; the anxiety is redoubled, for now the child must obtain a good piece of paper. School is the place where one obtains (or does not obtain) this piece of paper; it is simply instrumental—it no longer is the place that is supposed to make the child a human being. Thirty years ago, in Greece, the traditional expression was: "I am sending you to school so that you may become a human being—*anthropos*." (p. 34)

On the other hand, educational institutions have become a principal target of marketization agendas that have sought to discursively reconstitute and redefine the nature of education by transforming it from a collective public good into an individualistic commodity that can be bought and sold in the marketplace. Education, as an ideological state apparatus, insidiously works to ensure the perpetuation of the dominant ideology by immersing students in ideologically determined practices like measuring student learning and the quality of teaching by percentage improvement of test scores and standardized tests. Then funding of education is based on this measurement. This fact ignores a basic thesis of sociology of education: that the social background of students reflects competence. As Macedo so repetitively argues, when a student goes hungry to school, it is impossible to learn. So instead of working on the source of their underperformance, schools under the neoliberal regime are to be punished. One thing is sure: This will contribute even more to increasing inequalities of education, leading the poor to become poorer and more ignorant and the rich richer.

Markets have gradually taken over education as a commodity. Many governments, under pressure from the International Monetary Fund (IMF) and the World Bank to cut government funding, have imposed fees for public schooling—a de facto privatization. In the U.S., neoliberalism has taken a variety of forms in education; perhaps the most important of these being the running of formally public school systems by private, for-profit companies. In order for schools to be taken over by the market, standardized testing has been used:

> While ensuring accountability through standardized testing may seem somewhat paradoxical—since education is meant to extend far beyond standardized test scores and graduation rates—this craze with standardized testing not only promotes teaching to the test, but has also become a vehicle to restrict educational opportunities from those who need those opportunities the most. (Makris, 2009, p. 2).

Contrary to these recent changes, societies have long designed school systems to meet a broad set of social needs—including the creation of social equality, social cohesion, common values and language. When schooling is privatized and education becomes a commodity, these broader social needs take second place before the need of the private-school operators to make a profit and the decisions of individuals who are buying an education to meet their particular needs. As education becomes a commodity, the nature of this "product" gets transformed. As Kincheloe writes (in this book), "In this milieu, students are transformed from citizens into consumers, capable of being bought and sold." Democratic control over what goes on in the schools is harshly curtailed, if not eliminated entirely.

Schools increasingly resemble prisons, and policing is the only pedagogy the system is able to apply. Since there is no more intention of creating jobs, security, or a viable future of any kind, as Giroux (2004) supports, the system insidiously promotes the limitation of personal creativity and freedom, while it attempts to create a culture of fear to ensure that the Youth will not resist the dominant ideology in its various manifestations. The system's ultimate goal is to subordinate the Youth, which, left to their own devices, will perform actions, the implications of which the system definitely wants to avoid. In other words, they want to kill the soul of the Youth before it becomes expressive or offensive. At the same time, since the Youth is no longer a social "investment" and it has lost its established cultural position, schooling is restricted to utilizing mainly policing facilities, which is hard for society to swallow. Giroux (2004) notes this: "As despairing as these conditions appear at the present moment, they increasingly have become a basis for a surge of political resistance on the part of many Youth, intellectuals, labor unions, educators and social movements" (p. 103).

Marcuse (1989), a major figure in the Frankfurt school, so insightfully points out, "No qualitative social change, no socialism, is possible without the emergence of a new rationality and sensibility in the individuals themselves: no radical social change without a radical change of the individual agents of change." As for the radicalization of individual agents, education is a site for struggle. According to Freire (2004), "If education alone cannot transform society, without it society cannot change either" (p. 47). The final crucial issue refers to what Castoriadis called "the riddle of politics," i.e., how within a heteronomous society and a heteronomous education we may create autonomous institutions and the infrastructure of *paideia*.

This is where critical pedagogy seems to be a necessary component of awareness, resistance, and social struggle. Critical pedagogy is about how to be in the world with the world, and as Macedo (2007) so correctly remarks, it is a "never-ending process that involves struggle and pain, but also hope and joy maintained by a humanizing pedagogy." Critical pedagogy, according to Giroux(1994), signals how questions of audience, voice, power, and evaluation actively work to construct particular relations between teachers and students, institutions and society, and classrooms and communities. Pedagogy in the critical sense illuminates the relationship between knowledge, authority, and power (Giroux, 1994, p. 30). It is at this place where critical pedagogy becomes an important vehicle for social resistance and social transformation.

Critical Pedagogy as Democratic Practice

Since education is the ideological apparatus of the state, according to Althusser (1994), the aim of education is explicit: It is the construction of the desired citizen. Under neoliberalism, this person has become a passive citizen who accepts the neoliberal agenda. It is for teachers to change that. Critical pedagogy as a social theory necessitates that the teacher has taken a stand and has recognized his/her ideological basis. It means that whatever and however they teach (as Aronowitz supports in this book, critical pedagogy is not about method), they connect knowledge to the social and political agenda and instill democratic values to their students in an effort to make them agents of social change.

According to Castoriadis(2003), the goal of emancipation is individual and social autonomy. In order to achieve an autonomous society, an autonomous activity of collectivities is required. At the individual level, a democratic ethos needs to be cultivated. Commenting on the crisis of democracy, Castoriadis(2003) says:

> Democracy is possible only where there is a democratic *ethos*: responsibility, shame, frankness (*parressia*), checking up on one another, and an acute awareness of the fact that the public stakes are also personal stakes for each one of us. And without such an ethos, there can no longer be a "Republic of Letters," but only pseudotruths *administered* by the State, by the clergy (whether monotheistic or not), or by the media. (p. 6)

What is needed then is a critical pedagogy in the classroom cultivating the democratic ethos of the student and creating the conditions for a citizen, through conscientization, to struggle for a just world. In such an emancipating pedagogy, egocentrism, narcissist certainties, and the constant accumulation of experiences are put into question. Instead, communitarian values are to be developed. According to Aristotle in *Nicomachean Ethics* (1.2.1094b7–10), a life guided by moral virtue is a political life. He maintains that the good person and the good citizen are one, at least in the ideal state. To be a good person is simply to use one's faculties well, and political activity constitutes a way in which one can exercise one's faculties well. Hence, to perform one's tasks as a citizen is to exercise one's faculties for the sake of the community that one shares in (Harper, 1995, p. 81). Aristotle claims that the good of the community is nobler and more divine than the good of any individual; to secure and preserve the former is greater and more complete than the latter. Since the good person is someone who leads a good life, and since one who works with other citizens improves his own life too, the good person should be a good citizen. On the other hand, not only is the good citizen a good person, but it is through acts incumbent upon citizens that they can realize their human potential. In an ideal state, personal and civic interest, private and public interest converge. In other words, the individual cannot be happy alone, but only within a community, and the community cannot prosper without its citizens' contribution.

Educating the active, critical citizen to participate in the *polis* is considered by critical pedagogy as an essential means for the emancipation of society. In Castoriadis's words:

> Only the education (paideia) of the citizens as citizens can give valuable, substantive content to the "public space." This paideia is not primarily a matter of books and academic credits. First and foremost, it involves becoming conscious that the polis is also oneself and that its fate also depends upon one's mind, behaviour, and decisions; in other words, it is participation in political life.

According to Freire (2004), "Dealing with the city—the polis—is not simply a technical matter; it is above all a political one" (p. 17). The polis is an area for political action. Also, as an expression of individual autonomy, it secures more than human survival. Politics makes possible man's development as a creature capable of genuine autonomy, freedom, and excellence, according to ancient Greek practice. Education as a means of cultivating the democratic ethos for a genuine democracy to be realized needs to open up pedagogical spaces, where interaction between the educators and the students promotes this self-realization and self-institution of society.

Critical pedagogy contributes to a democratic ethos for the benefit of both the individual and the collective. Critical pedagogy is about acquiring both knowledge and the ability to maximize individual *and* social autonomy, as a means of individual *and* social liberation.

This democratic ethos is cultivated in a sense of freedom. Freedom cannot be taken for granted; it is something that needs to be taught. Aristotle claims that freedom is not a means; it is a coordinated end. According to Freire (2004):

> Freedom is not a gift given, but is rather earned by those who enrich themselves through the struggle for it. That is true to the extent that there can be no life without at least a minimal presence of freedom. Even though life in itself implies freedom, that does not mean in any way that we can give it gratuitously. (p. 120)

Giroux (2004) argues, "Democracy necessitates forms of education that provide a new ethic of freedom and a reassertion of collective identity as central preoccupations of a vibrant democratic culture and society" (p. 53). This necessitates commitment to the democratic project with passion. Democracy is impossible without a democratic passion, a passion for the freedom of each and of all, a passion for common affairs, which become, as a matter of fact, the personal affairs of each individual. Freedom facilitates the understanding of human conditionality and the potential of humankind to shake off any kind of oppression and exploitation. Freedom, personal initiatives, and resistance to any form of compliance and to any form of power should be an integral part of the educational process.

However, using Reason to teach freedom is a paradox, as "Reason itself presupposes freedom—autonomy. Reason is not a mechanical device or a system of ready-made truths; it is the movement of a thought that doesn't recognize any authority other than its own activity" (Castoriadis, 2003, p. 292). The sense of freedom necessitates Reason because excessive freedom can lead to selfishness, hedonism, and egoism, that is, people who love and strive for their own freedom but ignore the freedom of others. This neoliberal egoistic notion of freedom that equates freedom with personal interests has been successfully cultivated by capitalism through competition and individualism.

In a state of freedom, autonomy is cultivated. Autonomy according to Castoriadis is not hedonic fulfillment of desires: doing whatever one wants, whenever one wants. The word is a combination of Greek words *auto* (self) and *nomos* (law). So there is a law, but the question is who lays down the law (p.158). Critical pedagogy aids the subject in becoming as autonomous as possible in a collective autonomy. As Freire (2004) commented, "It is necessary for the child to learn that his/her own autonomy can only attain legitimacy if it respects the autonomy of others" (p. 38).

Freedom and autonomy have to be based on the cultivation of *nous* and embedded in a communitarian context—to use Castoriadis's (2003) words, "in a collective identity—of a whole with which one might, in key respects, identify, in which one participates and about which one might bear some concern, and for whose fate one feels oneself responsible" (p. 98).

According to Castoriadis (1988), for the self-institution of society, *nous* as critical thinking and praxis as critical outcome, are required. This distinction resembles Freire's concept of conscientization. As Freire (1970) stressed, conscientization focuses on achieving an in-depth understanding of the world, allowing for the perception and exposure of social and political contradictions. This conscientization, as *nous*, is an inner-self-procedure and cannot be indoctrinated. Conscientization also includes praxis, taking action against the oppressive elements in one's life that are illuminated by that understanding. So we see that this conscientization has two dimensions: conscientization as *nous*, which has to do with the realization of circumstances and praxis, which has to do with forms of resistance.

This freedom and autonomy (through the creation of a democratic ethos) is essential for conscientization as *nous*. Conscientization within a democratic ethos is about an agent who wants to belong to a community based on equality (regardless of race, age, sex, culture, class, disability, sex orientation), feeling responsibility for the injustices of this world. This responsibility feeling is not a state; it is a procedure. This "responsibilization" grows with conscientization and makes us feel that we are an organic part of what is going on around us, that we are equally liable for the injustices being done in this world as they evolve, unless we speak up and strive for their elimination. It is clear that "responsibilization" based on autonomy does not mean imposing one's value system upon others, but implementing dialogue and maintaining empathy, an attitude of openness in order to understand others, while always respecting them. It dictates justice as each individual contributes to the community, according to each one's capabilities and needs. Personal freedom in society is inextricably and dialectically linked with personal responsibility. The existence of either is dependent on the existence of the other. However, responsibility needs to be seen in a context of community feeling, since it is essential not only for the defense against neoliberal global capitalism, but mainly for humanization, according to Freire (2004). He says, "If I lack responsibility, I cannot speak of ethics or of hope" (Freire, 2004, p. 99). Feeling responsible for social exclusions is an inextricable feature of human dignity. "Responsibilization" in this form becomes an essential component of social prosperity, and it is a prerequisite for unity and mutual support. Responsibility, though, is not to be founded on guilt. Guilt immobilizes the individual, neutralizes every tendency for freedom, and overshadows and numbs human feelings.

Conscientization as praxis means acting with solidarity, where the collectivity by no means consists of homogenized and identical masses. Solidarity can become an enriching experience. It makes sense when its definition takes into account the needs of *all* the exploited and oppressed. It must be based not only on unity in struggle but also on learning from other people about the forms of oppression and exploitation that they face. Capitalism has destroyed previous forms of community and solidarity. Castoriadis (2003) says this: "The only value in liberal-capitalist societies is money, media notoriety, or power in the most vulgar, most derisory sense of the term. Here, community is destroyed. Solidarity is reduced to a few administrative measures" (p. 78).

Responsibilization, as a procedure of conscientization, concludes to solidarity, to a communal feeling, connecting to society and working towards a common goal, which is defined by society and not the markets. This is where responsibilization connects conscientization as *nous* with conscientization as praxis. Conscientization as praxis is a revolutionary action. When Castoriadis was asked if he was a revolutionary, he replied, "Revolution does not mean torrents of blood, the taking of the Winter Palace, and so on. Revolution means a radical transformation of society's institutions. In this sense, I certainly am a revolutionary(1988) ." This is where critical pedagogy comes along as an essential emancipatory device for social self-institution (auto-thesmisis, to use Castoriadis's term). Challenging neoliberal hegemony as a form of domination is crucial to reclaiming an alternative notion of the political and rearticulating the relationship between political agency and substantive democracy (Giroux, 2004, p. 53).

Critical Pedagogy as Pedagogical Practice

Critical pedagogy as Aronowitz argues in this book remains the only emancipatory vision of a democratic, libertarian future we have. Aronowitz points out that the term Freire employed to summarize his approach to education, "pedagogy," is often interpreted as a "teaching" method rather than a philosophy or a social theory. As Aronowitz points out:

> Sometimes it merely connotes that teachers try to be "interactive" with students; sometimes it signifies an attempt to structure classtime as, in part, a dialogue between the teacher and students; some even mean to "empower" students by permitting them to talk in class without being ritualistically corrected as to the accuracy of their information, their grammar, or their formal mode of presentation—or to be punished for dissenting knowledge. All of these are commendable practices, but they hardly require Freire as a cover. (p. 254)

Pedagogy is not about the how of teaching; it is about the why. It forms the foundation of teaching, and it constitutes a basis for answering difficult questions or dilemmas of education: Why am I teaching? What is my scope or aim? How is knowledge selected? What are the consequences of my actions? Who benefits from this kind of education? Who gets left out? Am I really helping my students become adults who will be responsible and agents in society? Will society improve if my students grow up to be the citizens the system wants them to be? And the list of crucial questions could go on and on. . . . Pedagogy certainly has implications on teaching. One's teaching approach is inextricably linked to one's pedagogical ideas. The "why" influences the "how." As Pykett (2009) describes:

> Teaching may be considered a direct relationship between student and teacher whereas pedagogy is a prescribed mode of address, which places some critical distance (both temporally and spatially) between teacher and the person taught. Teaching is what happens in schools, but pedagogy involves thinking about teaching, strategizing, discriminating for/against the particular demands of specific students, and consideration of the interplay between a teacher's intentions, the social conditions in which students and teachers interact and the desired outcomes of each actor within the pedagogic event. Hence pedagogy produces novel subjects and is active in constituting actors, but there is some deferral in producing its powerful effects. (p. 102)

At the same time, the teacher is not the same as the pedagogue. A pedagogue may not teach in the classical sense in classes, and a teacher may not be a pedagogue in a true meaning but merely a technocrat who performs on demand. For John Dewey, pedagogy is "that reconstruction or reorganization of experience which adds to the meaning of experience, and which increases ability to direct the course of subsequent experience" (Pykett, 2009, p. 102). In this way, pedagogy is concerned with developing students' capacities and competences, rather than limiting their access to critical consciousness.

This does not mean that critical pedagogues do not teach the curriculum. But there is the need to take advantage of the educational system and its pedagogical spaces, enlarge them, and work on the critical conscious. In order to do so, as Bartolomé (1998) writes in this book, we need to deny in our pedagogy the false dichotomy between context-bound and decontextualized discourse. Overall, as Freire (1995) stated:

> Educators who are mesmerized by the neoliberal pragmatic discourse are not educating in the full sense of the word. When these educators accept the notion that what is important is the acquisition of facts without the educational background to critically analyze these facts, they produce a type of training that reduces students to narrow technical professionals. It is worth saying that an educational practice devoid of dreams, dissent, and pronouncements is neutral and accommodating. On the other hand, we should stress something, which is also true. That is, the fact that an educational practice reduced to simple dissent and pronouncements and the inspiration of dreams, which minimizes the technical preparation of students for the world of work, is not worth much.

It is important to convince the hesitant teachers who understand that education is a political site but need to see an alternative solution, which also yields positive results. For as Apple (2009) said:

By showing successful struggles to build a critical and democratic education in real schools and real communities with real teachers and students today, attention is refocused on action not only in charter schools but on local elementary, middle, and secondary schools in communities much like those in which most of us spend our lives. Thus, publicizing such 'stories' makes critical education seem actually 'doable,' not merely a utopian vision dreamed up by 'critical theorists' in education. (p. 98)

This is where critical pedagogy as an ideological and social site has to be recognized as such by educators. In other words, neoliberalism, with its sharp contradictions leading to the elimination of human rights and the possibility of social prosperity, has made it inevitable for educators to take a stand. The time of innocence is over. Despite the fact that there is an attempt to "kill ideology ideologically" as Macedo and Freire (in press) so insightfully claim, neoliberalism has made things clearer, since the problems that humanity is facing are sharper and more acute than ever. Teachers have to understand the full picture that there is no apolitical pedagogy. If they define themselves as "neutral," then what they are really doing is taking a stand with the neoliberal ideas, and they must understand the consequences and therefore take their share of responsibility in the condition of this world. But if they are discontented with the emerging polarities and increasing inequalities, the breaking of the social canvas and the continuing suffering of the majority of humankind in order for the ruling elite to prosper, then critical pedagogy becomes one of a limited number of solutions. As Althusser (1994) so rightly illustrates:

I feel for those teachers who in horrible conditions try to go against the dominant ideology, against the system and its practices, where they have been trapped, with their scarce armory that they find their place in history and the knowledge they "teach." They are heroes. But they are rare, whilst how many are there (the majority) who are totally unsuspecting of the kind of "work" the system makes them do (which overpasses them and crushes them) or worse, do their best to do their "duty" (with the so-called new methods). They are so sure about what they are doing, that they contribute, with their devotion, to the maintenance and the ideological conservatism of education, that wants to present today's school as "natural," useful, necessary, even beneficial. (p. 95).

Critical pedagogy attempts to disrupt the effects of oppressive regimes of power both in the classroom and in the society at large. The classroom is a site where new knowledge, grounded in the experiences of students and teachers alike, is produced through meaningful dialogue. As Trifonas and Balomenos comment in this book:

The summative goal of critical pedagogy is to empower students with the ability to think and act reflectively as individual subjects of a society or a culture who have formed a conscious self-awareness of the meanings of their multiple affiliations and the significance of their worldly transactions with the other. (p. 223)

The shift of the locus of the learning process from the teacher to the student means that critical pedagogy signifies an altered power relationship, not only in the classroom but in the broader social canvas as well. This purpose is inextricably linked to the fulfillment of what Freire (1970) defined as our "vocation"—to be truly humanized social agents in the world.

Critical pedagogy in these New Dark Ages also needs to be connected with hope for change and resistance. Teachers must recognize how schools unite knowledge and power and how through this function they can work to influence or thwart the formation of critically thinking and socially active individuals (Darder & Mirón, 2006). Teachers, who have connected education with the political, have hope that, through their actions, change can occur since they have come to be aware of their role as historical agents. This hope battles and wins over pessimism, hopelessness, surrender. For as Freire (2001) writes, "I am not angry with people who think pessimistically. But I am sad because for me they have lost their place in history" (p. 26).

Through linking teaching to the political, critical pedagogy aims to create individuals who will fight to eliminate injustices in this world. As Darder writes in this book, "Given this approach, any classroom situation can potentially be converted into a critical environment as educators discover the multitude of pedagogical possibilities in their disposal." Critical pedagogy is about cultivating the critical consciousness and empowering the creation of the citizen as social agent. And as Freire (2001) so endlessly stresses, critical pedagogy is about respect, love, and hope and not another mold-making process.

Epilogue

Paulo Freire (1970) started his magnum opus, *Pedagogy of the Oppressed,* by commenting that, "While the problem of humanization has always, from an axiological point of view, been humankind's central problem, it now takes on the character of an inescapable concern."

Since then, things have turned from bad to worse, and neoliberalism is the driving force behind that. Neoliberalism has been wreaking havoc in education. For one, it has promoted a pathological sense of a citizen as a consumer rather than as historical agent. Neoliberalism has made the true face of global capitalism so obvious and so ugly. It is clear now that we are trapped in walls, to use Cavafy's metaphor, and that something radical has to be done. Teachers are now confronted with an inevitable choice: Which stand do they take? Are they with the victimizers or the victims? Do they choose to support the vulnerable, the excluded, and those who suffer, or do they insist in performing an act, which is not apolitical but has deep social consequences and deepens social injustices? As Darder and Mirón (2006) suggest:

> There is no question that we are living in a time when we must stretch the boundaries of critical educational principles to infuse social and institutional contexts with its revolutionary potential. It is a moment when our *emancipatory theories must be put into action,* in our efforts to counter the hegemonic fear-mongering configurations of a national rhetoric that would render teachers, students, parents, and communities voiceless and devoid of social agency. Hence, critical pedagogical ideas and practices in the interest of democratic schooling must be central to our efforts to confront the powerlessness and uncertainty that is so much the reality in many public schools today. (p. 7)

Critical pedagogy comes to bring hope to these New Dark Ages, since it is revolutionary and reintroduces the potential for struggles to promote social justice. So, as despairing as the conditions created by neoliberalism can be, they are also a basis for hope. And hope is needed in education, especially for the teachers. Hope is based on a human-centric worldview. It behooves us to imagine that humanity deserves better than this; that humanity can make it work right. As Castoriadis said (1988), societies are self-instituted. The difficult thing is for this idea to be conscientized. Besides, along with dark ages comes renaissance, hope for a better condition for humanity.

Hope can be further cultivated when teachers have proof that critical pedagogy has not only a liberating impact but also profound educational outcomes. Teachers need encouragement toward their decision to take a stand, to fight for ideology. And good examples of combining critical pedagogy with teaching are very much needed. As Apple (2009) adds, "In the absence of this, we are left standing on the sidelines while the right reconstructs not only common sense but the schools that help produce it" (p. 99). We can always learn from everyday lives in schools, in society, and in nature and improve our practice. Overall, building and defending a truly democratic and critical education is a collective project. We have much to learn from each other.

Notions of pedagogy, teaching, didactics, methodology, education, culture and power apparently overlap. Critical pedagogy is about pedagogy and cannot be enshrined in teaching methods. That by no means demonstrates that it is not connected to teaching. How we teach is obviously determined by our pedagogical theory. Freire (2001) said, "The educator with a democratic vision or posture cannot avoid insisting on the critical capacity, curiosity and autonomy of the learner in his teaching praxis" (p. 33). First of all we have to look closer at the pedagogy inscribed in the classroom for the cultivation of a democratic ethos within each individual student. We must think of ways to pedagogically contribute to the creation of a human being who is autonomous, more humane, author of his/her decisions, dignified, with social solidarity, responsibility, and a sense of freedom that negates every dehumanizing practice. This means that critical pedagogy promotes a teaching culture that will foster the development of a young generation with a democratic ethos, which will inevitably negate the capitalist system. To nourish and practice a democratic ethos is to deal primarily with the inner self, in the belief that the social expression of this self as praxis will follow accordingly. An essential step to take toward building a democratic ethos is to instigate in students a desire for freedom and a rejection of oppression as values. We must also link, rigorously and with perseverance, our labor within schools, universities, and communities to actual conditions and events, with the clear purpose and intent of transforming these conditions collectively in very concrete and meaningful ways. A critical pedagogy in the classroom also necessitates that practice employed confirm an agenda, according to which people and nature coexist harmonically.

In this context critical pedagogy in the New Dark Ages must promote the sense of freedom, an inner sense that radicalizes and revolutionizes interpersonal and group relations, an inner revolution, which will express itself outwardly and will transform the existing structures, relations, and modes of communication. In essence, the democratic ethos is the starting point of a reflective praxis. This democratic ethos evolves into conscientization, which in turn becomes responsibilization with hope, culminating in solidarity,love, dignity, and mutual support through praxis, inevitably reinforcing the same democratic ethos. It is time for critical pedagogy to assist students in developing the capabilities to further their involvement in the process, in a search for a more just world.

Notes

1. European "socialism" rapidly conformed to the rules of neoliberalism, consisting a "social neo-liberalism."
2. Although, of course, Athenian democracy was partial because of the narrow definition of citizenship, which excluded women and allowed the existence of slaves.

Bibliography

Althusser, L. (1994). *Ideology and ideological mechanisms. Σύγχρονη Σκέψη, 5*, 69–95.
Apostolopoulos, A. (2008). Poverty, charity and NGOs. *Diaplous, August-September,* p. 49.
Apple, M. (2009). Some ideas on interrupting the right: On doing critical educational work in conservative times. *Education, Citizenship and Social Justice, 4*, 87.
Aristotle. (1964). *Politics* (W. D. Ross, Trans.). Oxford, England: Clarendon Press.
Bartolomé, L. (1998). *The misteaching of academic discourses: The politics of language in the classroom.* Boulder, CO: Westview Press.
Beder, S. (2008). The corporate assault on democracy. *The International Journal of Inclusive Democracy, 4*(1). Retrieved: http://www.inclusivedemocracy.org/journal/vol4/vol4_no1_beder.htm
Bourdieu, P. (1998). The essence of neoliberalism. *Le Monde,* . Retrieved from http://www.analitica.com/Bitblio/bourdieu/neoliberalism.asp

Castoriadis, C. (1988). *The revolutionary problem today.* Athens, Greece: Ypsilon.

Castoriadis, C. (2005). *Figures of the thinkable.* Retrieved from http://www.costis.org/x/castoriadis/Castoriadis-Figures_of_the_Thinkable.pdf

Castoriadis, C. (2003). *The rising tide of insignificancy.* Retrieved from http://www.notbored.org/RTI.pdf.

Castoriadis, C. (2007). *The rationality of capitalism.* Retrieved from http://indy.gr/library/kornlios-kastoriadis-i-orthologikotita-toy-kapitalismoy/kastoriadis-i-orthologikotita-toy-kapitalismoy.

Darder, A., & Mirón, L. F. (2006). Critical pedagogy in a time of uncertainty: A call to action. *Cultural Studies- Critical Methodologies, 6*(1), PP: 5–20., .

Dewey, J. (1954). *The public and its problems.* Chicago, IL: The Swallow Press Inc.

Fotopoulos, T. (2008a). The globalization of poverty. *Diaplous,* August –September . Also retrieved from: http://www.inclusivedemocracy.org/fotopoulos/greek/grvarious/diaplous_aug_08.htm

Fotopoulos, T. (2008b). Values, the dominant social paradigm and neoliberal globalisation. *The International Journal of Inclusive Democracy, 4*(1). Retrieved from http://www.inclusivedemocracy.org/journal/vol4/vol4_no1_takis_values.htm

Freire, P. (1970). *Pedagogy of the oppressed.* London, England: Penguin.

Freire, P. (1985). *Politics of education: Culture, power and liberation.* Westport, CT: Bergin & Garvey Publishers.

Freire, P. (1995). *Letters to Christina: Reflections on my life and work.* New York, NY: Routledge.

Freire, P. (2001). *Pedagogy of freedom.* Lanham, MD: Rowman and Littlefield Publishers.

Freire, P. (2004). *Pedagogy of indignation.* Boulder, CO: Paradigm.

Freire, P., & Macedo, D. (2002). *Ideology matters.* Lanham, MD: Rowman & Littlefield Publishers.

Giroux, H. (1994) *Disturbing pleasures: Learning popular culture.* New York, NY: Routledge.

Giroux, H. (2004). *The terror of neoliberalism-authoritarianism and the eclipse of democracy.* Boulder, CO: Paradigm.

Giroux, H., & Giroux, S. (2008). Beyond bailouts: On the politics of education after neoliberalism. Retrieved from http://www.truthout.org/123108A

Giroux, H., & McLaren, P. (1994). *Between borders: Pedagogy and the politics of cultural studies.* New York, NY: Routledge.

Gounari, P. (2006). Contesting the cynicism of neoliberal discourse: Moving towards a language of possibility. *Studies in Language and Capitalism, 1,* 77–96.

Gounari, P. (2010) Manufacturing fear: The violence of anti-politics. In J. Schostak & J. Schostak (Eds.), *Researching violence, democracy and the rights of people* (pp. 180–195). London, England: Routledge.

Habermas, J. (1986). *Autonomy and solidarity.* Athens, Greece: Ypsilon.

Harper, E. C. (1995). Virtue and the state. In K. I. Boudouris (Ed.), *Aristotelian political philosophy* (pp. 79–90). Athens, Greece: Boudouris.

Harvey, D. (2003). *The newimperialism.* Oxford University Press.

Macedo, D., & Gounari, P. (Eds.). (2006). *Globalization of racism.* Boulder, CO: Paradigm.

Macedo, D. (2006). *Literacies of power: What Americans are not allowed to know.* Boulder, CO: Westview Press.

Macedo, D. (2007). In P. McLaren & J. Kincheloe (Eds.), *Critical pedagogy: Where are we now?* New York, NY: Peter Lang.

MacEwan, A. (2005). Neoliberalism and democracy: Market power versus democratic power. In A. Saad-Filho & D. Johnston (Eds.), *Neoliberalism: A critical reader.* London, England: Pluto Press.

Makris, V. (2009). The dominance of neoliberal ideology in public schooling and possibilities for reconstructing the common good in education. Unpublished Master's thesis. University of Alberta, Edmonton, Canada.

Marcuse, H. (1989). *Counterrevolution and revolt.* Boston, MA: Beacon Press.

McLaren, P., & Kincheloe, J. (Eds.). (2007). *Critical pedagogy: Where are we now?* New York, NY: Peter Lang.

Oikonomou, Y. (2005). Plato and Castoriadis: The concealment and the unravelling of democracy. *The International Journal of Inclusive Democracy, 2*(1).

Orwell, G. (1949). *1984*. New York, NY: Harcourt, Brace and Company.

Polanyi, K. (1957). *The great transformation*. Boston, MA: Beacon Press.

Pykett, J. (2009). Pedagogical power: Lessons from school spaces. *Education, Citizenship and Social Justice, 4*(2), 102–116.

Ronaldi, R. (2008). The movements against poverty. *Diaplous*, August-September

Rousseau, J. (1762). *The social contract*. Amsterdam, TNT: Chez M. M. Rey.

Stavrianos, L. (1976). *The promise of the coming dark age*. San Francisco, CA: Freeman.

Steinberg, S. (2007). Preface. In P. McLaren & J. Kincheloe (Eds.), *Critical pedagogy: Where are we now?* New York, NY: Peter Lang.

Trifonas, P., & Balomenos, E. (2003). *Good taste: How what you choose defines who you are*. Cambridge, England: Icon.

The World Bank Group. (2001). *Administrative and civil service reform*. Retrieved from http://www1.worldbank.org/publicsector/civilservice/center.htm

Wood, E. M. (1995). *Democracy against capitalism*. Cambridge University Press.

Two

Living in the Time of Monsters

Slavoj Žižek

In China, so they say, if you really hate someone, the curse you address him with is: "May you live in interesting times!" In our history, "interesting times" are effectively the times of unrest, war, and power struggle with millions of innocent bystanders suffering the consequences. Today, we are clearly approaching a new epoch of interesting times. After decades of the (promise of) Welfare State, when financial cuts were limited to short periods and sustained by a promise that things will soon return to normal, we are entering a new period in which the crisis is permanent. This crisis—or, rather, a kind of economic state of emergency—with the need for all sorts of austerity measures (cutting benefits, diminishing free health and education services, making jobs more and more temporary, etc.) is turning into a constant, becoming simply a way of life.

What does this mean for today's Left? In psychoanalytic treatment, one learns to clarify what one desires: Do I really want what I think I want? Take the proverbial case of a husband engaged in a passionate extramarital affair, dreaming all the time about the moment when his wife will disappear (die, divorce him, or whatever), so that he will then be able to fully live with his mistress. When this finally happens, all his world breaks down, and he discovers that he also doesn't want his mistress. As the old proverb says, there is one thing worse than not getting what one wants—to really get it. Leftist academics are now approaching such a moment of truth: You wanted real change; now you can have it! Back in 1937, in *The Road to Wigan Pier*, George Orwell perfectly characterized this attitude when he pointed out "the important fact that every revolutionary opinion draws part of its strength from a secret conviction that nothing can be changed." Radicals invoke the need for revolutionary change as a kind of superstitious token that will achieve its opposite, *prevent* the change from really occurring. If a revolution is taking place, it should occur at a safe distance: Cuba, Nicaragua, Venezuela . . . so that, while my heart is warm when I think about the events far away, I can go on promoting my academic career.

This new situation in no way demands that we abandon the patient intellectual work with no immediate "practical use." Today, more than ever, one should bear in mind that communism begins with what Kant called the "public use of reason," with thinking, with the egalitarian universality of thought. When Paul says that, from a Christian standpoint, "there are no men and women, no Jews and Greeks," he thereby claims that ethnic roots, national identity, etc., are *not a category of truth*. Or, to put it in precise Kantian terms, when we reflect upon our ethnic roots, we engage in a *private use of reason*, constrained by contingent dogmatic presuppositions, i.e., we act as "immature" individuals, not as free human beings who dwell in the dimension of the universality of reason. For Kant, the public space of the "world-civil-society" designates the paradox of the universal singularity, of a singular subject who, in a kind of short-circuit, bypassing the mediation of the particular, directly participates in the Universal. In this view, "private" is not the stuff of our individuality as opposed to communal ties, but the very communal-institutional order of our particular identification.

Our struggle should thus focus on those aspects that pose a threat to the trans-national public space. In the European Union, the ongoing Bologna reform of higher education is one big concerted attack on the "public use of reason." The underlying idea of this reform—the urge to subordinate higher education to the needs of society, to make it useful toward finding solutions for concrete problems we are facing—aims at producing expert opinions meant to answer problems posed by social agents. However, what disappears here is the true task of thinking: not only to offer solutions to problems posed by "society" (state and capital), but to reflect on the very form of these "problems," to reformulate them, to discern a problem in the very way we perceive a problem. The reduction of higher education to the task of producing socially useful expert knowledge is the paradigmatic form of the "private use of reason" in today's global capitalism.

It is crucial to link the ongoing push towards *Gleichschaltung* of higher education—not only in the guise of direct privatization or links with business, but also in the more general sense of orienting education towards its "social use" (the production of expert knowledge which will help to solve problems)—to the process of enclosing the commons of intellectual products, of privatizing the general intellect. This process has set in motion a global transformation in the hegemonic mode of ideological interpellation. The capitalist modernity imposed the twin hegemony of legal ideology and education (state school system): Subjects were interpellated as patriotic free citizens, subjects of the legal order, while individuals were formed into legal subjects through the compulsory universal education. The gap was thus maintained between bourgeois and citizen, between the egotist-utilitarian individual concerned with his private interests and the citizen dedicated to the universal domain of the state. And insofar as, in the spontaneous ideological perception, ideology is limited to the universal sphere of citizenship, while the private sphere of egotist interests is considered "preideological," the very gap between ideology and nonideology is thus transposed into ideology. What happens in the latest stage of the post-68 "postmodern" capitalism is that *economy itself (the logic of market and competition) is progressively imposing itself as the hegemonic ideology.*

In education, we are witnessing the gradual dismantling of the classical bourgeois school ISA. The school system is less and less the compulsory network elevated above market and organized directly by state, bearer of enlightened values (*liberté, égalité, fraternité*); on behalf of the sacred formula of "lower costs, higher efficiency," it is progressively penetrated by different forms of PPP (public-private partnership).

In the organization and legitimization of power, the electoral system is more and more conceived on the model of market competition: Elections are like a commercial exchange in which the voters "buy" the option that offers to do the job of maintaining social order, prosecuting crime, etc., in the most efficient way. On behalf of the same formula of "lower costs, higher efficiency," even some functions which should be the exclusive domain of the state power (like running prisons) can be privatized; the army is no longer based on universal conscription, but composed of hired mercenaries, etc.

Even the process of engaging in emotional relations is more and more organized along the lines of a market relationship. Alain Badiou deployed the parallel between today's search for a sexual (or marital) partner through appropriate dating agencies and the ancient procedure of marriages prearranged by parents. In both cases, the proper risk of "falling in love" is suspended; there is no contingent "fall" proper. The risk of the real "love encounter" is minimized by preceding arrangements which take into account all material and psychological interests of the concerned parties. This is the reason why marital agencies are an antilove device par excellence: Their wager is that they will organize love as an actual free choice—upon reviewing the list of selected candidates, I choose the most appropriate one.

And, quite logically, insofar as economy is considered the sphere of nonideology, this brave new world of global commodification considers itself postideological. The Ideological State Apparatuses are, of course, still here, more than ever. However, as we have already seen, insofar as, in its self-perception, ideology is instilled in subjects in contrast to preideological individuals, this hegemony of the economic sphere cannot but appear as the absence of ideology. What this means is not that ideology simply directly reflects economy as its actual base. We fully remain within the sphere of ISA. Economy functions here as an ideological model, so that we are completely justified to say that economy is here operative as an ISA—in contrast to the "real" economic life which definitely does not follow the idealized liberal market model.

This full naturalization (or self-erasure) of ideology imposes a sad but unavoidable conclusion with regard to today's global social dynamic. Today, it is capitalism, which is properly revolutionary; it changed our entire landscape in the last decades, from technology to ideology, while conservatives as well as social democrats were mostly reacting to these changes, desperately trying to maintain old gains. In such a constellation, the very idea of a radical social transformation may appear as an impossible dream. However, the term "impossible" should make us stop and think. Today, impossible and possible are distributed in a strange way, both simultaneously exploding into an excess. On the one hand, in the domains of personal freedoms and scientific technology, the impossible is more and more possible (or so we are told). "Nothing is impossible." We can enjoy sex in all its perverse versions; entire archives of music, films, and TV series are available for downloading; going to space is available to everyone (with money). There is the prospect of enhancing our physical and psychic abilities, of manipulating our basic properties through interventions into genome, up to the tech-gnostic dream of achieving immortality by fully transforming our identity into a software which can be downloaded from one hardware to another. . . . On the other hand, especially in the domain of socioeconomic relations, our era perceives itself as the era of maturity in which, with the collapse of Communist states, humanity has abandoned the old millenarian utopian dreams and accepted the constraints of reality (read: the capitalist socioeconomic reality) with all its impossibilities. *You cannot* engage in large collective acts (which necessarily end in totalitarian terror), cling to the old Welfare State (it makes you noncompetitive and leads to economic crisis), isolate yourself from the global market, etc. (In its ideological version, ecology also adds its own list of impossibilities, so-called threshold values—i.e., no global warming in excess of 2° C, etc.—based on "expert opinions.") The reason is that we live in the postpolitical era of naturalization of economy: Political decisions are as a rule presented as matters of pure economic necessity—when austerity measures are imposed, we are repeatedly told that this is simply what has to be done. So perhaps the time has come to rearrange our possibilities: Something is wrong with the world where it is possible to become immortal but impossible to spend a little bit more for education.

The problem here is deeper than it may appear: One of the key features of today's capitalism is *the privatization of (what Marx called) the "general intellect" itself*. This is what is at the core of the struggle for "intellectual property." Within this frame, exploitation in the classic Marxist sense is no longer possible, which is why it has to be enforced more and more by direct legal measures, i.e., by a noneconomic force. This is why, more and more, direct authority is needed: It is needed to impose the (arbitrary) legal conditions for extracting rent, conditions which are no longer "spontaneously" generated by the market. Perhaps, therein resides the fundamental "contradiction" of today's "postmodern" capitalism: While its logic is deregulatory, "antistatal," nomadic, deterritorializing, etc., its key tendency of the "becoming-rent-of-the-profit" signals the strengthening role of the state, whose (not only) regulatory function is increasingly all-present. Dynamic deterritorialization coexists with and relies more and more on authoritarian interventions of the state and its legal and other apparatuses. What one can discern at the horizon of our historical becoming is thus a society in which personal libertarianism and hedonism coexist with (and are sustained by) a complex web of regulatory state mechanisms. Far from disappearing, the state is strengthening today.

To put it in a slightly different way, today's capitalism generates situations in which fast large-scale interventions are needed, but the problem is that parliamentary-democratic institutional frames do not allow such quick radical interventions. Sudden financial crises, ecological catastrophes, large-scale reorientations of economy, etc.—they all call for a body with full authority to react quickly with appropriate countermeasures, bypassing the niceties of long democratic negotiations. Recall the financial meltdown in the fall of 2008: The panic was absolute, a transnational and nonpartisan unity was immediately established, and world leaders momentarily forgot all grudges in order to avert *the* catastrophe. What the much-praised "bipartisanship" in the U.S. effectively meant is that democracy was *de facto* suspended: There was no time to engage in proper democratic procedures. Those who opposed the plan in the U.S. Congress were quickly made to march with the majority. Bush, McCain, and Obama all quickly got together and explained to the confused masses that there was no time for prolonged democratic debates—we are in a state of emergency; things simply must be done quickly. No wonder authoritarian regimes like the one in China are more efficient than Western democracies.

Is the fact that Communists in power today are the most dynamic capitalists not the ultimate sign of the triumph of capitalism? Another sign of this triumph is the very fact that the ruling ideology can afford what appears to be ruthless self-critique. There is no lack of anticapitalism today. We are even witnessing an overload of the critique of capitalism's horrors: Books, in-depth newspaper investigations, and TV reports abound with stories about companies ruthlessly polluting our environment, corrupted bankers continuing to get fat bonuses while their banks must be saved by public money, and sweatshops working children overtime, etc. There is, however, a catch to all this overflow of critique: What is as a rule not questioned in this critique, ruthless as it may appear, is the democratic-liberal frame of fighting against these excesses. The (explicit or implied) goal is to democratize capitalism, to extend the democratic control onto economy through the pressure of the public media, parliamentary inquiries, harsher laws, honest police investigations, etc.—but never questioning the democratic institutional frame of the (bourgeois) state of law. This remains the sacred cow that even the most radical forms of this "ethical anticapitalism" (the Porto Allegre forum, the Seattle movement) do not dare touch.

It is here that Marx's key insight remains valid, today perhaps more than ever. For Marx, the question of freedom should not be located primarily in the political sphere proper (does a country have free elections? Are the judges independent? Is the press free from hidden pressures? Are human rights respected? And other similar questions different "independent"—and not so independent—Western institutions apply when they want to pronounce a judgment on a country). The key to actual freedom rather resides in the "apolitical" network of social relations, from the market to the family, in which the change needed if we want an actual improvement is not a political reform but a change in "apolitical" social relations of production—*which means* revolutionary class struggle, not democratic elections or other political measures in the narrow sense of the term. We do not vote about who owns what, about relations in a factory, etc. All this is left to processes outside the political sphere, and it is illusory to expect that one can effectively change things by "extending" democracy into this sphere, say, by organizing "democratic" banks under the people's control. Radical changes in this domain should be made outside the sphere of legal "rights." In such "democratic" procedures (which, of course, can play a positive role), no matter how radical our anticapitalism is, the solution is sought in applying the democratic mechanisms which, one should never forget, are part of the state apparatuses of the "bourgeois" state that guarantee undisturbed functioning of the capitalist reproduction. Closely linked to this need to de-fetishize democracy is the need to de-fetishize its negative counterpart, violence. Badiou recently proposed the formula of "defensive violence": One should renounce violence (i.e., the violent taking over of state power) as the principal *modus operandi* and rather focus on building free domains at a distance of state power, subtracted from its reign (like the early Solidarity in Poland) and only resort to violence when the state itself uses violence to crush and subdue these "liberated zones." The problem with this formula is that it relies on the deeply problematic distinction between the "normal" functioning of the state apparatuses and the "excessive" exercise of state violence. One cannot separate violence from the very existence of market and state. In his intervention at the 2010 Left Forum in London, John Holloway, just returning from Greece, mentioned an example of practicing communism in a park in Athens, which was taken over by demonstrators and proclaimed a liberated zone, with protestors at its entrances announcing, "No entry to capitalism!" No commercialization was allowed inside. People just freely gathered, danced, debated. Capitalists would have no doubt celebrated such islands as zones of relaxation which made workers fitter when they had to return to their jobs. We should thus critically analyze this space of the subtraction from state power where Badiou meets Holloway. It is easy to say that, in view of the catastrophic results of the 20th-century Communist movement focused on taking state power, we should abandon violence, limiting it to the protection of the free spaces of subtraction. However, one should also take into account how those who exert the state monopoly on violence always love those who claim that problems are "deeper" than those who hold power, since they pose no threat to their hold on power.

So where are we today? Badiou wonderfully characterized the postsocialist situation as "this troubled situation, in which we see Evil dancing on the ruins of Evil." There is no question of any nostalgia. The Communist regimes were "evil." The problem is that what replaced them is also "evil," albeit in a different way. If, in these conditions, the Communist project is to be renewed as a true alternative to global capitalism, we should start from the beginning again, enacting a clear break from the 20th-century Communist experience. One should also bear in mind that 1990 was not only the defeat of the Communist State-Socialism, but also the defeat of the Western Social Democracy. This is why it is totally erroneous to put the hopes on strong, fully sovereign nation-states (which can defend the acquisitions of the Welfare State) against transnational bodies like the European Union which, so the story goes, serve as the instruments of the global capital to dismantle whatever remained of the Welfare State. From here, it is only a short step to accept the "strategic alliance" with the nationalist Right worried about the dilution of national identity in transnational Europe.

Walls that are now arising all around the world are not of the same nature as the Berlin Wall, the icon of the Cold War. Today's walls appear not to belong to the same notion, since even the same wall often serves multiple functions: defense from terrorism, illegal immigrants, and smuggling; a cover for colonial land grabbing; etc. However, in spite of this appearance of multiplicity, Wendy Brown is right to insist that we are dealing with the same phenomenon (although its examples are usually not perceived as cases of the same notion). Today's walls are a reaction to the threat to nation-state sovereignty posed by the ongoing processes of globalization:

> Rather than resurgent expressions of nation-state sovereignty, the new walls are icons of its erosion. While they may appear as hyperbolic tokens of such sovereignty, like all hyperbole, they reveal a tremulousness, vulnerability, dubiousness, or instability at the core of what they aim to express—qualities that are themselves antithetical to sovereignty and thus elements of its undoing.

What cannot but strike us is the theatrical, and rather inefficient, nature of these walls: Basically, they consist of old-fashioned material (concrete and metal) fences, a weirdly medieval countermeasure to the immaterial forces that effectively threaten national sovereignty today (digital and commercial mobility, modern weapons). Brown is also right to add organized religion to global economy as the principal trans-statal agency which poses a threat to state sovereignty. One can argue that, for example, China, in spite of its recent opening to religion as an instrument of social stability, opposes so ferociously some religions (Tibetan Buddhism, the Falun Gong movement) precisely insofar as it perceives them to be a threat to national sovereignty and unity (Buddhism yes, but under the Chinese state control; Catholicism yes, but the bishops nominated by the Pope should be screened by Chinese authorities).

On October 17 2010, Angela Merkel wrote, "This multicultural approach, saying that we simply live side by side and live happily with each other, has failed. Utterly failed." The least one can say is that she was consistent, echoing the debate about *Leitkultur* (the dominant culture) from a couple of years ago, when conservatives insisted that every state is based on a predominant cultural space which the members of other cultures who live in the same space should respect. Instead of playing the Beautiful Soul bemoaning the newly emerging racist Europe such statements suggest, we should turn the critical eye upon ourselves, asking to what extent our own abstract multiculturalism contributed to this sad state of things. If all sides do not share or respect the same civility, then multiculturalism turns into legally regulated mutual ignorance or hatred. The conflict about multiculturalism already *is* a conflict about *Leitkultur*: It is not a conflict between cultures, but a conflict between different visions of how different cultures can and should coexist, about the rules and practices these cultures have to share if they are to coexist. One should thus avoid getting caught into the liberal game of "how much tolerance can we afford the Other"—should we tolerate if they beat their women? if they pre-arrange marriages of their children? if they brutalize gays among their ranks? etc. At this level, of course, we are never tolerant enough, or we always are—already too tolerant, neglecting the rights of women, etc. The only way to break out of this deadlock is to propose and fight for a positive universal project shared by all participants. This is why a crucial task of those who fight for emancipation today is to move beyond mere respect for others to a positive emancipatory *Leitkultur,* which can only sustain authentic coexistence and immixing of different cultures, and accept the forthcoming battle for *Leitkultur.*

In Western and Eastern Europe, there are signs of a long-term rearrangement of the political space. Until recently, the political space was dominated by two main parties, which addressed the entire electoral body, a Right-of-center party (Christian-Democrat, liberal-conservative, populist's. . .) and a Left-of-center party (socialist, social-democratic), with smaller parties addressing a narrow electorate (ecologists, liberals, etc.). Now, there is one party progressively emerging. It stands for global capitalism, usually with relative tolerance toward abortion, gay rights, religious and ethnic minorities, etc. Opposing this party is a stronger and more intensely anti-immigrant populist party, which, on its fringes, is accompanied by directly racist neo-Fascist groups. The exemplary case here is Poland: After the disappearance of the ex-Communists, the main parties are the "antiideological" centrist liberal party of the prime minister Donald Dusk and the conservative Christian party of the Kaczynski brothers. Berlusconi in Italy is proof that even this ultimate opposition is not insurmountable: The same party, his *Forza Italia*, can integrate both global capitalism and populist anti-immigrant tendencies. In the de-politicized sphere of postideological administration, the only way to mobilize people is to awaken fear (of immigrants, i.e., of the *neighbor*).

Is the Tea Party movement in the U.S. not its own version of this Rightist populism that is gradually emerging as the only true opposition to the liberal consensus? The Tea Party movement has, of course, some features specific to the U.S., which allows us to safely predict that its rise will be strictly correlated with the further decline of the U.S. as a world power. More interesting is the conflict between the GOP establishment and the Tea Party, which is already exploding here and there. Heads of the big banks have already met leaders of the GOP who promised to repeal the Volcker rule, which limits the speculations that led to the 2008 meltdown. The Tea Party set as its first task to extend the Bush tax cuts for the very rich, thus adding hundreds of billions of dollars to the deficit it wants to abolish. In the middle of April 2009, I was sitting in a hotel room in Syracuse, jumping between two channels: a documentary on Pete Seeger, the great American folk singer of the Left, and a Fox News report on the antitax "tea party" in Austin, Texas, with a country singer performing an anti-Obama populist song full of complaints about how Washington is taxing hard-working ordinary people to finance the rich Wall Street moneymakers. The short-circuit between the two programs had an electrifying effect on me, with two especially noticeable features. First, there was the weird similarity between the two singers, both formulating an antiestablishment populist complaint against the exploitative rich and their state, calling for radical measures, up to civil disobedience—another painful reminder that, with regard to the form or organization, today's radical-populist Right strangely resembles the old radical-populist Left. (Are today's Christian survivalist-fundamentalist groups, with their half-illegal status and their view of the oppressive state apparatus as the main threat to their freedom, not organized like the Black Panthers back in the 1960s?) How long will this masterful ideological manipulation continue to work? How long will the Tea Party stick to the fundamental irrationality of its agenda to protect the interests of the hard-working ordinary people by way of privileging the "exploitative rich," thus literally countering its own interests? It is here that the ideological struggle begins: The blatant irrationality of the Tea Party protests bears witness to the power of the ideology of the "freedom of the individual against state interference," which can blur even the most elementary facts.

One often hears that the true message of the Greek crisis is that not only the euro, but the project of the united Europe itself, is dead. But before endorsing this general statement, one should add a Leninist twist to it: Europe is dead, okay, but *which* Europe? The answer is the postpolitical Europe of accommodation to the world market, the Europe which was repeatedly rejected at referendums, the Brussels technocratic-expert Europe. The Europe which presents itself as standing for the cold European reason against Greek passion and corruption, for mathematics against pathetics. But, utopian as it may appear, the space is still open for another Europe, a repoliticized Europe, a Europe founded on a shared emancipatory project, a Europe that gave birth to ancient Greek democracy, to French and October revolutions. This is why one should avoid the temptation to react to the ongoing financial crisis with a retreat to fully sovereign nation-states, easy prey of the freely floating international capital which can play one state against the other. More than ever, the reply to every crisis should be even *more* internationalist and universalist than the universality of global capital. The idea of resisting global capital on behalf of the defense of particular ethnic identities is more suicidal than ever, with the specter of the North Korean *juche* idea lurking behind.

In his intervention at the 2010 Marxism Today conference in London, Alex Callinicos evoked his dream of a future communist society in which there will be museums of capitalism, displaying to the public artifacts of this irrational and inhuman social formation. The unintended irony of this dream is that today, the only museums of this kind are the museums of Communism, displaying its horrors. So, again, what to do in such a situation? Two years before his death, when it became clear that there would be no all-European revolution and that the idea of building socialism in one country was nonsense, Lenin wrote,

> What if the complete hopelessness of the situation, by stimulating the efforts of the workers and peasants tenfold, offered us the opportunity to create the fundamental requisites of civilization in a different way from that of the West European countries?

Is this not the predicament of the Morales government in Bolivia, of the Aristide government in Haiti, of the Maoist government in Nepal? They came to power through "fair" democratic elections, not through insurrection, but once in power, they exerted it in a way that is (partially, at least) "nonstatal": directly mobilizing their grassroots supporters and bypassing the party-state representative network. Their situation is "objectively" hopeless: The whole drift of history is basically against them, they cannot rely on any "objective tendencies" pushing in their way, and all they can do is to improvise, do what they can in a desperate situation. Nonetheless, does this not give them a unique freedom? And are we—today's Left—not all in exactly the same situation? One is tempted to apply here the old distinction between "freedom from" and "freedom for": Does their freedom *from* history (with its laws and objective tendencies) not sustain their freedom *for* creative experimenting? In their activity, they can rely only on the collective will of their supporters. Badiou wrote:

> The model of the centralized party made possible a new form of power that was nothing less than the power of the party itself. We are now at what I call a "distance from the State." This is first of all because the question of power is no longer "immediate": nowhere does a "taking of power" in the insurrectional sense seem possible today.

Does he thereby not get caught in an all too simple alternative? What about heroically assuming whatever power one can, with full awareness that "objective conditions" are not "mature" for radical changes, and—against the grain—do what one can?

To conclude, let me return to Greece, where the popular discontent brought about the discreditation of the entire political class and the country seems to approach a power void. The danger is, of course, that the capitalist system (if we may permit ourselves this personification) will gleefully allow the Left to take over and then allow Greece to end up in economic chaos, destined to serve as a lesson to all future similar temptations. Nonetheless, if there effectively is an opening for taking power, the Left should seize the opportunity and confront the problems, making the best of the worst situation (renegotiating the debt, mobilizing European solidarity and popular support for its predicament). The tragedy of politics is there will never be a "good" proper moment to grab power; the opportunity to seize power will always offer itself in the worst possible moment (of economic fiasco, ecological catastrophe, civil unrest, etc.), when the ruling political class loses its legitimacy and the Fascist-populist threat lurks behind. For example, the Scandinavian countries, which continue to maintain high equality and Welfare State standards, also score very well on global competitiveness, occupying top posts—proof that:

> generous, relatively egalitarian Welfare States should not be seen as utopias or protected enclaves, but can also be highly competitive participants in the world market. In other words, even within the parameters of global capitalism there are many degrees of freedom for radical social alternatives.

Perhaps the most succinct characterization of the epoch which began with the First World War is the well-known phrase attributed to Gramsci: "The old world is dying away, and the new world struggles to come forth: now is the time of monsters." Are Fascism and Stalinism not the twin monsters of the twentieth century, one emerging out of the desperate endeavor of the old world to survive and the other out of the misbegotten endeavor to build a new one? And what about the monsters we are engendering now, propelled by the tech-gnostic dreams of a society with biogenetically controlled populations? All the consequences should be drawn from this paradox. Perhaps there is no direct passage to the new, at least not in the way we imagined it, and monsters emerge necessarily in any attempt to enforce the passage to the New.

Signs of the growth of the ruling political class to dominate are multiplying not only in Greece, but even at the top, in the U.S. In the last two millennia, Christians in the Middle East survived a series of calamities, from the end of the Roman Empire through the defeat in the Crusades, the decolonization of the Arab countries, the Khomeini revolution in Iran, etc. (with the notable exception of Saudi Arabia, the main U.S. ally in this region, where there are no autochthonous Christians). In Iraq, there were approximately 1 million of them under Saddam, leading exactly the same lives as other Iraqi subjects, with one of them, Tariq Aziz, even occupying the high post of the foreign minister and Saddam's confidante. But then, something weird happened to Iraqi Christians, a true catastrophe—a Christian army occupied (or liberated, if you want) Iraq. The Christian occupation army dissolved Iraqi secular armed forces and thus left the streets open to the Muslim fundamentalist militias to terrorize each other and the Christians. No wonder roughly half of the Christians soon left the country, preferring even the terrorist-supporting Syria to the liberated Iraq under Christian military control.

In 2010, things took a turn for worse. Tariq Aziz, who survived the previous trials, was condemned to death by hanging by a Shia court for his "persecution of Muslim parties" (i.e., fighting against Muslim fundamentalism) under Saddam. Bomb attacks on Christians and their churches followed one after the other, leaving dozens dead, so that finally, at the beginning of November 2010, the Baghdad archbishop Atanasios Davud appealed to his flock to leave Iraq: "Christians have to leave the beloved country of our ancestors and escape the intended ethnic cleansing. This is still better than getting killed one after the other." And to dot the *i*, as it were, in November 2010 media reported that al Maliki was confirmed as Iraqi prime minister thanks to Iranian support. So the result of the U.S. intervention is that Iran, the prime agent of the Axis of Evil, is getting close to politically dominating Iraq. It is as if, in a contemporary display of the "cunning of reason," some invisible hand of destiny repeatedly arranges it so that a U.S. intervention strengthens the very cause against which it intervened.

Where does this invisible hand come from? *The problem with today's U.S. is not that it is a new global empire, but that it is* not: *While pretending to be, it continues to act as a nation-state, ruthlessly pursuing its interests.* It is as if the guideline of the

U.S. foreign policy is a weird reversal of the well-known motto of the ecologists: *act globally, think locally*. This contradiction was best exemplified by the two-sided pressure the U.S. was exerting on Serbia back in 2003. The U.S. representatives simultaneously demanded of the Serbian government to deliver the suspected war criminals to the Hague court (in accordance with the logic of the global empire which demands a global judicial institution) *and* to sign the bilateral treaty with the U.S. obliging Serbia not to deliver to any international institution (i.e., to the *same* Hague court) U.S. citizens suspected of war crimes or other crimes against humanity (in accordance with the nation-state logic). No wonder the Serb reaction was one of perplexed fury. The U.S. policy is thus definitely approaching a stage of madness and not only in domestic affairs where the Tea Party proposes to fight the national debt by lowering taxes, i.e., by increasing the debt. (One cannot but recall here Stalin's well-known thesis that, in the Soviet Union, the state is withering away through the strengthening of its organs, especially its organs of police repression.) In foreign policy also, the spread of Western Judeo-Christian values is organized by setting conditions for the expulsion of Christians, who, maybe, could move to Iran. . . . This is definitely not a clash of civilizations, but a true dialogue and cooperation between the U.S. pragmatists and the Muslim fundamentalists.

Our situation is thus the very opposite of the classical twentieth-century predicament when we knew what we had and wanted to do (establish the dictatorship of the proletariat, etc.), but had to wait patiently for the proper moment when the opportunity would offer itself. Now, we do not know what we have to do. But we have to act now because the consequence of our inaction could be catastrophic. We will have to risk taking steps into the abyss of the New in totally inappropriate situations. We will have to reinvent aspects of the New just to maintain what was good in the Old (education, healthcare, etc.). The journal in which Gramsci published his texts in the early 1920s was called *Il ordine nuovo, The New Order*, a title which was later fully appropriated by the extreme Right. Instead of seeing in this later appropriation the "truth" of Gramsci's use, so that we should abandon the term as running counter to the rebellious freedom of the authentic Left, we should return to it as a sign of the hard problem of defining the new order that a revolution should generate after its success. In short, our time is like what none other than Stalin said about the atom bomb: not for those with weak nerves.

Communism is today not the name of a solution, but the name of a *problem*: the problema of *commons* in all its dimensions—the commons of nature as the substance of our life, the problema of our biogenetic commons, the problema of our cultural commons ("intellectual property"), and, last but not least, directly the problema of commons as the universal space of humanity from which no one should be excluded. Whatever the solution, it will have to solve *this* problem.

THREE

On the Right and the Duty to Change the World

Paulo Freire

If someone reading this text were to ask me, with an ironic smile, whether I believe that in order to change Brazil it is enough to surrender to the fatigue of constantly stating that change is possible and that human beings are not mere spectators, but also actors in history, I would say no. But I would also say that changing implies knowing that it is possible to do it.—Paulo Freire

It is certain that men and women can change the world for the better, can make it less unjust, but they can do so only from the starting point of the concrete reality they "come upon" in their generation. They cannot do it on the basis of reveries, false dreams, or pure illusion.

What is not possible, however, is to even think about transforming the world without a dream, without utopia, or without a vision. Pure illusions are the false dreams of those who, no matter how plentiful their good intentions, propose fancies that cannot be realized. World transformation requires dreaming, but the indispensable authenticity of that dream depends on the faithfulness of those who dream to their historic and material circumstances and to the levels of technological scientific development of their context. Dreams are visions for which one fights. Their realization cannot take place easily, without obstacles. It implies, on the contrary, advances, reversals, and at times, lengthy marches. It implies struggle. In reality, the world transformation that dreams aspire to is a political act, and it would be naïve of anyone not to recognize that dreams also have their counter-dreams. The time a generation belongs to, since it is historic, reveals old marks involving understandings of reality, special interests, class interests, prejudices, and the gestation of ideologies that have been perpetuated in contradiction to more modern aspects. For this reason, there is no today that is devoid of long-enduring "presences" in the cultural atmosphere that characterizes its concrete reality. Thus, the nature of all reality is contradictory and process oriented. In this sense, the rebellious impetus against the aggressive injustice that characterizes land possession among us, which is eloquently embodied in the landless workers movement, is as current as the indecent reaction of landowners—who are obviously much more supported by the law, which is primarily at the service of their interests—to any agrarian reform, no matter how timid it may be. The struggle for agrarian reform in my country, Brazil, represents a necessary advance, opposed by the immobilizing backwardness of conservatism. It is necessary to make clear that immobilizing backwardness is no stranger to reality. There is no present that is not the stage for confrontations between forces opposed to advancement and those that struggle for it. In this sense, the strong marks of our colonial, slavery-ridden past are contradictorily present in our current reality and intent on posing obstacles to advancement toward modernity. Those are marks of a past that, while incapable of enduring much longer, insist on prolonging their presence to the detriment of change. Precisely because immobilizing reaction is part of present reality, it is effective on the one hand, but, on the other, it can be contested. The ideological, political, pedagogical, and ethical fight put up by those who position themselves in line with a progressive option chooses no particular time or place. It takes place at home, in the relations between fathers, mothers, sons, and daughters, as well as in school, at any level, and within work relationships. What is fundamental, if one is consistently progressive, is to give testimony, as a father, teacher, employer, employee, journalist, soldier, scientist, researcher, or artist, as a woman, mother, or daughter, no matter what one is, to one's respect for the dignity of the other. It is fundamental to give testimony to one's respect for the other's right to be in relation to his or her right to have.

Possibly, the most fundamental knowledge required in the exercise of that sort of testimony is one's certainty that while change is difficult, it is possible. That is what makes us refuse any fatalist position that may lend a *determinant* power, before which nothing can be done, to this or that *conditioning* factor.

As great as the conditioning power of the economy may be over our individual and social behavior, I cannot accept being completely passive before it. To the extent that we accept that the economy, or technology, or science, it doesn't matter what, exerts inescapable power over us, there is nothing left for us to do other than renounce our ability to think, to conjecture, to compare, to choose, to decide, to envision, to dream. When reduced to the act of making viable what has already been determined, politics loses the sense of being a struggle toward the realization of different dreams. Our presence in the world becomes devoid of any ethics. In this sense, while I recognize the undeniable importance of how society organizes its production in order to understand how we are being, it is not possible for me to ignore or minimize human beings' reflective and decision-making capacity. The very fact that human beings have become equipped to recognize how conditioned or influenced they are by economic structures also makes them capable of intervening in the conditioning reality. Knowing oneself to be conditioned but not fatalistically subjected to this or that destiny opens up the way for one's intervention in the world. The opposite of intervention is adaptation, is to settle, or to purely adapt to a reality that is thus not questioned. It is in this sense that, among us, men and women, *adaptation* is only a moment in the process of *intervention* in the world. That is the foundation of the primordial difference between *conditioning* and *determination.* It is only possible, in fact, to speak of ethics if there is choice resulting from one's capacity for comparing, and if there is responsibility taken. It is also for these reasons that I negate the *deproblematization of the future,* which I often refer to and which implies its inexorability. The deproblematization of the future, within a mechanistic understanding of history whether from the right or from the left, necessarily leads to an authoritarian death or negation of the dream, of utopia, of hope. Within a mechanistic and thus deterministic understanding of history, the future is already known. The struggle for a future already known a priori requires no hope. Deproblematizing the future, no matter in the name of what, is a breaking away from human nature, which is socially and historically constituted.

The future does not make us. We make ourselves in the struggle to make it.

Mechanists and humanists alike recognize the power of today's globalized economy. However, while for the former there is nothing to be done about this untouchable power, for the latter, it is not only possible but also necessary to fight against the robust power of the powerful, which globalization has intensified, as it has the weakness of the fragile.

If economic structures indeed dominate me in such a masterful manner as to shape my thinking, to make me a docile object of their power, how can I explain political struggle, and above all, how can struggle be undertaken and in the name of what? To me, it should be undertaken in the name of ethics, obviously not the ethics of markets but rather the universal ethics of human beings—in the name of the needed transformation of society that should result in overcoming dehumanizing injustice.[1] That is so because, while conditioned by economic structures, I am not determined by them. If it is not possible, on the one hand, to ignore the fact that political struggle and transformation are gestated within the material conditions of society, it is not possible, on the other, to deny the fundamental importance of subjectiveness in history. Subjectiveness does not all-powerfully create objectiveness, nor does the latter irreversibly construct the former. To me, it is not possible to speak of subjectiveness except if understood within its dialectic relationship to objectiveness. There is no subjectiveness in the hypertrophy that turns it into the maker of objectivity, nor in the minimization that sees it as mere result of objectivity. In this sense, I can only speak of subjectiveness among beings that, while *unfinished,* become able to know themselves as unfinished; among beings that have equipped themselves to go beyond *determination,* thus reducing it to conditioning; and among beings who, taking responsibility for being objects, while conditioned, were able to risk being subjects, because they are not determined. One cannot speak, therefore, of subjectiveness within an objectivistic or mechanistic understanding of history, nor within a subjectivistic one. Only within a view of history as possibility rather than determination can subjectiveness be realized and lived in its dialectic relationship with objectiveness. It is by realizing and living history as possibility that one can fully experience the capacity to compare, to make judgments, to choose, to decide, and to break away. That is how men and women make the world ethical, yet they also remain capable of being transgressors of ethics.

Choice and decision—a subject's actions of which we cannot speak within a mechanistic understanding of history, whether from the right or the left but must rather understand as time of possibility—necessarily underscore the importance of education. Education, which must never be neutral, can be at the service either of decision, of world transformation and of critical insertion within the world, or of immobility and the possible permanence of unjust structures, of human beings' settling for a reality seen as untouchable. That is why I always speak of education and never of pure training. I not only speak of, but also live and defend, a radical educational practice, one that encourages critical curiosity and that always seeks the reason or reasons for being of facts. It is easy to understand why such practice cannot be accepted and must be rejected, by those who, to a greater or lesser extent, see in the permanence of the *status quo* the protection of their interests. It must also be rejected by those who, tied to the interests of the powerful, serve them. However, because I recognize the limits of education, be it formal or informal, I recognize its power as well, and because I realize the possibility human beings have to take on historic tasks, I return to writing about certain commitments and duties we must not neglect if our option is progressive. There is the duty, for example, to never, under any circumstances, accept or encourage fatalist positions. There is also the duty of rejecting, for that reason, statements such as: "It is a pity that there are so many among us who go hungry, but that is what reality is." "Unemployment is a fatality of the end of the century." "You can't teach an old dog new tricks." Our testimony, on the contrary, if we are progressive, if we dream of a less aggressive, less unjust, less violent, more human society, must be that of saying "no" to any impossibility determined by the "facts" and that of defending a human being's capacity for evaluating, comparing, choosing, deciding, and finally intervening in the world.

Children need to grow in the exercise of this ability to think, to question and question themselves, to doubt, to experiment with hypotheses for action, and to plan, rather than just following plans that, more than proposed, are imposed upon them. Children's right to learn how to decide, which can only be achieved by deciding, must be ensured. If liberties are not constituted on their own, but rather in the ethical observance of certain limits, the ethical observance of these limits cannot be accomplished without putting liberties themselves and the authority or authorities to which they dialectically relate at a measure of risk as well.

Recently, I closely participated in the "well-addressed" frustration of a grandmother, my wife, who had spent several days nursing the joyous expectation of having Marina, her beloved granddaughter, with her at home. On the eve of the awaited day, the grandmother was notified by her son that her granddaughter would not come. She had made plans with some friends in her neighborhood to meet to create a recreation and sports club.

By planning, the granddaughter is learning how to plan, so the grandmother did not feel denied or unloved that her granddaughter's decision, through which she is learning how to decide, did not correspond to her wishes.

It would have been regrettable if the grandmother had, with a long face, expressed undue discomfort in light of her granddaughter's legitimate decision, or if the father, revealing his dissatisfaction, had attempted to insist, in authoritarian fashion, that the daughter do something she did not want to do. That does not mean, on the other hand, that in her learning of her own autonomy, the child in general does not need to learn as well that at times, it is necessary to respond to the expectations of others without incurring any disrespect for her own autonomy. Further, it is necessary for the child to learn that her own autonomy can only attain legitimacy as it observes the autonomy of others. The progressive task is thus to encourage and make possible, in the most diverse circumstances, the ability to intervene in the world—never its opposite, the crossing of arms before challenges. It is clear and imperative, however, that my advocacy for intervention in the world never turn me into a whimsical inconsequent who does not take into account the existence and the power of conditioning. Refusing determination does not imply negating conditioning.

In the final analysis, if I am a consistent progressive, I must give permanent testimony to my children, my students, my friends, and whomever else, of my certainty that social and economic facts do not take place in this or that manner because so they had to be. Further, I must be certain that the facts are not immune to our action upon them. We are not mere objects of their "necessity"; while we can adapt to them, we remain historic subjects as well, as we fight for a different will or desire—to change the world. It does not matter that this struggle may last such a long time that generations may succumb in the process.

The Landless Movement in Brazil, as ethical and pedagogical as it is full of beauty, did not start just now, nor ten or fifteen, nor twenty years ago. Its most remote roots are found in the rebelliousness of the *kilombos*,[2] and more recently, in the bravery of their fellows in the Peasant Leagues (*Ligas Camponesas*),[3] which were crushed forty years ago by the same backward forces of perverse reactionary colonial immobilism.

What matters, however, is to recognize that the *kilombos*, as well as the peasants from the Leagues and the landless workers of today, all in their own time, yesterday and before, and now, dreamed and dream the same dream; they believed and believe in the imperative necessity to fight for the making of history as a "deed of freedom." Deep down, they would never surrender to the ideological falsity of the statement: "Reality is what it is, and it is useless to fight." On the contrary, they bet on intervening in the world to rectify it, not to maintain it more or less as it is.

If the landless workers had bought into the "death of history," the death of utopia and of the dream, if they had bought into the vanishing of social classes, into the inefficacy of testimonies of love for freedom, if they had believed that criticizing neoliberal fatalism was an expression of "neo-foolishness," if they had believed in the despotic politics built into the discourse which asserts that today is a time for "little talk, less politics, and more results," if they had bought into the official rhetoric and given up their land occupations and returned not to their homes but to their self-negation, agrarian reform would have been shelved one more time.

We owe more to those men and women, the landless workers, and to their uncompromising determination to help the democratization of this country, than at times we are able to think. How great it would be for the expansion and consolidation of our democracy, above all with respect to its authenticity, if other marches were to follow theirs: marches of the unemployed, of the disenfranchised, of those who protest against impunity, of the ones who decry violence, lying, and disrespect for public property. Let us not forget as well the marches of the homeless, of the school-less, of the healthless, of the renegades, and the hopeful march of those who know that change is possible.

Notes by Ana Maria Araújo Freire

While still in Jaboatão, Paulo started this second letter and was only able to complete it after we returned from Cambridge, Massachusetts, on April 7, 1997. We had gone there via New York, in late March 1997, precisely on the twenty-second, to finalize the details with Harvard University of the course he would have taught at the Harvard Graduate School of Education (HGSE) in the fall semester of 1997. Everything was set with Donaldo Macedo, professor at the University of Massachusetts in Boston, whom Paulo had invited to assist with the course. The class would have had as its central axis the book Pegagogy of Freedom, *which had been translated into English with this immediate objective in mind. We were approached by a few students and several professors in Harvard Square, and they all expressed their joy and surprise at the fact that such a conservative and status-quo maintaining university was opening up the opportunity for critical professors to offer a critical-reflective and conscience-building course.*

We returned happy with our expectations about the critical work Paulo would do. We were certain that it would be undertaken with seriousness, honesty, and transparency, even if reluctantly allowed by the prestigious American university. Such "openness" was part of the "democratic frame" that the United States has to uphold because it proclaims itself democratic, Paulo used to say. We were planning out the time we would have in New England to read, write, and reflect, at the warm home, we dreamed, which would protect us from the usually cold fall and winter temperatures experienced in that region. From within its comfort, however, we would be able to see through the windows two things, he would repeat boyishly, two natural phenomena, that had enchanted him ever since he had first experienced them. Green leaves gradually turn more and more yellow until they go down, almost brown, and fall to the ground that embraces them, even if covered in the snow that petrifies and freezes them, so that they continue to be part of the cycle of life. The snow itself softly falls as if it were made of cotton flakes or tiny pieces of white paper. Those were whims of nature that Paulo so loved in their different forms and functions. We discussed, above all, what it would be like to understand the issues of our country from a distance, while being in another so very different politically, economically, and culturally.

Around that time, Paulo concerned himself, in a very special manner, with the world's situation as tied to a neoliberal political model and to economic globalization. He reflected a great deal and never tired of saying, and of writing, that he believed in the political-ideological option and the nonviolent actions undertaken by the MTS— the Landless Movement—as historic possibility, as a way out of our colonialism and our miseries, as a tactic toward a strategy for Brazilian democracy. He would write and discuss this letter, and become more enthusiastic each day about the testimony on "respect for the dignity of others." In fact, I must emphasize, Paulo would never forgive anyone for deliberately moving away from that. We were happy to see that "these fearless people are giving us, through their struggle, the hope of better days for Brazil," he would repeat, filled with hope.

I must and want to give testimony here to Paulo's emotion, on April 17, 1997, when the March of the Landless entered Brasilia in orderly fashion, coming from different parts of our country and making itself into one body containing the bodies of children, the elderly, the young, whites, blacks. He had invited me to join him to watch the political event on television, since we were not there at the capital with all of them in the march where many had pilgrimaged for three months. When Paulo saw that multitude entering the ministerial mall, with pride and discipline, he stood up and paced back and forth in the room, with all the hairs on his body standing up, pores open, and warm perspiration. He would repeat, in an emotional voice, speaking to the landless marchers and not to me, his words filled with his understanding of the world: "That is my people, my masses, my Brazilian people. This Brazil belongs to all of us, men and women. Let us move forward with the nonviolent struggle, with conscious resistance, with determination, so we can take it back in order to build, in solidarity, the country of all men and women born here or who joined it to make it greater. This country must not go on belonging to the few. Let us fight for the democratization of this country. March on, people of our country."

Paulo finished this second letter on that same day. In it he called for other marches. Given his usual humility, he did not say, did not even mention, that this march also had its roots in his liberating understanding of education, nor that the Brazilian social movements, not only the Landless Movement, undeniably gained consciousness in their praxis through what he, Paulo, proposed in his theoretical anthropological-ethical-ideological-political-educational work—what he proposed with his life.

Notes

1.   See Paulo Freire, "Necessary Knowledge to the Educational Practice," in *Pedagogy of Freedom* (Boulder, CO: Rowman & Littlefield, 1998).

2.   Translator's note: The Portuguese word *quilombo* has been used in English with the spelling *kilombo*. It refers to groups of rebellious, escaped slaves who gathered to form agricultural communities that lived for generations hidden and resistant to the tyranny of slavery.

3.   Translator's note: *Ligas Camponesas* has been translated in English as the Peasant Leagues. It refers to a leftist-organized, pro-agrarian reform movement in Brazil in the early 1960s.

Rethinking Democracy and Education

FOUR

Democracy and Education

Noam Chomsky

The topic that was suggested, which I'm very happy to talk about, is "Democracy and Education." The phrase *democracy and education* immediately brings to mind the life and work and thought of one of the outstanding thinkers of the past century, John Dewey, who devoted the greater part of his life and his thought to this array of issues. I guess I should confess a special interest. His thought was a strong influence on me in my formative years—in fact, from about age two on, for a variety of reasons that I won't go into but are real. For much of his life—later he was more skeptical—Dewey seems to have felt that reforms in early education could be in themselves a major lever of social change. They could lead the way to a more just and free society, a society in which, in his words, "the ultimate aim of production is not production of goods, but the production of free human beings associated with one another on terms of equality." This basic commitment, which runs through all of Dewey's work and thought, is profoundly at odds with the two leading currents of modern social intellectual life; one, strong in his day—he was writing in the 1920s and 1930s about these things—is associated with the command economies in Eastern Europe, the systems created by Lenin and Trotsky and turned into an even greater monstrosity by Stalin. The other, the state capitalist industrial society being constructed in the U.S. and much of the West, with the effective rule of private power. These two systems are similar in some fundamental ways, including ideologically. Both were, and one of them remains,

This paper was published in Macedo, D. (ed). (2000). *Chomsky on miseducation.* Lanham, MD: Rowman and Littlefield. This article was originally delivered as a lecture at Loyola University, Chicago, 19 October 1994.

deeply authoritarian in fundamental commitment, and both were very sharply and dramatically opposed to another tradition, the Left libertarian tradition, with roots in Enlightenment values, a tradition that included progressive liberals of the John Dewey variety, independent socialists like Bertrand Russell, leading elements of the Marxist mainstream, mostly anti-Bolshevik, and of course libertarian socialists and various anarchist movements, not to speak of major parts of the labor movement and other popular sectors.

This independent Left, of which Dewey was a part, has strong roots in classical liberalism. It grows right out of it, in my opinion, and it stands in sharp opposition to the absolutist currents of state capitalist and state socialist institutions and thought, including the rather extreme form of absolutism that's now called conservative in the U.S., terminology that would have amused Orwell and would have caused any genuine conservative to turn over in his grave, if you could find one.

I need not stress that this picture is not the conventional one, to put it rather mildly, but I think it does have one merit, at least—namely, the merit of accuracy. I'll try to explain why.

Let me return to one of Dewey's central themes, that the ultimate aim of production is not production of goods but the production of free human beings associated with one another on terms of equality. That includes, of course, education, which was a prime concern of his. The goal of education, to shift over to Bertrand Russell, is "to give a sense of the value of things other than domination," to help create "wise citizens of a free community," to encourage a combination of citizenship with liberty and individual creativeness, which means that we regard "a child as a gardener regards a young tree, as something with a certain intrinsic nature, which will develop into an admirable form, given proper soil and air and light." In fact, much as they disagreed on many other things, as they did, Dewey and Russell did agree on what Russell called this "humanistic conception," with its roots in the Enlightenment, the idea that education is not to be viewed as something like filling a vessel with water but, rather, assisting a flower to grow in its own way—an eighteenth-century view that they revived. In other words, providing the circumstances in which the normal creative patterns will flourish.

Dewey and Russell also shared the understanding that these leading ideas of the Enlightenment and classical liberalism had a revolutionary character, and retained it right at the time they were writing, in the early half of this century. If implemented, these ideas could produce free human beings whose values were not accumulation and domination but, rather, free association on terms of equality and sharing and cooperation, participating on equal terms to achieve common goals that were democratically conceived. There was only contempt for what Adam Smith called the "vile maxim of the masters of mankind, all for ourselves, and nothing for other people," the guiding principle that nowadays we're taught to admire and revere, as traditional values have eroded under unremitting attack, the so-called conservatives leading the onslaught in recent decades.

It's worth taking time to notice how sharp and dramatic is the clash of values between, on the one hand, the humanistic conception that runs from the Enlightenment up to leading twentieth-century figures like Russell and Dewey and, on the other hand, the prevailing doctrines of today, the doctrines that were denounced by Adam Smith as the "vile maxim" and also denounced by the lively and vibrant working-class press of over a century ago, which condemned what it called the "new spirit of the age, gain wealth, forgetting all but self"—Smith's vile maxim. It's quite remarkable to trace the evolution of values from a precapitalist thinker like Adam Smith, with his stress on sympathy and the goal of perfect equality and the basic human right to creative work, and contrast that and move on to the present to those who laud the "new spirit of the age," sometimes rather shamelessly invoking Adam Smith's name. For example, Nobel Prize–winning economist James Buchanan, who writes that what each person seeks in an "ideal situation" is "mastery over a world of slaves." That's when you seek, in case you hadn't noticed, something that Adam Smith would have regarded as simply pathological.

The best book I know of on Adam Smith's actual thought *(Adam Smith and His Legacy for Modern Capitalism)* is written by a professor here at Loyola, Patricia Werhane. Of course, it's always best to read the original.

One of the most dramatic illustrations of the "new spirit of the age" and its values is the commentary that's now in the press on the difficulties we face in uplifting the people of Eastern Europe. As you know, we're now extending to them, our new beneficiaries, the loving care that we've lavished on our wards elsewhere in Latin America and the Philippines and so on, with consequences that are dramatically clear and consistent in these horror chambers but also are miraculously free of any lessons about who we are and what we do. One might ask why. In any event, we are now proceeding to uplift the people liberated from communism as we've in the past liberated Haitians and Brazilians and Guatemalans and Filipinos and Native Americans and African slaves and so on. The *New York Times* is currently running an interesting series of articles on these different problems. They give some interesting insight into the prevailing values. There was an article on East Germany, for example, written by Steven Kinzer. It opens by quoting a priest who was one of the leaders of the popular protests against the communist regime in East Germany. He describes the growing concerns there about what's happening to the society. He says, "Brutal competition and the lust for money are destroying our sense of community, and almost everyone feels a level of fear or depression or insecurity" as they master the new spirit of the age in which we instruct the backward peoples of the world.

The next article turned to what we regard as the showplace, the real success story, Poland, written by Jane Perlez. The headline reads, "Fast and Slow Lanes on the Capitalist Road." The structure of the story is that some are getting the point but there are also some who are still backwards. She gives one example of a good student and one example of a slow learner. The good student is the owner of a small factory that is a "thriving example" of the best in modern capitalist Poland. It produces intricately designed wedding gowns sold mostly to rich Germans and to that tiny sector of super-rich Poles. This is in a country where poverty has more than doubled since the reforms were instituted, according to a World Bank study last July, and incomes have dropped about 30 percent. However, the people who are hungry and jobless can look at the intricately designed wedding gowns in the store windows, appreciating the new spirit of the age, so it's understandable that Poland is hailed as the great success story for our achievements.

A good student explains that "people have to be taught to understand they must fight for themselves and can't rely on others." She is describing a training course she's running that's trying to instill American values among people who are still brainwashed with slogans like "I'm a miner. Who else is better?" They have got to get that out of their heads. A lot of people are better, including people who can design wedding gowns for rich Germans. That's the chosen illustration of the success story of American values. Then there are the failures, still on the slow lane on the capitalist road. Here she picks one as her example, a forty-year-old coal miner who "sits in his wood-paneled living room admiring the fruits of his labor under communism—a television set, comfortable furniture, a shiny, modern kitchen," and he wonders "why he's at home, jobless and dependent on welfare payments," having not yet absorbed the new spirit of the age, gain wealth, forgetting all but self, and not "I'm a miner. Who else is better?" The series goes on like that. It's interesting to read and to see what's taken for granted.

What's happening in Eastern Europe recapitulates what's gone on in our Third World domains for a long time and falls into place in a much longer story. It's very familiar from our own history and the history of England before us. There's a recent book, by a distinguished Yale University labor historian, David Montgomery, in which he points out that modern America was created over the protests of its working people. He's quite right. Those protests were vigorous and outspoken, particularly in the working-class and community press that flourished in the U.S. from the early nineteenth century up until the 1950s, when it was finally destroyed by private power, as its counterpart in England was about ten years later. The first major study of this topic was in 1924 by Norman Ware. It still makes very illuminating reading. It was published here in Chicago and reprinted very recently by Ivan Dee, a local publisher. It's very much worth reading. It's a work that set off very substantial study in social history.

What Ware describes, looking mostly at the labor press, is how the value system that was advocated by private power had to be beaten into the heads of ordinary people, who had to be taught to abandon normal human sentiments and to replace them with the new spirit of the age, as they called it. He reviews the mainly mid-nineteenth century working-class press, often, incidentally, run by working-class women. The themes that run through it are constant for a long period. They are concerned with what they call "degradation" and loss of dignity and independence, loss of self-respect, the decline of the worker as a person, the sharp decline in cultural level and cultural attainments as workers were subjected to what they called "wage slavery," which they regarded as not very different from the chattel slavery they had fought to uproot during the Civil War. Particularly dramatic and quite relevant to today's problems was the sharp decline in what we call "high culture," reading of classics and contemporary literature by the people who were called the factory girls in Lowell and by craftsmen and other workers. Craftsmen would hire somebody to read to them while they were working because they were interested and had libraries. All that had to go.

What they described, paraphrasing the labor press, is that when you sell your product, you retain your person. But when you sell your labor, you sell yourself, losing the rights of free men and becoming vassals of mammoth establishments of a "moneyed aristocracy" that "threatens annihilation to every man who dares to question their right to enslave and oppress." "Those who work in the mills ought to own them," not have the status of machines ruled by private "despots" who are entrenching "monarchic principles on democratic soil" as they drive downward freedom and rights, civilization, health, morals, and intellectuality in the new commercial feudalism.

Just in case you are confused, this is long before any influence of Marxism. This is American workers talking about their experiences in the 1840s. The labor press also condemned what they called the "bought priesthood," referring to the media and the universities and the intellectual class, that is, the apologists who sought to justify the absolute despotism that was the new spirit of the age and to instill its sordid and demeaning values. One of the early leaders of the AFL, Henry Demarest Lloyd, about a century ago, late nineteenth century, expressed the standard view when he described the mission of the labor movement as to overcome "the sins and superstitions of the market" and to defend democracy by extending it to control over industry by working people.

All of this would have been completely intelligible to the founders of classical liberalism, people like Wilhelm von Humboldt, for example, who inspired John Stuart Mill and who, very much like his contemporary Adam Smith, regarded creative work freely undertaken in association with others as the core value of a human life. So if a person produces an object on command, Humboldt wrote, we may admire what he did but we will despise what he is, not a true human being who acts on his own impulses and desires. The bought priesthood has the task of undermining these values and destroying them among people who sell themselves on the labor market. For similar reasons, Adam Smith warned that in any civilized society governments would have to intervene to prevent the division of labor from making people "as stupid and ignorant as it is possible for a human creature to be." He based his rather nuanced advocacy of markets on the thesis that if conditions were truly free, markets would lead to perfect equality. That was their moral justification. All of this has been forgotten by the bought priesthood, who has a rather different tale to tell.

Dewey and Russell are two of the leading twentieth-century inheritors of this tradition, with its roots in the Enlightenment and classical liberalism. Even more interesting is the inspiring record of struggle and organization and protest by working men and women since the early nineteenth century as they sought to win freedom and justice and to retain the rights that they had once had as the new despotism of state-supported private power extended its sway.

The basic issue was formulated with a good deal of clarity by Thomas Jefferson around 1816. This was before the Industrial Revolution had really taken root in the former colonies, but you could begin to see the developments. In his later years, observing what was happening, Jefferson had rather serious concerns about the fate of the democratic experiment. He feared the rise of a new form of absolutism that was more ominous than what had been overthrown in the American Revolution, in which he was of course a leader. Jefferson distinguished in his later years between what he called "aristocrats" and "democrats." The aristocrats are "those who fear and distrust the people, and wish to draw all powers from them into the hands of the higher classes." The democrats, in contrast, "identify with the people, have confidence in them, cherish and consider them as the honest and safe depository of the public interest," if not always "the most wise." The aristocrats of his day were the advocates of the rising capitalist state, which Jefferson regarded with much disdain, clearly recognizing the quite obvious contradiction between democracy and capitalism, or more accurately what we might call really existing capitalism, that is, guided and subsidized by powerful developmental states, as it was in England and the U.S. and indeed everywhere else.

This fundamental contradiction was enhanced as new corporate structures were granted increasing powers, not by democratic procedures but mainly by courts and lawyers who converted what Jefferson called the "banking institutions and monied incorporations," which he said would destroy freedom and which he could barely see the beginnings of in his day. They were converted, mainly through courts and lawyers, into "immortal persons" with powers and rights beyond the worst nightmares of precapitalist thinkers like Adam Smith or Thomas Jefferson. Half a century earlier, Adam Smith already warned against this, though he could barely see the beginnings of it.

Jefferson's distinction between aristocrats and democrats was developed about a half a century later by Bakunin, the anarchist thinker and activist. It was actually one of the few predictions of the social sciences ever to have come true. It ought to have a place of honor in any serious academic curriculum in the social sciences and the humanities for this reason alone. Back in the nineteenth century, Bakunin predicted that the rising intelligentsia of the nineteenth century would follow one of two parallel paths. One path would be to exploit popular struggles to take state power, becoming what he called a "Red bureaucracy" that will impose the most cruel and vicious regime in history. That's one strain. The other strain, he said, will be those who discover that real power lies elsewhere, and they will become its "bought priesthood," in the words of the labor press, serving the real masters in the state-supported private system of power, either as managers or apologists "who beat the people with the people's stick," as he put it, in the state capitalist democracies. The similarities are pretty striking, and they run right up to the present. They help account for the rapid transitions that people make from one to the other position. It looks like a funny transition, but in fact it's a common ideology. We're seeing it right now in Eastern Europe with the group that's sometimes called the Nomenklatura capitalists, the old communist ruling class, now the biggest enthusiasts for the market, enriching themselves as the societies become standard Third World societies. The move is very easy because it's basically the same ideology. A similar move from Stalinist apologist to "celebration of America" is quite standard in modern history, and it doesn't require much of a shift in values, just a shift in judgment as to where power lies.

Fear of democracy is deeply entrenched. Alexander Hamilton put it clearly when he described the people as a "great beast" from which governing elites have to be protected. These ideas have become ever more entrenched in educated circles as Jefferson's fears and Bakunin's predictions were increasingly realized. The basic attitudes coming into this century were expressed very clearly by Woodrow Wilson's secretary of state, Robert Lansing—attitudes that led to Wilson's Red Scare, as it was called, which destroyed labor and independent thought for a decade. Lansing warned of the danger of allowing the "ignorant and incapable mass of humanity" to become "dominant in the earth" or even influential, as he believed the Bolsheviks intended. That's the hysterical and utterly erroneous reaction that's pretty standard among people who feel that their power is threatened.

Those concerns were articulated very clearly by progressive intellectuals of the period, maybe the leading one being Walter Lippmann in his essays on democracy, mainly in the 1920s. Lippmann was also the dean of American journalism and one of the most distinguished commentators on public affairs for many years. He advised that "the public must be put in its place" so that the "responsible men" may "live free of the trampling and the roar of a bewildered herd," Hamilton's beast. In a democracy, Lippmann held, these "ignorant and meddlesome outsiders" do have a "function." Their function is to be "interested spectators of action" but not "participants." They are to lend their weight periodically to some member of the leadership class, that's called elections, and then they are supposed to return to their private concerns. In fact, similar notions became part of mainstream academic theory at about the same time.

In the presidential address to the American Political Science Association in 1934 William Shepard argued that government should be in the hands of "an aristocracy of intellect and power," while the "ignorant, the uninformed and the antisocial elements" must not be permitted to control elections, as he mistakenly believed they had done in the past. One of the founders of modern political science, Harold Lasswell, one of the founders of the field of communications, in fact, wrote in the *Encyclopedia of Social Sciences* in 1933 or 1934 that modern techniques of propaganda, which had been impressively refined by Wilsonian liberals, provided the way to keep the public in line.

Wilson's World War I achievements in propaganda impressed others, including Adolf Hitler. But crucially they impressed the American business community. That led to a huge expansion of the public-relations industry which was dedicated to controlling the public mind, as advocates used to put it in more honest days, just as, writing in the *Encyclopedia of Social Sciences* in 1933, Lasswell described what he was talking about as propaganda. We don't use that term. We're more sophisticated.

As a political scientist, Lasswell advocated more sophisticated use of this new technique of control of the general public that was provided by modern propaganda. That would, he said, enable the intelligent men of the community, the natural rulers, to overcome the threat of the great beast who may undermine order because of, in Lasswell's terms, "the ignorance and stupidity of the masses." We should not succumb to "democratic dogmatisms about men being the best judges of their own interests." The best judges are the elites, who must be ensured the means to impose their will for the common good. Jefferson's aristocrats, in other words.

Lippmann and Lasswell represent the more liberal, progressive fringe of opinion, which grants the beast at least a spectator role. At the reactionary end you get those who are mislabelled conservatives in contemporary newspeak. So the Reaganite statist reactionaries thought that the public, the beast, shouldn't even have the spectator role. That explains their fascination with clandestine terror operations, which were not secret to anybody except the American public, certainly not to their victims. Clandestine terror operations were designed to leave the domestic population ignorant. They also advocated absolutely unprecedented measures of censorship and agitprop and other measures to ensure that the powerful and interventionist state that they fostered would serve as a welfare state for the rich and not be troubled by the rabble. The huge increase in business propaganda in recent years, the recent assault on the universities by right-wing foundations, and other tendencies of the current period are other manifestations of the same concerns. These concerns were awakened by what liberal elites had called the "crisis of democracy" that developed in the 1960s, when previously marginalized and apathetic sectors of the population, like women and young people and old people and working people and so on, sought to enter the public arena, where they have no right to be, as all right-thinking aristocrats understand.

John Dewey was one of the relics of the Enlightenment classical liberal tradition who opposed the rule of the wise, the onslaught of the Jeffersonian aristocrats, whether they found their place on the reactionary or the liberal part of this very narrow ideological spectrum. Dewey understood clearly that "politics is the shadow cast on society by big business," and as long as this is so, "attenuation of the shadow will not change the substance." Meaning, reforms are of limited utility. Democracy requires that the source of the shadow be removed not only because of its domination of the political arena but because the very institutions of private power undermine democracy and freedom. Dewey was very explicit about the antidemocratic power that he had in mind. To quote him, "Power today"—this is the 1920s—"resides in control of the means of production, exchange, publicity, transportation and communication. Whoever owns them rules the life of the country," even if democratic forms remain. "Business for private profit through private control of banking, land, industry reinforced by command of the press, press agents and other means of publicity and propaganda," that is the system of actual power, the source of coercion and control, and until it's unraveled we can't talk seriously about democracy and freedom. Education, he hoped, of the kind he was talking about, the production of free human beings, would be one of the means of undermining this absolutist monstrosity.

In a free and democratic society, Dewey held, workers should be "the masters of their own industrial fate," not tools rented by employers. He agreed on fundamental issues with the founders of classical liberalism and with the democratic and libertarian sentiments that animated the popular working-class movements from the early Industrial Revolution, until they were finally beaten down by a combination of violence and propaganda. In the field of education, therefore, Dewey held that it is "illiberal and immoral" to train children to work "not freely and intelligently, but for the sake of the money earned," in which case their activity is "not free because not freely participated in." Again the conception of classical liberalism and the workers' movements. Therefore, Dewey held, industry must also change "from a feudalistic to a democratic social order" based on control by working people and free association, again, traditional anarchist ideals with their source in classical liberalism and the Enlightenment.

As the doctrinal system has narrowed under the assault of private power, particularly in the past few decades, these fundamental libertarian values and principles now sound exotic and extreme, perhaps even anti-American, to borrow one of the terms of contemporary totalitarian thought in the West. Given these changes, it's useful to remember that the kinds of ideas that Dewey was expressing are as American as apple pie. They have origins in straight American traditions, right in the mainstream; not influenced by any dangerous foreign ideologies; in a worthy tradition that's ritually lauded, though it's commonly distorted and forgotten. And all of that is part of the deterioration of functioning democracy in the current age, both at the institutional and at the ideological level, in my opinion.

Education is, of course, in part a matter of schools and colleges and the formal information systems. That's true whether the goal of education is education for freedom and democracy, as Dewey advocated, or education for obedience and subordination and marginalization, as the dominant institutions require. The University of Chicago sociologist James Coleman, one of the main students of education and effects of experience on children's lives, concludes from many studies that the total effect of home background is considerably greater than the total effect of school variables in determining student achievement. So it's therefore important to have a look at how social policy and the dominant culture are shaping these factors, home influences and so on.

That's a very interesting topic. The inquiry is much facilitated by a UNICEF study published a year ago called *Child Neglect in Rich Societies,* written by a well-known American economist, Sylvia Ann Hewlett. She studies the preceding fifteen years, the late 1970s up through the early 1990s, in the rich nations. She's not talking about the Third World but about the rich countries. She finds a sharp split between the Anglo-American societies on the one hand and continental Europe and Japan on the other hand. The Anglo-American model, spearheaded by the Reaganites and Thatcher, has been a disaster for children and families, she says. The European-Japanese model, in contrast, has improved their situation considerably, from a starting point that was already considerably higher, despite the fact that these societies lack the huge advantages of the Anglo-American societies. The U.S. has unparalleled wealth and advantages, and while the United Kingdom, Britain, has severely declined, particularly under Thatcher, it has the economic advantage, at least, of being a U.S. client as well as being a major oil exporter in the Thatcher years. That's something that makes the economic failure of Thatcherism even more dramatic, as authentic British conservatives like Lord Ian Gilmour have shown.

Hewlett describes the Anglo-American disaster for children and families as attributable "to the ideological preference for free markets." Here she's only half right, in my opinion. Reaganite conservatism opposed free markets. It did advocate markets for the poor, but it went well beyond even its statist predecessors in demanding and winning a very high level of public subsidy and state protection for the rich. Whatever you choose to call this guiding ideology, it's unfair to tarnish the good name of conservatism by applying it to this particular form of violent and lawless and reactionary statism. Call it what you like, but it's not conservatism. It's not the free market. However, Hewlett is quite right in identifying the free market for the poor as the source of the disaster for families and children. And there isn't much doubt of the effects of what Hewlett calls the "anti-child spirit that is loose in these lands," in the Anglo-American lands, most dramatically in the U.S., but also Britain. This "neglect-filled Anglo-American model" based on market discipline for the poor has largely privatized child rearing while making it effectively impossible for most of the population to rear children. That's been the combined goal and policy of Reaganite conservatism and the Thatcherite analogue. The result is, of course, a disaster for children and families.

Continuing, Hewlett points out, "in the much more supportive European model," social policy has strengthened rather than weakened support systems for families and children. It's no secret, except as usual to readers of the press. As far as I'm aware, this 1993 study, rather critically relevant to our current concerns, has yet to be reviewed anywhere. It's not been, say, featured in the *New York Times,* although the *Times* did devote last Sunday's book review section largely to this topic, with somber forebodings about the fall of IQs, the decline of SAT scores, and so on and what might be causing it. Say, in the city of New York, where the social policies that have been pursued and backed by the *Times* have driven about 40 percent of the children below the poverty level, so that they're suffering malnutrition, disease, and so on. But it turns out that that is irrelevant to the decline in IQs, as is anything that Hewlett discusses in this Anglo-American neglect-filled model. What's relevant, it turns out, is bad genes. Somehow people are getting bad genes, and then there are various speculations about why this is. For example, maybe it's because black mothers don't nurture their children, and the reason is maybe they evolved in Africa, where the climate was hostile. So those are maybe the reasons, and this is really serious, hardheaded science, and a democratic society will ignore all this at its peril, the reviewer says. Well-disciplined commissars know well enough to steer away from the obvious factors, the ones rooted in very plain and clear social policy. They are perfectly evident to anybody with their head screwed on and happen to be discussed in considerable detail by a well-known economist in a UNICEF study that's not likely to see the light of day around here.

The facts are no secret. A blue-ribbon commission of the State Boards of Education and the American Medical Association reported, "Never before has one generation of children been less healthy, less cared for or less prepared for life than their parents were at the same age." That's a big shift in an industrial society. It's only in the Anglo-American societies where this antichild, antifamily spirit has reigned for fifteen years under the guise of conservatism and family values. That's a real triumph for propaganda.

A symbolic expression of this disaster is that when Hewlett wrote her book a year ago, 146 countries had ratified the international Convention on the Rights of the Child, but one had not: the U.S. That's a standard pattern for international conventions on human rights. However, just for fairness, it's only proper to add that Reaganite conservatism is catholic in its antichild, antifamily spirit. The World Health Organization voted to condemn the Nestle Corporation for aggressive marketing of infant formula, which kills plenty of children. The vote was 118 to 1. I'll leave you to guess the one. However, this is quite minor compared with what the World Health Organization calls the "silent genocide" that's killing millions of children every year as a result of the free-market policies for the poor and the refusal of the rich to give aid. Again, the U.S. has one of the worst and most miserly records among the rich societies.

Another symbolic expression of this disaster is a new line of greeting cards by the Hallmark Corporation. One of them says, "Have a super day at school." That one, they tell you, is to be put under a box of cereal in the morning, so that when the children go off to school they'll have a warm and caring message. Another one says, "I wish I had more time to tuck you in." That's one that you stick under the pillow at night when the kid goes to sleep alone. [Laughter] There are other such examples. In part this disaster for children and families is the result simply of falling wages. State corporate policy has been designed for the last years, especially under the Reaganites and Thatcher, to enrich small sectors and to impoverish the majority, and it succeeded. It's had exactly the intended effect. That means that people have to work much longer hours to survive. For much of the population both parents have to work maybe fifty hours merely to provide necessities. Meanwhile, incidentally, corporate profits are zooming. *Fortune* magazine talks about the "dazzling" profits reaching new heights for the Fortune 500 even though sales are stagnating.

Another factor is job insecurity, what economists like to call "flexibility in the labor markets," which is a good thing under the reigning academic theology but a pretty rotten thing for human beings, whose fate doesn't enter into the calculations of sober thinking. Flexibility means you better work extra hours, without knowing whether you have a job tomorrow, or else. There are no contracts and no rights. That's flexibility. We've got to get rid of market rigidities. Economists can explain it. When both parents are working extra hours, and for many on falling incomes, it doesn't take a great genius to predict the outcome. The statistics show them. You can read them in Hewlett's UNICEF study if you like. It's perfectly obvious without reading them what's going to happen. She reports that contact time, that is, actual time spent by parents with children, has declined sharply in the last twenty-five years in the Anglo-American societies, mostly in recent years. That's actually ten to twelve hours a week. What they call "high-quality time," time when you're not just doing something else, is declining. That leads to the destruction of family identity and values. It leads to sharply increased reliance on television for child supervision. It leads to what are called "latchkey children," kids who are alone, a factor in rising child alcoholism and drug use and in criminal violence against children by children and other obvious effects in health, education, ability to participate in a democratic society, even survival, and decline in SATs and IQs, but you're not supposed to notice that. That's bad genes, remember.

None of these things is a law of nature. These are consciously selected social policies designed for particular goals, namely, enrich the Fortune 500 but impoverish others. In Europe, where conditions are more stringent but policy is not guided by the same antifamily, antichild spirit, the tendencies are in the opposite direction, and the standards for children and families are much better.

It's worth mentioning, and let me stress, that this is not just true in the Anglo-American societies themselves. We're a big, powerful state. We have influence. It's very striking to notice what happens when other countries within the range of our influence try to undertake policies that benefit families and children. There are several striking examples.

The region that we control most completely is the Caribbean and Central America. There are two countries there that did undertake such policies—Cuba and Nicaragua—and with considerable success, in fact. Something which should surprise no one is that those are the two countries that were primarily targeted for U.S. assault. And it succeeded. So in Nicaragua, the rising health standards and the improvement in literacy and the reduction in child malnutrition have been reversed thanks to the terrorist war that we fought in Nicaragua, and now it's proceeding to the level of Haiti. In the case of Cuba, of course, the terrorist war has been going on a lot longer. It was launched by John F. Kennedy. It had nothing to do with communism. There weren't any Russians around. It had to do with things like the fact that these people were devoting resources to the wrong sectors of the population. They were improving health standards. They were concerned with children, with malnutrition. Therefore we launched a huge terrorist war. A bunch of CIA documents were just released recently filling in some of the details of the Kennedy period, which was bad enough. It continues up to the present. Actually, there was another assault just a couple of days ago. On top of that there's an embargo to try to ensure that they'll really suffer. For years the pretext was that this had to do with the Russians, which is completely fraudulent, as you can see by what was going on when the policies were instituted and as is demonstrated conclusively by what happened after the Russians disappeared. Here was a real job for the bought priesthood. They have to not notice that after the Russians disappeared we harshened the attack against Cuba. Kind of odd if the reason for the attack was that they were an outpost of communism and the Russian Empire. But we can handle that.

So after the Russians disappeared from the scene and it really became possible to strangle them, the conditions got harsher. A proposal was sent through Congress by a liberal Democrat, Representative [Robert] Torricelli, calling for a cutoff of any trade with Cuba by any subsidiary of any American corporation or any foreign corporation that used any parts produced in the U.S. That is so obviously in violation of international law that George Bush vetoed it. However, he was forced to accept it when he was outflanked from the right by the Clintonites in the last election, so he did then allow it to go through. That went right to the United Nations, where the U.S. position was denounced by just about everybody. In the final vote, the U.S. could pick up only Israel, which is automatic, and they got Rumania for some reason. Everyone else voted against it. The U.S. position was defended by no one. It is an obvious violation of international law, as even Britain and others pointed out. But it doesn't matter. It's extremely important to carry out our antichild, antifamily spirit and our insistence on highly polarized societies everywhere we can go. If a foreign country under our control tries to go a different way, we'll take care of them, too.

That's now continuing. It's the kind of thing you can actually do something about if you like. In Chicago there are the Pastors for Peace and the Chicago–Cuba Coalition, which have another caravan going to Cuba to try to undermine the embargo and bring humanitarian aid, medicines, medical books, powdered milk for infants, and other assistance. They're in the phone book under Chicago–Cuba Coalition. You can look them up. Anyone who is interested in countering the antichild, antifamily spirit that reigns here and that we're exporting by violence elsewhere can do that, just as they can do plenty of things at home.

I should say that the effects of this latest Democratic proposal, which went through, to strangle Cuba have recently been reviewed in this month's issues, October, of two leading American medical journals, *Neurology* and the *Florida Journal of Medicine,* which simply review the effects. They point out the obvious thing. It turns out that about 90 percent of the trade that was cut off by the Clinton–Torricelli bill was food and humanitarian aid, medicine, and things like that. For example, one Swedish company that was trying to export a water filtration device to create vaccines was blocked by the U.S. because there's some part in it that's American made. We really have to strangle them badly. We have to make sure that plenty of children die. One effect is a very sharp rise in infant mortality and child malnutrition. Another is a rare neurological disease that's spread over Cuba that everyone pretended they didn't know the reasons for. It's a result of malnutrition, a disease which hasn't been seen since Japanese prison camps in World War II. So we're succeeding in that one. The antichild, antifamily spirit is not just directed against kids in New York, but much more broadly.

I stress again that it is different in Europe, and there are reasons for it. One of the differences is the existence of a strong trade union movement. That's one aspect of a more fundamental difference—namely, the U.S. is a business-run society to quite an unparalleled degree, and as a result the vile maxim of the masters prevails to an unprecedented extent, pretty much as you'd expect. These are among the means that allow democracy to function formally, although by now most of the population is consumed by what the press calls "antipolitics," meaning hatred of government, disdain for political parties and the whole democratic process. That, too, is a great victory for the aristocrats in Jefferson's sense, that is, those who fear and distrust the people and wish to draw all power from them into the hands of the higher classes. By now that means into the hands of transnational corporations and the states and quasi-governmental institutions that serve their interests.

Another victory is the fact that the disillusionment, which is rampant, is antipolitics. A *New York Times* headline on this reads, "Anger and Cynicism Well Up in Voters as Hope Gives Way. Mood Turns Ugly as More People Become Disillusioned with Politics." Last Sunday's magazine section was devoted to antipolitics. Notice, not devoted to opposition to power and authority, to the easily identifiable forces that have their hands on the lever of decision making and that cast their shadow on society as politics, as Dewey put it. They have to be invisible. The *Times* has a story today again about this topic where they quote some uneducated person who doesn't get the point. He says, "Yeah, Congress is rotten, but that's because Congress is big business, so of course it's rotten." That's the story you're not supposed to see. You're supposed to be antipolitics. The reason is that whatever you think about government, it's the one part of the system of institutions that you can participate in and modify and do something about. By law and principle you can't do anything about investment firms or transnational corporations. Therefore nobody better see that. You've got to be antipolitics. That's another victory.

Dewey's observation that politics is the shadow cast on society by big business, which was incidentally also a truism to Adam Smith, has now become almost invisible. The force that casts the shadow has been pretty much removed by the ideological institutions and is so remote from consciousness that we're left with antipolitics. That's another severe blow to democracy and a grand gift to the absolutist and unaccountable systems of power that have reached levels that a Thomas Jefferson or John Dewey could scarcely imagine.

We have the usual choices. We can choose to be democrats in Thomas Jefferson's sense. We can choose to be aristocrats. The latter path is the easy one. That's the one that the institutions are designed to reward. It can bring rich rewards, given the locus of wealth and privilege and power and the ends that they very naturally seek. The other path, the path of the Jeffersonian democrats, is one of struggle, often defeat, but also rewards of a kind that can't even be imagined by those who succumb to the new spirit of the age, gain wealth, forgetting all but self. It's the same now as it was 150 years ago when there was an attempt to drive it into the heads of the factory girls in Lowell and the craftsmen in Lawrence and so on. Today's world is very far from Thomas Jefferson's. The choices it offers, however, have not changed in any fundamental way.

FIVE

Paideia and Democracy

Cornelius Castoriadis

I would like to talk to you about an issue that should concern all of us, both intellectually and politically. It's the issue of *paideia* in a democratic society. First, let me explain the term *paideia*. If I were speaking a foreign language,[1] I would say *culture*, but this term is both outlandish and ill sounding in Greek and became somewhat infamous lately. I will explain further down what I mean by the word *paideia* and I would like to remind you that nothing should be in principle more self-evident than the subject of this discussion.

To live in a democratic society means that we wonder about all those surrounding us inside this society, thus we wonder for our *paideia* itself. That very wondering is part of our *paideia* as a process and an ethos. Of course, as soon as we formulate this sentence—the status of *paideia* in a democratic society—a series of questions rises up. What do we mean by the word *paideia*? What do we mean by the word society? Or, what do we mean by the word *democracy*? I won't elaborate on these matters; I will only refer to them. But I would like to stress that the core of our topic is this: What is so special about *paideia* in a democratic society and what is its relation to the society and Democracy, compared to other societies, all of which, even the most primitive ones, had what I want to call *paideia*, or some kind of culture? I will name *paideia* anything that in a given society, within its public domain, goes beyond what is simply functional or instrumental and,

This paper is published in Castoriadis, C. (2001). *Anthropology, politics, philosophy*. Athens: Ypsilion (in Greek). My own translation (Maria Nikolakaki). From a Lecture that took place on February 24, 1993, in Alexandroupolis, in a ceremony during which Castoriadis received an honorary doctorate at Democritus University of Thrace.

most importantly, presents an invisible dimension, positively vested by the society members. In other words, *paideia* is what pertains to the public presence of this society's imaginary, *stricto sensu*, and the imaginary of the poeitic, *senso lato*, as this poeitic imaginary is substantiated and embodied in works, attitudes and actions that go beyond what is functional and instrumental.

I referred to an invisible aspect. When we have a book or a music score in front of us, or when we listen to what's written on that score, or when we see a painting, a statue, a monument, even though they are visible, what interests and excites us is this very invisible aspect beyond the visible, the non perceptible dimension beyond what is directly heard (or seen)—which, of course, can only exist through the visible, the audible or the tangible; but this visibility, this audibility or this tangibility is a precondition of this dimension.

Now, *democracy* is certainly a term that requires by nature much more discussion, because it has been, since a long time ago, since centuries, since millenniums, jeopardized in political debates and struggles, and also because it has since decades been prostituted, either in mild or in violent ways. Let's not forget that one of the most oppressive states in human history, until its collapse three years ago, had as its name four words that were all false: Union of Soviet Socialist Republics.

In order to avoid this cacophony, we will return to etymology. Democracy is the *kratos* of *demos*, which means the power of the people. Of course, philology cannot settle political conflicts, but at least it does allow us to formulate this question: Where in the world, in which country, does anyone dare to say that the power of the people is being realized? However, this power is written in the constitutions of Western countries, among them Greece, under the heading of "sovereignty of the people." Leaving aside, for now, the hypocrisy of this law affirmation, I will rely on the letter of the law to infer a meaning that only few could contest. In a democracy, the people are sovereign, that is to say, they make laws and the Law. Or, put in another way, society makes its institutions and institutes itself . It is autonomous, it is self-instituted obviously and explicitly, it works on itself its own rules, values and meanings. Autonomy or freedom entails and presupposes the autonomy, the freedom of the individuals, and is at the same time impossible without the latter. This very autonomy comprises the core target of our political project. But autonomy, which is, at least in appearance, guaranteed by law, by the constitutions, by declarations of human and civil rights, is based, all things considered, both *de jure* and *de facto*, on the collective law, the Law in the formal, as well as in the informal sense.

Real individual freedom—I'm not referring to philosophical or psychical freedom, but for the freedom we can realize through our private life and our social action—should be a matter of decision and entrenchment by a law that no individual could put or ratify on his own. And within the framework of this law, the individual can in turn define and determine for himself the norms, the values and the significations on which, and through which, he will then try to order his own life and give that life a meaning. As we all know, autonomy, this explicit self-institution, emerges for the first time in the Greek democratic cities. It reemerges later in a different—according to some aspects broader, in others stricter—way in the modern Western world. So, this autonomy marks the break that the creation of democracy bears with all previous social-historic regimes, because all earlier social-historical regimes are regimes of instituted heteronomy: Namely, in this regimes, the source and foundation of the law, as well as the source and foundation of each norm, value and signification, are considered transcendent in relation to the society; transcendent in an absolute way, as in monotheistic societies, and transcendent, in any case, with regard to the reality of the living society, as it happens in mythical or primitive societies (mythical not in the sense that they are societies narrated by myths, but in the sense that they are societies that base their institution on myths). And heteronomy goes hand in hand with something that is quite important for us and I will call it, for now, closure of signification; that means that the word of God or the provisions that our ancestors bestowed are not debatable and they are established once and for all. In heteronomous societies, this also holds for individuals. The meaning of their life is given, pre-determined and, thus, guaranteed. There is no possibility for discussion concerning institutions, nor is there any possibility for discussion, for questioning what is worthy and what is not, what is good and what is bad, what one should do and what one should not do.

Thus, in a heteronomous or traditional society, the closure of significance and of power or value shuts off in advance not only the political or philosophical question, but also the aesthetic (issue) or moral question. What must be said in each case is dictated, without possible appeal, by the law and by collective norms; and nothing changes in this situation when the huge, sophisticated, wise and endless commentaries of the law in the Talmud, in the Christian or the Islamic theology are introduced.

The same stands for *paideia*, in the way I use this term. Undoubtedly, the heteronomous societies have produced and created immortal works, which would be impossible and useless to recite. But those works, these monuments, in the broader sense of the term, are always found within the horizon of the instituted imaginary significations. Those works are always, all things considered, coordinated with the divine, the sacred, the holy, whether we take the divine, the sacred, and the holy in the current sense, or we consider them the sacred and holy of the domain of politics. These works reinforce the instituted significations, whether it concerns the worship of the divine or it's about the deification or glorification of heroes or the ancestors' gallantry and so on. Of course, it is roughly described here, but this is the substantial core of the great works that the primitives, the great traditional monarchies of the East, the real European Middle Ages, Eastern or Western, or the traditional Islam bequeathed to us.

That said, if these works and their creators act in the service of instituted significations, their public sees in them the confirmation and the glorification of its own significations and values, which are simply the collective and traditional values. And this is consonant with the specific mode of societies' cultural temporality", namely the particularly slow rhythm of change and the underground, secret character of the manner, style and context alteration. This also goes hand in hand with the impossibility to individualize the creators, something that doesn't derive from our lack of information. Under the dynasty of the Tang in China, they paint in this way and not differently; it's not perceivable otherwise. Under the twentieth dynasty of the Pharaoh, sculpture is done that way and not the other way; one should be specialized in order to discern the works of the Tang dynasty from the works of the Song or the Ming dynasty, or to discern the works of the twentieth dynasty from those of the twenty first or the nineteenth dynasty of Pharaonic Egypt. Thus, there are arranged and normative patterns: the forms—just as in our own Byzantine icons, for quite some time, even the smallest details are canonically set when it comes for the life of a saint or a given moment in the life of Virgin Mary. However, I outrun you, it is impossible to confuse a verse by Sappho with a verse by Archilochus. It is impossible for us, even if we're not philologists, but we just know how to read, to take a verse by Aeschylus for a verse by Sophocles; or, if we are to talk about the modern era, it is impossible not to distinguish a piece of Bach from a piece of Handel, even though both are Germans, lived in the same period and wrote with the same counterpoint technique. The founding of democracy, the emergence of the project of autonomy in history, no matter if it's just a mere seed, no matter how imperfect it is, radically alters the previous state, from this aspect too.

It is necessary here to make a short philosophical digression. When, in a way, we consider, speculate and contemplate whatever we can consider, speculate and contemplate, we reach to the conclusion that Being is chaos, abyss, the bottomless, but at the same time it is creation; it is a *vis formandi*, as we would say in Latin, a force of formation or figuration, which is not predetermined and which superposes on chaos, if I may say so, a *cosmos*—in the ancient Greek meaning— namely an entity that is more or less organized and regulated.

Similarly, when we finish, if we can finish at all, contemplating, speculating, thinking of the human sphere, we arrive to the conclusion that man, in the general, collective sense, which is both a society and an individual that takes naturally part in the Being, is also himself abyss, chaos and bottomless. And that, because man is a being of imagination and imaginary; and as a being of imagination and imaginary, of individual imagination and collective and social imaginary, man is also a force of formation (*vis formandi*). But he is also something that we certainly couldn't say (or perhaps could we?) for the Being as a whole is libido formandi, as we would say in Latin, he is *eros* and passion for formation and figuration, he is a force of creation, but also a desire for creation and formation or figuration.

This force and desire or passion is what I call the poeitic element of the man; a poeitic element of which even the Reason itself is nothing but an offshoot. Reason is a poeitic creature of man. The meaningful man wants and necessarily has to vest the world, the society, his face and his life with, is nothing else but this very education, in the strict sense of the term, not in the sense of conventional education, the *Bildung* as we would say in German (*Bild* means "image"), the constant effort to combine in an order, in an organization, in a world, all the things that appear and all those man himself causes to emerge. To give form to chaos—I think that is the best possible definition of *paideia* and, of course, this is (appears with more lucidity) even more obvious when it comes to art. The shape we give to chaos is the meaning and the signification, both of which, of course, are not simply a matter of ideas or presentations, but it should once again combine together, namely to capture (συν-λάβει) the depiction and the desire and the feeling, within a figure, within a form.

Of course, we can't say that this is what all religions and each religion have always done. Religion has a double nature, due to the fact that it attempts, on the one hand, to give shape and meaning to chaos, to abyss, to the bottomless, but, on the other hand, it does so by restricting chaos, abyss and the bottomless; by giving it a form, an image, a name, a Reason, certain dictates or certain qualities, things that religion probably names God. What especially concerns us here, since we don't talk all that philosophically but rather social-historically, is that religion can only achieve something like that, which is typical of it, by offering and at the same time by binding the form it gives to chaos, not only with the transcendent guarantee of signification—a guarantee that obviously human beings greedily need—but also with the closure, which only seemingly appears to be coessential with the very idea of the meaning. It establishes this guarantee and this closure—and I'm not talking only about monotheistic religions—by denying mankind the possibility to create meaning. For every religion, meaning has already been created once and for all and has been created elsewhere; man can, at most, accept this.

So, the creative force, *vis formandi*, is restrained and channeled, if I may say so, in a certain way, as is also the passion of formation restrained and channeled, which from then on is limited in enjoying its previous creations without even knowing that they're its own, since it attributes them to a transcendent being.

But democratic creation destroys any transcendent source of signification, as least as far as the public domain is concerned and, I would say, even for the private individual too, if it's complete. It breaks the closure of signification and, thus, it gives to the living society, to the people who exist "here and now," the possibility to think of their creative force, *vis formandi*, and to allow *libido formandi*, the passion and the desire (lust?) for formation and creation, to take effect. Of course, this presupposes a philosophical stance that in a way, I think, is the contact point of philosophy and politics or, if you prefer, of philosophy and democracy despite appearances. This will probably sound like a paradox, but I think that's the way it is. Both require an acknowledgment of the fact that there is no signification in Being, as if it were a hidden treasure that should be found; nor inside Being, nor into the world, nor into history, nor into our personal life and that it is us who create the signification and the meaning, based on what has no basis, relying on the bottomless; and that in this way it is us who give shape to chaos with our thought, our action, our works—therefore, this signification has no external guarantee. It is in the same way that El Greco's *The burial of Count Orgath* doesn't draw its beauty from the sky on the upper part of the painting, but from the entirety of the synthesis and the painting process itself.

This means that we are alone in the Being; alone, yet not solipsists. We are already alone, strangely enough though, because we talk and we talk to each other, whereas Being doesn't talk, not even to recite the Riddle of the Sphinx. But we're not solipsists, because our creation and our word is based on Being and constantly bounces due to our confrontation with it; and this word and creation of ours maintains its motion by trying to form what is only elusively and fragmentarily offered for formation and so it can, sometimes momentarily, sometimes long-lastingly, but always under danger to form what's presented.

If this is how things are, in a democratic society our cultural, or paidic (παιδειακή), if I may use this neologism, creation appears to be completely changed in relation to the pre-democratic societies—and so, we reach at last at the core of our subject. To put it briefly, the work is no longer inscribed in a domain of already instituted and collectively accepted significations. It doesn't find in this domain neither the norms of its form or its context, nor can its creator simply draw from this domain his norms, the material of his work and the method of his labor, and nor can the public base its acceptance of the new work on something that's simply delivered.

The community, society, creates openly, its norms and significations itself—and so the individual is called, at least *de jure*, to create within formally unlimited frameworks the meaning of his life and, for example, to judge with his own criteria the cultural creations that are presented to him. Of course, we shouldn't think of this passage as being absolute, because we are always, and we will always be, in an autonomous democratic society, in a social domain of signification that is not just formal. We will always have some kind of relation with tradition and no one can avoid this, not even the most original artist: he can only contribute to their creative alteration. These are the essential characters of this domain that alter when a democratic society is being established—as we can see this in the democratic societies, however limited that were established during the two phases of history I mentioned earlier: that is, the case of ancient Greece and the case of Western Europe.

We can see this clearly for ourselves in ancient Greece; I won't talk about it, because I think that it's very familiar to you, but I will talk about the case of Western Europe. Let's consider the strictly modern phase of the Western world: let's say, from the middle eighteenth century, with the Enlightenment, and after the great democratic revolutions and the subsequent decline of religion, at least as a political and social force, until 1950—a totally symbolic date, which, however, marks the entrance to a new phase.

What is the domain of significations of the unprecedented and inconceivable cultural creation that characterized both these centuries? Let's take the creator's point of view. Who is the creator here? He's not a Byzantine hagiographer or a builder, someone who works for his God's glory, such as Isidore of Miletos and Anthemius of Tralles when they built the Hagia (Saint) Sophia, or an unknown, nameless Western artist, when he created equally great masterpieces, namely the Gothic temples, for the glory of his God. For the great artists we know of from this period have no or almost no relation to religion. Where is this artist? I think that what moves him and makes him live is what I would call sober exhilaration of freedom. It's the exhilaration of exploring, of freedom concerning the creation of new forms, new forms which he seeks as such. Of course, new forms emerge and in other historical periods, e.g. when the Romantic style gives way to the Gothic, but this new form appears, if we could put it that way, redundantly. In the modern era, we have this freedom of exploring new forms as such. But this freedom remains tied up to its object, in other words it is exploration and, in a way, establishment of a meaning within the new form. Of course, the artist seeks, like the Ancients did, the κλέος (kleos) and the κύδος (kydos), the fame and the glory. But a great artist, Proust, had talked about what one can think and what one should think: the action itself, the artist's practice, alters him so deeply that he no longer pays attention to his motives—and neither do we. For, as Proust says, the artist began working for glory and got so carried away by his work that he doesn't care anymore for glory. I think that this is what distinguishes the true artist, as well as the true politician and the true philosopher. The realization of freedom here, and the realization of *vis formandi* and *libido formandi*, is the freedom of creating norms, of creating examples, as Kant remarks correctly in *The Critique of Judgement*, and as such, it is destined to endure.

This is par excellence the case of modern art during the two-century period I mentioned earlier, which explores and creates forms, in the strong and strict sense of the term; I would say that, on this account, it is democratic, namely liberating, even when those representing it are or could be reactionary, such as Chateaubriand, Balzac, Flaubert, Dostoyevsky, Degas, Rilke and others. But it is especially the artist who remains attached to an object. Modern art ceased to be religious and became philosophical in a way. It certainly isn't philosophy, but it is philosophical since it is exploration of constantly newer layers of the psyche, the society, the visible, and the audible. It is, of course, the exploration of these layers that aspires, with the unique way of art, to give form to chaos.

Once again, this doesn't mean that art is philosophy, but that it can only exist as such by creating meaning, while a religious art, for example, has no obligation to do so. It acquires its meaning from the religious faith and the context of religion. And I will remind you again of Proust: This is exactly the subject of the author's extensive reasoning and contemplation with himself in *Le temps retrouvé*, in the time that has been found again, where Proust finally makes it his object, in his own words, "to find the essence of things."

And from this aspect Kant had seen something very important, though he had distorted it, if I may say so, by saying that the work of art is a presentation inside the intuition of the ideas of reason. It's a presentation of chaos or abyss or the bottomless, to which it gives form. And through this presentation, art is a kind of window to chaos, through with it destroys for the rest of us the quiet and silly certainty of our everyday life. And it reminds us that we will always live on the edge of the abyss—which is exactly the first and last knowledge of an autonomous being. A knowledge that doesn't prevent him from living like, to cite for the third and last time Proust, "the atheist artist [. . .] who considers himself obliged to restart twenty times a piece, while he knows quite well that the admiration this piece probably raises, will be totally immaterial in his worm-eaten body. Just as this small piece of yellow wall, painted with such wisdom and finesse by a painter that will always remain unknown to us and that we simply call him today by the name Vermeer."

The public, on its turn, participates indirectly in this freedom, during that period, with the artist's intervention. However, it is seized by the new meaning that the work presents it with—and that can happen only because, in spite of the inertias, the delays, the resistances, this public, the Western public of those two centuries, when all is said and settled, is a public that is creative itself. The acceptance of a new work is never and can never be just a passive acceptance; it's recreation. The people who, for instance, understood and applauded for the first time Wagner's music, his music of the second era after *Tristan*, were the people who, in a way, recreated socially what we understand as music and what music is.

And thus, both the artist's freedom and its products, its works, are socially vested. And I conclude wondering: Are we still living in that era? It's a dangerous question, which, however, I will try not to avoid. I think that, in spite of appearance, this rupture of the closure that the great democratic and political movements of the two centuries between 1750 and 1950 brought about runs a deadly risk of being masked. If we look at the real function of society, the "power of the people" serves as a curtain that covers up the power and dominion of money, of technoscience, of political parties and state bureaucracy, of mass media. On the level of individuals, a new closure is established that takes the form of a generalized conformism. I assert that we live in one of the most conformist phases of Greek-Western history. We are told that every person is free; while in reality all persons passively accept the only meaning the institutions and the social domain propose to them and, in fact, imposes on them. It's the meaning one could call tele[2]–consumption; it's not just the television consumption, but a consumption taking place from a distance, because its object is constantly drifting away.

If, now, we are to discuss the cultural creation—where, of course, judgments are most uncertain, most debatable and most dangerous—one cannot underestimate the remarkable growth of eclecticism, the collage, in the broader sense of the term, of a spineless syncretism, and especially the loss of the *object* and the loss of the *meaning*, which go hand in hand with an abandonment of the search for form. For the form and for what the form is—and, as you may see, I used this term during this speech not in the formalistic sense, but in the sense of the Platonic and Aristotelian *eidos*, namely the unity of an appearance with what this appearance expresses—as Victor Hugo profoundly said, it is the bottom that rises to the surface; and I think no-one can say it better or say anything more than that.

From this respect, all the pessimistic prophets and the contemporary era prophets, of this modern era, are now in the process of being fulfilled—from Tocqueville, who talked about "mediocrity," the mediocre value of what he called "democratic" individual, namely the modern person, passing on from Nietzsche and nihilism (as Nietzsche put it, "What does nihilism signify? Those higher values are being devalued. It lacks a goal, it is missing the answers to the question 'Why?'"), and then on to Spengler and Heidegger. Perhaps we could say that all these prophecies have been reversed, meaning that they are in the process of being theorized in the silly trend that today is called postmodernism, through which our era is self-praised, or rather the insignificance of our time.

I don't want to keep you much longer; I will just stress once again that the so-called individualism, the triumph of which various insignificant journalists and politicians celebrate, is not, nor can it be, a void form, because individuals don't do whatever they want, but they do what the composed society or the institutionalized society, the establishment as we usually say, imposes on them. And a real individualism can never be the void form of individualism, just like a real democracy can never be simply procedural. Democratic proceedings today, for example, as a shape, as a form, are filled with the oligarchic context of the modern social composure and the individualistic forms are filled with the capitalist imaginary of the unlimited expansion of production, of consumption and of a mendacious, pseudo-rational pseudo-sovereignty over things and over people.

If these statements are, partly at least, accurate, then we can say that *paideia* in such a democratic society runs the greatest of risks—not, of course, the pseudo—*paideia* that appears in the form of multi-knowledge, or museum-oriented or tourist, when people visit the Acropolis or the temples of Cambodia or Hagia Sophia and then visit the area's restaurants with the same attitude and gravity, not from this aspect, but as far as its creational essence is concerned. And I think that, as far as I'm concerned, society consists a "whole"—albeit it is certainly disintegrated, highly complicated and enigmatic. Thus, as the current evolution of *paideia* is not wholly irrelevant to the inertia and the social and political passivity characteristic of our world today, a renaissance of its vitality,, will be indissociable from a great new politico-social movement that will reactivate democracy and will give it at once the form and the contexts the idea of democracy requires, should it take place.

Of course, one might ask what could be the context of such a new democracy, but the question would be unapt. When Cleisthenes and his companions were establishing a democracy, they neither could have—nor should have—foreseen, nor was their aim to foresee Aeschylus, Sophocles and Euripides, the Parthenon or the Athenian huge creation that followed, any more than the French *Constituants* or Jefferson and other Americans, when establishing democratic or quasi democratic regimes, could have foreseen that after 20, 30 or 40 years people like Stendhal, Balzac, Flaubert or like Poe, Melville and Whitman would appear.

Philosophy shows us, and I conclude shortly, that it would be silly and absurd to believe that we might ever exhaust the thinkable, the feasible or the formable, just as it shows it would be silly and absurd to set limits on the power of formation that is always present within people's psychical imagination and within the collective socio-historical imaginary. But philosophy doesn't stop us from ascertaining that humanity has already been through periods of decay and lethargy, much more insidious, to the degree they were followed, i.e., during the Roman Empire era, by what we usually call material well-being. But to the degree, frail or not, that this depends on us, and especially on those among us that think and try, as long as what we think and try to do and show to others remains true to the idea of human autonomy, then we could at least contribute to making this phase of slow lethargy as short as possible. Thank you.

Notes

1. This refers to the fact that the speech was given in Greek.
2. Tele in Greek means from distance.

SIX

From (Mis)Education to *Paideia*

Takis Fotopoulos

Democracy, Paideia and Education

Culture, the Dominant Social Paradigm and the Role of Education

Education is a basic component of the formation of culture,[1] as well as of the socialisation of the individual, i.e., the process through which an individual internalises the core values of the dominant social paradigm.[2] Therefore, culture in general and education in particular play a crucial role in the determination of individual and collective values. This is because as long as individuals live in a society, they are not just individuals but *social* individuals, subject to a process which socialises them and induces them to internalise the existing institutional framework and the dominant social paradigm. In this sense, people are not completely free to create their world but are conditioned by History, tradition and culture. Still, this socialisation process is broken, at almost all times—as far as a minority of the population is concerned—and in exceptional historical circumstances even with respect to the majority itself. In the latter case, a process is set in motion that usually ends with a change of the institutional structure of society and of the corresponding social paradigm. Societies therefore are not just "collections of individuals" but consist of social individuals, who are both free to create their world (in the sense that they can give birth to a new set of institutions and a cor-

Reprinted from the *The International Journal of Inclusive Democracy*, Vol. 2, No.1 (September 2005)

responding social paradigm), and are created by the world (in the sense that they have to break with the dominant social paradigm in order to recreate the world).

A fundamental precondition for the reproduction of every kind of society is the consistency between the dominant beliefs, ideas and values on the one hand and the existing institutional framework on the other. In other words, unlike culture[3] which has a broader scope and may express values and ideas that are not necessarily consistent with the dominant institutions (this has frequently been the case in arts and literature), the dominant social paradigm has to be consistent with the existing institutions for society to be reproducible. In fact, institutions are reproduced mainly through the internalisation of the values consistent with them rather than through violence by the elites which benefit from them. This has always been the case. The values, for instance, of the present system are the ones derived by its basic principles of organisation: the principle of heteronomy and the principle of individualism which are built into the institutions of the market economy and representative 'democracy.' Such values involve the values of inequity and effective oligarchy (even if the system calls itself a democracy), competition and aggressiveness.

Still, what is wrong is not the very fact of the internalisation of some values but the internalisation of such values that reproduce an heteronomous society and consequently heteronomous individuals. Paideia will play a crucial role in a future democratic society with respect to the internalisation of its values, which would necessarlily be the ones derived by its basic principles of organisation: the principle of autonomy and the principle of community, which would be built into the institutions of an inclusive democracy.[4] Such values, as we shall see in the third section, would include the values of equity and democracy, respect for the personality of each citizen, solidarity and mutual aid, caring and sharing.[5]

However, the institutions alone are not sufficient to secure the non-emergence of informal elites. It is here that the crucial importance of education, which in a democratic society will take the form of paideia, arises. Paideia was of course at the centre of political philosophy in the past, from Plato to Rousseau. Still, this tradition, as the late Castoriadis[6] pointed out, died in fact with the French Revolution. But, the need to revisit paideia today in the context of the revival of democratic politics, after the collapse of socialist statism, is imperative.

Education, Paideia and Emancipatory Education

Education is intrinsically linked to politics. In fact, the very meaning of education is defined by the prevailing meaning of politics. If politics is meant in its current usage, which is related to the present institutional framework of representative 'democracy,' then politics takes the form of statecraft, which involves the administration of the state by an elite of professional politicians who set the laws, supposedly representing the will of the people. This is the case of a heteronomous society in which the public space has been usurped by various elites which concentrate political and economic power in their hands. In a heteronomous society education has a double aim:

- First, to help in the internalisation of the existing institutions and the values consistent with it (the dominant social paradigm). This is the aim of explicit school lessons like History, introduction to sociology, economics, etc., but, even more significantly—and insidiously—of schooling itself, which involves the values of obedience and discipline (rather than self-discipline) and unquestioning of teaching.

- Second, to produce 'efficient' citizens in the sense of citizens who have accumulated enough 'technical knowledge'[7] so that they could function competently in accordance with 'society's aims, as laid down by the elites which control it.

On the other hand, if politics is meant in its classical sense that is related to the institutional framework of a direct democracy, in which people not only question laws but are also able to make their own laws, then we talk about an autonomous society.[8] This is a society in which the public space encompasses the entire citizen body that in an inclusive democracy will take all effective decisions at the 'macro' level, i.e., not only with respect to the political process but also with respect to the economic process, within an institutional framework of equal distribution of political and economic power among citizens. In such a society we do not talk about education anymore but about the much broader concept of *paideia*. This is an all-round civic education that involves a life-long process of character development, absorption of knowledge and skills and—more significant—practicing a 'participatory' kind of active citizenship, that is a citizenship in which political activity is not seen as a means to an end but an end in itself. Paideia therefore has the overall aim of developing the capacity of all its members to participate in its reflective and deliberative activities, in other words, to educate citizens as citizens so that the public space could acquire a substantive content. In this sense, paideia involves the specific aims of civic schooling as well as personal training. Thus,

- *Paideia as civic schooling* involves the development of citizens' self-activity by using their very self-activity as a means of internalising the democratic institutions and the values consistent with them. The aim therefore is to create responsible individuals that have internalized both the necessity of laws and the possibility of putting the laws into question, i.e., individuals capable of interrogation, reflectiveness, and deliberation. This process should start from am early age through the creation of educational public spaces that will have nothing to do with present schools, at which children will be brought up to internalize, and therefore to accept fully, the democratic institutions and the values implied by the fundamental principles of organisation of society: autonomy and community.

- *Paideia as personal training* involves the development of the capacity to learn rather than to teach particular things, so that individuals become autonomous, that is, capable of self-reflective activity and deliberation. A process of conveying knowledge is of course also involved but this assumes more the form of involvement in actual life and the multitude of human activities related to it, as well as a guided tour to scientific, industrial and practical knowledge rather than teaching, as it is simply a step in the process of developing the child's capacities for learning, discovering, and inventing.

Finally, we may talk about *emancipatory education* as the link between present education and paideia. Emancipatory education is intrinsically linked to transitional politics, i.e., the politics that will lead us from the heteronomous politics and society of the present to the autonomous politics and society of the future. The aim of emancipatory education is to give an answer to the 'riddle of politics' described by Castoriadis,[9] i.e., how to produce autonomous (that is capable of self-reflective activity) human beings within a heteronomous society, and beyond that, in the paradoxical situation of educating human beings to accede to autonomy while—or in spite of—teaching them to absorb and internalize existing institutions. No less than the breaking of the socialisation process, which will open the way to an autonomous society, is involved here. The answer to this riddle proposed by this essay is to help the collectivity, within the context of the transitional strategy, to create the institutions that, when internalized by the individuals, will enhance their capacity for becoming autonomous.

Therefore, autonomy politics, i.e., the kind of politics implied by a transitional strategy towards a democratic society,[10] emancipatory education and paideia form an inseparable whole through the internal dynamic that leads from the politics of autonomy and emancipatory education to an autonomous society and paideia. It is therefore clear that as paideia is only feasible within the framework of a genuine democracy, an emancipatory education is inconceivable outside a democratic movement fighting for such a society, as we shall see in the final section.

However, before we discuss the nature and content of a democratic paideia and the transition to it through emancipatory education we have to examine the nature of present miseducation as it evolved in modernity—the topic of the next section.

Education in Modernity

The Shift to Modernity

The rise of the present system of education has its roots in the nation-state, which did not start to develop until the fourteenth to sixteenth centuries. The idea of a 'nation' was unknown in antiquity and even in the Middle Ages. Although in the territorial regnum of the Middle Ages some monarchies did indeed have their national territories and made claims to sovereign power within them, these monarchies were just part of European Christendom, so that there was little of a national state or indeed of any sort of state. In fact, it was not until the end of the Middle Ages and specifically in the seventeenth century that the present form of the nation-state emerged. The nation-state, even in its early absolutist form, extended its control beyond the political and into the religious (with the creation of an established church) and educational fields as well as to almost all other aspects of human life. As the state bureaucracy was expanding, the need for well-educated civil servants was significant and universities of the time became more and more training institutions for higher civil servants whereas, at the same time, elementary education for the middle classes developed further, particularly in the seventeenth and eighteenth centuries. A basic distinguishing characteristic of pre-modern schools and universities compared to modern ones was that whereas up to the seventeenth century the aim of education was conceived as a religious one, in the eighteenth century the ideas of secularism and progress, which constituted the fundamental components of the emerging new dominant social paradigm, began to prevail.

As I attempted to show elsewhere,[11] the two main institutions which distinguish premodern society from modern society are, first, the system of the market economy and, second, representative 'democracy,' which are also the ultimate causes for the present concentration of economic and political power and, consequently, for the present multidimensional crisis. In this *problematique*, industrial production constituted only the necessary condition for the shift to modern society. The sufficient condition was the parallel introduction—through decisive state help—of the system of the market economy that replaced the (socially controlled) local markets that existed for thousands of years before. In both cases, it was the emergence of the nation-state, which played a crucial role in creating the conditions for the 'nationalisation' of markets (i.e., their de-localisation), as well as in freeing them from effective social control—the two essential preconditions of marketisation. Furthermore, it was the same development, i.e., the rise of the nation-state that developed from its early absolutist form at the end of the Middle Ages into the present 'democratic' form, which led to the establishment of the political complement of the market economy: representative 'democracy.'

The shift to modernity therefore represented in more than one way a break with the past. The new economic and political institutions in the form of the market economy and representative 'democracy' as well as the parallel rise of industrialism marked a systemic change. This change was inescapably accompanied by a corresponding change in the dominant social paradigm. In premodern societies, the 'dominant social paradigms' were characterised mainly by religious ideas and corresponding values about hierarchies, although of course there were exceptions like the Athenian democracy. On the other hand, the dominant social paradigm of modernity is dominated by market values and the idea of progress, growth and rational secularism. In fact, the flourishing of science in modernity has played an important ideological role in 'objectively' justifying the growth economy—a role that has been put under severe strain in neoliberal modernity by the credibility crisis of science. Thus, just as religion played an important part in justifying the feudal hierarchy, so has science, particularly social 'science,' played a crucial role in justifying the modern hierarchical society. In fact, from the moment science replaced religion as the dominant worldview, it had 'objectively' justified the growth economy, both in its capitalist and 'socialist' forms.

However, although the fundamental institutions which characterize modernity and the main tenets of the dominant social paradigm have remained essentially unchanged since the emergence of modernity more than two centuries ago (something that renders as a myth the idea of postmodernity, into which humanity supposedly has entered in the last three decades or so), there have, nevertheless, been some significant *nonsystemic* changes within this period that could usefully be classified as the three main phases of modernity. We may distinguish three forms that modernity took since the establishment of the system of the market economy: liberal modernity (mid to end of nineteenth century) which, after the World War I and the 1929 crash, led to statist modernity (mid-1930s to mid-1970s) and finally to today's neoliberal modernity (mid-1970s to date).

The various forms of modernity have created their own dominant social paradigms, which in effect constitute sub-paradigms of the main paradigm, as they all share a fundamental characteristic: the idea of the separation of society from the economy and polity, as expressed by the market economy and representative 'democracy'—with the exception of Soviet statism in which this separation was effected through central planning and Soviet 'democracy.' On top of this main characteristic, all forms of modernity share, with some variations, the themes of reason, critical thought and economic growth. As one could expect, the nonsystemic changes involved in the various forms of modernity and the corresponding sub-paradigmatic changes had significant repercussions on the nature, content and form of education, on which I now turn.

Education in Liberal Modernity

During the period of liberal modernity, which barely lasted half a century between the 1830s and the 1880s, the grow-or-die dynamic of the market economy led to an increasing internationalisation of it, which was accompanied by the first systematic attempt of the economic elites to establish a purely liberal internationalised market economy in the sense of free trade, a 'flexible' labour market and a fixed exchange rates system (Gold Standard)—an attempt that, as I tried to show elsewhere,[12] was bound to fail given the lack of the objective conditions for its success and in particular the fact that markets were dominated by national-based capital, a fact that led to two world wars with the main aim to redivide them.

The rise of the system of the market/growth economy in this period created the need to expand the number of pupils/students in all stages of education: at the primary level, because the factory system that flourished after the Industrial Revolution required an elementary level of literacy; at the secondary level, because the factory system led to the development of various specialisations that required further specialised training; and, finally, at the tertiary level, because the rapid scientific developments of the era required an expansion of the role of universities to train not just civil servants, as before, but also people who would be able to be involved in applied research on new methods of production, both as regards its physical and its administrative/organisational aspects.

All these developments had significant repercussions on education, one of the most significant ones being the gradual acceptance of the view that education ought to be the responsibility of the state. Countries such as France and Germany began the establishment of public educational systems early in the nineteenth century. However, this trend was in contradiction to the dominant social (sub) paradigm of liberal modernity. This paradigm was characterised by the belief in a mechanistic model of science, objective truth, as well as some themes from economic liberalism such as laissez faire and minimisation of social controls over markets for the protection of labour. This is why countries such as Great Britain and the United States, in which the dominant social paradigm has been better internalised, hesitated longer before allowing the government to intervene in educational affairs. The prevailing view among the elites of these countries was that "free schools" were to be provided only for the children of the lowest social groups, if at all, whereas general taxation (which was the only adequate way to provide education for all) was rejected. Still, when liberal modernity collapsed at the end of the nineteenth century, for the reasons mentioned above, governments across Europe and the US legislated to limit the workings of laissez-faire—first by inspecting factories and offering minimal standards of education and later by providing subsistence income for the old and out of work."[13] As a result, by the beginning of the twentieth century, social legislation of some sort was in place in almost every advanced market economy.[14]

However, it was not only the access to education that changed during the nineteenth century. The nature of education changed as well, as the new social and economic changes also called upon the schools, public and private, to broaden their aims and curricula. Schools were expected not only to promote literacy, mental discipline, and good moral character but also to help prepare children for citizenship, for jobs, and for individual development and success. In other words, schools and educational institutions in general were expected to help in the internalisation of the existing institutions and the values consistent with it (i.e., the dominant social paradigm), on top of producing 'efficient' citizens in the sense of citizens who have accumulated enough technical knowledge so that they could function competently in accordance with 'society's aims, as laid down by the elites which control it. Similarly, the practice of dividing children into grades or classes according to their ages—a practice that began in eighteenth-century Germany— was to spread everywhere as schools grew larger. Massive schooling, which was to characterize the rest of modernity to date, was set in motion.

Statist Modernity, Education and Social Mobility

Statist modernity took different forms in the East (namely the regimes of Eastern Europe, China, etc.) and the West. Thus, in the East,[15] for the first time in modern times, a 'systemic' attempt was made to reverse the marketisation process and create a completely different form of modernity than the liberal or the social-democratic one—in a sense, another version of liberal modernity. This form of statism, backed by Marxist ideology, attempted to minimise the role of the market mechanism in the allocation of resources and replace it with a central planning mechanism. On the other hand in the West,[16] statism took a social-democratic form and was backed by Keynesian policies which involved active state control of the economy and extensive interference with the self-regulating mechanism of the market to secure full employment, a better distribution of income and economic growth. A precursor of this form of statism emerged in the inter-war period but it reached its peak in the period following World War II, when Keynesian policies were adopted by governing parties of all persuasions in the era of the social-democratic consensus, up to the mid-1970s. This was a consensus involving both conservative and social-democratic parties, which were committed to active state intervention with the aim of determining the overall level of economic activity, so that a number of social-democratic objectives could be achieved (full employment, welfare state, educational opportunities for all, better distribution of income, etc.).

However, statist modernity, in both its social-democratic and Soviet versions, shared the fundamental element of liberal modernity, namely, the formal separation of society from the economy and the state. The basic difference between the liberal and statist forms of modernity concerned the means through which this separation was achieved. Thus, in liberal modernity this was achieved through representative 'democracy' and the market mechanism, whereas in statist modernity this separation was achieved either through representative 'democracy' and a modified version of the market mechanism (Western social democracy), or, alternatively, through Soviet 'democracy' and central planning (Soviet statism). Furthermore, both the liberal and the statist forms of modernity shared a common growth ideology based on the Enlightenment idea of progress—an idea that played a crucial role in the development of the two types of 'growth economies': the 'capitalist' and the 'socialist' growth economy.[17] It is therefore obvious that although the growth economy is the offspring of the dynamic of the market economy, still, the two concepts are not identical since it is possible to have a growth economy which is not also a market economy—notably the case of 'actually existing socialism.' However, the Western form of statist modernity collapsed in the 1970s when the growing internationalisation of the market economy, the inevitable result of its grow-or-die dynamic, became incompatible with statism. The Eastern form of statist modernity collapsed a decade or so later because of the growing incompatibility between, on the one hand, the requirements of an 'efficient' growth economy and, on the other, the institutional arrangements (particularly centralised planning and party democracy) which had been introduced in the countries of 'actually existing socialism' in accordance with Marxist-Leninist ideology.[18]

The dominant (sub)paradigm in the statist period still features the same characteristics of liberal modernity involving a belief in objective truth and (a less mechanistic) science, but includes also certain elements of the socialist paradigm and particularly statism, in the form of Soviet statism based on Marxism-Leninism in the East and a social-democratic statism based on Keynesianism in the West. Both types of statism attempted to influence the education process although Soviet governments, particularly in the early days after the 1917 Revolution, had much wider aims than Western social democrats who mainly aimed at widening the access to education in order to improve social mobility.

Thus, the Soviets, immediately after the Revolution, introduced free and compulsory general and polytechnical education up to the age of 17, pre-school education to assist in the emancipation of women, the opening of the universities and other higher institutions to the working class, even a form of student-self management. On top of this, a basic aim of education was decreed to be the internalisation of the new regime's values. No wonder that, as soon as a year after the Revolution, the Soviet government had ordered by decree the abolition of religious teaching in favour of atheistic education.

As regards the social democrats, their main achievement was the welfare state which represented a conscious effort to check the side effects of the market economy as far as covering basic needs (health, education, social security) was concerned. An important characteristic of the ideology of the welfare state was that its financing (including education) was supposed to come from general taxation. Furthermore, the progressive nature of the tax system, which was generalised during this period, secured that the higher income groups would take the lion's share of this financing, improving thereby the highly unequal pattern of income distribution that a market economy creates. However, the expansion of education opportunities was not simply necessitated by ideological reasons. Even more important was the post-war economic boom that required a vast expansion of the labour base, with women and, sometimes immigrants, filling the gaps. On top of this, the incessant increase in the division of labour, changes in production methods and organisation, as well as revolutionary changes in information technology required a growing number of highly skilled personnel, scientists, high-level professionals, etc. As a result of these trends, the number of universities in many countries doubled or trebled between 1950 and 1970, whereas technical colleges, as well as part-time and evening courses, spread rapidly, promoting adult education at all levels.

Still, despite the fact that massive education flourished in this period, the effects of this rapid growth of education opportunities on social mobility have been insignificant. If we take as our example Britain, in which a bold social-democratic experiment was pursued in the post-war period to change social mobility through education—a policy pursued (in various degrees) by both Labour and Conservative governments—the results were minimal. Thus, an extensive study by three prominent British academics concluded that the post-war expansion of education opportunities brought Britain no nearer to meritocracy or equality of opportunity.[19] Another study, also carried out during the period of social-democratic consensus, concluded that despite the 'propitious' circumstances, 'no significant reduction in class inequality has in fact been achieved'[20]—a situation that has worsened in today's neoliberal modernity in which, as Goldthorpe showed, the chances of manual workers' sons not doing anything but manual work have risen. But, if the results of social-democratic education policies on social mobility and social change in general have been so meagre, one could easily imagine the effects of neoliberal policies to which I now turn.

Neoliberal Modernity and the Privatisation of Education

The emergence of neoliberal internationalisation was a monumental event which implied the end of the social democratic consensus that marked the early post-war period. The market economy's grow-or-die dynamic and, in particular, the emergence and continuous expansion of transnational corporations' (TNC) and the parallel development of the Euro-dollar market, which led to the present neoliberal form of modernity, were the main developments which induced the economic elites to open and liberalise the markets. In other words, these elites mostly institutionalised (rather than created) the present form of the internationalised market economy.

An important characteristic of the neoliberal form of modernity is the emergence of a new 'transnational elite'[21] which draws its power (economic, political or generally social power) by operating at the transnational level—a fact which implies that it does not express, solely or even primarily, the interests of a particular nation-state. This elite consists of the transnational economic elites (TNC executives and their local affiliates), the transnational political elites, i.e., the globalising bureaucrats and politicians, who may be based either in major international organisations or in the state machines of the main market economies, and, finally, the transnational professional elites, whose members play a dominant role in the various international foundations, think tanks, research departments of major international universities, the mass media etc. The main aim of the transnational elite, which today controls the internationalised market economy, is the maximisation of the role of the market and the minimisation of any effective social controls over it for the protection of labour or the environment, so that maximum 'efficiency' (defined in narrow techno-economic terms) and profitability may be secured.

Neoliberal modernity is characterised by the emergence of a new social (sub)paradigm which tends to become dominant, the so-called 'post-modern' paradigm. The main elements of the neoliberal paradigm are, first, a critique of progress (but not of growth itself), of mechanistic and deterministic science (but usually not of science itself) and of objective truth, and, second, the adoption of some neoliberal themes such as the minimisation of social controls over markets, the replacement of the welfare state by safety nets and the maximisation of the role of the private sector in the economy.

As regards scientific research and education, neoliberal modernity implies the effectual privatisation of them. As a result, the non-neutral character of science has become more obvious than ever before, following the 'privatisation' of scientific research and the scaling down of the state sector in general and state spending in particular.[22] As Stephanie Pain, an associate editor of *New Scientist* (not exactly a radical journal) stresses, science and big business have developed ever closer links lately:

> Where research was once mostly neutral, it now has an array of paymasters to please. In place of impartiality, research results are being discreetly managed and

massaged, or even locked away if they don't serve the right interests. Patronage rarely comes without strings attached.[23]

Also, as regards education in general, as Castoriadis pointed out,[24] for most educators it has become a bread-winning chore, and, for those at the other end of education, a question of obtaining a piece of paper (a diploma) that will allow one to exercise a profession (if one finds work)—the royal road of privatization, which one may enrich by indulging in one or several personal crazes.

The effects of the neoliberal privatisation of education on access to education in general and social mobility in particular are predictable. Thus, as regards the former, it is not surprising that, as a result of increasing poverty and inequality in neoliberal modernity, the reading and writing skills of Britain's young people are worse than they were before World War I. Thus, a recent study found that 15 per cent of people aged 15 to 21 are 'functionally illiterate,' whereas in 1912, school inspectors reported that only 2 per cent of young people were unable to read or write.[25] Similarly, as regards the access to higher education, the UK General Household Survey of 1993 showed that, as the education editor of the *London Times* pointed out, 'although the number of youngsters obtaining qualifications is growing rapidly, the statistics show that a child's socio-economic background is still the most important factor in deciding who obtains the best higher educa-tion. Thus, according to these data, the son of a professional man was even more likely to go to university in the early 90s than one from the same background in the early 60s (33 percent versus 29 percent). Finally, an indication of the marginal improvement to access to education achieved by social democracy is the fact that whereas at the end of the 1950s the percent of the sons of unskilled workers going to university was too small to register, by the early 90s this percentage has gone up to 4%![26] Needless to add that the situation has worsened further since then. The difference between the proportion of professionals and unskilled workers going to university has widened 10 points during the nineties and by the end of this decade fewer than one in six children from the bottom rung were going to university compared to nearly three-quarters of the top.[27]

No wonder therefore that social mobility in Britain has declined in neoliberal modernity. This is because, although the working class has declined in size follow-ing neoliberal globalisation, the middle classes have not been displaced. As a re-sult, over the 20th century, the trapdoor beneath the upper social groups became less and less the worry it was in Victorian society, and as sociologist Peter Saun-ders[28] put it, the safeguards against failure enjoyed by dull middle-class children are presently strengthening. Despite, therefore, a small increase in social mobility for children from lower social strata, at the same time, as a team led by Stephen Machin of University College London has found, more children from higher-class backgrounds have remained in the same social class as their parents. This could explain the paradox that the amount of 'equality of opportunity' may actually have fallen in recent years, despite the expansion of educational opportunity.[29] Another study by Abigail McKnight[30] of the University of Warwick confirms this. Thus, whereas between 1977 and 1983, a full 39 per cent of workers in the bottom quarter of the earnings distribution had progressed into the top half by 1983, in the period between 1991 and 1997, that had dropped to 26 per cent.

Similar trends are noted everywhere, given the universalisation of neoliberal modernity. Predictably, the effects are even worse in the South where education was seen by those nations newly liberated from their colonial ties nations as both an instrument of national development and a means of crossing national and cultural barriers. No wonder that, worldwide, 125 million children are not attending school today (two-thirds of them girls) despite a decade of promises at UN conferences to get every child in the world into a classroom. Thus, as cash-strapped governments have cut education budgets, forcing schools to charge fees, 'schools have become little more than child minding centres.'[31]

The Preconditions of *Paideia*

As I attempted to show in the first section, paideia in a democratic society is seen both as *civic schooling* and as *personal training*. In the first sense, paideia is intrinsically linked with a set of institutional preconditions at society's level whereas in the second sense it is linked with the institutional preconditions at the educational level itself. Apart, however, from the institutional preconditions it is clear that paideia presupposes a radical change in value systems—the main aim of emancipatory education—which would lead to a new dominant social paradigm. This conception of paideia clearly differentiates it from the stand on education usually adopted by liberals, but also by some Marxists and many more libertarians, who separate education from the system of market economy and representative 'democracy' and suggest that an alternative education is feasible even in the existing system. Thus, in contrast to the fathers of anarchism like Bakunin who insisted that a libertarian education is impossible in existing society,[32] supporters of Stirner's individualistic tendency within anarchism like Ivan Illich, adherents to the 'anarchy in action' current like Colin Ward and others[33] propose various schemes of libertarian education within the existing system of capitalist market economy. No wonder that a recent article published in *Social Anarchism* does not hesitate to adopt the neoliberal arguments of cost effectiveness in attacking state schools ['of the two forms (public and private) . . . public school is by far the most expensive in direct cost'][34] in order to support a simplistic case for deschooling! At the other end, many Marxists, as well as anarchists and supporters of autonomy like Castoriadis, talk only about paideia *after* the revolutionary change in society, ignoring the crucial stage of the transitional period and the need to develop an emancipatory education for it.

In this section, I will attempt to describe the institutional preconditions of paideia whereas in the next section the issue of emancipatory education (i.e., the transition from present modernity education to a democratic paideia) will be discussed in an effort to show that any attempt to create an alternative education within the existing system is doomed, unless it is implemented at a significant social scale and is an integral part of an antisystemic project.

Institutional Preconditions at Society's Level

The institutional preconditions of paideia at society's level are summarised by the inclusive democracy (ID) conception, described in detail elsewhere,[35] so I will only attempt here to briefly describe the main elements of this conception that are relevant to the question of paideia.

The conception of inclusive democracy, using as a starting point the classical definition of it, expresses democracy in terms of direct political democracy, economic democracy (beyond the confines of the market economy and state planning), as well as democracy in the social realm and ecological democracy. In short, inclusive democracy is a form of social organisation which re-integrates society with economy, polity and nature. In this sense, democracy is seen as irreconcilable with any form of inequity in the distribution of power, that is, with any concentration of power, political, social or economic. Consequently, democracy is incompatible with commodity and property relations, which inevitably lead to concentration of power. Similarly, it is incompatible with hierarchical structures implying domination, either institutionalised (e.g., domination by men, educators and so on), or 'objective' (e.g., domination of the South by the North in the framework of the market division of labour), and the implied notion of dominating the natural world.

The ID conception draws a fundamental distinction between public and private, which is particularly important with respect to the paideia issue. The public realm, contrary to the practice of many supporters of the republican or democratic project (Arendt, Castoriadis, Bookchin et al.) includes not just the political realm, but any area of human activity where decisions can be taken collectively and democratically. So, the public realm includes the political realm which is defined as the sphere of political decision-taking, the area where political power is exercised; the economic realm which is defined as the sphere of economic decision-taking, the area where economic power is exercised with respect to the broad economic choices that any scarcity society has to make; the social realm which is defined as the sphere of decision-taking in the workplace, the education place and any other economic or cultural institution that is a constituent element of a democratic society; and, finally, the 'ecological realm,' which is defined as the sphere of the relations between the natural and the social worlds.

Correspondingly, we may therefore distinguish between four main types of democracy that constitute the fundamental elements of an inclusive democracy: political, economic, ecological and 'democracy in the social realm.' Political, economic and democracy in the social realm may be defined, briefly, as the institutional framework that aims at the equal distribution of political, economic and social power, respectively, in other words, as the system which aims at the effective elimination of the domination of human being over human being. Similarly, we may define ecological democracy as the institutional framework that aims at the elimination of any human attempt to dominate the natural world, in other words, as the system which aims to reintegrate humans and nature.

In the political realm there can only be one form of democracy, what we may call *political* or *direct democracy*, where political power is shared equally among all citizens. So, political democracy is founded on the equal sharing of political power among all citizens, the self-instituting of society. This means that certain conditions have to be satisfied for a society to be characterised as a political democracy, i.e., that democracy is grounded on the conscious *choice* of its citizens for individual and collective autonomy and not on any divine or mystical dogmas and preconceptions, or any closed theoretical systems involving social/natural 'laws,' or tendencies determining social change; that no institutionalised political *processes* of an oligarchic nature exist so that all political decisions (including those relating to the formation and execution of laws) are taken by the citizen body collectively and without representation; that no institutionalised political *structures* embodying unequal power relations exist which implies specificity of delegation, rotation of delegates who are re-callable by the citizen body, etc., and that all residents of a particular geographical area and of a viable population size beyond a certain age of maturity (to be defined by the citizen body itself) and irrespective of gender, race, ethnic or cultural identity, are members of the citizen body and are directly involved in the decision-taking process.

The above conditions instutionalise a public space in which all significant political decisions are taken by the entire citizen body. However, one should clearly distinguish between democratic *institutions* and democratic *practice* which may still be non-democratic, even if the institutions themselves are democratic. It is therefore clear that the institutionalisation of direct democracy is only the necessary condition for the establishment of democracy. As Castoriadis puts it: "the existence of a public space (i.e., of a political domain which belongs to all') is not just a matter of legal provisions guaranteeing rights of free speech, etc. Such conditions are but conditions for a public space to exist."[36] Citizens in Athens, for instance, before and after deliberating in the assemblies, talked to each other in the *agora* about politics.[37] The role of paideia in the education of individuals as citizens is therefore crucial since it is only paideia that can "give valuable, substantive content to the 'public space.'"[38] As Hansen[39] points out on the crucial role of paideia:

> [T]o the Greek way of thinking, it was the political institutions that shaped the 'democratic man' and the 'democratic life,' not vice versa: the institutions of the *polis* educated and moulded the lives of the citizens, and to have the best life you must have the best institutions and a system of education conforming with the institutions.

The basic unit of decision making in a confederal inclusive democracy is the *demotic* assembly, i.e., the assembly of *demos*, the citizen body in a given geographical area, which delegates power to demotic courts, demotic militias, et cetera. However, apart from the decisions to be taken at the local level, there are a lot of important decisions to be taken at the regional or confederal level as well as at the workplace or the educational place to which we will come next. So, confederal democracy is based on a network of administrative councils whose members or delegates are elected from popular face-to-face democratic assemblies in the various *demoi,* which, geographically may encompass a town and the surrounding villages or even neighbourhoods of large cities. The members of these confederal councils are strictly mandated, recallable, and responsible to the assemblies that choose them for the purpose of co-ordinating and administering the policies formulated by the assemblies themselves. Their function is thus a purely administrative and practical one, not a policy-making one like the function of representatives in representative 'democracy.'[40]

Therefore, the institutional preconditions described create only the preconditions for freedom. In the last instance, individual and collective autonomy depend on the internalisation of democratic values by each citizen. This is why *paideia* plays such a crucial role in the democratic process. It is paideia, together with the high level of civic consciousness that participation in a democratic society is expected to create, which will decisively help in the establishment of a new moral code determining human behaviour in a democratic society. It is not difficult to show, as I attempted to do elsewhere,[41] that the moral values which are consistent with individual and collective autonomy in a *demos*-based society are those that are based on co-operation, mutual aid and solidarity. The adoption of such moral values will therefore be a conscious choice by autonomous individuals living in an autonomous society, as a result of the fundamental choice for autonomy, and not the outcome of some divine, natural or social 'laws,' or tendencies.

However, political democracy does not make sense, particularly in a society based on a market economy, until it is supplemented by economic democracy. Given the definition of political democracy as the authority of the people (*demos*) in the political sphere—which implies the existence of political equality in the sense of equal distribution of political power—we may correspondingly define economic democracy as the authority of *demos* in the economic sphere—which implies the existence of economic equality in the sense of equal distribution of economic power. Economic democracy therefore relates to a social system which institutionalises the integration of society and the economy and may be defined as an economic *structure* and a *process* which, through direct citizen participation in the economic decision-taking and decision-implementing process, secures an equal distribution of economic power among citizens. This means that, ultimately, the demos controls the economic process, within an institutional framework of *demotic* ownership of the means of production. Therefore, for a society to be characterised as an economic democracy there should be no institutionalised economic *processes* of an oligarchic nature, which implies that all 'macro' economic decisions, namely, decisions concerning the running of the economy as a whole (overall level of production, consumption and investment, amounts of work and leisure implied, technologies to be used, etc.) are taken by the citizen body collectively and without representation, although 'micro' economic decisions at the workplace or the household level may be taken by the individual production or consumption unit. Also, there should be no institutionalised economic *structures* embodying unequal economic power relations, which implies that the means of production and distribution are collectively owned and directly controlled by the *demos* so that any inequality of income is therefore the result of additional voluntary work at the individual level. Thus, *demotic ownership* of the economy provides the economic *structure* for democratic ownership, whereas direct citizen participation in economic decisions provides the framework for a comprehensively democratic control *process* of the economy. The *demos*, therefore, becomes the authentic unit of economic life, since economic democracy is not feasible today unless both the ownership and control of productive resources are organised at the local level. Briefly,[42] the main characteristic of the proposed model, which also differentiates it from socialist planning models, is that it explicitly presupposes a stateless, moneyless and marketless economy that precludes the institutionalisation of privileges for some sections of society and private accumulation of wealth, without having to rely on a mythical post-scarcity state of abundance or having to sacrifice freedom of choice.

The satisfaction of the above conditions for political and economic democracy would represent the re-conquering of the political and economic realms by the public realm, that is, the re-conquering of a true social individuality, the creation of the conditions of freedom and self-determination, both at the political and the economic levels. But, political and economic power are not the only forms of power and therefore political and economic democracy do not, by themselves, secure an inclusive democracy. In other words, an inclusive democracy is inconceivable unless it extends to the broader social realm to embrace the workplace, the household, the educational place and indeed any economic or cultural institution which constitutes an element of this realm.

A crucial issue that arises with respect to democracy in the social realm in general and paideia in particular refers to relations in the household. Women's social and economic status has been enhanced during, particularly, the statist and neoliberal phases of modernity, as a result of the expanding labour needs of the growth economy on the one hand and the activity of women's movements on the other. Still, gender relations at the household level are mostly hierarchical, especially in the South where most of the world population lives. However, although the household shares with the public realm a fundamental common characteristic, inequality and power relations, the household has always been classified in the private realm. Therefore, the problem that arises here is how the 'democratisation' of the household may be achieved.

One possible solution is the dissolution of the household/public realm divide. Thus, some feminist writers, particularly of the eco-feminist variety, glorify the *oikos* and its values as a substitute for the *polis* and its politics, something that, as Janet Biehl observes, 'can easily be read as an attempt to dissolve the political into the domestic, the civil into the familial, the public into the private.'[43] Similarly, some green thinkers attempt to reduce the public realm into an extended household model of a small-scale, co-operative community.[44] At the other end, some Marxist feminists[45] attempt to remove the public/private dualism by dissolving all private space into a singular public, a socialised or fraternal state sphere. However, as Val Plumwood points out, the feminists who argue for the elimination of household privacy are today a minority although most feminists stress the way in which the concept of household privacy has been misused to put beyond challenge the subordination of women.[46] Another possible solution is, taking for granted that the household belongs to the private realm, to define its meaning in terms of the freedom of all its members. As Val Plumwood points out this means that "household relationships themselves should take on the characteristics of democratic relationships, and that the household should take a form which is consistent with the freedom of all its members.[47]

To my mind, the issue is not the dissolution of the private/public realm divide. The real issue is how, maintaining and enhancing the autonomy of the two realms, such institutional arrangements are adopted that introduce democracy in the household and the social realm in general (workplace, educational establishment, et cetera) and at the same time enhance the institutional arrangements of political and economic democracy. In fact, an effective democracy is inconceivable unless free time is equally distributed among all citizens, and this condition can never be satisfied as long as the present hierarchical conditions in the household, the workplace and elsewhere continue. Furthermore, democracy in the social realm, particularly in the household, is impossible, unless such institutional arrangements are introduced which recognise the character of the household as a needs-satisfier and integrate the care and services provided within its framework into the general scheme of needs satisfaction.

Although therefore nobody disputes the fact that the family plays a crucial role in the socialisation of an individual at an early age, still, the usual libertarian discussion of the 1960s and 1970s on whether family should be abolished raises the issue in simplistic, if not Manichaic terms. It is obvious today that living in a family is an individual choice which strictly belongs to the private realm. The crucial issue therefore is how democratic relations are created at the household or the educational place to support and enhance the democratic institutions created at society's level.

Finally, coming to ecological democracy the issue here is how we may envisage an environmentally friendly institutional framework that would not serve as the basis of a Nature-dominating ideology. Clearly, if we see democracy as a process of social self-institution where there is no divinely or 'objectively' defined code of human conduct, there are no guarantees that an inclusive democracy will also be an ecological one. The replacement of the market economy by a new institutional framework of inclusive democracy constitutes only the *necessary condition* for a harmonious relation between the natural and social worlds. The sufficient condition refers to the citizens' level of ecological consciousness. Still, the radical change in the dominant social paradigm that will follow the institution of an inclusive democracy, combined with the decisive role that *paideia* will play in an environmentally friendly institutional framework, could reasonably be expected to lead to a radical change in the human attitude towards Nature. In other words, a democratic ecological *problematique* cannot go beyond the institutional preconditions that offer the best hope for a better human relationship to Nature. However, there are strong grounds to believe that the relationship between an inclusive democracy and Nature would be much more harmonious than could ever be achieved in a market economy, or one based on socialist statism, as a result of the new structures and relations that will follow the establishment of political and economic democracy in the social realm.

The above conditions for democracy imply a new conception of citizenship: economic, political, social and cultural citizenship which involves new political and economic structures and relations, self-management structures at the workplace, democracy in the household and the educational place, as well as new democratic structures of dissemination and control of information and culture (mass media, art, etc.) that allow every member of the demos to take part in the process and at the same time develop his/her intellectual and cultural potential. The conception of citizenship adopted here, which could be called a democratic conception, is based on the above definition of inclusive democracy and presupposes a 'participatory' conception of active citizenship, like the one implied by the work of Hannah Arendt.[48] In this conception, "political activity is not a means to an end, but an end in itself; one does not engage in political action simply to promote one's welfare but to realise the principles intrinsic to political life, such as freedom, equality, justice, solidarity, courage and excellence."[49] It is therefore obvious that this conception of citizenship is qualitatively different from the liberal and social-democratic conceptions which adopt an 'instrumentalist' view of citizenship, i.e., a view which implies that citizenship entitles citizens with certain rights that they can exercise as means to the end of individual welfare.

In conclusion, as it was stated above, the institutional conditions described are just necessary conditions for democracy. The sufficient condition so that democracy will not degenerate into some kind of "demago-cracy," where the demos is manipulated by a new breed of professional politicians, is crucially determined by the citizens' level of democratic consciousness, which, in turn, is conditioned by *paideia*. Therefore, there is a continuous interaction between paideia and democracy both of which should be seen as dynamic processes rather than as simply static structures. The institutional preconditions of paideia at the social level secure the institutional framework for paideia, as they provide the public space for the education of individuals as citizens. In other words, these conditions are the necessary conditions for an *autonomous* paideia which presupposes autonomous individuals (in contrast to libertarians who talk about a moral paideia instead of an autonomous one). At the same time, a democratic paideia is the necessary condition for the reproduction of democracy itself so that it does not degenerate in practice into a new kind of oligocracy.

Change in Values as a Precondition and Consequence of Paideia

An inclusive democracy does not simply presuppose a set of institutional conditions that secure social and individual autonomy. It also assumes a set of values that are compatible with the democratic organisation of society. Therefore, the democratic project is incompatible with irrationalism because, democracy, as a process of social self-institution, implies a society which is open ideologically, namely, which is not grounded on any closed system of beliefs, dogmas or ideas. "Democracy," as Castoriadis puts it, "is the project of breaking the closure at the collective level."[50] In a democratic society, dogmas and closed systems of ideas cannot constitute parts of the dominant social paradigm, although, of course, individuals can have whatever beliefs they wish, as long as they are committed to uphold the democratic principle, namely the principle according to which society is autonomous, institutionalised as inclusive democracy.

So, the democratic project cannot be grounded on any divine, natural or social 'laws' or tendencies, but on our own conscious and self-reflective choice between the two main historical traditions: the tradition of heteronomy which has been historically dominant, and the tradition of autonomy. The choice of autonomy implies that the institution of society is not based on any kind of ir-rationalism (faith in God, mystical beliefs, etc.), or on 'objective truths' about social evolution grounded on social or natural 'laws.' This is so because any system of religious or mystical beliefs (as well as any closed system of ideas), by defini-tion, excludes the questioning of some fundamental beliefs or ideas and, there-fore, is incompatible with citizens setting their own laws. In fact, the principle of 'non-questioning' some fundamental beliefs is common in every religion or set of metaphysical and mystical beliefs from Christianity up to Taoism. This is important if we take particularly into account the fact that today's influence of irrationalist trends on libertarian currents has resulted in the silly picture of scores of libertarian communes organised democratically and inspired by various kinds of irrationalism (not unlike similar religious sects in the past, e.g., the Christian Catharist movement extolled by libertarians as democratic![51]). Classical anarchists like Bakunin on the other hand were explicit in their hostility towards religious or other dogmas:

> Education of children and their upbringing must be founded wholly upon the scientific development of reason and not that of faith; upon the development of personal dignity and independence, not upon piety and obedience; on the cult of truth and justice at any cost; and above all, upon respect for humanity, which must replace in everything the divine cult…. All rational education is at bottom nothing but the progressive immolation of authority for the benefit of freedom, the final aim of education necessarily being the development of free men imbued with a feeling of respect and love for the liberty of others.

The fundamental element of autonomy is the creation of our own truth, something that social individuals can only achieve through direct democracy, that is, the process through which they continually question any institution, tradition, or 'truth.' In a democracy, there are simply no given truths. The practice of indi-vidual and social autonomy presupposes autonomy in thought, in other words, the constant questioning of institutions and truths. Democracy is therefore seen not just as a structure institutionalising the equal sharing of power but also as a process of social self-institution, in the context of which politics constitutes an ex-pression of both social and individual autonomy. Thus, as an expression of social autonomy, politics takes the form of calling into question the existing institutions and of changing them through deliberate collective action. Also, as an expression of individual autonomy, "the polis secures more than human survival. Politics makes possible man's development as a creature capable of genuine autonomy, freedom and excellence," as Cynthia Farrar[52] points out referring to the thought of the Sophist philosopher Protagoras. Therefore, a democratic society will be a social creation, which can only be grounded on our own conscious selection of those forms of social organisation that are conducive to individual and social autonomy.

It is clear that democratic paideia needs a new kind of rationalism, beyond both the 'objectivist' type of rationalism we inherited from the Enlightenment and the generalised relativism of postmodernism. We need a *democratic rationalism*, i.e., a rationalism founded on democracy as a structure and a process of social self-institution. Within the context of democratic rationalism, democracy is not justified by an appeal to objective tendencies with respect to natural or social evolution but by an appeal to reason in terms of *logon didonai* (rendering account and reason), which explicitly denies the idea of any 'directionality' as regards social change. Therefore, as I tried to show elsewhere,[53] what is needed today is not to jettison science, let alone rationalism altogether, in the interpretation of social phenomena but to transcend 'objective' rationalism (i.e., the rationalism which is grounded on 'objective laws' of natural or social evolution) and develop a new kind of democratic rationalism.

All this has very important implications directly on technoscience and indirectly on paideia. As regards technoscience, as I tried to show elsewhere[54] modern technoscience is neither 'neutral' in the sense that it is merely a 'means' which can be used for the attainment of whatever end, nor autonomous in the sense that it is the sole or the most important factor determining social structures, relations and values. Instead, it is argued that technoscience is conditioned by the power relations implied by the specific set of social, political and economic institutions characterising the growth economy and the *dominant social paradigm*. What is therefore needed is the reconstitution of both our science and technology in a way that puts at the centre of every stage in the process, in every single technique, human personality and its needs rather than, as at present, the values and needs of those controlling the market/growth economy. This presupposes a new form of socio-economic organisation in which citizens, both as producers and as consumers, do control effectively the types of technologies adopted, expressing the general rather than, as at present, the partial interest. In other words, it presupposes first, a political democracy, so that effective citizen control on scientific research and technological innovation can be established; economic democracy, so that the general economic interest of the confederated communities, rather than the partial interests of economic elites, could be effectively expressed in research and technological development; ecological democracy, so that the environmental implications of science and technology are really taken into account in scientific research and technological development; and last, but not least, democracy in the social realm, that is, equal sharing in the decision-taking process at the factory, the office, the household, the laboratory and so on, so that the abolition of hierarchical structures in production, research and technological development would secure not only the democratic content of science and technology but also democratic procedures in scientific and technological development and collective control by scientists and technologists.

It should be clear, however, that the democratisation of science and technology should not be related to a utopian abolition of division of labour and specialisation as, for instance, Thomas Simon suggests, arguing that democratising technology means abolishing professionals and experts: "the extent to which a professional/expert is no longer needed is partially the extent to which a process has become democratised. It is the extent to which we are able to make the professional terrain a deliberative assembly."[55] But, although it is true that the present extreme specialisation and division of labour has been necessitated by the needs of 'efficiency,' which are imposed by the dynamics of the growth economy, still, there are certain definite limits on the degree of reduction in specialisation which is feasible and desirable, if we do not wish to see the re-emergence of problems that have been solved long ago (medical problems, problems of sanitation, etc.). The nature of the technology to be adopted by a democratic society does not just depend on who owns it or even who controls it. Not only, as History has shown, it is perfectly possible that 'socialist' bureaucrats may adopt techniques which are as environmentally destructive and life damaging (if not more) as those adopted by their capitalist counterparts, but also the possibility cannot be ruled out that citizens' assemblies may adopt similar techniques. So, the abolition of oligarchic ownership and control over technology, which would come about in a marketless, moneyless, stateless economy based on an inclusive democracy, is only the necessary institutional condition for an alternative pro-life and pro-nature technology. The sufficient condition depends, as always, on the value system that a democratic society would develop and the level of consciousness of its citizens. One therefore can only hope that the change in the institutional framework together with a democratic paideia would play a crucial role in the formation of this new system of values and the raising of the level of consciousness.

In conclusion, a democratic paideia should promote the values consistent with the new democratic institutions and particularly the principles of autonomy and community on which they are based. Thus, out of the fundamental principle of autonomy one may derive a set of moral values involving equity and democracy, respect for the personality of every citizen (irrespective of gender, race, ethnic identity etc.) and of course respect for human life itself which, as Castoriadis puts it, 'ought to be posited as an absolute because the injunction of autonomy is categorical, and there is no autonomy without life.'[56] Also, out of the same fundamental principle of autonomy, we may derive values involving the protection of the quality of life of each individual citizen—something that would imply a relationship of harmony with nature and the need to re-integrate society with nature. Similarly, out of the fundamental principle of community we may derive a set of values involving not only equity but also solidarity and mutual aid, altruism/self-sacrifice (beyond concern for kin and reciprocity), caring and sharing.[57]

Institutional Preconditions at the Educational Level

As the discussion of the institutional preconditions for paideia at society's level hopefully has made clear, the establishment of a democratic paideia is impossible within the existing system of capitalist market economy and representative 'democracy.' The next crucial issue is how we see the educational institutions of the future and the nature of education in general.

Paideia in a democratic society is seen as a means of achieving equal distribution of power, rather than, as at present and in any heteronomous society, as a means of maintaining and reproducing the concentration of power at the hands of privileged social groups. If paideia is seen as a means of achieving equal distribution of power it complements the institutions of political and economic democracy, which aim at an equal distribution of political and economic power respectively, so that a genuine classless society could be achieved.

As I mentioned in the first section, paideia in a democratic society should play the double role of *civic schooling* and *personal training*. The concrete forms that a democratic paideia will take are of course a matter for the democratic assemblies of the future to decide, and all we can do is outline some proposals that, in our view, would better implement these two fundamental aims. However, these two fundamental aims about the role of paideia in a democratic society have some definite implications on the nature, content and methodology of the education process, which are helpful in formulating some concrete proposals on the matter. On the basis of these aims the following should be basic features of a democratic paideia:

- *Public spaces in education.* The education process should create new public spaces in which students (who up to a certain age of maturity to be decided by demotic assemblies will not be able to be members of them) will experience and live democracy in running the educational process, as far as it affects them. This will involve educational assemblies for each area of study (general knowledge and specific areas of study/training), under the general guidance of demotic assemblies. Students in these assemblies will decide collectively, on an equal basis with their educators, the curriculum, the place/form of education/training and so on.

- *Free generalised and integral education for life.* This means that the education process for all children starts at an early age (to be decided individually within a reasonable age range) and continues for life. Furthermore, it is a process which does not distinguish in principle between intellectual and manual work that enjoy an equal social status. This, however, should not prevent an individual citizen from concentrating his/her training in a particular area of intellectual or manual work at some stage in his/her life, although all citizens should be able to do both types of work, so that they could effectively participate in the collective effort to meet the basic needs of the community.[58] The aim therefore will be to provide citizens with the general knowledge to understand the world, as well as the tools to carry out any activity they select to do in covering their basic and non-basic needs.

- *Individual and social autonomy.* The education methods used and the content of education itself should aim to promote freedom in the sense of individual and social autonomy both in the everyday educational practice as well as in the knowledge transmitted to students. The former should involve non-hierarchical relations in education (see below) whereas the latter should involve a systematic effort to create free self-reflective minds who would reject any dogmas and closed systems of thought and particularly any irrational belief systems, i.e., systems whose core beliefs are not derived by rational methods (i.e., reason and/or an appeal to 'facts') but by intuition, instinct, feeling, mystical experience, revelation etc. In this sense, education is seen as the principal means of encouraging the growth of the creative and autonomous person.

- *Non-hierarchical relations.* Paideia is a double-edged process in which students learn from educators and vice versa. Educators do not enjoy any hierarchical status as a result of their position and, therefore, their authority[59] over students is grounded on temporary differences in knowledge. In the democratic paideia which characterises an autonomous society, the instituted equality in the distribution of power at society's level rules out any hierarchical authority; so, the only kind of discipline that exists is the self-discipline created by freedom and activity themselves, which, in turn, enhance the creative spontaneity of the individual. This is in contrast to the hierarchical paideia which characterises any heteronomous society in which the authority of the educator is based on power relationships and is imposed through coercive discipline that does not recognise the right and ability to dissent. An implication of the non-hierarchical character of democratic paideia is that grades, diplomas and credentials have no place in it since they simply cultivate competition and create new hierarchies between trainees. The 'authority' of a person in his/her activity is confirmed by his/her knowledge and experience rather than by grades and diplomas.

- *Balance between science and the aesthetic sensibility.* Students should be encouraged in all areas of study and particularly in the general knowledge area to appreciate all forms of art and to be actively involved in practising creative art so that a meaningful balance could be achieved between scientific/practical knowledge on the one hand and aesthetic sensibility/ creativity on the other; this will be a crucial step in developing balanced personalities.

The final critical issue refers to the form paideia will take and in particular whether it will take the form of formal schooling in specifically designated educational institutions as today or whether instead it will take the form of 'de-schooling,' as many libertarians of the individualistic trend within the anarchist movement suggest. It should be stressed at the outset that Marxists and classical anarchists like Bakunin did not reject schooling but adopted the view that a socialist 'schooling' is impossible within the capitalist system. The resolution adopted by the First International in its Congress of Brussels in 1867 explicitly stated the need for the organisation of the 'schooling' of workers:

> Recognizing that for the moment it is impossible to organize a rational system of education, the Congress urges its various sections to organize study courses which would follow a program of scientific, professional, and industrial education, that is, a program of integral instruction, in order to remedy as much as possible the present-day lack of education among workers. It is well understood that a reduction of working hours is to be considered an indispensable preliminary condition.

Although the system of massive state education, which was organised everywhere during modernity, supposedly provided education to all as we saw in the second section of this chapter, the type of education provided had very different aims from the aims of socialist education, or of the democratic paideia discussed above. In fact, we may call the present form of education 'miseducation' to distinguish it from emancipatory education and paideia. However, the authoritarian type of education that developed particularly during the statist phase of modernity both in the East and the West gave rise to the counter-culture of the 1960s and an attack against not only the content but also the form of education. Authoritarian schooling carried out by professional teachers, using fixed curricula determined 'from above' rather than through any democratic decision-taking process, were particular targets of this attack. Paul Goodman's ideas on libertarian education and particularly Ivan Illich's 'deschooling' thesis were especially influential, and it seems that they still inspire 'life-style' anarchists today.

Thus, Matt Hern[60] stresses that 'what is needed is a vast, asystematically organized fabric of innumerable kinds of places for kids to spend their time' on the grounds that 'compulsory schooling is a culture that reifies the centralized control and monitoring of our daily lives.' However, this statement makes clear that the author, throwing away the baby with the bath-water, confuses control and organisation of education (which, of course, do not have to be centralised) with education itself. Next, he confuses the content with the form of schooling when he states, for instance, that 'schools are institutions with their own particular ideologies and pedagogical approaches, and they are devoted to schooling, or imparting a certain set of values, beliefs and practises upon their clients.' Still, as I tried to show above, in a democratic system of education, the values taught could be decided democratically rather than by elites as today. Furthermore, the individualistic trend which the article expresses (a trend which today seems to be dominant among 'anarchists'—a clear illustration of the degradation of this movement[61]) is evident in the following statement by the same author:

> The deschooling argument I want to make here presumes that each and every individual is best able to define their own interests, needs and desires. Schools and education assume that children need to be taught what is good, what is important to understand I refuse to accept this. Kids do not need to be taught. . . . Deschooling suggests the renunciation of not only schooling, but education as well, in favour of a culture of self-reliance, self-directed learning, and voluntary, non-coercive learning institutions.

Thus, according to this passage, 'each and every individual' is best able to define the content and form of education in accordance with his/her own interests, needs and desires. Clearly, there is no society in this scheme, as the guru of neoliberalism, Mrs. Thatcher, has declared twenty years earlier! There are no social individuals but simply self-reliant individuals of the Robinson Crusoe type—the typical example used by orthodox neoclassical economists to justify the market system. Finally, the author, in an obvious confusion of what a direct democracy means, stresses that a directly democratic agenda has to include an explicit renunciation of the other-controlled mentality of compulsory schooling because:

> If we want and expect our kids to grow up to be responsible creatures capable of directing their own lives, we have to give them practice at making decisions. To allow authority to continually rob our kids of basic decisions about where and how to play is to set our kids up for dependence and incompetence on a wide scale. If we are to truly counter the disabling effect of schools, this is indeed our fate. A genuine democracy, a society of self-reliant people and communities, has

to begin by allowing children and adults to shape themselves, to control their own destinies free of authoritarian manipulation.

It is clear that direct democracy is distorted here to mean *individual* rather than collective decision-taking by assemblies of educators and trainees. The distortion attempted here becomes even more obvious when it is made clear that the author confuses also the form and content of learning with learning itself, as for instance when he declares that 'Learning is like breathing. It is a natural human activity: it is part of being alive. . . . Our ability to learn, like our ability to breathe, does not need to be tampered with. It is utter nonsense, not to mention deeply insulting to say that people need to be taught how to learn or how to think.' However, although nobody would deny that learning is a natural ability this does not mean that a dentist, a pilot, or a pianist do not have to be taught how to learn (i.e., to be given a curriculum) dentistry, flying or playing the piano! The issue therefore is who determines the curriculum, i.e., the program of study, and this clearly can neither be left to the individual student to decide, as proposed by libertarian supporters of deschooling, nor, of course, to the elites, as it happens today, but to the democratic assemblies of educators and pupils/students.

So, given the fundamental aims of democratic paideia and their implications we considered above and given the objections to the deschooling thesis, as far as it rejects the very idea of a curriculum, how do we see the education 'institutions' of a democratic society? To my mind, the best way out of the present strictly structured miseducation, which aims to produce career people who have internalised the values of the heteronomous society, is the creation of 'education groups' as the basic units within which the education process will take place. I would propose three categories of such groups which I will call 'primary,' 'secondary' and 'tertiary' groups although, as we shall see, their relationship to today's three grades of education under similar names is almost nil.

'Primary' education groups consist of pupils of an early age (to be determined by the demotic assemblies, e.g., 6–15) and educators. Every child of this age has to join one of these groups, as this represents the only compulsory stage in the education process. The reason for this compulsory element is that, given the accumulated knowledge of the 21st century, a minimum of knowledge is required for all citizens to be able to participate in the production of the 'basic' goods and services (i.e., the ones covering basic needs) which secure the survival of their self-reliant communities and themselves. Therefore the basic aim of primary educational groups is to provide the minimum knowledge required for this purpose, which would include industrial skills, if group assemblies decide so, as well of course as the general knowledge and aesthetic sensibility we described above. Furthermore, the knowledge provided by these primary educational groups would provide a sufficient background for attending secondary or tertiary groups. The

curriculum, as mentioned above, would be decided by each educational group democratically. 'Educators' would consist not only of trained educators but also of citizens involved in every kind of activity who could offer their knowledge and experience. There would be no fixed time-tables or specifically designed 'schools' since education would take place in the actual areas of activity, linking knowledge and learning to real-life processes. Still, specially designed public buildings with various facilities would be available to these educational groups for their assembly meetings, in which the curriculum, the planning of their activity in implementing their curriculum, etc., would be determined. Therefore, much of the group's activity would take place in laboratories, science centres, factories, farms, offices, shops, as well as in museums, libraries, theatres, cinemas, etc. Pupils, who would not be able during this education stage to participate in the production of the basic goods and services necessary for the survival of the community, would be allocated 'basic vouchers,'[62] in exactly the same way as any other citizen, for the satisfaction of their basic needs and, on top of them, any 'non-basic vouchers' allocated to them by the confederal assembly on the basis of the resources available to the confederal democracy.

Citizens who have finished attending the primary groups and do not wish to join a specialised tertiary group but want to extend their knowledge of particular areas, or simply wish to update their general knowledge acquired at primary groups, could do so either on an individual basis through 'open education' programmes offered by TV, the internet, etc., or collectively, by voluntarily joining *'secondary' education groups,* which could be done at any age. These groups are distinguished from 'tertiary' groups on the basis of the degree of specialisation involved. In contrast to 'tertiary' groups which aim at a clearly specialised education, secondary groups aim at providing semi-specialised education, beyond the level provided within primary groups. Citizens attending the secondary groups are entitled to their basic and non-basic vouchers as any other citizen, according to need and labour offered to the community respectively, which implies that students attending such groups would still have to contribute to the community the minimum 'basic' hours of labour required for covering their basic needs. As regards educators, places of education, curricula, etc., similar arrangements to the ones proposed for primary groups could be adopted by these groups.

Finally, *'tertiary' educational groups* aim at providing the specialised knowledge required in areas of activity which necessitate a high degree of specialisation (e.g., medicine, engineering, physics, education, etc.). Joining these groups is also voluntary and can take place at any age after attending the primary education groups. Educators in tertiary groups are specialised in a particular area of knowledge and constitute the only 'teachers,' in the sense of professionals, within the democratic system of paideia. Given, however, the time requirements of attending the tertiary groups, students are exempted from communal work in the production of basic goods and services, but they are entitled, like pupils in primary groups, to the same basic and non-basic vouchers as they are. Clearly, given the burden on communal resources that specialised education involves, the time allowance granted by the community to attend such groups should be fixed within a reasonable range and determined by the decisions of the assemblies of educators and students in each area of study and the resources available. Similarly, the curriculum is determined by the same assemblies in which, however, the vote of educators, given the specialised knowledge required for this purpose, will have an increased weight. Finally, the places of education will necessarily be determined by the needs of each area of study. The education provided within the tertiary groups, would therefore effectively be, given their specialised needs, the only 'structured' education in a democratic system of paideia.

The proposed scheme could avoid both the Scylla of statist education, which characterised modern capitalist and socialist societies (particularly the latter), with all its authoritarianism and suppression of the individual, as well as the Charybdis of individualistic education like the one proposed by libertarians of the individualistic trend (Illich, Spring, Hern et al.) according to whom (as Illich put it) the most pressing problem of the modem world is to change the style of institutions and technology so that they work for the benefit of the individual.[63] Instead, a democratic paideia should work for the benefit of both the collectivity and the individual. A democratic paideia is therefore neither the present miseducation and schooling nor the individualistic affair of 'anything goes' proposed by some 'libertarians' aiming at maximising individual autonomy. A democratic paideia could only mean gaining knowledge and ability to maximize individual *and* social autonomy as a means of individual *and* social liberation.

Emancipatory Education as the Transition from Modernity Education to a Democratic Paideia

The final crucial issue refers to what Castoriadis called 'the riddle of politics,' i.e., how within an heteronomous society and an heteronomous education we may create autonomous institutions and the infrastructure of paideia, or what I would call the conditions for an emancipatory education, i.e., the conditions for the transition from present modernity miseducation to a democratic paideia. This would involve the breaking of the socialisation process on a massive scale so that the activist minorities who have managed to internalise the values of an alternative democratic society would be joined by the majority. The problem has engaged in the past the radical Left and is still, of course, unresolved. I would classify the main stands on this issue as follows. First, there are those who in effect do not propose any transitional strategies because they believe that only after a revolutionary change in society would it be possible to introduce a paideia. Second, there are those who propose a transition through various schemes of libertarian education, and finally there is the inclusive democracy approach, which proposes linking emancipatory education to the transitional political strategy and setting up emancipatory educational institutions as an integral part of the political and economic institutions being created during the transition.

The 'Paideia After the Revolution' Thesis

The classical position of the radical Left on the matter was one of rejecting the possibility of paideia within the existing system of the capitalist market economy and representative 'democracy.' The position was best summarised by Bakunin but stressed also by other Marxist and anarchist writers of the past and explicitly or implicitly repeated by contemporary radicals like Bookchin, Castoriadis et al. Thus, Bakunin explicitly links the advent of a socialist education with the socialist transformation of society[64]:

> Public education, not fictitious but a real one, can exist only in a truly equalitarian society. . . . Socialist morality is altogether contrary to existing morality, the teachers who are necessarily dominated to a greater or lesser extent by the latter, will act in the presence of the pupils in a manner wholly contrary to what they preach. Consequently, socialist education is impossible in the existing schools as well as in present-day families. But integral education is equally impossible under existing conditions. The bourgeois have not the slightest desire that their children should become workers, and workers are deprived of the means necessary to give their offspring a scientific education. . . . It is evident that this important question of the education and upbringing of the people depends upon the solution of the much more difficult problem of radical reorganization of the existing economic conditions of the working masses.

The same author gives perhaps the best answer to many contemporary anarchists who advocate various schemes of free schools and vouchers as a means of creating the conditions of a 'libertarian' paideia[65]:

> If it were even possible to found in the existing environment schools which would give their pupils instruction and education as perfect as we can imagine, would those schools succeed in developing just, free, and moral men? No, they would not, for upon leaving school the graduates would find themselves in a social environment governed by altogether contrary principles, and since society is always stronger than individuals, it would soon come to dominate them, and it would demoralize them.

Similarly, Castoriadis,[66] to mention just one of the contemporary radical writers who have explicitly dealt with the issue of paideia, stresses that:

Only the education (paideia) of the citizens as citizens can give valuable, substantive content to the 'public space.' This paideia is not primarily a matter of
books and academic credits. First and foremost, it involves becoming conscious
that the polis is also oneself and that its fate also depends upon one's mind, behaviour, and decisions; in other words, it is participation in political life.

As 'participation in political life' for Castoriadis has nothing to do with today's
liberal representative 'democracy,' which he appropriately called liberal 'oligarchy,'
it is obvious that Castoriadis too saw as non-feasible the creation of institutions of
paideia under the present system.

Libertarian Education as a Transition 'Strategy'

Next, we may refer to various proposals, usually made by supporters of the individualistic trend within the anarchist movement, 'life-style anarchists' and adherents of 'anarchy in action,' who adopt various schemes of 'libertarian education'
within the existing framework of the market economy and representative 'democracy.' The common element in all those proposals is that they are not suggested
as an integral part of the program of an antisystemic movement. In fact, most
if not all of those proposals, implicitly or sometimes explicitly, reject any idea
of action within a political movement to overthrow the present system and describe instead various schemes to maximise individual autonomy in education, as
a kind of desired life-change rather than as means to create the consciousness for
a systemic change. No wonder that these proposals do not link the suggested institutional changes at the 'micro' educational level with the required institutional
changes at the 'macro' social level. In this sense, one may classify these proposals
to what Murray Bookchin aptly called 'life-style anarchism,'[67] which could easily
be considered as a kind of libertarian reformism, given that most if not all of the
proposed changes could easily be integrated within the present system—as they
actually have been, whenever implemented.

As Joel Spring, the author of *A Primer of Libertarian Education* and an ad-
herent of the individualistic trend within the anarchist movement, described the
free school movement that flourished in the 1950s and 1960s, it was an attempt
to establish an environment for self-development in a world that was considered
overly structured and rationalized, with precursors (among others) to the 'free
playground' movement in the 1940s. It was seen 'as an expression of libertarian
concern about reshaping the world so that people could control and use it for
their own purposes,' or even as 'an oasis from authoritarian control and as a means
of passing on the knowledge to be free,' with the overall aim to providing a free
and unstructured environment.[68] As the same author points out, the American
libertarian Paul Goodman was one of the major spokesmen for the free school
movement who advocated the decentralization of large and cumbersome school

systems and the establishment of small-scale schools. As is obvious, the establishment of 'free schools' had nothing to do with any antisystemic political movement or a transition strategy but simply aimed at providing a kind of libertarian education (presumably to hippy middle-class parents who could afford the luxury of paying the fees). Anecdotal evidence has it that most of these children who attended the 'free schools' have by now moved from ex-hippies to yuppies who flourish within the neoliberal 'new economy'!

Ivan Illich in the late 1960s took a step further and rejected the 'free school' movement in order to promote his 'deschooling' thesis. But, Illich, as far as I know, never challenged the very system of the capitalist market economy and representative 'democracy' which are the foundations of the present system. His 'revolution' was basically against bureaucracy and technocracy with particular emphasis on the industrial culture (as deep ecologists do today) rather than against the system itself. It is not therefore surprising that he sees the abolition of the right to corporate secrecy as 'a much more radical political goal than the traditional demand for public ownership or control of the tools of production' and that he comes out in favour of a 'subsistence economy' whose feasibility, as he stresses, 'depends primarily on the ability of a society to agree on fundamental, self-chosen, anti-bureaucratic and anti-technocratic restraints.'[69] The inevitable conclusion is that a 'subsistence economy' and a 'deschooled society' could also develop within the present system as long as the appropriate culture has been created!

Then, in the 1970s, the 'anarchy in action' libertarian current inspired by Colin Ward made similar proposals for maximisation of individual autonomy as regards education, through a voucher scheme. According to this scheme, each citizen at birth receives an actual or notional book of vouchers or coupons (representing his/her share of nation's educational budget) which entitle him/her to so many units of education which can be bought any time in his/her life.[70] Ward argued that such a scheme would allow libertarians to exploit the existing system with the aim of providing 'genuine' alternatives. However, such a scheme in fact does not 'exploit' the existing system but could instead be used by it not only to marginalise and integrate the 'alternative' schools within a supposedly 'pluralistic' education system but also to reproduce and enhance the vast inequalities the system creates. It is obvious that those coming from elite social groups will have a clear comparative advantage at school/college and in later life with respect to those coming from non-privileged ones, despite the fact that they attended the same education institutions—the experience of social democracy is illuminating. Even more important is the fact that the voucher scheme by itself not only does nothing at all to create an antisystemic consciousness among pupils/students but in fact cultivates the liberal/neoliberal mythology of a 'genuine' freedom of choice that the market system supposedly creates, which (with the libertarian approval!) should extend to education as well. Colin Ward himself stressed that his voucher scheme would "appeal to those who would like to see a genuine freedom of choice with competition on equal terms between radically different kinds of learning, and who want to see the education made more responsive to the expressed needs of students."[71] No wonder that even neoliberals and social-liberals proposed similar voucher schemes in neoliberal modernity! The voucher scheme is therefore another scheme to maximise individual rather social autonomy, which could easily end up with a reformist improvement of the system.

In this context, Matt Hern's recent proposals may be seen as the 'dialectical synthesis' of the views expressed by supporters of "libertarian education as a transition strategy"—something that in fact, for the reasons discussed, constitutes neither a strategy nor a transition to a libertarian society.

The ID Strategy for the Transition to Paideia

The ID strategy for the transition from present modern miseducation to a democratic paideia is an integral part of the ID transitional strategy to an inclusive democracy as described in Vol. 8, No. 1 of *D&N*.[72] Briefly, the ID strategy involves the building of a mass programmatic political movement, like the old socialist movement, with an unashamedly universalist goal to change society along genuine democratic lines, beginning here and now. Therefore, such a movement should explicitly aim at a systemic change as well as at a parallel change in our value systems. This strategy would entail the gradual involvement of increasing numbers of people in a new kind of politics and the parallel shifting of economic resources (labour, capital, land) away from the market economy. The aim of such a strategy should be to create changes in the institutional framework, as well as to value systems, which, after a period of tension between the new institutions and the state, would, at some stage, replace the market economy, representative 'democracy,' and the social paradigm "justifying" them, with an inclusive democracy and a new democratic paradigm, respectively.

The rationale behind this strategy is that, as systemic change requires a rupture with the past, which extends to both the institutional and the cultural level, such a rupture is only possible through the development of a new political organisation and a new comprehensive political program for systemic change that will create a clear anti-systemic consciousness at a massive scale. This is in contrast to the statist socialist strategy, which ends up with the creation of a clear anti-systemic consciousness only with respect to an avant-garde, or to the life-style activities which, if they create any antisystemic consciousness at all, it is restricted to the few members of various libertarian 'groupuscules.' However, the creation of a new culture, which has to become hegemonic before the transition to an inclusive democracy could be effected, is only possible through the parallel building of new political and economic institutions at a significant social scale. In other words, it is only through action to build such institutions that a mass political movement with a democratic consciousness could be built. Such a strategy creates the conditions for the transition, both the 'subjective' ones, in terms of helping the development of a new democratic consciousness, and the 'objective' ones, in terms of creating the new institutions which will form the basis of an inclusive democracy. At the same time, the establishment of these new institutions will crucially assist here and now the victims of the concentration of power which is associated with the present institutional framework, and particularly the victims of neoliberal globalisation, to deal with the problems created by it.

Therefore, the objective of an ID strategy is the creation, from below, of 'popular bases of political and economic power,' that is, the establishment of local inclusive democracies, which, at a later stage, will confederate in order to create the conditions for the establishment of a new confederal inclusive democracy. A crucial element of the ID strategy is that the political and economic institutions of inclusive democracy begin to be established immediately after a significant number of people in a particular area have formed a base for 'democracy in action'—preferably, but not exclusively, at the significant social scale that is secured by winning in local elections under an ID program. It is because the *demos* is the fundamental social and economic unit of a future democratic society that we have to start from the local level to change society. Therefore, participation in local elections is an important part of the strategy to gain power, in order to dismantle it immediately afterwards, by substituting the decision-taking role of the assemblies for that of the local authorities, the day after the election has been won. Furthermore, contesting local elections gives the chance to start changing society from below, as against the statist approaches that aim to change society from above through the conquest of state power, and the 'civil society' approaches that do not aim at a systemic change at all. However, the main aim of direct action, as well as of the participation in local elections, is not just the conquest of power but the rupture of the socialisation process and therefore the creation of a democratic majority 'from below,' which will legitimise the new structures of inclusive democracy.

It is at the stage when power has been won at the local level through contesting local elections that the transition to a democratic paideia could begin. The creation of ID institutions at the local level involves the development not only of political institutions of direct democracy and cultural institutions controlled by *demos* but also of a 'demotic' sector, which involves production units that are owned and controlled collectively by the citizens, as well as institutions of demotic welfare, education and health which are self-managed and indirectly controlled by the *demos*. A new *demotic tax system* (i.e., a tax system directly controlled by the demos) would finance: programmes for the demoticisation of the local productive resources, providing employment opportunities for local citizens; social spending programs that will cover the citizens' welfare needs which include educational needs; various institutional arrangements that will make democracy in the household effective (e.g., payment for work at home, for the care of children and the elderly, etc.). The combined effect of the above measures will be to redistribute economic power within the community, in the sense of greater equality in the distribution of income and wealth. This, combined with the introduction of democratic planning procedures, should provide significant ground for the transition towards full economic democracy.

In this system, assemblies would have significant powers in determining the allocation of resources in the demoticised sector, namely, the demotic enterprises and the demotic welfare system. As a first step, demotic assemblies could introduce a voucher scheme with respect to social services which could take the form of a *demotic free credit card scheme* with the aim of covering the welfare needs of all citizens in a *demotic welfare system*, i.e., a welfare system controlled by the demos that would provide important social services (education, housing, etc.) locally, or regionally in cooperation with other demoi in the area.

As regards the content and nature of the education process as well as the form education institutions will take, the proposals made in the last section about the way a democratic paideia would be organised could provide a guideline about the way emancipatory education could be organised and the aims it should pursue. The overall aims of emancipatory education would be to break the socialisation process in a significant social scale, maximise social and individual autonomy and create the infrastructure for a democratic paideia.

In cases where education is already controlled by local authorities, as it still happens in some countries, a program of establishing primary, secondary and tertiary education groups, as described above, could be set in motion immediately after local power has been won. In that case, citizens would be credited, through the *demotic free credit card scheme,* a certain amount to be determined by the demotic assemblies in relation to the demos' resources, which could be spent at any age to cover their education needs.

In cases where education is still controlled by the state, a full system of emancipatory education cannot be set up until enough *demoi* have been created so that a confederal inclusive democracy could be established. However, even before that happens, demotic assemblies should fight not only to create a decentralised education system but also to create alternative education opportunities within the existing system. A demoticised education system could implement the obligatory national curriculum in a way that would challenge the imposed national system of education both in theory (interpreting prescribed textbooks on the basis of the democratic social paradigm and its values, contrasting the officially prescribed program with alternative programs of knowledge based on democratic values, etc.) and in practice (creating educational public spaces to run these institutions).

The provision of supplementary educational facilities promoting the alternative democratic world-view through, e.g., a demoticised 'open-education' TV-operated system, the free distribution of alternative education material (books, videos, etc.) would be an important part of emancipatory education.

However, apart from the creation of alternative education opportunities, which would be supplemented by the free provision of a democratic culture through a system of demoticised mass media, theatres, cinemas, etc., the very fact that citizens would, for the first time in their lives, be able to have a real say in the running of their everyday life, through the new political and economic institutions being created, would be the most important means of emancipatory education towards a democratic paideia and an inclusive democracy.

Notes

1. Culture is frequently defined as the integrated pattern of human knowledge, belief, and behavior. This is a definition broad enough to include all major aspects of culture: language, ideas, beliefs, customs, taboos, codes, institutions, tools, techniques, works of art, rituals, ceremonies and so on.

2. By this I mean the system of beliefs, ideas and the corresponding values which are dominant (or tend to become dominant) in a particular society at a particular moment of its history, as most consistent with the existing political, economic and social institutions. The term "most consistent" does not imply, of course, any kind of structure/superstructure relationship a la Marx. Both culture and the social paradigm are time- and space-dependent, i.e., they refer to a specific type of society at a specific time. Therefore, they both change from place to place and from one historical period to another and this makes any "general theory" of History, which could determine the relationship between the cultural and the political or economic elements in society, impossible.

3. For the differences between culture and dominant social paradigm, see T. Fotopoulos, 'Mass Media, Culture and Democracy,' *Democracy & Nature*, Vol. 5, No. 1 (March 1999), pp. 33–64.

4. See T. Fotopoulos, *Towards an Inclusive Democracy* (London/N.Y.: Cassell/Continuum, 1997).

5. See T. Fotopoulos, 'Towards a Democratic Liberatory Ethics,' *Democracy & Nature*, Vol. 8, No. 3 (Nov. 2002), pp. 361–396.

6. C. Castoriadis, *Philosophy, Politics, Autonomy* (Oxford: Oxford University Press, 1991), p. 162.

7. 'Technical knowledge' here means the absorption of some general skills (reading, writing) as well as the introduction, at the early stages of schooling, to some general scientific and technological ideas to be supplemented, at later stages, by a higher degree of specialisation.

8. Following Castoriadis, we may call autonomous "a society that not only knows explicitly that it has created its own laws but has instituted itself so as to free its radical imaginary and enable itself to alter its institutions through collective, self-reflective, and deliberate activity." On the basis of this definition Castoriadis then defines politics as "the lucid activity whose object is the institution of an autonomous society and the decisions about collective endeavours"—something that implies, as he points out, that the project of an autonomous society becomes meaningless if it is not, at the same time, the project of bringing forth autonomous individuals, and vice versa. In the same sense, he defines democracy as the regime of collective reflectiveness (C. Castoriadis, *World in Fragments*, (Stanford: Stanford University Press, 1997) p. 132.)

9. C. Castoriadis, *World in Fragments*, p. 131

10. See T. Fotopoulos, 'Transitional Strategies and the Inclusive Democracy Project,' *Democracy & Nature*, Vol. 8, No. 1 (March 2002), pp. 17–62.

11. See T. Fotopoulos, 'The Myth of Postmodernity,' *Democracy & Nature*, Vol. 7, No. 1 (March 2001), pp. 27–76.
12. See T. Fotopoulos, *Towards an Inclusive Democracy*, ch. 1.
13. Will Hutton, *The State We're In* (London: Jonathan Cape, 1995), p. 174.
14. See Nicholas Barr, *The Economics of the Welfare State* (London: Weidenfeld & Nicolson, 1987), ch. 2.
15. See T. Fotopoulos, *Towards an Inclusive Democracy*, pp. 75–79.
16. See T. Fotopoulos, *Towards an Inclusive Democracy*, pp. 21–33.
17. See T. Fotopoulos, *Towards an Inclusive Democracy*, ch. 2.
18. See T. Fotopoulos, *Towards an Inclusive Democracy*, pp. 73–85 and 100–104 See also, T. Fotopoulos, 'The Catastrophe of Marketisation', *Democracy & Nature*, Vol. 5, No. 2 (July 1999), pp. 275–310.
19. A. H. Halsey et al,. *Origins and Destinations, Family, Class and Education in Modern Britain* (Oxford: Clarendon Press, 1980).
20. J. J. Goldthorpe, *Social Mobility & Class Structure in Modern Britain* (Oxford: Clarendon Press, 1980), p. 252.
21. See T. Fotopoulos, 'Globalisation, the Reformist Left and the Anti-Globalisation Movement,' *Democracy & Nature*, Vol. 7, No. 2 (July 2001), pp. 233–280.
22. Takis Fotopoulos, *Towards an Inclusive Democracy*, pp 33–46.
23. Stephanie Pain, "When the Price Is Wrong," *The Guardian* (27 Feb. 1997).
24. See *The Castoriadis Reader*, ed. By David Ames Curtis (Oxford: Blackwell, 1997), p. 260.
25. Tracy McVeigh, 'Level of Illiteracy among Young Is Above That of 1912,' *The Observer* (August 19, 2001).
26. Ian Murray, 'Class and Sex Still Decide Who Goes to University,' *The Times* (29 April 1993).
27. Will Woodward, 'Students Are the New Poor,' *The Guardian* (June 27, 2001).
28. David Walker, 'Snakes and Ladders,' *The Guardian* (March 28, 2002).
29. Ibid.
30. See Will Hutton, 'The Class War Destroying Our Schools,' *The Observer* (May 26, 2002).
31. Charlotte Denny, Paul Brown and Tim Radford. 'The Shackles of Poverty,' *The Guardian* (August 22, 2002).
32. See G.P. Maximoff, *The Political Philosophy of Bakunin* (New York: The Free Press, 1953), pp. 334–336.
33. Most of the contributors in *Education Without Schools* ed. by Peter Buckman (London: Souvenir Press, 1973) support similar views.
34. Matt Hern, 'The Promise of Deschooling: Politics, Pedagogy, Culture, Self-design, Community Control,' *Social Anarchism*, issue no 25, (1998).
35. See T. Fotopoulos, *Towards an Inclusive Democracy*, chs. 5–6.
36. Cornelius Castoriadis, *Philosophy, Politics, Autonomy*, p. 113.
37. Mogens Herman Hansen, *The Athenian Democracy in the Age of Demosthenes*, p. 311.
38. Cornelius Castoriadis, *Philosophy, Politics, Autonomy*, (Oxford: Oxford University Press, 1991), p. 113.
39. Mogens Herman Hansen, *The Athenian Democracy in the Age of Demosthenes*, (Oxford: Blackwell, 1991), p. 320.
40. Murray Bookchin has described a similar scheme which, however, is based on communities and does not involve a proper economic democracy since it assumes a moral economy that assumes away the problem of scarcity, see "The Meaning of Confederalism," *Society and Nature*, Vol. 1, No. 3 (1993), pp. 41–54.
41. See T. Fotopoulos, 'Towards a Democratic Liberatory Ethics.'
42. For the full version of this model see, *Towards an Inclusive Democracy*, chapter 6; see, also, Takis Fotopoulos, 'Pour une démocratie économique,' *Agone*, no 21 (1999), pp. 136-158.
43. Janet Biehl, *Rethinking Ecofeminist Politics* (Boston: South End Press, 1991), p. 140.
44. Ted Trainer, *Abandon Affluence!* (London: Zed Books, 1985).
45. Pat Brewer, *Feminism and Socialism: Putting the Pieces Together* (Sydney: New Course, 1992).

46. Val Plumwood, 'Feminism, Privacy and Radical Democracy,' *Anarchist Studies*, Vol. 3, No. 2. (Autumn 1995), p. 107.
47. Val Plumwood, 'Feminism, Privacy and Radical Democracy,' p. 111.
48. Maurizio Passerin d' Entreves, "Hannah Arendt and the Idea of Citizenship" in *Dimensions of Radical Democracy*, ed. by C. Mouffe (London: Verso, 1995 & 1992), pp. 145–68.
49. Maurizio Passerin d' Entreves, "Hannah Arendt and the Idea of Citizenship", p. 154.
50. Castoriadis, *Philosophy, Politics, Autonomy*, p. 21.
51. See G. Woodcock, 'Democracy, heretical and radical,' *Our Generation*, Vol. 22, Nos. 1–2 (Fall 1990–Spring 1991), pp. 115–16.
52. See Cynthia Farrar, "Ancient Greek Political Theory as a Response to Democracy" in *Democracy, the Unfinished Journey*, 508 BC to AD 1993, ed. by John Dunn (Oxford: Oxford University Press, 1992), p. 24.
53. Takis Fotopoulos, *Towards an Inclusive Democracy*, Chapt. 8.
54. See T. Fotopoulos, 'Towards a Democratic Conception of Science and Technology,' *Democracy & Nature*, vol. 4 no. 1, (1998) pp. 54–86.
55. Thomas W. Simon, "Beyond Technological Things," in *Renewing the Earth*, John Clark, ed. (London: Greenprint, 1990), p. 112.
56. *The Castoriadis Reader*, p. 400.
57. As Michael Taylor has shown, one of the core characteristics of a community is reciprocity, which covers 'a range of arrangements and relations and exchanges, including mutual aid, some forms of cooperation and some forms of sharing.' Michael Taylor, *Community, Anarchy, and Liberty* (Cambridge: Cambridge University Press, 1982) pp. 28–29.
58. See Takis Fotopoulos, *Towards an Inclusive Democracy*, ch. 6.
59. A usual gross error of many libertarians, as April Carter stresses, is that they confuse—not unlike conservatives—authority with authoritarian rule, April Carter, *Authority and Democracy* (London: Routledge & Kegan Paul, 1979) p. 67. As the same author points out, 'There are three spheres in which some form of authority is necessary and intrinsic: the relationship between adult and child, teacher and student, and professional and layman. Authority in these spheres may be abused or insufficiently authoritative, but unless it exists child rearing, education and professionalism are impossible' (ibid. p. 70).
60. Matt Hern, 'The Promise of Deschooling: Politics, Pedagogy, Culture, Self-design, Community Control.'
61. See Takis Fotopoulos, 'The End of Traditional Anti-systemic Movements and the Need for a New Type of Antisystemic Movement Today,' *Democracy & Nature*, Vol. 7, No. 3 (November 2001). pp. 415–456; see also, Murray Bookchin, *Social Anarchism or Lifestyle Anarchism* (Edinburgh: AK press, 1995).
62. See Takis Fotopoulos, *Towards an Inclusive Democracy*, ch. 6 for a detailed description of basic and non-basic needs satisfaction in an inclusive democracy.
63. Joel Spring, *A Primer of Libertarian Education* (New York: Free Life Editions, 1975), p. 57.
64. G.P. Maximoff, *The Political Philosophy of Bakunin*, pp. 335–336.
65. Ibid. p. 335.
66. C. Castoriadis, *Philosophy, Politics, Autonomy*, p. 113.
67. Murray Bookchin, *Social Anarchism or Lifestyle Anarchism*.
68. Joel Spring, *A Primer of Libertarian Education*, pp. 54–55.
69. See Ivan Illich, 'The Deschooled society' in *Education Without Schools*, ed. by Peter Buckman, p. 15 & p. 18.
70. See Colin Ward, 'The Role of the State' in *Education Without Schools*, pp. 39–48.
71. Ibid. pp. 44–45.
72. See Takis Fotopoulos, 'Transitional Strategies and the Inclusive Democracy Project.'

SEVEN

Schools and the Manufacture of Mass Deception

A Dialogue

Howard Zinn and Donaldo Macedo

MACEDO: In your 1967 book *Vietnam: The Logic of Withdrawal,* you called for an immediate withdrawal from Vietnam without any conditions. But of course that didn't happen, and we have learned that thousands and thousands of innocent victims, including women and children, could have been spared from the vicious violence unleashed by the U.S. military against the people of Vietnam that ranged from the wanton spraying of Agent Orange (a chemical warfare) to carpet bombing of civilians in densely populated areas, such as the bombing of Hanoi. Tragically, President Johnson did not adhere to your suggestions.

Now, here we are again, committing something that is fundamentally wrong in Iraq that revisionist historians will later whitewash as a mistake. In your recent piece published in *The Progressive,* you made a similar call for an immediate withdrawal from Iraq without any conditions, and you wrote a lovely and eloquent speech that could have been given by any of the Democratic candidates for president—a speech based on the very democratic fabric upon which this nation was built, at least in theory. Most of the Democratic presidential candidates would not have the courage to develop a presidential campaign based on ideals of true democracy and social justice. But even if they did, their political handlers would summarily argue against adhering to the democratic propositions in your speech because, according to them, a progressive discourse that celebrates true demo-

This dialogue between Howard Zinn and Donaldo Macedo took place in January 2004 in Cambridge, Massachusetts.

cratic ideals such as equity, social and racial justice, and peace would constitute political suicide. In fact, this is precisely what happened to the candidacy of Howard Dean when the mass media strangled his presidential aspirations overnight because he raised too many impertinent questions concerning the illegal war in Iraq and talked about protecting the majority against the economic tyranny of the few. As you know, Howard Dean is hardly the ideal progressive candidate, and many of his proposals could be considered center right. Nevertheless, he was considered too radical for the establishment.

The paradox for me is why—in a society that embraces the myth of democracy to the point that the majority of Americans supported the illegal war against Iraq so we can undemocratically impose democracy—are politicians who truly want to create conditions for the actual practice of democracy along the lines proposed by the Declaration of Independence hardly taken seriously? In fact the political pundits would really argue against adhering to your position because they see your proposals for equity, democracy, and social justice as being either out of touch with reality or, worse, subversive socialist propaganda. It is to this huge contradiction that I want to turn our attention. Of course we have the propaganda state, the media, and so on working to "manufacture consent" and docility, but in our conversation today I would like to hear what you have to say regarding the role that schools play in creating this paradox and the mechanisms schools use to maintain it so as to reproduce dominant values that, ultimately, work counter to the very democratic ideals that schools seemingly promote. Do you see the contradiction?

ZINN: It's interesting. In a way the educational system, the schools, prepare young people to live with those contradictions and to accept them and to think they're OK. Because the schools give the people the ideals. The schools teach people about the Declaration of Independence, and they teach young people that we live in a democracy and that there is equality and justice for all. These are the ideals, you see. And then at the same time the schools do not give the young people, or even older people if they're in adult education programs, the information that shows how these ideals are being violated every day. So that, on the one hand, the schools give students the ideals, but, on the other hand, they don't give students the analytical tools so that they can look at society today and see what the discrepancy is between the ideals and the reality.

Or, to put it another way, the schools don't give students an accurate picture of reality. If they did, then the glaring difference between the ideals and the state of people in this society would be very apparent to students. For instance, schools do not give students a real picture of the class divisions in society. They don't give students a picture of how money dominates every aspect of society. Money obviously dominates the economic system, but it also dominates the political system, the culture, and even the educational system itself. Schools don't give students a look at how wealth and corporate power are dominant in this society, nor do they give their students a picture of how the other classes, the less-than-wealthy classes—that is, the oppressed—live. Students do not get an accurate picture of homelessness, they don't get an accurate picture of how poor people live, they don't get an accurate picture of what it's like to be a tenant subject to the power of a landlord or what it's like to be an unemployed person looking for a job and being frustrated every day. They do not get a picture of what it is to be black, to be colored in this society—a real picture of what it's like—and that's why when students are given, for instance (this was my own experience), the *Autobiography of Malcolm X* to read, they are startled. Because it's such a vivid and compelling and personal story, they say, almost for the first time, "This is what it's like to be a black person in society." Before reading such a book, they have this idea, "Oh, yes, there's discrimination, segregation, and so on," but there are two ways of knowing something: you know something superficially or you know something that hits you in your gut. And it can hit you in your gut even if you are not a victim of it. If you yourself are a victim of it, you don't have to learn about it, you experience it. But if you are a white person living in society, it's possible for you to begin to feel what it's like to be a person of color. You don't know exactly what it's like, but you can at least begin to understand it. That's what literature does. People read Richard Wright's *Black Boy* or Ralph Ellison's *Invisible Man,* and it wakes them up to what it feels like to be black. So we have this enormous gap in our educational system, where young people learn about the ideals of liberty and democracy, but they don't learn about the reality of a class society in which a very small number of wealthy people dominate the society and in which, at the other end of the spectrum, there are huge numbers of people who live on the edge of survival, who are really struggling to stay alive, to feed their kids, and to send their kids to school.

MACEDO: And the middle-class folks usually blame the loss of their jobs on immigrants, high taxes, and the welfare state, as they castigate the poor for the meager social assistance they might get from the government—the welfare queen syndrome catapulted to the national stage by former President Ronald Reagan. However, most of the same middle-class individuals who feel insecure economically are seldom able (or willing) to link their job losses to the corporate greed that makes them redundant through "outsourcing" (a euphemism for job liquidation) in order to generate greater and greater profits for corporations and their investors. Members of the middle class also fail to understand that our government has a hand in their misery because it promotes the exportation of jobs abroad by providing tax breaks and subsidies to corporations that do so.

It is for this reason that it becomes imperative for educators to help students shorten the gap between a superficial understanding of reality and the knowledge, as you put it, of "something that hits you in your gut." However, this is not an easy task, given the weight of dominant pedagogy designed primarily to domesticate and create obedient workers. For example, when I was teaching a course at the Harvard Graduate School of Education called "Anti-Racist Multicultural Education," a heated discussion ensued concerning the value of the METCO program—a program designed to bus a small number of inner-city students (primarily students of color) to suburban schools so they can have a better chance at a quality education. To provoke further analysis, I suggested to the class that we should also create a METCO program in reverse, where well-to-do white suburban students would be bused to inner-city schools so they can experience firsthand and understand the human misery and economic deprivation of ghetto living. This class was made up of mostly well-intentioned, affluent, white women who had an interest in working in inner-city schools. However, with the exception of a small number of minority students, the majority of the students in the class saw no pedagogical value in my proposal. In fact, they perceived my proposal as contentious, provocative, and unworkable since most suburban parents would not allow their children to be bused into city schools. As one student noted, "that is why they fled to the suburbs in the first place." The reason that was given most often against busing rich, white students to inner-city schools was that these schools and the neighborhoods in which they are located are too dangerous. When I asked them whether these schools and neighborhoods are also dangerous for the poor and mostly nonwhite students trapped in them, they agreed but contended that my proposal would only inflame class warfare and controversy.

As you can see, it is OK, if not cool, to study poverty in elite and wealthy universities in order to later become managers of poverty, such as directors of Head Start programs and other social initiatives in the inner city, but it is altogether another matter to ask these same white, affluent students to allow themselves to be "hit in the gut" in order to truly learn what it means to experience deprivation, discrimination, and dehumanization. Many of the students in the class were part of the Risk and Prevention Program at Harvard, but they were unwilling to ask the simple question of who put these students at risk to begin with, nor were they interested in delving into the root cause of poverty and its social consequences.

ZINN: That is understandable if the class system in the United States is to remain invisible and the myth of a classless society intact. And your proposal to deconstruct the contradiction is even more threatening to what is called the middle class, since they also experience great alienation and insecurity. The middle class in this country is supposed to be the sign of America's prosperity; it is often pointed to as a sign of how successful capitalism is, because we have created a large middle class of people who have television sets, who have cars, who may even own their own homes, and so on. But what is not represented actively is the psychic insecurity of people in that class, because so long as there is a class society including both the very rich and the very poor, members of the middle class never know which way they are going. They never know whether their jobs will be there tomorrow because the middle class is not the ownership class. Even if they are professionals or run small businesses, members of the middle class live in a society where they are ruled by somebody more powerful than they are, and they can lose their livelihoods suddenly—we're seeing this now in the United States, where so many middle-class people are suddenly losing their jobs.

MACEDO: You are correct, and more and more this economic dislocation is breeding tremendous insecurity in a large number of middle-class people.

ZINN: For example, on my street there are three people who were earning very good salaries working in the computer industry, and suddenly all three of them are unemployed. And in the meantime they have contracted to build additions on their houses, they have bought more goods, and they have sent their kids to private schools. So suddenly the middle class is nervous and insecure in our class society. And there are ways, of course, of educating people about this. Some teachers do this; it can be done. But the educational system at large, in the main, does not educate students about the realities of living in a class society, and instead young people grow up thinking that this is a successful society and that the Horatio Alger myth still persists—that if you work hard and get educated, you will be prosperous and successful and, presumably, that then the ideals that you once learned about will have been obtained.

MACEDO: You made reference to class, which is one of the issues I was hoping that we could elaborate on in this dialogue. I am reminded of the conversation we had in the coffee shop in Harvard Square when your friend raised the issue of your role as a working-class intellectual. It amazes me that the vast majority of people in this society, including highly educated individuals, particularly in schools of education where teachers are prepared, continue to promote or to embrace the myth that we live in a classless society. When I read your piece *Being Left: Growing Up Class-Conscious*, I was incredibly touched and moved by your description of what it meant to grow up as a working-class kid, helping your dad, who was a waiter, during a New Year's Eve party. You helped him clear and clean the tables while the well-to-do enjoyed the celebration totally oblivious to what it meant for working-class folks to struggle because, by and large, the partygoers had never experienced working-class living conditions. Yet in most schools, even those teachers who grew up in the working class often find ways to block any substantive discussion concerning class analysis, and they often proceed to teach the myths of classlessness.

For instance, this myth of the classless society gets reproduced in the way we do research in education. The class variable is never really allowed because, according to pseudoscientist educators, it taints objectivity. Also, as you have mentioned earlier, we don't need to create an educational context where students begin to experience and explore what it means to be a part of the working class, what it means to be poor, and what it means to be homeless because the curriculum is about somebody else's reality; the educational objective in our schools is to assimilate everybody into a mythical middle-class ideal, even though most working-class students, particularly students of color, will never experience that promised middle-class reality. It's a form of colonialism in that the vast majority of working-class students are often betrayed by the promises of the school discourse. At most only a small percentage of students in each generation will truly enjoy the fruits of the ideal classless society promised by schools. The mechanisms used for the blind acceptance for class assimilation are not too dissimilar from the tools used by colonial powers to legitimize the disparity and the often inhumane conditions created by colonialism. In this respect, schools usually function to provide justification and legitimization of what would be otherwise considered inhumane, exploitative, and oppressive.

What do I want to say about the role of education in the promotion of this myth of classlessness in the United States? Let me be specific. I came to the United States from Cape Verde, in West Africa, a colonial possession of Portugal marked by a cruel class division that bothered me from a very early age. When I immigrated with my family to the United States we took residence in Dorchester, Massachusetts, in 1966. I remember feeling a sense of relief, almost an acquired freedom, because around me, outside the racial factor that was generating elevated levels of tension in the neighborhood, everybody seemed to be in the same class. I really thought that yes, the myth is true, in the United States there is no class. But what I did not realize until I went to college is that growing up in Dorchester I did not have access to the middle- and upper-class reality. I didn't experience class distinctions in the United States until I went to college, and some of my professors began to invite me over to their houses in Newton, Brookline, and Lexington, which are mostly white, middle- and upper-class echelons. Because I was locked into a working-class reality without realizing it, I had made the generalization that everybody is equal in terms of class, because I couldn't really conceive otherwise. Yes, there were rich people, but I believed that they didn't belong to a separate class, because we are all the same. After all, we all had televisions and cars, although ours was of an inferior model. And as I mentioned earlier, it took a graduate program to wake me up to the class reality in the United States. I find it fascinating that the system is able to engage us in the pedagogy of lies to the point that even educators, who should know better, continue to promote the false notion of a classless society even when the reproduction of this myth produces dire consequences for working-class students, such as providing them with a rationalization for their school failures through academically crafted deficit theories.

ZINN: It's interesting. When I think of my own education, there was nothing in it that talked about class differences, and of course all the symbols of early education are the kinds of symbols that dominate our culture: the flag, the Pledge of Allegiance, America, the words, the language. And it's always as if we all belong to one class. You're aware, even if you grow up in a working-class community, that somehow, somewhere in the distance—you see their pictures in the papers, or you see them on the screen, in the news—there's a rich class. But you actually don't think of, and nothing in your education prepares you for the fact that there is some connection between their wealth and your poverty. You're never asked to question, never led to question how it is that some people are rich and others are poor. To put it another way, you're taught to accept what is there, you're not taught to challenge what is there, you're taught to believe that this is all natural. It is natural that you should live this way, it is natural that some should live that way, there's no criticism of that and nobody raises the question of how it has come to be this way or raises the question of whether it can be different. I never assumed growing up that it could be different. I wasn't even led to think about it.

MACEDO: And if you begin to feel victimized by this "natural" order supported by a commonsense folk theory, the message then is "it's your own fault . . . if you work hard enough, you will get the goodies like everyone else."

ZINN: It begins in the elementary schools. When I went on from elementary school to junior high school to high school—all of this was in the working-class milieu—the educational system taught about the Founding Fathers and the Constitution, and it taught us pride in the American Revolution and the Civil War, the great presidents and the great military leaders. There was nothing in my education that suggested that there was anything wrong with the existing arrangements. And what was missing from my education was this: any notion that in addition to great presidents and military heroes in our history there were also dissidents, people who rebelled. Of course I never learned that there were mutineers in George Washington's army in the Revolutionary War, or about the class nature of the draft riots during the Civil War. I certainly never learned—because it was always very simple, the Confederacy was bad, the North was good—that in the Confederacy there was class conflict, that poor people deserted from the Confederacy, that the wives of soldiers in the Confederacy rioted in Georgia against the plantation owners who were growing cotton instead of food because it was more profitable. There was no class consciousness in any of my education, and this continued right up into college and graduate school. There was no notion at all, you see, that it was possible to live in a different way. So all of my education was kind of Machiavellian, that is, the schools taught that this is the way things are and therefore you have to be pragmatic and realistic and just be part of this system the way it is. Because you don't learn about people who question the system, because you haven't been given a reason to question the system, because you haven't been asked what causes these class differences, and you haven't been given a larger picture of class segmentation in society, even if you know your own background and your background was poor. So that you live in some small part of the country and that is what you know, but you don't generalize from that and you don't see how this is a social phenomenon, a national phenomenon, so you don't think about this in larger terms.

I'm trying to think of whether anywhere in my education, right up until graduate school, I was given any notion of class conflict and class struggle in society. There were little hints of it. You'd be told about a particular labor struggle very superficially, such as the Pullman strike of 1894. You were only told about that, really, because Eugene Debs was involved in it and he was a presidential candidate. Anybody who was a presidential candidate was important because the one thing that you were socialized in was to believe in the importance of elections and to pour all of your civic energy into elections. So somebody who ran for president, OK, he was important so we give him a little attention. But the great labor struggles of the United States are glossed over or ignored completely. Actually, the United States has a history of some of the most dramatic labor struggles; it is one of the most amazing stories in Western history, but that history was absent from my education right up through graduate school. And so if I hadn't gone out and looked for it on my own and been led to it because of my own background, not just as a working-class person but specifically as a young, radical, working-class person (because that made a difference, you know) I never would have learned about those dramatic labor struggles. I could have been a working-class person and simply put that behind me, but as a young, working-class person who read Marx, Upton Sinclair, Jack London, Lincoln Stephens, and so on—as a young working-class person who read about other possibilities—I looked in my courses for class conflict and didn't find it. So I went out and looked for it myself. When I was an undergraduate at New York University, there was nothing in the history classes about the great labor struggles. I had to create an individual program for myself, and I found an advisor who would accept this, and then I could go ahead and read about the great strikes in American history. But I had to go out of my way to do this on my own because the educational system didn't give me any of that.

MACEDO: This control of the curriculum that leads to selective erasure of history continues today in the false promotion and reproduction of the myth that the United States is a classless society where everybody is the same. What I find paradoxical is the failure of the labor movement, particularly of the Left, to fill the gap, since the educational system is partly a function of a white, middle-class reality designed to reproduce values in the service of the dominant ideology. Why is it that the labor movement, or the Left for that matter, did not exercise a greater influence by teaching and creating conditions that would provide critical tools or avenues to find the information not available to students, particularly those students who yearn to think otherwise? We are then left to find out about these things when we have grown up. I read last night, for instance, what you wrote about the fact that you discovered the bad and criminal side of Columbus only after you finished your Ph.D.

ZINN: That's right.

MACEDO: It's amazing that you can earn a Ph.D. and do historical work while continuing to perpetuate the myth of Columbus as the good guy, the great hero, ignoring the atrocities, the massacres that he committed. Where do you see the disjunction happening in this great labor struggle and its inability to penetrate into schools to make them more democratic, more open, and more accessible? Do you see where I'm trying to go in terms of the failure of the labor movement to influence schools?

ZINN: I see where you go. It's a difficult question, because going back in history to the trade union movement, the American Federation of Labor, which was the most powerful labor union in the United States between the 1880s and the 1930s, was not interested particularly in this kind of class-oriented history. The American Federation of Labor consisted of skilled workers who had been successful in the system and who were taught to be very narrowly concerned with their own conditions and their own wages, not concerned with people outside their trades or crafts, not concerned with unskilled workers, immigrant workers, blacks, or women. And so the idea of a class-oriented education didn't mean anything to members of the American Federation of Labor, because in a sense they represented a certain class of privileged workers who did not have a larger view. Now there were trade unions in the history of the United States that did have a larger view—the Industrial Workers of the World (IWW), for instance, but the IWW was never able to penetrate or have any connection with the U.S. educational system. Remember, until the end of World War II and until millions of working-class guys entered the educational system under the GI Bill, the educational system after elementary school was closed to most working-class people. After laws were passed to provide a high school education to everybody, you know what happened: working-class students usually got the worst possible schools.

MACEDO: Well, that's what happened to you—you benefited from GI Bill assistance to further your schooling. Was this also a form of affirmative action?

ZINN: Yeah, exactly. But the educational system was a very limited system, and the IWW had no connection with that world of education. The people who were in the IWW might have been educated themselves, self-educated, but that never penetrated into the formal educational system. When the Congress of Industrial Organizations (CIO) was formed in the 1930s, it began to organize unskilled workers, black workers, and women workers and to organize the mass industries of the 1930s, auto and rubber. At that point you had for the first time a connection between radicalism and the labor movement and the idea of education; that is, a number of the unions, particularly left-wing unions of the 1930s, set up educational programs. These unions had education directors, and the National

Maritime Union had an educational program that was led by left-wing people, first the son of Daniel De Leon, who was an important socialist of the nineteenth century, and then Leo Huberman, who was a left-wing writer of history and economics, and they carried on educational programs for their members. There are still vestiges of that today; Local 1199 in New York still carries on educational and cultural programs. But that was always a separate educational system within the union, and it only involved a relatively small number of union members and never really penetrated the formal educational system.

Now why is this?

MACEDO: Yes, that's the question.

ZINN: Why is this? I've been dodging that question because I don't know the answer, except to say that the educational system was resistant to that kind of knowledge. I mean, how could the labor movement have an impact on schools? It could only happen if people in the educational system saw what was going on in the trade union movement, looked at these educational programs, and said, "oh, we need that as part of education." But no, the educational system has always been dominated by people who are not looking for change, who do not want to acknowledge the U.S. class system, who are looking for safety. Taking pointers from the labor movement would not have been a safe thing for schools to do. People in the educational system, like middle-class professionals anywhere, are very concerned about their security, their safety; they're subject to people above them. They're not of the upper rungs in the hierarchy of authority, so they worry about their standing and what can happen to them, and therefore they have admissions standards to the educational system. They don't want to rock the boat, they don't want to draw attention to themselves.

We're sitting here in the offices of the Trade Union Program of Harvard University. The Trade Union Program brings together union leaders from all over the country and even other parts of the world. They get together for eight-week periods, and they discuss all sorts of important things. It's an education, a real education here, for union people. They bring these trade union people here, and they bring Noam Chomsky, and they bring economists, and they bring even me in, and it's a concentrated educational thing for trade unionists. It's a totally separate thing from Harvard University. The students at Harvard University do not know of the existence of this program.

MACEDO: I never knew about the existence of this program until today. However, I am not a bit surprised that Harvard University would keep this program a secret and that most students don't know about its existence. On the other hand, this program functions also to promote the myth of academic freedom, openness, and rigorous inquiry espoused by Harvard in its promotional literature.

ZINN: Yeah, you were in the schools of education, and here we are, like we're in a prison cell and they won't allow visiting hours. And this is the way it's been.

The world of education is its own world, it does not want outsiders, it has immigration restrictions. It doesn't want people who will trouble the system, who will get in the way of turning out people whose one aim is to become successful in America in some way. And if you rock the boat, if you introduce troubling questions about the system, they're not ready for this, they won't accept this.

MACEDO: Do you think that this form of educational domestication also could be part of the reason that led to my initial question to you—why was the labor movement not aggressive enough to infiltrate in order to help transform education? Could it be that the movement itself, perhaps, was not quite willing to challenge the basic principle of capitalism? In other words, the labor movement was unwilling to transform and envision a society beyond capitalism. Instead, the labor movement focused mostly and narrowly on the need to make the lot of workers better and to share minimally the profits generated through their labor. The movement never intended to raise questions concerning the control of means of production, to raise issues regarding ownership, or to promote racial, class, and gender equity. These challenges would have to be met squarely and promptly but, unfortunately, this did not occur. The underlying belief is that you don't really want to educate young radicals who would push the envelope of social justice and equity and go beyond the narrow proposals set forth, a priori, by a labor movement that had an aversion toward any socialist-sounding proposals to begin with. Could this be a partial explanation for the narrowness of the labor movement in the United States?

ZINN: No question. I was dealing with one half of it. That is, here are these two entities, here is the educational system and here is, you might say, a class-oriented view of the world, which you find in some parts of the labor movement, and the two don't come together. And I was just talking about how the educational establishment itself closes the door to that. But what you were just talking about is the other side of it, that is, that the labor movement itself has had such a narrow vision. . . .

MACEDO: That's my point. One could also add that, in certain moments, the labor movement had no vision at all outside the struggle for a modicum of reform to better the working conditions of workers (not all workers, especially not ethnic and racial workers) and to secure a modest share of the profit generated through their labor. The labor leadership never sought to exercise substantive control over the means of production and promote issues of social justice and social welfare for all workers regardless of race, ethnicity, gender, and creed.

ZINN: The labor movement in the United States has had such a narrow vision. You know, in Britain the Labour Party at least called itself a socialist party, it accepted the idea of socialism. In many countries in the world, trade union movements are radical in their orientation; socialist, anticapitalist, they have deep critiques. In the United States, you might say that the labor movement—except for that brief period of the IWW in the early twentieth century and except for a small number of the unions in the CIO, some of which were destroyed by the 1950s. During the Cold War, with the emergence of the McCarthy period and the promulgation of the Taft-Hartley Act that enabled unions to purge communists and radicals, the trade union movement in the United States purged itself of left-leaning leaders in order to ingratiate itself with the establishment and to move closer to the seat of power. The trade union movement went along with purging those unions and those union leaders who had a larger vision, a class-conscious vision of society. So I mean the problems, yes, are not just the obstacles set up by the educational system but also the limitations of the trade union movement in the United States. Of course that raises a difficult question, which is why the trade union movement in the United States is so limited in its vision as compared to those of other countries. And one possible answer is that the United States, with all its wealth, has been able to, you might say, bribe a certain section of the working class, giving it just enough privilege, just enough benefits to make the trade union movement collaborators with the system, and so the incentive for trade unions to present a broader vision has not been there because they felt that we can do all right within the system. And the answer was, yes, some of them could do all right within the system, a minority, but in addition, the trade union movement of the United States has always been a minority of the working class. There are other countries in which a much larger percentage of the working class belongs to trade unions. In France, 80 percent of the workers belong to some trade union. In the United States, it never exceeded 30 percent, and now it's down to 10 percent, 12 percent. So yes, in the United States, the trade union movement itself has had a very limited vision, and the most potentially radical workers, the most potentially radical and troublesome members of the working class, have generally been outside the trade union movement, and that's certainly true today.

MACEDO: The creation of this accommodated class of laborers, who were given certain privileges (one could argue bones to chew on) due to the immense resources and wealth of the United States, anesthetized the labor movement's ability to connect with, for instance, our foreign policy, which has always been designed to exploit workers from poor and underdeveloped countries, thus enabling U.S. society to maintain and enjoy a higher standard of living. The exploitation of both workers and natural resources in other countries provides the U.S. market with the means to provide its workers with some privileges, albeit limited ones, not enjoyed by workers from the countries that are being exploited. The ability to maintain a higher standard of living within the United States functions as a form of co-optation of U.S. workers, who then become complacent and indifferent to the imperialistic exploitation of third-world workers, including children. If, on the other hand, schools would provide students with the critical tools to make the necessary linkages in order to better comprehend a particular reality and its raison d'être, the level of complacency and indifference on the part of U.S. citizens toward the suffering of third-world people would, perhaps, drastically change.

Take, for example, high school teacher Bill Bigelow's use of a soccer ball in his global studies classroom, designed to encourage students to read multiple realities linked with the ball. Bigelow began the lesson with a beat-up soccer ball and asked students to write a description. As expected, he was greeted with "puzzlement and annoyance" because, according to one student, "it's just a soccer ball." The students' "accounts were straightforward and accurate if uninspired."[1] Although Bigelow's students provided an accurate description of the ball, their depictions remained purely physical, with little connection to a "deeper reality associated with this ball—a reality that advertising and consumption-oriented rhythms of U.S. daily life discouraged students from considering, 'Made in Pakistan.'"[2]

Bigelow then invited his students to inquire about the "human lives hidden in 'just a soccer ball'—a clue to the invisible Pakistanis whose hands crafted the ball."[3] Aware of the importance of making linkages, Bigelow used Bertolt Brecht's poem "A Worker Reads History" to engage his students in a deeper meaning contained in the hidden stories of the soccer ball:

> Each page a victory
> At whose expense, the victory ball?
> Every ten years a great man,
> Who paid the piper?

By using Brecht's poem, Bigelow eclipsed the criticism alleging that the development of political clarity politicizes education and invariably waters down the curriculum. Who would argue that reading Brecht waters down education? After reading the poem, Bigelow asked his students to "re-see" the soccer ball. Students raised questions: Who made this soccer ball? Where did the real people go after the ball was made? One student, Sarah, wrote: "I sew together these shapes of leather. I stab my finger with my needle. I feel a small pain, but my fingers are so callused. Everyday I sew these soccer balls together for 5 cents, but I've never once had a chance to play soccer with my friends. I sew and sew all day long to have these balls shipped to another place where they represent fun. Here, they represent the hard work of everyday life."[4]

When we compare the first description of the soccer ball that focused on accurately describing the physical properties of the ball with Sarah's in-depth reading of the world of exploitation and suffering contained within the soccer ball, we see how political clarity not only expands the range of possibilities for making meaning but also improves the quality of writing. Sarah's understanding that her privilege comes at the high cost of someone else's sweat and suffering enabled her to develop the necessary empathy that could easily lead to action against all forms of oppression and exploitation. What Bill Bigelow's lesson shows is that it is possible to imagine a better world and that new pedagogical structures can be created where students become critical agents rather than mere objects to be filled with official myths and ideas. Then it is not a coincidence, nor is it innocent, that both schools and trade unions in the United States neglect to make the necessary linkages that could unveil the inherent exploitative nature of capitalism. The development of critical tools to make linkages to better comprehend the world would necessarily unveil U.S. imperialism, even though after the invasion of Iraq imperialism is now presented in the mass media as a national goal while the majority of the citizenry remains indifferent to its ramifications and consequences.

ZINN: But, of course, that failure to make connections to other countries is true in the trade union movement, and it's even more true in the educational system. Though I must say in the trade union movement we are beginning to see a small breakthrough with the globalization issue—we're beginning to see that because, for the first time, workers are looking at what's happening to them domestically, and they're having to confront our connections with foreign workers and to see, for instance, in Mexico, that the free trade agreement has been hurtful both to Mexican workers and to American workers, and so they're the seeds of solidarity. And we now see that there is a global movement; along with the globalization of the great economic powers, there's a globalization of resistance, and we now see international gatherings, the World Social Forum, which met in Porto Alegre, Brazil, as well as Seattle, Washington. The people participating in this globalization of resistance are still the minority, of course, still a small minority, but it's the beginning of consciousness about the connection between class exploitation here and class exploitation in other countries. But in the educational system it hasn't even gone that far. Probably the most egregious, the most flagrant failure in the American educational system, even beyond what I spoke about before, the failure to talk about class in the United States, has been the failure to understand the relations between the United States and other countries in the world, that is, American foreign policy. And the thing you pointed to, about the connections between the goodies that Americans can get, even the small goodies that Americans can get at the expense of workers in other countries, and W. E. B. Du Bois. . . .

MACEDO: He's one of the first American intellectuals to have raised this issue and it cost him dearly, forcing him to seek exile in Africa. The doctrinal reward system makes sure that dissent and a language of critique are not tolerated, and the cost of dissent, particularly a critique of capitalism, is usually very high, including one's life, as was the case with Martin Luther King Jr. The effectiveness of the doctrinal reward system to muffle dissent was painfully displayed after the 9/11 attacks, when all pretense of political opposition and critique in the United States just collapsed. Criticizing Bush administration policies for the war against Iraq was viewed as un-American. Members of Congress, including the Democratic opposition, understood that criticizing the president would have raised exponentially the possibility of their losing the next election. Thus, Congress became a rubber stamp to ratify all the policies on the conservative agenda, including tax cuts that benefited mostly the rich, while the distinction between the Republicans and Democrats simply disappeared.

ZINN: Yeah, that's right. W. E. B. Du Bois raised that issue and unfortunately we don't have a Du Bois in Congress now. And it's sort of natural that a black intellectual would raise that issue; after all, the relations between whites and blacks in the United States were a microcosm of the relations between Americans and people in other parts of the world because you might say that some white workers were benefiting from exploitation of black people in this country and Du Bois could see that connection. But the educational system teaches nothing about American foreign policy, teaches nothing that would suggest a critical look at American foreign policy. I mean, the general effect of the teaching of foreign policy, and this goes right up through graduate school, is to say that the United States has been a force for good in the world, basically that's the idea. There may have been a few aberrations, a few things. . . .

MACEDO: These aberrations are later whitewashed as mistakes, as McNamara described the Vietnam War. McNamara and other policy hawks would never admit that what they call "mistakes" constitute a wrong—a violation of international law and, in some cases, outright crimes against humanity, as was the case in Vietnam with the My Lai Massacre, even though the perpetrators of these crimes are seldom punished for their crimes. These same war hawks and policy makers would have no difficulty identifying these crimes against humanity and violations of international law if a country that they considered to be a "rogue nation" committed them. They would also have no qualms calling for the fullest application of the law. In fact, they might even recommend that the United States invade these "rogue nations" to indict these criminals, as was the case with Noriega when the United States invaded Panama. Never mind that Noriega was a thug and drug dealer created by the United States and protected and paid for years by the CIA.

ZINN: Exactly. That's right. In fact I was listening to, maybe you heard it too, an interview of the guy who made the film about McNamara, and the interviewer asked the filmmaker, "Well, did you ask McNamara about the Vietnam War?" And the filmmaker said, "Well, McNamara admits there were some mistakes." It's all mistakes, you see, and not something that's inherent in the system and persistent throughout our policy. But this critical examination of American foreign policy is absent. You can see this most flagrantly in the lack of education about Latin America. I mean, I didn't even think about this until I got out of graduate school, it didn't occur to me that I'd learned nothing about Latin America. There was a required one-year course for history majors on the history of England, but nothing in the curriculum, required or not required, on our relations with Latin

America. I mean, you would think, here are black students, well, what about Haiti, the first black republic? No, you could graduate after four years at a black college, and you'd never know that Haiti existed.

MACEDO: But we should not be at all surprised. After all, these countries are banana republics that we invade from time to time in order to whip them into shape to fend off altruistic and dangerous aspirations of sovereignty, social justice, and democratic ideals.

Linked to the absence of Latin America in the curriculum of U.S. schools is the total omission of analysis of the School of the Americas, and if one were to use President Bush's criteria in determining what constitutes a terrorist organization, one would have to classify this school as a terrorist training ground not too dissimilar to Osama bin Laden's, where Latin America's worst thugs and criminals were trained to commit the most horrendous crimes against their own populations (mostly civilians), such as the case with the slaughter of the Jesuit priests in El Salvador. But since these thugs were our thugs (these characterizations are never used by the administration, or the media, for that matter, to refer to these criminals; in fact, former President Reagan used to call them freedom fighters), not only are they never punished for their crimes and atrocities but also they are often rewarded. For example, Roberto D'Aubuisson, who as a major architect and sponsor of death squads in El Salvador, was responsible for the assassination of Archbishop Oscar Romero and was also implicated in the slaughter of the Jesuit priests, was given red-carpet treatment in Congress by former Senator Jesse Helms of North Carolina. Can you imagine American reaction if Cuba, or any other country for that matter, hosted a high official from al Qaeda? It was no secret that both the Reagan and Bush administrations were heavily involved in the civil war in El Salvador by supporting the ultra-right political faction and its death squads, which were responsible for all kinds of barbarous atrocities committed mostly against civilians. The civil war casualty count in El Salvador is approximately thirty thousand dead. For these victims and their relatives, our support of this unjust and cruel war is no less terrorism than the vicious tragedy in New York on 9/11.

ZINN: Yeah, but you knew nothing about that. Americans could not, after graduating from college, tell you where Ecuador was or whether Guatemala was in the Western Hemisphere or in Africa. They couldn't tell you that. So the educational system brings up whole generations of Americans who do not understand what we have done to other countries. I must say that—and I haven't talked about this at all, because I have only said negative things about our educational system, and I'll continue, of course—since the 1960s we have begun to have a sort of smattering of people coming into the educational system with a broader social view, and people are teaching about Latin America—you know, somebody teaching at a privileged college like Wellesley who has been in Central America and has a progressive point of view about it—and African studies programs are just beginning. So we have now a small minority of teachers in the educational world, on the college level at least, I'm not even sure it's gotten into the high schools, who are beginning to teach something critical about American foreign policy. But in the main? No, Americans do not learn about this, and of course what this does is it leads Americans to accept uncritically what their government tells them about current foreign policy.

MACEDO: But they do this even when the evidence points to the contrary, which is really amazing. The last time we met, we talked about the fact that some 60-odd percent of college students continued to believe that Iraq had something to do with 9/11, even when President Bush himself has denied publicly such links and intelligence agencies all over the world have also come to the same conclusion. This shows you the power of the propaganda state, on the one hand, and, on the other, the total lack of critical thinking found in schools to counterbalance the propaganda apparatus. And this is very dangerous; it does not really bode well for the democratic ideals to which we claim to aspire. It also shows a high level of domestication that turns students into obedient automatons who eagerly move according to the marching orders given by the doctrinal system.

ZINN: I'm not surprised that 60 percent of college students would think something like the linkage between al Qaeda and Iraq is absolutely true, because they didn't get anything in their education that would prepare them to look critically at what the government says, so they listen to the government say again and again and again that something is true or hint and suggest and make connections, and then when the president denies it in one statement, it's not enough to penetrate what has already become a mountain of lies. I suppose it's encouraging—but then again, I'm easily encouraged, one might say desperate for encouragement—that *only* 60 percent of college-educated people believe that, since from what they get from the educational system, it should be 95 percent. So it means that there is, despite the educational system and despite the propaganda system, a countervailing network of underground information in this country that somehow seeps through to a fairly large number of Americans. And that is some cause for hope, because it shows that it may be possible to break through this control. In fact that possibility was realized during the Vietnam War, because during the Vietnam War, certainly, the educational system gave students no information, no background, on Vietnam. You could graduate from college and have no idea where Vietnam was. . . .

MACEDO: Neither did they have any idea about the cruel and violent U.S. policy toward Vietnam.

ZINN: And certainly nothing about our policy toward Vietnam. And what happened is that at the beginning of the Vietnam War, two-thirds of Americans supported the Vietnam War, and a few years later two-thirds of Americans opposed the war. What happened in between to make that change? Not the government, not the press. What happened in between was the effects of what I call the underground network, the counterculture, the underground newspapers, the community radio stations, the teach-ins, the rallies, the work of small radical groups (even though they did not have the major means of communication at hand)—the power of the truth was so strong that it overcame the government and media propaganda machines and reached a large number of Americans. So I'm suggesting that it wasn't the educational system itself that did it. The fact that we had to have teach-ins is a sign of that. What did the 1960s produce? Not only teach-ins but also alternative little schools within a school; we even had programs—voluntary programs, extracurricular programs—that were set up by the students themselves to teach about what was going on in the world because they couldn't get that information in their regular classes.

MACEDO: You mentioned this counterculture, and, of course, it gets manifested at least at the university level as ethnic studies, women's studies, African American studies, and so on, and these developments are great—no question in my mind—for a more pluralistic, multicultural society. And because these university developments often question the doctrinal systems, such as the interrogation of patriarchy by feminists, they are often under attack. In fact, the backlash is real. For instance, at the University of Massachusetts, where I teach, the College of Public and Community Services (CPCS), which is a community-oriented, highly progressive college, is currently under assault by the present university administration, which always points to the low enrollments as justification to withdraw resources from the college. Because CPCS now lacks adequate resources for recruitment, you end up with a vicious cycle that will progressively strangle it. One senior administrator at the university who shows a total distaste for CPCS and the democratic values it espouses, which are rooted in the ideals of the 1960s, remarked, "The problem with CPCS is that it is stuck in the Sixties vision of social justice and students are mostly interested in jobs"—which means that social justice in our society, which was founded on democratic ideals of social justice, is now considered something outdated and passé. So if CPCS wants to really get on with the program, it has to abandon its social justice orientation, which includes community programs that study issues of homelessness, housing for the poor, and other social issues that are very much pertinent for the underclass residents of Roxbury, Dorchester, and other economically depressed areas near Boston. It amazes me that an educator or an administrator in an urban and public educational system that was created with the primary goal of working toward social justice for the oppressed citizens of Boston and the surrounding areas would think that social justice is passé. It is scary, but that is a fact. So, although I am hopeful on the one hand, on the other hand there are tremendous obstacles that present real and difficult challenges for those of us who yearn to imagine a world that is less discriminatory and more just.

ZINN: Although the challenges, as you said, are difficult, it is important to think that change is possible, and we should remain always hopeful.

MACEDO: I wanted to ask you a question that I had also asked Paulo Freire many years ago in New York, which points to another paradox. The United States is one of the wealthiest countries in the world; it has the largest resources for education, both private and public; it has the highest level of teacher training compared to any other country in terms of the amount of money and number of courses and degrees that we give in education, and yet it produces staggering failures like in New York. As I had asked Paulo, how does one reconcile the fact that all this wealth, all these material and technological advancements in education, and all of this training end up producing huge educational failures, particularly among minority students that sometimes reach unacceptable dropout rates? Freire sort of smiled at me and said, "Donaldo, don't be naive. What you are calling failure is the ultimate victory of the system, because the system was never designed to educate those who are failing to begin with." And then he asked me, "Who are those who are failing? They are your blacks, your working-class whites, your ethnic folks, your immigrants." I had never really thought of it in this light. What we call the failure question should basically really be inverted—we are talking about the victory of the system, and I've been thinking a lot about it lately. Let's take New York, for example, which spends billions of dollars to maintain a system that generates largely failure. We tolerate this blatant failure in education, but let's say we had the same rate of failure in health care. The society would not tolerate that. For instance, if the *Boston Globe* revealed on its front page that 57 percent of the patients admitted to Massachusetts General Hospital died, immediately administrators, politicians, and the society in general would be calling for blue ribbon commissions to study the problem. In fact Massachusetts General Hospital would be closed, because no one would go there. Yet, we are willing to spend billions of dollars to support an educational system that generates failure, and nobody really cares. Again, we shouldn't be surprised since most of the white, middle- and upper-class students in Boston don't go to the Boston public schools anyhow. Do you see my point?

ZINN: Yeah. Of course the only reason the people on top would care in your example about the health care system is because people in the larger society would be rebellious against such extreme health care failure. And the question is, why aren't people in the larger society rebellious against what is happening in the educational system?

MACEDO: Because those who are victims of the educational system are considered to be disposable bodies who were never supposed to be educated in the first place. The ruling class would never tolerate dysfunctional educational programs for their children. That is why they pay large sums of money to send their children to private schools while they remain content that inner-city schools become containment centers for the underclass students who are, by and large, non-white. While the dominant class finds it unacceptable to, as they say, "throw more money" at educating poor, inner-city students (the Boston public school system spends approximately $8,000 per student per year), it has no difficulty bankrolling approximately $30,000 per person per year to contain a large percentage of the under-class "school dropouts" in jails. Perhaps they rationalize that $30,000 for each prisoner is a good investment in that it keeps a potentially large number of black and minority voters from exercising their right to vote, as was the case during the 2000 presidential election in Florida where thousands upon thousands of black voters were unfairly and illegally disqualified from voting. Jail will do the trick more easily, although it is more costly.

ZINN: Exactly. And it's a vicious cycle, because the people who are the victims of the system don't have the resources or the wherewithal to rebel against the system. Or their rebellion comes in another form: they go out into the streets, and they become dysfunctional people in society, and they're the ones who become the two million people in prison, or they're the ones who become the homeless. And they don't become an organized force. And the people who have the resources to resist and complain are the people whose children are the successful ones in the system. So it's representative of the larger problem in the society, which is true not only of education but also of the economy, and that is that the people who are the greatest victims of the economy—that is, the forty million people without health care, and the people who are unemployed, and the people who are living in the ghettos of the country—are the people who have the least resources to rebel. And every once in a while, of course, there is an upsurge, such as the riots of blacks in the 1960s; every once in a while there's something like that. The system puts them away, it puts them out of sight. And so the question is, at what point can there be a breakthrough in this? Will it require that the people who are successful in the system realize that they are not really successful, that they also will suffer from this, that the fact that there's an underclass undercuts the security of the people in the middle class? How and when this breakthrough will take place is very hard to say, because it's a kind of self-perpetuating system, and it will take something critical, troublesome, dangerous—some crisis—to make people who think they are succeeding in the system realize that they're not, that they are succeeding in a system that ultimately makes them insecure. And I don't know the answer to breaking through that kind of self-perpetuating cycle.

MACEDO: Which I think largely education promotes, sustains, and maintains in some direct way. This goes back to the question that your friend raised during our conversation in the coffee shop in Harvard Square. Growing up working class and being face-to-face with all kinds of deprivations, humiliation, and alienation, as you discussed in your essay that I read the other day, can you remain working class in the academy? I know that lots of working-class folks who have "made it" then behave as if the system functions justly and normally without much problem. My friend Henry Giroux, who is also a friend of yours, once told me very clearly when we were both teaching at Boston University that there's no such thing as a working-class intellectual in the academy. According to him, if you remain true to your working-class values, even in the way you behave and the way you are in the world and with the world, the academy will weed you out. And that's what happened to him. In your case, you already had tenure so John Silber couldn't get rid of you. But your presence, and Henry's presence, along with the presence of others, particularly those who are radicals and activists and whose goal is to change the system, are not welcome in the academy; the academy imposes a level of censorship even while claiming to espouse a free and open education.

And I wanted to ask you, in particular, about your relationship with John Silber, the former president of Boston University, where you taught for many years. In my view, John Silber behaved always like the ultimate fascist and was, at the same time, always rewarded by the dominant system with accolades from the *New York Times,* the *Boston Globe,* and other media outlets that portrayed him as a great educator, even though he's never written a book on education, and as a Kantian scholar, even though he wrote and published just two articles on Kant taken largely from his doctoral dissertation. The doctrinal system created a myth around him, elevating him to stardom, making him into someone who can go on television and dismiss scholars like you and Noam Chomsky—all the while providing no proof for his tirades and getting away with it. In fact, Silber was often rewarded for his falsehoods. Given this level of censorship of progressive thinkers in the academy, I am trying to grapple with how this works and how institutions of higher learning can promote people like John Silber, who bragged about having kept the Frankfurt School of thought out of Boston University, eliminated studies dealing with sexual orientation, and attempted to weed out all progressive thinkers (labeled leftists) from the faculty while spouting platitudes about scientific rigor in the pursuit of truth. Of course, it is his own version of the pursuit of scientific knowledge and democratic ideals. Can you talk about a society that enables people like John Silber to be who they are and rewards them and promotes them to the highest levels?

ZINN: After all, who has the controlling voice in universities? It's not the faculty; it's not the students; it's certainly not the janitors, the cleaning people, the secretaries; it's the trustees of the universities or the boards of regents. And who are these people? In the case of boards of trustees, they're businesspeople, in the case of boards of regents, they're still businesspeople, they're people in the upper reaches, very often they're not people who have much to do with education. They're people who have political connections, people who have business connections, and they are the people who make the important decisions in the university. They decide who will be the president of the university. Ultimately they can decide which professors get tenure and which do not.

We go into the university naïvely, thinking it is a different place than the rest of society, an oasis; even if we have a critical view of society, the university is an oasis within this society. And I've known even radical people in the university who saw the university that way. Therefore in the 1960s, when people rebelled against the university they said, "You're destroying *our* university." I remember specifically a professor at Boston University who considered himself a Marxist saying, "Remember, it's our university." But it was never our university. So there's this naïveté about the university. But the university has always really been a part of the capitalist world in microcosm, controlled by business, controlled by people who have power and wealth and who make the ultimate decisions. And so it's possible for radical professors to occasionally make their way into the system and stay there and get tenure, but there are two things to note about them: one, there are not that many of them, and two, they can be used as examples of the tolerance of the system, of how democratic the system is. If Chomsky says the educational system is an undemocratic system, you can say, well, *you're* there, you have a position at MIT. Well, it's perfectly attuned to the American system of control, a very sophisticated system of control that allows just enough dissidence so that those in power can point to the fact that the university is democratic but not enough dissidence to create a real danger to the system. And so it operates like the world outside, with the same hierarchy of power, with the same bare margin of toleration for some people. And, at the same time, while some people, some radicals who become embedded in the system, you might say, retain their radicalism and teach in a different way and become active in outside political activities, there are many people who start out as radicals, enter the system, and while holding on to their reputations as radicals remain radicals only on a very abstract intellectual level. They might even teach a course in Marxism, but they are not dissidents— they are not dissidents in the society outside, and they are not dissidents in the university because they consider themselves part of the university and they hold to the idea, and therefore perpetuate the idea, that the university is basically a decent institution.

MACEDO: These are the intellectuals that Chomsky often refers to as "commissars," because ultimately their major function is to legitimize and reproduce those very values that, as intellectuals, they should work against. This leads to my last question. What do you see as the role of intellectuals not only in universities but also in K–12 education, since, in the view of many progressive thinkers, teachers are, or should be, first and foremost intellectuals who must also always be vigilant and willing to critique any form of social injustice? Teachers must also courageously work toward conditions that promote a society that is less dehumanizing and more humane. How can we accept the label *intellectual,* when in fact one is unable to ethically intervene to ameliorate a wrong? With rare exceptions of courageous and coherent intellectuals like you, Noam Chomsky, bell hooks, and Henry Giroux, among others, the vast majority of professors seem to cling to the naïve notion, as you put it, that "it's our system," "it's our school," "it's our university," even though these institutions do not belong to us. Intellectuals should always aim for a world that rejects all forms of dehumanization while celebrating the liberation of all people, regardless of race, religion, ethnicity, and gender. What can you say about the role of intellectuals in the United States and their obvious complicity with the power structure as they, through their work, end up legitimizing values that are unjust, exploitative, undemocratic, and, in final analysis, unethical?

ZINN: Well, the chief problem is that if intellectuals who do have a radical vision of this society, and who even present that vision in the education system in their teaching through the books they assign or what they say in their lectures, are not at the same time involved in the world outside, in the real social struggles that go on—if the classroom remains a sealed, intellectual entity—then they are teaching their students that this classroom radicalism is sufficient. They're teaching their students to be content with being intellectually dissident and then, maybe, to become teachers who will perpetuate the role of the intellectual dissident but without venturing into the world outside. . . .

MACEDO: Which is also a form of dilettantism.

ZINN: Yes, yes, certainly, a form of dilettantism. And in a way it's a marvelous way for the system to perpetuate itself, to contain dissent by giving people the illusion of being critics of the system without acting out that criticism in the society at large. And so for every radical social critic in the academy who is also out in the world acting out, exemplifying his or her ideas, there are many, many, many more radicals in the system who confine their radical critiques to the intellectual level and thereby teach passivity to their students. They teach contentment with the role they play, feeling that they are doing something important when actually they are perpetuating the barrier between the radical intellectual inside the university and the world outside. I know that every year there's a meeting in New York of socialist scholars. Several thousand people come, and I wonder how many of those several thousand people are actively involved outside of the academy, how many of them are just scholars, you see, and how many of them go outside. . . .

MACEDO: Well, the very label is telling—they're socialist scholars, and scholarship is not about engagement in action. So what you're saying, and I agree with you, is that reflection alone is not enough, and awareness alone is also not enough in that awareness must always be coupled with action, and action forces you outside the ivory tower. But this is also very much a class issue that informs and ultimately shapes the behaviors of many liberal professors. Many of these professors that you just described could even have a turbulent relationship with an activist like you because, at some level, they will feel threatened to the degree that your praxis becomes a mirror that shows their own complicity with the dominant system. That is, your praxis may make them realize that what they're doing is not sufficient and that their work is not part of a political project that collectively points to mechanisms to transform an unjust reality. In fact, their work would, invariably, reproduce the very dominant values they claim through their liberal discourse to interrogate. Unfortunately, it often ends up being a form of interrogation without action. Furthermore, because they adopt a liberal discourse that accommodates rather than liberates, even when they teach, let's say, a course on Marxism, this fact is, in turn, used by the dominant institutions to say: "See, we are open and democratic, and we tolerate dissent."

Notes

1. Bill Bigelow, "The Human Lives behind the Labels: The Global Sweatshop, Nike, and the Race to the Bottom," *Rethinking Schools* (1997): 1.
2. Bigelow, "The Human Lives behind the Labels," 1.
3. Bigelow, "The Human Lives behind the Labels," 1.
4. Bigelow, "The Human Lives behind the Labels," 12.

Trends in Critical Pedagogy

EIGHT

Critical Pedagogy in the Twenty-First Century: Evolution for Survival

Joe L. Kincheloe

I am dedicated to the basic themes of critical pedagogy. I have been for years and assume I will continue to be for the rest of my life. At the same time because I am dedicated to the principles of criticality, I am by necessity a vehement critic of the tradition. Adherence to such critical notions, many believe, requires those of us within the tradition to criticize and move it to new plateaus while recognizing our own failures and the failures of the domain. It is in this spirit that Peter and I entered into our work on *Critical Pedagogy: Where Are We Now?* Bound by our enduring friendship and common commitment to a wide range of critical concepts, together we move into the next phase of critical pedagogy. As I reference my role as a "vehement critic" of the critical tradition, I offer such criticism in the spirit of Paulo Freire's radical love. I don't want to assess the successes and failures of critical pedagogy in the posture of one who knows best where we should be going—I don't possess such prescience. In the spirit of Paulo I offer my critiques humbly, painfully aware of my own shortcomings as a teacher-scholar.

Concurrently, I refuse to attack my fellow critical pedagogues in some mean-spirited, ad hominem way simply because they might disagree with me. I find that on the vast majority of issues I am a committed ally of proponents of critical pedagogy with whom I have profound disagreements. In such contexts I seek a synergistic conversation, knowing that any disagreement we have around a theo-

First published in McLaren, P. & J. Kincheloe. (2007). *Critical Pedagogy—Where Are We Now?* NY: Peter Lang.

retical or social action-oriented concept can be analyzed within a larger context of sociopolitical and pedagogical solidarity. With this critical harmony and radical love as the foundation that grounds my conception of critical pedagogy, I offer this chapter as a call for critical solidarity in an era that might be described as "less than friendly" to many of our perspectives on social, cultural, political, economic, epistemological, ontological, psychological, social, theoretical, and pedagogical issues of the day. Didn't Ben Franklin once say something about it being better to hang together than to hang separately? In this era of a new U.S. empire, political economic globalization, a corporatized politics of knowledge, a "recovered" dominant race, class, gender, sexual, and religious supremacy, and a grotesque anti-intellectualism, I would argue that Franklin's eighteenth-century perspective on the dynamics of hanging is quite relevant for twenty-first-century practitioners of critical pedagogy.

Keeping Critical Pedagogy Relevant: Diverse Dialects—Open-Access Writing and Speaking

If critical pedagogy is to matter as we move toward the second decade of the twenty-first century, if it is to be more than a historical blip on the educational landscape of the late twentieth and early twenty-first centuries, then it must meet several contemporary challenges. From my perspective a vibrant, relevant, effective critical pedagogy in the contemporary era must be simultaneously intellectually rigorous and accessible to multiple audiences. In an era when open-access publishing on the Internet is a compelling issue in the politics of knowledge (Willinsky, 2006), I contend that open-access writing and speaking about critical pedagogy are also profoundly important. Such a populist form of criticality does not in any manner undermine our intellectual rigor and theoretical sophistication; instead, it challenges our pedagogical ability to express complex ideas in a language that is understandable and germane to wide audiences.

Make no mistake, there is a central place in the lives of academic critical pedagogues for scholarly, peer-reviewed publications—such an enterprise is a dynamic dimension of being a scholar and improving our intellectual skills. Such a practice occupies a central place in the cultivation of the intellect and in all of our efforts to become adept transformative intellectuals. In the research and scholarship of every critical pedagogue there is an important role for both scholarly peer-reviewed journal publication and writing aimed at diverse audiences: teachers, social workers, parents, students at a variety of grade levels, labor groups, women's groups, sexual groups, racial/ethnic groups, religious organizations, etc. Our imagination is the only limit to the audiences critical pedagogues might address. Indeed, we have important insights to pass along to diverse groups; consequently we need to seek out these audiences, publish for them, and convince university tenure and promotion committees of the significance of such work in our larger research and publishing agendas.

Critical pedagogues are public intellectuals, public activists, and as such we need to develop diverse languages to address divergent audiences. Many African Americans, Latinos/as, indigenous peoples, and first-generation college students from all racial backgrounds know that the language they speak at the university is significantly different from the "dialect" they speak at home and in their communities. As a Southern Appalachian, I knew that the way I spoke with my three Aunt Effies back in Tennessee and Virginia was profoundly different from my presentation on critical postformal thinking at an academic conference. And when I screwed up and talked in too academic a language for my Aunt Effie Kincheloe Bean, she let me know it. "Think you're pretty smart, don't you, Mr. Professor," she would tell me in her best exaggerated East Tennessee mountain accent. I listened to her loving chiding carefully, trying to devise a better way to tell her about the topic at hand. Though she is long departed from this planet, I often write to her in some of my books and essays about critical pedagogy. Some folks see dead people; I write to them.

In a related context I analyze why critical pedagogy as a discourse doesn't speak to many different subcultural groups in divergent societies. When I attend and speak at critical pedagogical conferences around the world, I see far too few indigenous peoples, individuals of African descent, and Asians. In the North American context I am simply appalled by the small numbers of African Americans at critical pedagogical events. Indeed, one of the greatest failures of critical pedagogy at this juncture of its history involves the inability to engage people of African, Asian, and indigenous backgrounds in our tradition. I call for intense efforts in the coming years to bring more diversity into our ranks for two purposes: 1) Critical pedagogy has profound insights to pass along to all peoples; and 2) Critical pedagogy has much to learn from the often subjugated knowledges of African, African American, Asian, and indigenous peoples.

Indeed, a significant dimension of the future of critical pedagogy rests with the lessons to be learned from peoples around the world. Thankfully, critical pedagogy is supported and informed by numerous Latin and South American peoples. My fear, however, is that critical pedagogy has become too much of a North American (and often European) "thing," as White North American scholars appropriate a South American discourse. North Americans must be demanding in their efforts to make sure that Paulo Freire and his South/Latin American colleagues and progeny are viewed as the originators of this hallowed tradition. In the spirit of Paulo, a confident yet humble approach to our work—a critical humility—seems to serve us well. Critical pedagogy does not find its origins as a North American phenomenon, and if critical pedagogues cannot learn this simple lesson, then they will have little positive impact on the world.

In addition, despite what proponents of different positions might argue, critical pedagogy is not simply for one interest group. Critical pedagogy serves both teachers and cultural workers who engage in social activism outside the boundaries of schools. Some of the most depressing moments I have spent engaged in critical pedagogy have occurred either when teachers view the classroom as the central if not only domain for critical pedagogical analysis and action or when cultural workers see schools as "lost places" where nothing matters because the institution is flawed. In these cases, I have actually seen cultural worker/social activists roll their eyes at one another when teachers reference classroom practice. My god, the activist labor that critical pedagogically informed cultural workers perform is profoundly important and has much to teach teachers—and teachers, of course, have much to teach such cultural workers.

Those academics who study the politics of knowledge, the macrodynamics of education, cultural pedagogies promoted in the twenty-first-century global marketplace, and many other ideological/educational phenomena have much to teach everyone. My point here is obvious: until we come to see the work of these different groups of critical pedagogues as synergistic rather than hierarchical, the achievements of the tradition will be acutely undermined. Qualitative hierarchies of importance segregating those who engage in critical pedagogy into status-laden groups will destroy our efforts to address power inequities and the human suffering such disparity causes. We are too smart to allow such egocentric status seeking to subvert our struggle for justice. If we're not able to overcome such pathology, then to hell with us—we don't deserve to survive.

Getting Started: The Origins of Critical Pedagogy and Its Uses in a Conflicted, Complex World

With these concerns in mind, let's briefly examine the origins of critical pedagogy. In the early twenty-first century it has become a cliche among many pedagogical scholars to describe education as a Janus-faced institution with its two faces looking toward opposite goals and outcomes: in one direction, a democratic, inclusive, socially sensitive objective concerned with multiple sources of knowledge and socioeconomic mobility for diverse students from marginalized backgrounds; and in the other, a standardized, exclusive, socially regulatory agenda that serves the interest of the dominant power and those students most closely aligned with the social and cultural markers associated with such power.

Thus, in the contemporary era educational scholars on faculties of education at colleges/universities and educators in elementary and secondary schools walk through a complex terrain of contradictions in their everyday professional pursuits, as educational researchers tend to find evidence of both progressive and regressive purposes in most educational institutions. As critical pedagogues observe such phenomena, they understand that the notion of "becoming a teacher" or a cultural worker concerned with social justice involves far more complex bodies of knowledge and conceptual insights than is sometimes found in teacher education and educational research programs, not to mention the knowledge that the mass media make available to the public.

Emerging from Paulo Freire's work in poverty-stricken northeastern Brazil in the 1960s, critical pedagogy amalgamated liberation theological ethics and the critical theory of the Frankfurt School in Germany with progressive impulses in education. Critical pedagogy gained an international audience with the 1967 publication of Freire's *Pedagogy of the Oppressed* and its English translation in 1970. By the mid-1970s several scholars in education and other disciplines adapted Freire's conception of critical pedagogy into a so-called first-world context. Over the next decade, critical pedagogy influenced pedagogical practice, teacher education, and sociopolitical and educational scholarship in South and North America. In the twenty-first century, the field is at a conceptual crossroads as researchers contemplate the nature of its movement to the next phase of its evolution. *Critical Pedagogy: Where Are We Now?* is intent on providing a series of speculations and tentative answers to questions concerning where we are now and where we go from here.

In my own work I have explored this "next phase" of critical pedagogy in relation to the issues raised at the beginning of this chapter and in recognition of the complexity of everyday life (Kincheloe, 2004). Attention to this complexity with the rigorous scholarship it demands—multiple forms of knowledge coming from around the globe as well as diverse research methodologies—forces proponents of critical pedagogy to ask revealing questions about the purposes of existing educational practices and their consequences. Such questions and the answers scholars provide will help shape the next phase of critical pedagogy. In this context we move to a new terrain of intellectually rigorous and highly practical cultural and educational work.

What is the relation between classroom practice and issues of justice? How do schools reflect or subvert democratic practices and the larger culture of democracy? How do schools operate to validate or challenge the power dynamics of race, class, gender, sexuality, religion, indigenous/aboriginal issues, physical ability-related concerns, etc.? How do such processes play out in diverse classrooms located in differing social, cultural, and economic domains? How do the knowledges schools and other social institutions choose to transmit replicate political relationships in the larger society and affect the academic performance of students from dissimilar socioeconomic and cultural backgrounds? What roles do diverse media play in the ideological education of societies? What is the pedagogical role of popular culture? What are the hegemonic and counter-hegemonic dimensions of new technologies? How do we use critical methodologies and understandings to tap into the libidinal energy of individuals in a way that will produce joy and happiness as they pursue learning and transformative social action? The ability to provide well-informed and creative answers to such questions that lead to practical educational policy and practice is a key dimension of critical pedagogy.

As we look back from the perspective of the first decade of the twenty-first century to the innovative scholarly work on epistemology and research of the last several decades, one understanding becomes increasingly clear: producing knowledge about the world and understanding the cosmos are more complex than we originally thought. What we designate as facts is not as straightforward a process as it was presented to us. Critical pedagogues operating with this understanding of complex multilogicality or what many have called "the bricolage" (Kincheloe, 2001; Kincheloe and Berry, 2004; Kincheloe, 2005) know that what most people consider the natural social world is a conceptual landmine wired with assumptions and inherited meanings.

Critical researchers have learned that what is unproblematically deemed "a fact" has been shaped by a community of inquirers and sociopolitical forces. All of these researchers accept, often unconsciously, a particular set of theoretical assumptions. Engaging in knowledge work without a deep understanding of the tacit sociopolitical rules of the game is not a manifestation of rigor. Indeed, such a lack of knowledge profoundly undermines the effort to produce compelling and useful data about the world around us (Horn, 2004; Fischer, 1998). Great scholars in diverse historical and cultural settings have admonished individuals not to take fixed viewpoints and concepts as reality (Varela, 1999). Critical pedagogues as bricoleurs heed such a warning as they move into a zone of critical complexity.

Roymeico Carter (2004) extends this critical complex concept into the world of the visual. The complexity of researching the visual domain is often squashed by the formal methods of Cartesian aesthetics. Carter reminds us that the intricate layers of visual meaning must be studied from numerous perspectives as well as diverse cultural and epistemological traditions. But such diversity of perception lets the cat out of the bag; it relinquishes control of how we are to see the world. According to Ilya Prigogine, complexity demands that researchers give up the attempt to dominate and control the world. The social and physical worlds are so complex that they can only be understood like human beings themselves: not machine-like, but unpredictable, dependent upon context, and influenced by minute fluctuations (Capra, 1996). Thus, bricoleurs focus their attention on addressing the complexity of the lived world, understanding in the process that the knowledge they produce should not be viewed as a transhistorical body of truth. In this framework, knowledge produced by bricoleurs is provisional and "in process." Bricoleurs know that tensions will develop in social knowledge as the understandings and insights of individuals change and evolve (Blackler, 1995).

A critical researcher, for example, who returns to an ethnographic study only a few years later may find profound differences in what is reported by subjects. The categories and coding that worked three years ago may no longer be relevant. The most important social, psychological, and educational problems that confront us are untidy and complicated. As we wade through the swamp of everyday life, research methods that fail to provide multiple perspectives at macro-, meso-, and microlevels do not provide the insights that we need.

It is one thing to find out that schools, for example, do not provide many poor students a path to social mobility. It is quite another thing to take this macro finding and combine it with the mesodynamics of the ways particular schools and school leaders conceptualize the relationship between schooling and class mobility. It is also important that these findings be viewed in a context informed by everyday classroom and out-of-classroom interactions between teachers and students and students and their peers. Obviously, different research methodologies will be used to explore the differing questions emerging at the different levels. Once data from these diverse layers are combined we begin to discern a picture of the multiple dynamics of the relationship between socioeconomic class and education. Only a multidimensional, complex picture such as this can help us formulate informed and just strategies to address such issues.

Critical Complications: A Research and Pedagogical Agenda for a Globalized, Multilogical World

If critical pedagogical scholars/researchers refuse to move into the multileveled swamp of complexity or to integrate the diverse forms of data found at its different levels, they may find themselves asking pedestrian questions of profoundly complicated issues. Simple, unproblematic questions about the domain of schooling and socioeconomic class, for example, tend to be the least significant to the society at large. Positivistic standards of rigor as presently employed by many social, psychological, and educational researchers actually preclude the complex, multidimensional, multimethodological work necessary to producing meaningful and usable research data (Schon, 1995). Francisco Varela (1999) writes about "the situated embodiments of simple acts" (p. 8), maintaining that such complexity in everyday life undermines total reliance on computational methods where "knowledge is a manipulation of symbols by logic-like rules, an idea that finds its fullest expression in modern digital computers" (p. 7).

In the domain of cognitive science, Varela concludes, even the simplest acts—even those performed by insects—rest outside the understanding of the computational strategy. Varela's pronouncements tell critical bricoleurs not to throw out computational strategies but to understand what they can and cannot tell us and to carefully consider how we might use them in the bricoleur's pursuit of complexity in the social, political, psychological, and educational spheres. As we examine "where we are now" in critical pedagogy, we must understand these elements of complexity in order to become more rigorous scholar-researcher educators and more effective agents of socially just political and educational change. We have no choice if we want to remain relevant in the emerging era. Hyperreality, with its bombardment of communicative messages and ideologically inscribed images, demands no less.

Even simple acts of cognition, social interaction, learning, and textual analysis are more complex than researchers first suspected. "Just give me the facts" is not as simple a command as it seemed to appear to Cartesian sensibilities. The situated nature of knowledge questions a variety of Cartesian assumptions. When we pick particular attributions of meaning about specific phenomena, we must consider a variety of factors. Such choices are inevitably political and ideological and have nothing to do with efforts to be objective. Even the decisions researchers make about what to study reflect these same political and ideological dynamics. In the highly ideologically charged first decade of the twenty-first century, do educational researchers study how to improve student test scores in the suburbs or the impact of racism on lower-socioeconomic-class African American students in urban schools? The problems and issues that are chosen by researchers are marked by subjective judgments about whose problems are deemed most important.

These interpretative decisions are always complex and influenced by a plethora of social, cultural, political, economic, psychological, discursive, and pedagogical dynamics. As a critical discourse, the bricolage always considers the normative dimension of what should be as well as what is. When Horkheimer and Adorno's concept of immanence (the examination of what is in relation to what should be) is added to the complex dynamics surrounding decision making and interpretation in the realm of research, critical pedagogues as bricoleurs move to yet a higher domain of complexity. Reflecting on the research process from a perspective shaped by these concerns, critical bricoleurs gain new insights into the ideological consequences of reductionism. For example, when rational inquiry is positioned in opposition to the emotional, affective, and value-laden dimensions of human activity, then it has removed itself as a means of gaining insight into the social, psychological, and educational domains. Life in these domains simply cannot be understood without careful attention to the emotional, affective, and value-laden aspects of human behavior (Williams, 1999; Reason and Bradbury, 2000). Indeed, a rational inquiry that devalues the role of irrationality will sink under the weight of its own gravitas.

Because of this damned complexity, advocates of a critical pedagogy understand that no simple, universally applicable answers can be provided to the questions of justice, power, and praxis that haunt us. Indeed, such questions have to be asked time and again by teachers and other educational professionals operating in different historical times and diverse pedagogical locales. Critical pedagogy understands that no educator who seeks to promote individual intellectual development, sociopolitical and economic justice, the production of practical transformative knowledge, and institutional academic rigor can escape the complex contextual specificity of these challenging questions. The pedagogical and research agenda of a complex critical pedagogy for the twenty-first century must address these realities as it constructs a plan to invigorate the teaching and study of such phenomena in the new phase of critical pedagogy that I am proposing for North America and around the world.

Proponents of a complex critical pedagogy appreciate the fact that all educational spaces are unique and politically contested. Constructed by history and challenged by a wide variety of interest groups, educational practice is an ambiguous phenomenon as it takes place in numerous settings, is molded by numerous and often invisible forces and structures, and can operate under the flag of democracy and justice in oppressive and totalitarian ways. Practitioners of critical pedagogy report that some teacher education students, educational leaders, parents, and members of the general public often have difficulty appreciating the fact that schooling can be hurtful to particular students from specific backgrounds in unique social, cultural, and economic settings—for example, indigenous and aboriginal students. Many individuals often have trouble empathizing with students harmed by such negative educational dynamics because schooling in their experience has played such a positive role in their own lives.

Thus, a complex critical pedagogy is a domain of research and practice that asks much from those who embrace it. Critical pedagogical teacher education and leadership, for example, involve more than learning pedagogical techniques and the knowledge required by the mandated curriculum. In addition to acquiring teaching methods, teachers and leaders steeped in critical pedagogy also understand the social, economic, psychological, and political dimensions of the schools, districts, and systems in which they operate. They also possess a wide range of knowledge about information systems in the larger culture that serve as pedagogical forces in the lives of students and other members of society: television, radio, popular music, movies, the Internet, podcasts, and youth subcultures; alternative bodies of knowledge produced by indigenous, marginalized, or low-status groups; the ways different forms of power operate to construct identities and empower and oppress particular groups; and the modus operandi of the ways sociocultural regulation operates.

Democracy is a fragile entity, advocates of critical pedagogy maintain, and embedded in educational policy and practice are the very issues that make or break it. Understanding these diverse dimensions and structures that shape schooling and the knowledge it conveys is necessary, critical pedagogues believe, to the very survival of democratic schooling—not to mention the continued existence of democracy itself. The analysis of the ways these complex forces evolve in a globalized, technological, electronic communications-based era marked by grand human migrations is central to the complex critical pedagogy proposed here.

The future of critical pedagogy involves addressing this complexity head on and making sure—as I maintained at the beginning of this chapter—that critical pedagogues listen carefully to marginalized groups from diverse corners of the planet. In such a context, a complex, humble critical pedagogy for a new era promotes research, analysis, and the use of subjugated, repressed, and indigenous knowledges in relation to the academy in general, teaching and learning, and epistemological and ontological understandings central to educational policy and practice. Indigenous knowledge has been and continues to be difficult to define. Always aware of the possibility of Western exploitation of particular forms of indigenous knowledge, this new phase of critical pedagogy views its usage with respect and reverence for its producers. For the millions of indigenous peoples of Africa, Latin America, Asia, Oceania, and North America, indigenous knowledge is an everyday way of making sense of the world, the self, and the relationship between them that rewards individuals who live in a given locality.

In this context indigenous knowledge reflects the dynamic way in which the residents of an area have come to understand themselves in relationship to their natural environment and how they organize their knowledge of flora and fauna, cultural beliefs, history, and teaching and learning to enhance their lives (Keith & Keith, 1993; Dei, 1995; Semali and Kincheloe, 1999; Dei and Kempf, 2006). Paulo Freire—among many other scholars—was committed to the potential transformative power of subjugated and indigenous knowledges and the ways that such information and its accompanying conceptual frameworks could be used to foster empowerment and justice in a variety of cultural contexts—for both indigenous peoples themselves and Western scholars who came to understand indigenous epistemologies and ontologies.

As Paulo Freire and Antonio Faundez (1989) wrote, indigenous knowledge is a rich social resource for any justice-related attempt to bring about social change. In this context, indigenous ways of knowing become a central resource for the work of academics, whether they be professors in the universities or teachers in elementary and secondary schools. Intellectuals, Freire and Faundez conclude, should "soak themselves in this knowledge . . . assimilate the feelings, the sensitivity" (p. 46) of epistemologies that move in ways unimagined by many Western academic impulses. Thus, a central dimension of the new phase of critical pedagogy involves researching subjugated and indigenous knowledges, incorporating them into the development of the discipline of critical pedagogy, and using them to enhance education in general and indigenous/aboriginal education in particular in a multilogical, globalized world.

Critical Pedagogy and the Contemporary Challenge to Democracy

Critical theory—especially in the post-9/11 era of global political, economic, and military empire building—questions the assumption that societies such as the United States, Canada, Australia, New Zealand, and the nations in the European Union, for example, are unproblematically democratic and free. Over the twentieth century, especially after the early 1960s, individuals in these societies were acculturated to feel uncomfortable with equality and independence and more content with relations of social regulation and subordination. Given the social and technological changes of the last half of the century that led to new forms of information production and access, critical theorists argued that questions of self-direction and democratic egalitarianism should be reassessed. In this context critical researchers informed by the "post-discourses" (e.g., critical feminism, poststructuralism, post-colonialism, indigenous studies) came to understand that individuals' views of themselves and the world were even more influenced by social and historical forces than previously believed. Given the changing social and informational conditions of late twentieth-century and early twenty-first-century media-saturated Western culture, critical theorists have needed new ways of researching and analyzing the construction of identity and selfhood (Agger, 1992; Flossner & Otto, 1998; Leistyna, Woodrum, & Sherblom, 1996; Smith & Wexler, 1995; Sunker, 1998; Steinberg, 2001; Wesson & Weaver, 2001). Thus, one begins to understand the need for an evolving notion of criticality—a critical social theory—in light of these changing conditions.

In this context it is important to note that a social theory as used in this context is a map or a guide to the social sphere. A social theory should not determine how we see the world but should help us devise questions and strategies for exploring it. A critical social theory is concerned in particular with issues of power and justice and the ways that the economy, matters of race, class, and gender, ideologies, discourses, education, religion and other social institutions, and cultural dynamics interact to construct a social system (Beck-Gernsheim, Butler, & Puigvert, 2003; Flecha, Gomez, and Puigvert, 2003). Critical theory and critical pedagogy—in the spirit of an evolving criticality—are never static; they are always evolving, changing in light of new theoretical insights, fresh ideas from diverse cultures, and new problems, social circumstances, and educational contexts.

The list of concepts making up this description of an evolving critical theory/critical pedagogy indicates a criticality informed by a variety of discourses emerging after the work of the Frankfurt School of Social Theory in post-World War I Germany. Indeed, some of the theoretical discourses, while referring to themselves as critical, directly call into question some of the work of Frankfurt School founders Max Horkheimer, Theodor Adorno, and Herbert Marcuse. Thus, diverse theoretical traditions have informed our understanding of criticality and have demanded understanding of diverse forms of oppression including class, race, gender, sexual, cultural, religious, colonial and ability-related concerns. In this context critical theorists/critical pedagogues become detectives of new theoretical insights, perpetually searching for new and interconnected ways of understanding power and oppression and the ways they shape everyday life and human experience. They become sleuths on the trail of those ever-mutating forces that threaten power-sensitive forms of democracy around the world.

Thus, criticality and the knowledge production and pedagogy it supports are always evolving, always encountering new ways to engage dominant forms of power and to provide more evocative and compelling insights. It is in this context that a pervasive theme of this chapter and book emerges yet again: criticalists must engage with diverse peoples around the world and listen carefully to and humbly learn from them. Employing these diverse cultural knowledges, the forms of social change an evolving critical pedagogy supports position it in many places as an outsider, an awkward detective always interested in uncovering social structures, discourses, ideologies, and epistemologies that prop up both the status quo and a variety of forms of privilege.

In the epistemological domain White, male, class-elitist, heterosexist, imperial, and colonial privilege often operates by asserting the power to claim objectivity and neutrality. Indeed the owners of such privilege often own the "franchise" on reason, rationality, and truth. An evolving criticality possesses a variety of tools to expose such power politics. In this context it asserts that criticality is well served by drawing upon numerous discourses and including diverse groups of marginalized peoples and their allies in the nonhierarchical collection of critical analysts. Here rests the heart of critical multilogicality, with its feet firmly planted in an understanding of political and economic conditions and its ear attuned to new ways of seeing the world. Moving these ideas to the cognitive domain, I have worked over the last couple of decades to produce a new mode of thinking, an alternate rationality labeled "postformalism" (Kincheloe and Steinberg, 1993; Kincheloe, Steinberg, and Hinchey, 1999; Thomas and Kincheloe, 2006; Kincheloe, 2007).

Obviously, an evolving criticality does not promiscuously choose theories to add to the bricolage of critical theories/pedagogies. It is highly suspicious of theories that fail to understand the workings of power, that fail to critique the blinders of Eurocentrism, that cultivate an elitism of insiders and outsiders, that do not understand the complexities and complications of what is referred to as democratic action, and that fail to discern a global system of inequity supported by diverse forms of hegemony and violence. It is uninterested in any theory—no matter how fashionable—that does not directly address the needs of victims of oppression and the suffering they must endure.

Indeed, the very origins of criticality—the tradition that lays the groundwork for critical pedagogy and is concerned with power and its oppression of human beings and regulation of the social order—are grounded on this concern with human suffering. Herbert Marcuse, one of the founders of the Frankfurt School of Critical Theory, and Paulo Freire were profoundly moved by the suffering they, respectively, witnessed in post-World War I Germany and Brazil of the 1950s and 1960s. The brilliant and critical racial insights of W.E.B. Du Bois, Ida B. Wells, Carter Woodson, Horace Mann Bond, and many others in the early decades of the twentieth century were grounded on their understanding of the suffering of their fellow African Americans. The insights these scholars produced constitute a powerful compendium of critical theoretical data—even though the scholars themselves did not employ the term critical.

Though my own notion of a critical pedagogy is one that continues to develop and operates to sophisticate its understandings of the world and the educational act, this evolving criticality in education should never lose sight of its central concern with human suffering. One does not have to go too far in this world to find people who are suffering: battered women, indigenous peoples attempting to deal with Western efforts to destroy their cultures, working-class people unable to find jobs, victims of racism and ethnic bias, individuals subjected to religious persecution, dirt-poor colonized peoples in poor nations, children with AIDS, men and women punished by homophobes, young women in developing countries working for less than subsistence wages from North American-owned transnational companies—unfortunately, the list goes on and on.

In the North American context suffering is often well hidden, but a trip to inner cities, specific rural areas, or indigenous reservations and reserves will reveal its existence. Outside of the North American context we can go to almost any region of the world and see tragic expressions of human misery. My articulation of critical pedagogy asserts that such suffering is a humanly constructed phenomenon and does not have to exist. Steps can be taken in numerous domains—education in particular—to eradicate such suffering if the people of the planet and their leaders have the collective will to do so. In recent years, however, globalized political economic systems with their de-emphasis on progressive forms of education and social policy have exacerbated poverty and its attendant suffering. An evolving criticality develops new ways to deal with such developments and new modes of education and political action to subvert their effects.

Critical Pedagogy in the Era with No Name: The Intersection of the Macrosocial with the Microindividual

If Clint Eastwood played "The Man with No Name," then we now live in an era with no name. Most of us by now understand that we live in a new era—but even after several decades of trying we still don't know what to call it. The postmodern condition? Hyperreality? Late capitalism? Late modernity? The post-9/11 world? The age of empire? The globalized world? The era of neocolonialism? Pax America? ad infinitum. Many will probably agree that this new era demands a new form of education that deals with macroglobal changes and the recursive dimension of the sociopsychological construction of the individual. In an evolving criticality, critical pedagogues have to come to terms with this new complex and unnamed world, developing insights and modes of praxis in the process that help educators, parents, students, and individuals around the world understand the complicated relationship between the larger sociopolitical domain and the life of the individual. As I asserted at the beginning of this chapter, this is where open-access publishing, speaking, and writing become central to our larger critical project. In this context, critical pedagogy works to develop both in-school and larger cultural pedagogies, always keeping in mind the omnipresent relationship between the social and individual.

I believe that a successful critical pedagogy for the future must be deeply concerned with the relationship between the sociopolitical domain and the life of the individual. A compelling synthesis of these provinces is necessary to catalyzing critical social action, civic contribution, and successful teaching from elementary to graduate school. In order to begin a rigorous analysis of a macro-micro evolving criticality—a critical pedagogy concerned with the sociopolitical realm, the individual, and the relationship that connects them—an appreciation of its critical social and educational theoretical traditions, its culture and the forces that are changing it, and its identity and the increasingly complex ways in which it is being shaped is necessary.

The attempt to make sense of contemporary culture and identity formation is enhanced by an appreciation of the critical social theoretical tradition. Peter and I have published versions of the following points elsewhere (Kincheloe, 2004; Kincheloe and McLaren, 2005) in our attempts to introduce critical theory to a wide audience. The following is an abbreviated version of the central points of critical theory. Keep in mind that in the spirit of an evolving criticality the subsequent points are part of an elastic, ever-evolving conceptual matrix. It changes with every theoretical innovation, integration of new cultural knowledge, and shifting of the zeitgeist. The points that are deemed most important in one time period may have little in common with the important points of a new era.

1. Critical enlightenment. In this context critical theory analyzes competing power interests between groups and individuals within a society—identifying who gains and who loses in specific situations. Privileged groups, criticalists argue, often have an interest in supporting the status quo to protect their advantages; the dynamics of such efforts often become a central focus of critical research.

2. Critical emancipation. Those who seek emancipation attempt to gain the power to control their own lives in solidarity with a justice-oriented community. Here, critical research attempts to expose the forces that prevent individuals and groups from shaping the decisions that crucially affect their lives. In this way greater degrees of autonomy and human agency can be achieved. In the first decade of the twenty-first century we are cautious in our use of the term "emancipation" because, as many critics have pointed out, no one is ever completely emancipated from the sociopolitical context that has produced him or her. Concurrently, many have used the term to signal the freedom an abstract individual gains by gaining access to Western reason—i.e., becoming reasonable. Our use of emancipation in an evolving criticality rejects any use of the term in this context.

3. The rejection of economic determinism. A caveat of a reconceptualized critical theory involves the insistence that the tradition does not accept the orthodox Marxist notion that "base" determines "superstructure"— meaning that economic factors dictate the nature of all other aspects of human existence. Critical theorists understand that in the twenty-first century there are multiple forms of power, racial, gender, and sexual axes of domination. In issuing this caveat, however, an evolving critical theory in no way attempts to argue that economic factors are unimportant in the shaping of everyday life.

4. The critique of instrumental or technical rationality. An evolving critical theory sees instrumental/technology rationality as one of the most oppressive features of contemporary society. Such a form of "hyperreason" involves an obsession with means in preference to ends. Critical theorists claim that instrumental/technical rationality is more interested in method and efficiency than in purpose. It delimits its questions to "how to" instead of "why should."

5. The impact of desire. An evolving critical theory appreciates poststructuralist psychoanalysis as an important resource in pursuing an emancipatory research project. In this context, critical researchers are empowered to dig more deeply into the complexity of the construction of the human psyche. Such a psychoanalysis helps critical researchers discern the unconscious processes that create resistance to progressive change and induce self-destructive behavior. A poststructural psychoanalysis, in its rejection of traditional psychoanalysis's tendency to view individuals as rational and autonomous beings, allows critical analysts new tools to rethink the interplay among the various axes of power, identity, libido,

rationality, and emotion. In this configuration the psychic realm is no longer separated from the sociopolitical one; indeed, desire can be socially constructed and used by power-wielders for destructive and oppressive outcomes. On the other hand, critical theorists can help mobilize desire for progressive and emancipatory projects.

6. The concept of immanence. Critical theory is always concerned with what could be, what is immanent in various ways of thinking and perceiving. Thus, critical theory should always move beyond the contemplative realm to concrete social reform. In the spirit of Paulo Freire, our notion of an evolving critical theory possesses immanence as it imagines new ways to ease human suffering and produce psychological well-being. Critical immanence helps us get beyond egocentrism and ethnocentrism and work to build new forms of relationships with diverse peoples.

7. A reconceptualized critical theory of power: hegemony. Our conception of a reconceptualized critical theory is intensely concerned with the need to understand the various and complex ways that power operates to dominate and shape consciousness. Power, critical theorists have learned, is an extremely ambiguous topic that demands detailed study and analysis. A consensus seems to be emerging among criticalists that power is a basic constituent of human existence that works to shape both the oppressive and productive nature of the human tradition. In the context of oppressive power and its ability to produce inequalities and human suffering, Antonio Gramsci's notion of hegemony is central to critical research. Gramsci understood that dominant power in the twentieth century was not always exercised simply by physical force but also through social psychological attempts to win people's consent to domination through cultural institutions such as the media, the schools, the family, and the church. Gramscian hegemony recognizes that the winning of popular consent is a very complex process and must be researched carefully on a case-by-case basis.

8. A reconceptualized critical theory of power: ideology. Critical theorists understand that the formation of hegemony cannot be separated from the production of ideology. If hegemony is the larger effort of the powerful to win the consent of their "subordinates," then ideological hegemony involves the cultural forms, the meanings, the rituals, and the representations that produce consent to both the status quo and to individuals' particular places within it. Ideology vis-a-vis hegemony moves critical inquirers beyond explanations of domination that have used terms such as

propaganda to describe the way media, political, educational, and other sociocultural productions coercively manipulate citizens to adopt oppressive meanings.

9. A reconceptualized critical theory of power: Linguistic/discursive power. Critical theorists have come to understand that language is not a mirror of society. It is an unstable social practice whose meaning shifts, depending upon the context in which it is used. Contrary to previous understandings, criticalists appreciate the fact that language is not a neutral and objective conduit for description of the "real world." Rather, from a critical perspective, linguistic descriptions are not simply about the world but serve to construct it. With these linguistic notions in mind, criticalists begin to study the way language in the form of discourses serves as a form of regulation and domination.

10. Focusing on the relationships among culture, power, and domination. In the last decades of the twentieth century, culture took on a new importance in the critical effort to understand power and domination. Critical theorists have argued that culture has to be viewed as a domain of struggle where the production and transmission of knowledge is always a contested process. Dominant and subordinate cultures deploy differing systems of meaning based on the forms of knowledge produced in their cultural domain. Popular culture, with its television, movies, video games, computers, music, dance, and other productions, plays an increasingly important role in critical research on power and domination. Cultural studies, of course, occupy an ever-expanding role in this context, as it examines not only popular culture but the tacit rules that guide cultural production.

11. The centrality of interpretation: Critical hermeneutics. One of the most important aspects of a critical theory-informed education and scholarship involves the often-neglected domain of interpretation. The critical hermeneutic tradition holds that in knowledge work there is only interpretation, no matter how vociferously many analysts may argue that the facts speak for themselves. The hermeneutic act of interpretation, in its most elemental articulation, involves making sense of what has been observed in a way that communicates understanding. Not only is all research merely an act of interpretation, but (hermeneutics contends) perception itself is an act of interpretation. Thus the quest for understanding is a fundamental feature of human existence, as encounter with the unfamiliar always demands the attempt to make meaning, to make sense.

12. The role of cultural pedagogy in critical theory. Cultural production can often be thought of as a form of education, as it generates knowledge, shapes values, and constructs identity. From the perspective of a book on critical pedagogy, such a framing can help critical teachers and students make sense of the world of domination and oppression as they work to bring about a more just, democratic, and egalitarian society. In recent years this educational dynamic has been referred to as cultural pedagogy. "Pedagogy" is a useful term that has traditionally been used to refer only to teaching and schooling. By using the term "cultural pedagogy," criticalists are specifically referring to the ways dominant cultural agents produce particular hegemonic ways of seeing. In our critical interpretive context, the notion of cultural pedagogy asserts that the new "educators" in the electronically wired contemporary era are those who possess the financial resources to use mass media. This is very important in the context of critical pedagogy, as teachers in the contemporary era must understand not only the education that takes place in the classroom but also that which takes place in popular culture.

Informed by these points, we are better able to conceptualize a critical pedagogy that cultivates a rigorous, intellectual ability to acquire, analyze, and produce both self-knowledge and social knowledge. Grounded by such knowledge and scholarly facility, individuals would be equipped to participate in the democratic process as committed and informed citizens. A basic assumption in this civic context involves the belief that, in terms of a democratic social education, Western public life and public education have failed. Corporations, transnational organizations, and other power-wielders have gained increasing control over the production and flow of information. Here, public consciousness is aligned in a complex and never completely successful process with the interests of power.

One of the most important goals of public life over the last few decades has been the cultivation of more and more social obedience and less democracy. The effort to win the consent of the public (hegemony), via appeals to both logic and affect, for privatization projects that may not be in the public's best interests has been frighteningly successful. In the same context, and driven by many of the same forces of power, public schooling has failed to promote a rigorous, democratic social education. Operating in the shadow of Frankfurt School critical social theorist Theodor Adorno, we reference his notion of "half-education" in which he described the way mainstream education perpetuates students' alienation from knowledge of the social and the self. In this process, the possibility of agency, of self-direction, is lost in a sea of social confusion (Sunker, 1994). To confront this alienation, social analysts must provide specific examples of formal and informal educational programs that promote a progressive education that fights alienation.

Understanding the affective dimensions of these programs, educators analyze why students and other individuals are emotionally invested in specific programs, why energy is produced and absorbed by participants, and why the disposition to imagine and create new projects is cultivated in some programs and not in others.

Schools as Venues for Critical Democracy: The Triumph of Standardization and Pseudo-democracy

In the contemporary Age of Empire—or whatever we may call it—Western schools have not been concerned with educating democratic citizens. Indeed, schools have not been particularly concerned with any positive public role in the larger society. The traditional public role of pedagogy has been undermined by a private corporate view of the role of education. In addition to their role as supplier of regulated labor to the economy, schools in this privatized view have come to be seen as commodities, subject to the dictates of the free market. In this milieu, students are transformed from citizens into consumers, capable of being bought and sold. The logic of this right-wing social reeducation involves the replacement of government service agencies with private corporate services, the redistribution of wealth from the poor to the wealthy, and the construction of a private market system that promotes the values of isolated individualism, self-help, corporate management, and consumerism in lieu of public ethics and economic democracy. Thus, the social curriculum being taught in twenty-first-century Western schools often involves a sanctification of the private sphere in a way that helps consolidate the power of corporations and the interests of the empire. In this context, the freedom of the corporation to redefine social and educational life in ways that serve its financial interests is expanded.

This conservative reeducation project with its corporatized politics has been difficult for critical pedagogy to counter because it has been adeptly couched in the language of public improvement and democratic virtue. The public sphere has failed, the apostles of privatization proclaim. The private market is a much more effective mechanism in the effort to achieve socioeconomic improvement. Since market forces govern the world, students, citizens, and schooling itself must learn to adapt to this reality. A key element of this conservative social education involves this adaptation, the attempt to promote a market philosophy. Corporations now sponsor schools or enter into school-business partnerships. Upon analysis, one begins to perceive a pattern in the lessons taught to students in the corporate curriculum of privatized schooling. Imperial education is grounded on a set of free-market goals. Schools are expected to graduate students who will help corporations: 1) increase worker output for the same wages; 2) reduce labor turnover; 3) decrease conflict with management, especially among the young workers; 4) convince citizens that labor and management share the same goals; and 5) create a workforce loyal to the corporation and the goals of the empire. Unfortunately, critical pedagogy must enter the conversation about the purposes of schools with these realities in mind.

This political process of privatization grounds a well-hidden ideological education embedded in the information environment of twenty-first-century Western societies (Sunker, 1994). In these societies, such an education occurs both in and outside of schools in a variety of social and cultural venues. Thus, the imperial ideological education takes into account the changing social conditions of an electronically mediated society, especially the new conditions under which information is produced. In this context, an imaginative critical pedagogy must understand that contemporary education and knowledge production emerge at the intersection of the political economy and the culture. Understanding these dynamics, an important aspect of a transformative critical pedagogy is its analytic project, its mapping of the ways political meanings are made in both schools and sociocultural locales. Here advocates of critical pedagogy initiate the important task of interpreting how domination takes place on the contemporary political economic, informational landscape. In an interpretive sense, an evolving critical pedagogy becomes a holographic (a dynamic where the whole is contained in all of its parts) hermeneutics that analyzes the ways oppressive ideologies produced by sociopolitical structures (the whole) embed themselves in the individual (the part). What is the relationship between macro-power and the subjectivity of individual human beings?

Understanding the Sociopolitical Construction of the Individual in Contemporary Education

This intersection of the social and the individual—the macro and the micro—is a central dimension in an evolving critical pedagogy. Indeed, as critical pedagogical analysis reintegrates the political, the economic, and the cultural on the new historical plane of the globalized, imperial, and "recovered" society of the twenty-first century, we work to rethink and reassert the importance of subjectivity (pertaining to the domain of personhood, consciousness) in this context. In many ways, such a move is controversial in the critical tradition, as numerous social analysts criticize—many times for good reason—the contemporary concern with individualism, self-actualization, and identity politics. Understanding the problems inherent within these often liberal dynamics, I still believe that there are emancipatory possibilities embedded within this emphasis on self-development. Drawing upon the work of Philip Wexler (1997) and my own work in developing a critical ontology (Kincheloe, 2003), a key feature of an evolving criticality involves the effort to extract the transformative elements in the education of the individual in the Age of Empire.

Since ideological education takes place in a variety of domains, study is demanded at not only the social (macro-) and individual (micro-) level but the institutional (meso-) one as well. In this integrative approach, the interactions of these three levels in the process of ideological education, the ways they operate in the construction of the social and individual, are significant. In such analysis, these multilevel concerns induce educators to avoid one-sided approaches of any variety. For example, I am concerned with not only the social construction of the individual's knowledge but also with the individual's responsibility for his or her actions. This attention to individual volition is often missing from some articulations of critical education. This notion of individual volition must be carefully reconsidered in light of liberal celebrations of individual freedom and deterministic laments of a totalized domination. Individuals frequently defeat the power of capital, White supremacy, homophobia, and patriarchy; at the same time, however, the structures of oppression too often induce individuals to acquiesce to dominant power's ways of viewing the world.

There is nothing simplistic about ideological education. How does one get across an understanding of the complementarity of the self-directed (autonomous) and the social individual? Such a complementarity refuses the collapse of the social and the collapse of the individual; instead, it seeks a third way. This third-way critical pedagogy embraces the complexity of the topic rather than avoiding it. It addresses head-on the contradictions inherent in the interaction of autonomy and belonging. The essence of this notion of the ideological education of selfhood involves the nature of the relationship between independence and interaction. The sociability of the individual within this complex relationship involves much more than just understanding the social context. While an appreciation of context is necessary, this articulation of ideological education involves the development of individual human senses. In this context, Philip Wexler's concept of "revitalization," emanating from the concern with "enlivenment" in contemporary society, is added to the critical theoretical mix. An evolving critical pedagogy takes Wexler's revitalization seriously, analyzing its problems and potentialities in relation to our larger concerns with equity and justice. The possibilities for social change and self-transformation offered by revitalization are compelling in this context.

The Ideological Construction of Subjectivity: Three "Takes"

The reconceptualized notion of the intersection of the social and the individual offered here can be used by critical teachers. Informed by the critical theoretical tradition as articulated by German social analyst Heinz Sunker (1994, 1998), the reconstruction of individual identity as developed by Philip Wexler (1997, 2000) and critical ontology (Kincheloe, 2003), and my own concerns with cultural pedagogy, a new concept of critical pedagogy for a hyper-real Age of Empire emerges.

Tradition

Heinz Sunker (1994, 1998) maintains that education is one social practice connected to and mediated by other social practices; in this context, he asks what is "good" in a good upbringing of youth. Utilizing theorists from both the Frankfurt School as well as German critical educational theorists Heinz-Joachim Hadorn and Georg Theunissen, a critical canon of ideological education is constructed. This body of work takes seriously one's contribution to the good life as a member of society, a contribution based on an awareness of the nature of the social construction of both consciousness and the social fabric. Such a canon understands the importance of intersubjectivity (relations of various individuals, interpersonal interaction) in the construction of subjectivity. In this context, historical educational efforts to act on such understandings are analyzed. Questions are asked about the reasons for their failures and successes and their relevance for contemporary practice. To better answer these questions, Sunker (1994) introduces Hadorn's articulation of *Bildung*, focusing on its concern with emancipation, maturity, and self-determination.

The tradition of *Bildung* is especially important to ideological education in its interest in the production of subjectivity in the context of intersubjective relations. Sunker advocates the relevance of *Bildung* to contemporary criticality by emphasizing two dimensions:

1) The mediating processes between the individual and society; and 2) the processes involved with the construction of the subjectivity of the individual. In this way, *Bildung* transcends hegemonic education's effort to normalize the individual so as to adjust him or her to the existing social order. Rejecting bourgeois liberalism's effort to form the individual without referencing extant social conditions, *Bildung* is interested in individual development in the context of relational consciousness and the development of social competencies. In this context, *Bildung* mediates materialist (political economic) understandings of the world and concerns with everyday life, connecting the macro to the micro in the process. According to the concept of *Bildung*, learning is conceived of as an activity taking place as part of a larger democratic struggle, with one eye on the cultivation of the intellect and the other on democracy.

With our critical canon of ideological education firmly grounded on a knowledge of *Bildung*, we move to other traditions for insights into our conception. As previously mentioned, our multidimensional model of critical education is also informed by Philip Wexler's efforts to reclaim ancient knowledges abandoned since the European Enlightenment and the birth of Cartesianism in the seventeenth and eighteenth centuries. If the modern era is ending (or at least changing), the problems we are called on to solve are mutating as well. As these social/cultural/political changes have occurred, Wexler points out the way religion has returned to the forefront of social practice and cultural consciousness. Moving in different directions simultaneously, religion moves backward, before modernity, and forward, past imperial hyperreality, to provide differing grounds for ways of seeing and acting. Wexler warns progressives and critical theorists not to reject such religious insights in a materialist knee-jerk presumption of religion as merely a tool of dominant ideology. Through the theological window, social educators can explore premodern modes of sacralization and mystical insights. Carefully avoiding commodified and distorted "New Age" articulations of these traditions, Wexler views them through the lenses of an exacting and rigorous critical socio-logical tradition. In his hands, new applications for such knowledge emerge.

Picking up on Wexler's theoretical move, I attempt to contribute to the canon of a transformative ideological education by bringing previously referenced sub-jugated and indigenous knowledges to the pedagogical table. Derived from dangerous memories of history that have been suppressed and information that has been disqualified by social and academic gatekeepers, subjugated and indigenous knowledges play an important role in a critical pedagogy concerned with the way dominant power inculcates ideology in the contemporary era. Through the conscious cultivation of these "low-ranking" knowledges, alternative democratic and emancipatory visions of society, politics, cognition, and social education are possible. The subjugated knowledge of Africans, indigenous peoples from around the world, women in diverse cultural contexts, working-class people, and many other groups have contested the dominant culture's view of reality. At the very least, such subjugated knowledges inform students operating within mainstream schools and society that there are multiple perspectives on all issues. A critical pedagogy that includes subjugated ways of seeing teaches a lesson on the complex-ities of knowledge production and how this process shapes our view of ourselves and the world around us.

Individuals from dominant social formations have rarely understood (or cared to understand) how they look to marginalized others. As a result, women often make sense of men's view of women better than men understand women's view of men; individuals from Africa, or with African heritages, understand the motivations of White people better than the reverse; and low-status workers fig-ure out how they are seen by their managers more clearly than the managers understand how they appear to workers. Obviously, such insights provide critical pedagogues and their students with a very different view of the world and the pro-cesses that shape it. Critical educators who employ such subjugated viewpoints become transformative agents who alert the community to its hidden features, its submerged memories, and in the process help specific individuals to name their oppression or possibly understand their complicity in oppression.

In this context, transformative critical educators search out specific forms of subjugated insights, such as indigenous knowledges. Indigenous knowledges are special forms of subjugated knowledges that are local, life-experience-based, and not produced by Western science. Such knowledges are transmitted over time by individuals from a particular geographical or cultural locality. Only now, in the twenty-first century, are European peoples just starting to appreciate the value of indigenous knowledges about health, medicine, agriculture, philosophy, spirituality, ecology, and education. Traditionally, these are the very types of knowledges Western ideological education have tried to discredit and eradicate. A transformative critical education works hard to save such knowledges, which are, unfortunately, disappearing from the face of the earth. Thankfully, many individuals from indigenous backgrounds and their allies are working to reverse this trend.

Culture

This section focuses on the expanding role of the cultural realm in the domain of contemporary ideological education. If a new era has dawned, then critical educators must search for the places where new ways of ideological education are taking place. The emergence of a new role, an expanded political and educational function for the cultural domain is a cardinal feature of the new social condition. The contemporary era confronts critical pedagogy with new contradictions and new ways of thwarting emancipation. In this new era, cultural capital has reorganized itself in ways that make it more flexible, innovative, and powerful. New technological and organizational developments have allowed capital greater access to both the world at large and human consciousness in particular. Reorganized transnational capital has embraced an aesthetic that celebrates the commodification of difference, ephemerality, spectacle, and fashion. In this observation, we uncover the central concern of the ideologically reorganized cultural realm: this new flexible aesthetic of capital gains its hegemonic force from its ability to employ the cultural realm for ideological indoctrination. Thus, the cultural domain emerges as a central political venue, a place where ideological consciousness is constructed, a new locale for ideological education.

Thus, in this context contemporary critical educators learn an invaluable lesson: everyday life takes place on a new ideological template—a semiotic matrix shaped in part by corporate-produced images. A new ideological education is produced by capital that is designed to regulate the population, as affectively charged consumers operating in a privatized domain lose consciousness of what used to be called the public sphere. This privatized domain is both globalized and decentralized/localized at the same time, distorting traditional concepts of space and time. The past is commodified and politicized, turning public memory into Disney's "Frontierland"—a powerful ideological educational venue. In this context, time is rearticulated and everyday life becomes an eternal present. Without critical intervention, the public space deteriorates and critical consciousness is erased. The disorientation that the informational overload of the new cultural condition induces moves individuals to seek more expert help, more therapeutic involvement in their everyday affairs. In the HBO series *The Sopranos*, for example, Tony, the Mafioso leader, is so distraught and confused by changing cultural conditions that he seeks psychological therapy and is prescribed Prozac for his depression. Even those who pride themselves on being self-sufficient outlaws cannot escape the effects of cultural disequilibrium. Working in the realm of information control and the production of pleasure, capital embeds positive images of itself at the deepest levels of our subconscious. Many come to associate the "good things in life" and happiness with the privatized realm of consumption. As powerful as crime boss Tony Soprano may be, for example, he cannot get his own son's attention while the boy (A.J.) plays his Nintendo video game.

Pleasure is a powerful social educator, and the pleasure produced by capital teaches a very conservative political lesson: since corporations produce pleasure, we should align our interests with them. In this way our "affect" is organized in the service of capital: lower corporate taxes, better business climates, equation of the corporate bottom line with social well-being, larger executive salaries, lower labor costs, fewer environmental regulations, and support for imperial wars, to name just a few. Hegemony in this new context operates where affect and politics intersect: the cultural realm. The revolutionary feature of this repressive, capital-driven ideological education is that culture shapes the political. Critical pedagogues have sometimes failed to appreciate this circumstance, not to mention its dramatic impact on the shaping of political consciousness and subjectivity.

Thus, transformative critical educators must understand the new affective dynamics at work in the production of selfhood. When we speak of the cultural realm, of course, a central feature of this domain involves popular culture and its relationship to power. Popular culture involves television, movies, video games, music, Internet, instant messaging, iPods, shopping malls, theme parks, etc. These are the sites of a contemporary cultural pedagogy of commodification that meets people where they exist in their affective fields. As it provides fun, pleasure, good feelings, passion, and emotion, this capital-inscribed ideological education connects ideology to these affective dynamics. In contemporary society, ideologies are only effective to the degree that they can be articulated along the affective plane. Affect is complex in that both pleasure and displeasure are affective responses. One's affective dislike of hip-hop, for example, can be inscribed ideologically with particular meanings about youth with African heritages around the world. Though complex, the power produced and deployed along this affective plane is profound in its ability to shape subjectivity and ways of seeing the world.

Our critical vision of a transformative education, an evolving critical pedagogy recognizes these contemporary politicocultural dynamics and analyzes their consequences at both the macro- and microlevels. One of the most important ef-

fects of this corporate colonization of affect has involved, of course, the phenomenon of depoliticization. At the heart of this phenomenon exists a paradoxical
reality: while many Westerners have invested affectively in the emerging privatization of the social order, they do not rationally buy into the political-economic
policies of conservatism. In this bizarre context, individuals remain politically un-
committed and civically inactive. Except for a significant minority of citizens on
the Right, individuals have removed themselves from the political realm. I don't
want to discount the importance of struggles such as janitors' fight for economic
justice, protests against the World Trade Organization, and the brief outpouring
of antiwar sentiment before the U.S. invasion and occupation of Iraq, but these
actions are still the exceptions. In addition, the depoliticization process. This ideological dynamic is so important that critical educators simply cannot do their jobs
if they don't understand it.

In the electronic mediated culture of the twenty-first century, youth are no
longer shielded from the esoteric knowledge of adulthood. Young people, in a
sense, know too much to retain the idealism traditionally associated with this
phase of life. In their knowledge of the world, many young people have become
jaded to the point that they know of nothing worthy of their faith outside the
intrinsic value of pleasure and affect in and of themselves. In their unshockability,
many young people (and many adults as well) become emotional only about emotion—certainly not about some complex political issue. In such a culture-driven
context, political discourse is reduced to "gut-level" emotion, to affective investments directly tied to self-interest. Politics becomes successful only when it is represented as "not politics." Questions of racial justice become important only when
many White citizens perceive that Blacks and government leaders, via affirmative
action, are taking their jobs away. Issues of social policy and public morality are
irrelevant in this context: "Non-Whites, aided by big government, are stealing
'our' jobs." Rational political debate is irrelevant; affirmative action is an affective
issue. Effective television campaign advertisements do not make a rational case for
ending affirmative action; they depict a Black hand taking a job application away
from a working-class White hand. Professional political consultants chant their
mantras: "Keep it on the affective plane, stupid." A transformative ideological
education in this media-saturated context can never be the same.

Identity

After having established a critical canon for a transformative ideological education
and explored the changing cultural conditions of a twenty-first-century electronic,
globalized society, attention needs to be focused on questions of identity and the
production of the individual. In this context, Philip Wexler's (1997, 2000) argument catalyzes our notion of an evolving criticality in an age of dominant power's

highly successful ideological education. The affect-centeredness of electronically mediated reality, Wexler posits, contains within it a decentered social movement that offers possibilities for emancipatory social education.

There is, he contends, an alternative rationality that often operates affectively to revitalize those caught in the commodified information environment of the present—a revitalization ignored by critical pedagogy. Just as affective measures can be used by power to hegemonize individuals and social groups, they can also be deployed by individuals to make certain things matter in ways that assert their self-direction and group solidarity by using the positive productive ability of power. From this conceptual foundation, Wexler moves to take critical advantage of what is available on the contemporary cultural landscape. If the self is the locus of historical change in the twenty-first century, then an evolving critical pedagogy must seize the opportunity to produce meaningful selves.

Aware of the politicocultural dimensions previously described, critical educators study the various ways individuals protect their identities from the power flows of capital. In such defensive actions, individuals not only shield themselves from the social earthquakes shaking the cultural terrain on which they live, but also forge new forms of collective alliances. Examples of such actions can be found on the Internet, as individuals morph their identities and connect with a wide range of similar web surfers. In such virtual lives, traditional boundaries of self are blurred in the interactions of dematerialized beings. In the electronic informational cosmos, Wexler's recognition of a retreat to a defensive inner world becomes an important understanding for the critical educator.

The revolution of social being described by Wexler is grounded on the possibilities offered by such an inward turn and the effort to reshape consciousness that accompanies it. At this important point there is a convergence of Sunker's *Bildung*-based assertion that consciousness is the central element of the educational process, new cultural technologies of consciousness construction, and Wexler's analysis of the consequences of the opportunities provided by the "inner turn." At this intersection, the new ideological education finds its purpose and the possibility for the construction of a new critical ontology—a transformative, self-aware way of being human. Central to this synthetic dynamic is Wexler's understanding of the potentialities of alternate rationalities and enlivenment in the emancipatory reconstruction of consciousness and identity.

Picking up on Wexler's theoretical move, I attempt to contribute to the canon of a transformative ideological education in a larger critical pedagogical context by bringing critical ontology to the recipe. In this context, critical educators engage in the excitement of attaining new levels of consciousness and "ways of being." In a critical ontology, individuals who gain such an awareness understand how and why their political opinions, religious beliefs, gender roles, racial positions, or sexual orientations have been shaped by dominant perspectives. They understand the nature and complexity of the ways dominant power works to construct subjectivity/consciousness via education, the media, and other cultural sites.

A critical ontological vision helps us in the effort to gain new understandings and insights as to who we can become. Such a vision helps us move beyond our present state of being—our ontological selves—as we discern the forces that have made us that way. The line between knowledge production and being is blurred, as the epistemological and the ontological converge around questions of identity and the social construction of selfhood. As we employ the ontological vision, we ask questions about ethics, morality, politics, emotion, and gut feelings, seeking not precise steps to reshape our subjectivity but a framework of principles with which we can negotiate. Employing the insights of ontology, we explore our being in the world. Thus, we join the quest for new, expanded, and more just and interconnected ways of being human.

A key dimension of a critical ontology involves freeing ourselves from the machine metaphors of Cartesianism. Such an ontological stance recognizes the reductionism of viewing the universe as a well-oiled machine and the human mind as a computer. Such "ways of being" subvert an appreciation of the amazing life force that inhabits both the universe and human beings. This machine cosmology has positioned human beings as living in a dead world, a lifeless universe. Ontologically, this Cartesianism has separated individuals from their inanimate surroundings, undermining any organic interconnection of the person to the cosmos. The life-giving complexity of the inseparability of human and world has been lost and social/cultural/pedagogical/psychological studies of people abstracted or removed from context. Such a removal has exerted disastrous ontological effects. Human beings, in a sense, lost their belongingness to both the world and to other people around them.

The importance of indigenous (Semali and Kincheloe, 1999) and other subjugated knowledges reemerges in this ontological context. With the birth of modernity and the Scientific Revolution, many premodern, indigenous ontologies were lost, ridiculed by Europeans as primitive. While there is great diversity among premodern worldviews and ways of being, there do seem to be some discernible patterns that distinguish them from modernist perspectives. In addition to developing systems of meaning and being that were connected to cosmological perspectives on the nature of creation, most premodern viewpoints saw nature and the world at large as living systems. Western Christian observers condescendingly labeled such perspectives as pantheism or nature worship and positioned them as an enemy of monotheism. Not understanding the subtlety and nuance of such indigenous views of the world, Europeans subverted the sense of belonging that accompanied these enchanted views of nature. European Christo-modernism transformed the individual from a connected participant in the drama of nature to a detached, objective, depersonalized observer.

The Western modernist individual emerged from the process, alienated and disenchanted. As Edmund O'Sullivan (1999) puts it, Cartesianism tore apart "the relationship between the microcosmos and the macrocosmos" (p. 18). Such a fragmentation resulted in the loss of cosmological significance and the beginning of a snowballing pattern of ontological imbalance. A critical ontology involves the process of reconnecting human beings on a variety of levels and in numerous ways to a living social and physical web of reality, to a living cosmos. Critical pedagogues with a critical ontological vision help students connect to the civic web of the political domain, the biotic web of the natural world, the social web of human life, and the epistemological web of knowledge production. In this manner, we all move to the realm of critical ontology where new ways of being and new ways of being connected reshape all people. In a critical ideological education, critical ontology sets the stage for alternative identities in a Western world with truncated possibilities for selfhood.

Here we can see the merger of Wexler's ideas and critical ontology. Grounded on his understanding of these ontological issues, Wexler contends that an intuitive disenchantment with this Cartesian fragmentation and its severing of the self-environment relationship are fueling a diffuse social revaluation. He employs the term revitalization for this mass, decentered movement taking place throughout Western societies. It constitutes an attempt, he contends, to resacralize our culture and our "selves." Such an effort exposes the impact of Eurocentrism and Cartesianism on what human beings (or our identities) have become, as, at the same time, it produces an ontological "change from within." Understanding the problems with Cartesianism's lack of self-awareness or concern with consciousness and inter-connectedness, Wexler's resacralization picks up on wisdom traditions, both premodern and contemporary, to lay the foundation for profound ontological change. In the emerging ontology the Cartesian bifurcation of the mind and body is repaired, and new relationships with the body, mind, and spirit are pursued. In the transcendence of modernist notions of bodily ego-greed, a new understanding of the body's role in meaning making and human being is attained. A new world of identity formation is constructed.

Picking up on these insights, a critical ontology positions the body in relation to the complexity of cognition and the process of life itself. The body is a corporeal reflection of the evolutionary concept of autopoiesis, self-organizing or self-making of life (Varela, 1999). Autopoiesis involves the production of a pattern-of-life organization. Cognition in this ontological context involves the process of self-production. Thus life itself, the nature of being, is a cognitive activity that involves establishing patterns of living, patterns that become the life force through self-organization. If life is self-organized, then there are profound ontological, cognitive, ideological, and pedagogical implications. By recognizing new patterns and developing new processes, humans exercise much more input into their own evolution than previously imagined. In such a context human agency and possibility are enhanced—we can overcome the neofascist elements of contemporary Western ideological oppression.

With these ideas and this hope in mind, it is important to note that Wexler maintains that one aspect of the electronic informational culture of the contemporary era involves the emergence of a new concern with the worldview and methods of classical mysticism. Even though this mediated culture has often served to shatter identities, Wexler identifies a new power in people's minds. Moving past the Cartesian Enlightenment, the new consciousness of social being emerges around a resacralization of cultural codes, the globalizing synthesis of cultural expressions that exposes the ethnocentrism of European science and epistemology, and a new historicism that reengages the premodern, the ancient, and the archaic. Revitalization of the self and the new identities it encourages takes shape in this synthetic context. Directly responding to the fragmenting effects of informational hyper-culture, revitalization uses imaginative power to protect the self from threats posed by informationalism in hyperreality. Fueled by these recognitions and an understanding of the traditions of critical theory and cultural studies, Wexler conceptualizes the synergy between a resacralized self-realization and a critical education.

The emancipatory power of this synergy hinges on the articulation of these conceptual intersections and the consciousness, agency, and praxis that emerge therein. Wexler understands that self-realization, in both its bodily and psychic expression, must transcend its roots in narcissism and plant itself firmly in the transcendent or the cosmological to be of benefit to what I call an evolving critical pedagogy. Employed at the sacred level, self-realization, a la revitalization, provides a compelling strategic grounding in the struggle against the alienation of commodification, rationalization, and ideological indoctrination. As it embraces desire and vitality in everyday life and discerns how to use them in an emancipatory rather than a manipulative way, self-realization reexamines the relationship between self and environment. A transformative ideological education takes advantage of this conceptual opening, drawing upon the vitality of this new individualism and connecting it to Sunker's canon and my own cultural concerns. Here self engages other in a strong union that constructs a vision for a reinvigorated, ever-evolving critical practice.

Key Dimensions of the Critical Synthesis

In a contemporary culture that finds it increasingly difficult to mobilize itself for political action, advocates of critical pedagogy must take place on uncharted social and cultural territory. In the complexity and high-speed change of hyperreality, efforts to address alienation, oppression, and ideological indoctrination seem somehow outside the spirit of the times. Our synthesis of these diverse domains must be not only conceptually compelling but also sufficiently contextually aware to operate on the bizarre sociocultural landscape that confronts us in the twenty-first century. The central features of our new evolving critical pedagogical synthesis of the critical theoretical tradition, an understanding of the power of dominant cultural pedagogies, and the importance of identity construction include:

1. The development of a socio-individual imagination. At the basis of our multilevel evolving critical pedagogy rests the ability to imagine new forms of self-realization and social collaboration that lead to emancipatory results. An important aspect of these emancipatory results involves the rethinking of educational practice, knowledge production, and engaged forms of citizenship. These dynamics interact to help us imagine new forms of consciousness and cognition grounded on creative images of a changing life. These new forms of consciousness cannot be separated from the educational realm and the democratic effort to reframe learning as part of the struggle against multiple forms of domination. Framed in this manner, an evolving criticality plays a central role in the development of our individual imagination. Here, an ideologically aware education induces individuals to rethink their subjectivities in order to emphasize the role of democratic community and social justice in the process of human development. An education for individual imagination becomes increasingly more important in a society torn asunder by commodified informationalism (McLaren, 1994, 2000, 2006).

2. The reconstitution of the individual outside the boundaries of abstract individualism. The reconstitution of the individual that is connected to our evolving critical pedagogy's celebration of self-realization must be articulated carefully in light of the use of the concept of individualism in the Western tradition. Our notion of self-realization is a corrective of both a critical tradition that rejects the possibilities of an authentic individuality and a market-based individualism that rejects the importance of social context. In critical communitarianism, the importance of the community consistently takes precedence over the interests of the individual—a position that poses great danger to the health of the democratic impulse. In the market context, egocentrism is equated with action for the common good, creating in the process powerful forms of regulatory power that ultimately destroy the social fabric. When our notion of criticality expresses its concern for individualism, this should by no means be interpreted as a naive acceptance of the Cartesian notion of the "abstract individual." This individual subject is removed from the effects

of complex power relations and endowed with abstract political rights that mean little when disconnected from the regulatory and disciplinary aspects of economic, social, and cultural forces.

3. The understanding of power and the ability to interpret its effects on the social and the individual. Of course one of the most important horizons within which critical educators analyze the world and its actors involves the context of power. Transformative educators are interested in both how power operates in the social order and the ways it works to produce subjectivity. In this context they focus on the nature of ideology and the process by which it imprints itself on consciousness, the ways hegemonic forces mobilize desire in the effort to win the public's consent to the authority of various power blocs, the means by which discursive powers shape thinking and behavior via the presences and absences of different words and concepts, and the ways that disciplines of knowledge are used to regulate individuals through a process of normalization. In this context an evolving critical pedagogy studies the methods individuals and groups use to assert their agency and self-direction in relation to such power plays. With this in mind, critical pedagogy is especially concerned with the complex relationship connecting individuals, groups, and power. Such an interaction never occurs around a single axis of power, and the ambiguity of the subjectivity that is produced never lends itself to simple description or facile prediction of ways of seeing or behaving. Mainstream forms of Western education have consistently ignored this effort, trivializing, in the process, the role of social analysis.

4. The provision of alternatives to the alienation of the individual. A central concern of our evolving critical pedagogy involves providing an alternative to social and educational alienation. Individuals in contemporary society experience social reality mainly as a world of consumerism and not as the possibility of human relations. In a consumerist hyperreality, both young people and adults are alienated from daily life and cultural and educational capital. Such alienation affects individuals from different social locations in divergent ways. Men and women from more-dominant locales suffer an informational alienation that erases issues of power, justice, and privilege. Those from less-dominant locales are denied access to institutions that provide tickets to social mobility by the use of a rhetoric of standards, excellence, and values. Less-privileged individuals are induced to blame themselves for their lack of access to various forms of capital via the deployment of such discursive strategies and regulatory forms. Such a reality can be described as a form of "second-degree alienation," a state

that is unconscious of the existence of alienation. In this alienated circumstance, the possibility of self-direction fades. In this context, our social education, drawing on the German *Bildung* tradition, provides individuals alternatives to their alienation. Here again Philip Wexler's concepts of resacralization and enlivenment and my concept of critical ontology become central to the generation of empowering alternatives.

5. The cultivation of a critical consciousness that is aware of the social construction of subjectivity. An evolving critical pedagogy produces conscious individuals who are aware of their self-production and the social conditions under which they live. With this in mind, our critical pedagogy is concerned not just with how individuals experience social reality but how they often operate in circumstances that they don't understand. A critical consciousness is aware of these dynamics, as it appreciates the complexity of social practices and their relationships with other practices and structures. Indeed, our education promotes a critical consciousness of self-production that not only understands the many planes of history on which an individual operates but how subjectivity is specifically colonized on these various planes. In this context, questions of the social construction of identity are viewed through the lenses of affect and emotion. Empowered by such knowledge, individuals with a critical consciousness are able to use their insights to overcome alienation and construct social and individual relations with other social actors. If democracy is to succeed, then large numbers of individuals need to reflect on the effects of the social on the individual. Via this consciousness-producing activity, the public space/political cultural is reconstructed.

6. The construction of democratic community-building relationships between individuals. The development of the individual coupled with the construction of a democratic community is central to a transformative pedagogy. Embracing a critical alterity (an awareness of difference) involving responsiveness to others, the new social education works to cultivate an intersubjectivity that develops both social consciousness and individual agency. The notion of an individual's relational existence becomes extremely important in this context as we focus attention on the power of difference in social education. Utilizing its understanding of how power relations shape individual subjectivity, an evolving critical pedagogy explores the power-inscribed nature of group difference. In this context, students learn how power shapes lives of privilege and oppression in ways that tear the social fabric and deny community. Students, workers, and other citizens who belong to diverse socioeconomic, racial,

ethnic, gender, and sexual groups can learn much from one another if provided the space to exchange ideas and analyze mutual difficulties. As such a powerful force, difference must not simply be tolerated but cultivated as a spark to human creativity and evolution. Relational existence is not only intrinsically important in a democratic society; it also holds cognitive and educational benefits for self-development. Understandings derived from the perspective of the excluded, the culturally different, or the colonized allow for an appreciation of the nature of justice, the invisibility of the process of oppression, and the difference that highlights our own social construction as human beings.

7. The reconceptualization of reason—understanding that relational existence applies not only to human beings but concepts as well. Drawing upon its critical roots, an evolving critical pedagogy understands the irrationality of what has sometimes passed for reason in the post-Enlightenment history of Western societies. Thus, an important aspect of our transformative education involves the reconstruction of reason. Such a process begins with the formulation of a relational reason. A relational reason understands conventional reason's propensity for conceptual fragmentation and narrow focus on abstraction outside of a lived context. The point here is not to reject rationality but to appreciate the limits of its conventional articulation in light of its relationship to power. Such a turn investigates various rationalities from the subjugated to the ancient, as it analyzes the importance of that deemed irrational by dominant Western power and its use-value in sociopolitical affairs and the construction of a critical consciousness. Such alternative ways of thinking are reappropriated via the realization of conventional decontextualization: individuals are separated from the culture, schools from society, and abstract rights from power. An evolving critical pedagogy critiques traditional Western reason's tendency—based on a Cartesian ontology—to view an entity as a thing-in-itself. All things are a part of larger interactive dynamics, interrelationships that provide meaning when brought to the analytical table. Indeed, our evolving critical pedagogy finds this relational reason so important and so potentially transformative that we see the interaction between concepts as a living process. These relational dynamics permeate all aspects of not only our social education but also of critical consciousness itself.

8. The production of social skills necessary to active participation in the transformed, inclusive democratic community. As a result of an evolving critical pedagogy, teachers and students will gain the ability to act in the role of democratic citizens. Studying the ideological in relation to self-

development, socially educated individuals begin to conceptualize the activities of social life. Viewing their social actions not only through the lenses of the political but also the economic, the cultural, the psychological, the epistemological, and the ontological, individuals analyze the forces that produce apathy and passivity. In this manner, critical pedagogy comes to embody the process of radical democratization, the continuing effort of the presently excluded to gain the right and ability to have input into civic life. As individuals of all stripes, ages, and backgrounds in contemporary hyperreality search for an identity, critical pedagogy provides them an affective social and individual vision in which to invest. Making connections between the political, the economic, the cultural, the psychological, the epistemological, the ontological, and the educational, individuals gain insight into what is and what could be as well as the disposition to act. Thus, as political agency is cultivated, critical pedagogy becomes a democratic social politic. Once again, social consciousness and the valorization of the individual come together to produce an emancipatory synergy.

Conclusion

I am always amazed with how quickly the world changes, the acceleration of the pace of change, and the expansion of the power of power. Given such dynamics it is inconceivable that critical pedagogy would not be ever-evolving, changing to meet the needs posed by new circumstances and unprecedented challenges. In such dire circumstances we need critical pedagogy more than ever. Wedged between an ideological rock and a hegemonic hard place with a relatively small audience, I believe critical pedagogy contains the imaginative, intellectual, and pragmatic power to free us from that snare. Such an escape is central to the survival of not just critical pedagogy but also to human beings as a species.

References

Agger, B. (1992). *The discourse of domination: From the Frankfurt School to postmodernism.* Evanston, IL: Northwestern University Press.

Beck-Gernsheim, E., Butler, J., & L. Puigvert. (2003). *Women and social transformation.* New York: Peter Lang.

Blackler, F. (1995). Knowledge, knowledge work, and organizations: An overview and interpretation. *Organization Studies, 16,* 6.

Capra, F. (1996). *The web of life: A new scientific understanding of living systems.* New York: Anchor Books.

Carter, R. (2004). Visual literacy: Critical thinking with the visual image. In J. Kincheloe & D. Weil (Eds.), *Critical thinking and learning: An encyclopedia for parents and teachers.* Westport, CT: Greenwood.

Dei, G. (1995). Indigenous knowledge as an empowerment tool. In N. Singh & V. Titi (Eds.) *Empowerment: Toward sustainable development*. Toronto: Fernwood Press.

Dei, G. & Kempf, A. (Eds.). (2006). *Anti-colonialism and education: The politics of resistance*. Rotterdam: Sense Publishers.

Fischer, F. (1998). Beyond empiricism: Policy inquiry in postpositivist perspective. *Policy Studies Journal*, 26(1), 129–46.

Flecha, R., Gomez, J., & Puigvert, L. (2003). *Contemporary sociological theory*. New York: Peter Lang.

Flossner, G., & Otto, H. (Eds.). (1998). *Towards more democracy in social services: Models of culture and welfare*. New York: de Gruyter.

Freire, P. & Faundez, A. (1989). *Learning to question: A pedagogy of liberation*. New York: Continuum.

Horn, R. (2004). Scholar-practitioner leaders: The empowerment of teachers and students. In J. Kincheloe & D. Weil (Eds.), *Critical thinking and learning: An encyclopedia for parents and teachers*. Westport, CT: Greenwood.

Keith, N. and Keith, N. (1993, November). Education, development, and the rebuilding of urban community. Paper presented at the Annual Conference of the Association for the Advancement of Research, Policy, and Development in the Third World, Cairo, Egypt.

Kincheloe, J. (2001). Describing the bricolage: Conceptualizing a new rigor in qualitative research. *Qualitative Inquiry*, 7(6), 679–92.

Kincheloe, J. (2003). Critical ontology: Visions of selfhood and curriculum. *JCT: Journal of Curriculum Theorizing*, 19 (1), 47–64.

Kincheloe, J. (2004). *Critical pedagogy*. New York: Peter Lang.

Kincheloe, J. (2005). On to the next level: Continuing the conceptualization of the bricolage. *Qualitative Inquiry*. 11(3), 323–350.

Kincheloe, J. (2007). *Critical pedagogy and cognition: An introduction to a postformal educational psychology*. Dordrecht, Netherlands: Springer.

Kincheloe J. & Berry, K. (2004). *Rigor and complexity in educational research: Conceptualizing the bricolage*. London: Open University Press.

Kincheloe, J. & McLaren, P. (2005). Rethinking critical theory and qualitative research. In N. Denzin and Y. Lincoln (Eds.), *Handbook of qualitative research* (3rd ed.). Thousand Oaks, CA: Sage.

Kincheloe, J. & Steinberg, S. (1993). A tentative description of post-formal thinking: The critical confrontation with cognitive theory. *Harvard Educational Review*, 63(3), 296–320.

Kincheloe, J., Steinberg, S., and Hinchey, P. (1999). *The postformal reader: Cognition and education*. New York: Falmer Press.

Leistyna, P., Woodrum, A., and Sherblom, S. (1996). *Breaking free: The transformative power of critical pedagogy*. Cambridge, MA: Harvard Educational Review.

McLaren, P. (1994). An interview with Heinz Sunker of Germany: Germany today—history and future (or dilemmas, dangers and hopes). *International Journal of Educational Reform*, 3(2), 202–209.

McLaren, P. (2000). *Che Guevara, Paulo Freire, and the pedagogy of revolution*. Lanham, MD: Rowman and Littlefield.

McLaren, P. (2006). *Rage and hope: Interviews with Peter McLaren on war, imperialism, and critical pedagogy*. New York: Peter Lang.

O'Sullivan, E. (1999). *Transformative learning: Educational vision for the twenty-first century*. New York: Zed.

Reason, P. & Bradbury, H. (2000). Introduction: Inquiry and participation in search of a world worthy of human aspiration. In P. Reason & H. Bradbury (Eds.), *Handbook of action research: Participative inquiry and practice*. Thousand Oaks, CA: Sage.

Schon, D. (1995). The new scholarship requires a new epistemology. *Change*, 27, 6.

Semali, L. & Kincheloe, J. (1999). *What is indigenous knowledge? Voices from the academy*. New York: Garland.

Smith, R., & Wexler, P. (Eds.). (1995). *After post-modernism: Education, politics, and identity*. London: Falmer.

Steinberg, S. (Ed.). (2001). *Multi/intercultural conversations*. New York: Peter Lang.

Sunker, H. (1994). Pedagogy and politics: Hadorn's "survival through education" and its challenge to contemporary theories of education (*Bildung*). In S. Miedema, G. Bieste, & W. Wardekke (Eds.) *The politics of human science*. Brussels, Belgium: VUB Press.

Sunker, H. (1998). Welfare, democracy, and social work. In G. Flosser & H. Otto (Eds.), *Towards more democracy in social services: Models of culture and welfare*. New York: de Gruyter.

Thomas, P. & Kincheloe, J. (2006). *Reading, writing, and thinking: The postformal basics*. Rotterdam: Sense Publishers.

Varela, F. (1999). *Ethical know-how: Action, wisdom, and cognition*. Stanford, CA: Stanford University Press.

Wesson, L. and Weaver, J. (2001). Administration—educational standards: Using the lens of postmodern thinking to examine the role of the school administrator. In J. Kincheloe and D. Weil (Eds.), *Standards and schooling in the United States: An encyclopedia*, 3 vols. Santa Barbara, CA: ABC-CLIO.

Wexler, P. (1997). Social research in education: Ethnography of being. Paper presented at the International Conference on the Culture of Schooling, Halle, Germany.

Wexler, P. (2000). *The mystical society: Revitalization in culture, theory, and education*. Boulder, CO: Westview.

Williams, S. (1999). Truth, speech, and ethics: A feminist revision of free speech theory. Genders, 30. http://www.genders.org

Willinsky, J. (2006). *The access principle: The case for open access to research and scholarship*. Cambridge, MA: MIT Press.

NINE

The Future of the Past

Reflections on the Present State of Empire and Pedagogy

Peter McLaren

H and-in-hand with his threat warnings, Bush keeps telling us how his War on
Terror has made us so much safer, bragging that there hasn't been a terrorist
attack in the United States in the five years since the one on September 11, 2001.
Marvelous. There wasn't a terrorist attack in the United States in the five years
before that day either (Blum, 2006).

In the twenty-first century, leaders of the dominant capitalist states have declared a permanent war on terror. Anti-democratic laws which grant extrajudicial
powers to hold citizens and immigrants without trial are moving modern democracies towards capitalist sovereignty congealed in the shape of totalitarianism. The
Patriot Act was extended in the United States, eviscerating basic constitutional
rights. Civil society is becoming militarized in the direction of a permanent security state, while political leaders on the right betray an unvarnished contempt for
any kind of criticism of U.S. foreign or domestic policy. Where comity among
nations was once lauded as a virtue, it is now seen as a weakness. The world's only
superpower seeks to rule by intimidation and brutality.

Marx's critique of political economy and his materialist conception of history
cannot be so easily discarded into the rag-and-bone shop of social history. Just
as in Marx's day, the development of capitalism is concomitant with the growth
and consolidation of commonplace understandings of how freedom of the market translates into democratic freedom. The prevailing categories and forms of

First published in McLaren, P. & J. Kincheloe. (2007). *Critical Pedagogy: Where Are We Now?* New York: Peter Lang.

thought used today to justify foreign and domestic policy in capitalist societies—such as those of "democracy"' and "freedom"—are shaped by the social relations of the societies that employ them. They have contributed to the perpetuation of a class-divided, racialized, and patriarchal social order. These forms of thought manifest a certain universality and often reveal the imprint of the ruling class (echoing Marx's famous dictum that the ideas of the ruling class prevail in every epoch as the ruling ideas). The market as a category in the vernacular of the ruling class is not conceived of as a crucible of exploitation but as a means of opportunity, a means of leveling the playing field, a means of achieving freedom and democracy. But Marx showed that precisely what we need is freedom from the market.

Marx demonstrated how the formal equality of political rights can exist, hand-in-hand, with brute exploitation and suffering. The separation of economic and political rights is the very condition of the impossibility of democracy, a separation that liberals have been stunningly unable to challenge in their discourses of reform. In fact, as Ellen Meiksins Wood (1995) and others have pointed out, the constitutive impossibility of democracy in a society built upon property rights significantly accounts for why democracy can be invoked against the democratic imperatives of the people in the gilded name of the global imperium. Property and the market must be served by ensuring that there is too little, not too much, democracy, and this cause can be advanced by leaders making sure that the world exists in a constant state of conflict. This, of course, can only occur when citizens are convinced that "freedom is not free" and that war will always be necessary to defend it (including "preventative wars" waged against those who are deemed to pose a threat sometime in the near or distant future). This is precisely how the United States secures its suzerainty: by ruling through the market, allowing limited autonomy to nations that adhere to the rules of the market and agree to keep their populaces subjugated as cheap labor. And by sending its warrior class into furious battle in those recalcitrant arenas where there is resistance to the rulers of the market as well as to the market rules, and hence to the conditions of freedom and democracy and its imperial agents and guardians. This is the real meaning of the freedom of the market. The market generates the conditions for the "winners" to create the necessary ideologies for justifying violence on the grounds of "us-against-them" theories of "inherent" competition and violence within the human species. And it provides them with the most formidable weapons available to carry out such violence and, in the case of the United States, to achieve the status (at least for the time being) as the organizing center of the world state.

A Reflection on Education under Attack

In 2006, the governor of Florida, Jeb Bush, approved a law (known as the Florida Education Omnibus Bill) barring the teaching of "revisionist" history in Florida public schools, including "postmodern viewpoints of relative truth." One chilling passage in the bill states: "American history shall be viewed as factual, not constructed, shall be viewed as knowable, teachable, and testable, and shall be defined as the creation of a new nation based largely on the universal principles stated in the Declaration of Independence." In a directive that brings to mind a cult of anti-intellectualism, teachers are charged to concentrate on the history and content of the Declaration and are instructed to teach the "history, meaning, significance and effect of the provisions of the Constitution of the United States and the amendments thereto" and to emphasize "flag education, including proper flag display and flag salute" and on the necessity of teaching "the nature and importance of free enterprise to the United States economy" (Craig, 2006). When seen in conjunction with President George W. Bush's 2003 attack on "revisionist historians" who challenged his justifications for using force against Saddam Hussein, and his 2005 warning on Veteran's Day in which he proclaimed that it is "deeply irresponsible to rewrite the history of how the war began" (Zimmerman, 2006), this inflammatory public demand for interpretive orthodoxy is designed to ward off any and all challenges to conventional understandings of history, understandings awash in information of suspicious provenance. In such a climate that is witnessing concerted attempts to blur the distinction between fact and value, collapsing them into official versions of events that carry the force of unbreachable dogma, disagreement can easily be equated with misinterpretation and misrepresentation, or even tantamount to deliberate falsification. The accolades heaped by the corporate media upon Ronald Reagan after his death were an index of just how little Americans know—or want to remember—about their presidents. Reagan's administration helped to establish the murderous Contra terrorists, who deliberately targeted innocent civilians, including women and children, in their attempt to overthrow Nicaragua's Sandinista rebels. And what about Gerald Ford? Ford gave the Indonesian dictator Suharto permission to invade East Timor, resulting in the massacre of 200,000 people, one third of the population of the country. Ford blocked the UN security council from enforcing its resolution respecting the right of self-determination and demanding the withdrawal of the Indonesian army. Ford also provided military and economic aid, including training for repressive internal security forces, to more than a dozen Latin American dictatorships, including that of Chile's infamous Augusto Pinochet. He sent large-scale arms aid and security assistance to numerous other brutal dictators, including Ferdinand Marcos in the Philippines and the Shah of Iran. He also allied with both the Mobutu dictatorship of Zaire and the apartheid regime in South Africa to arm rebel groups against the internationally recognized government of Angola (Zunes, 2006). And while these accounts barely scrape the surface of the horrendous policies of Reagan and Ford, it was difficult, if not impossible, to find any mention of them in the mainstream media accounts of Reagan and Ford's historical 'legacies.' After the deaths of these two "great" presidents, how many classroom discussions in the nation's schools centered around their egregious foreign and domestic policies? One wonders if the Florida Education Omnibus Bill is even necessary?

Reflections on Multicultural Education

The field of multiculturalism has, regrettably, overemphasized contingency and the reversibility of cultural practices at the level of the individual at the expense of challenging the structural determinations and productive forces of capital, its laws of motion, and its value form of labor—a move that has replaced an undialectical theory of economic determination with a poststructuralist theory of cultural determination, one that underestimates the ways in which the so-called autonomy of cultural acts is already rooted in the coercive relationships of the realm of necessity. Here, multiculturalists and antiracist scholars have often failed to acknowledge the considerable extent to which the objective of surplus labor grounds both cultural practices and social institutions. It is essential, therefore, that current realities we are witnessing in the national and international political arenas be understood in terms of their historical specificity and in terms of their functional imperatives for nation-states "administering a commodity-centered economy and its class-determining division of social labor" (San Juan, 2002). Despite the current rhetoric of positive nationalism, i.e., equal opportunity for all, these politics occlude both the racialized ideologies and economic interests of the capitalist class. But we also want to emphasize that we do not wish to limit counterhegemonic struggles against racism, patriarchy, and capitalist exploitation to a productivist framework of unilinear labor struggles involving the proletariat. Nor do we see the anti-globalization movement begun in Seattle as the global vanguard. Rather, we see current liberation struggles led not by the whitestream anti-capitalist vanguard, but by the world's most destitute: groups such as South Africa's *abantu abahlala emijondolo* (shackdweller movement) and the new movements of nondocumented workers throughout the world, including the United States.

A deepened understanding of the impact of global capitalism on aggrieved communities is essential for understanding the emergence of an acutely polarized labor market and the fact that disproportionately high percentages of people of color are trapped in the lower rungs of domestic and global labor markets. Difference in the era of global capitalism is crucial to the workings, movements, and profit levels of multinational corporations, but those types of complex relations cannot be mapped out without attending to capitalist class formations. Severing issues of difference from class analysis therefore conveniently draws attention away from the crucially important ways in which people of color (and more specifically women of color) provide capital with its superexploited labor pools—a phenomenon that is on the rise all over the world with the internationalization of migrant labor. In our call for a materialist analysis of the intersections of race, class, ethnicity, and gender, we are not arguing that proponents of cultural studies, post-Marxists or postcolonial theorists have all made their peace with capital, but they have exercised a "solidarity of defeat" insofar as they have limited their work to bad-faith reforms that have sidestepped the struggle against capital and pursued analysis compatible with the demands of neoliberal capitalism. Post-Marxists who are quick to celebrate the politics of difference, particularity, and historicity when they are discussing race quickly substitute these terms for those of universalizing, totalizing, or essentializing when they are discussing Marxist theory.

Joel Kovel (2002) has discussed the practice of prioritizing different categories of race, class, gender, species, etc., which he refers to as "dominative splitting." Kovel describes the process of establishing the priority of such categories as follows:

> Here we must ask, priority in relation to what? If we intend prior in time, then gender holds the laurel and, considering how history always adds to the past rather than replacing it, would appear as at least a trace in all further dominations. If we intend prior in existential significance, then that would apply to whichever of the categories was put forward by immediate historical forces as these are lived by masses of people: thus to a Jew living in Germany in the 1930s, anti-Semitism would have been searingly prior, just as anti-Arab racism would be to a Palestinian living under Israeli domination today, or a ruthless aggravated sexism would be to women living in, say, Afghanistan. As to which is politically prior, in the sense of being that which whose transformation is practically more urgent, that depends upon the preceding, but also upon the deployment of all the forces active in a concrete situation. . . . If, however, we ask the question of efficacy, that is, which split sets the others into motion, then priority would have to be given to class, for the plain reason that class relations entail the state as an instrument of enforcement and control, and it is the state that shapes and organizes the splits that appear in human ecosystems. (p. 123)

Kovel warns that we should not talk of "classism" to go along with "sexism," "racism," and "speciesism" because, he argues, "class is an essentially man-made category, without root in even a mystified biology." He maintains that historically the difference arises because "class"

> signifies one side of a larger figure that includes a state apparatus whose conquests and regulations create races and shape gender relations. Thus there will be no true resolution of racism so long as class society stands, inasmuch as a racially oppressed society implies the activities of a class-defending state. Nor can gender inequality be enacted away so long as class society, with its state, demands the super-exploitation of women. (pp. 123–124)

As I have acknowledged elsewhere (Scatamburlo-D'Annibale & McLaren, 2003, 2004), class is part of the "triptych formulation" that presumes to explain identity formation via intersecting relations of class, race, and gender in which people experientially locate themselves. Yet this formulation often reduces class to "classism" and fails to acknowledge its strategic centrality as a universal form of exploitation that provides the ground from which racialized and gendered social relations are produced. It fails to appreciate the conceptual fecundity of understanding race and racism within the context of class rule (which is not the same thing as reducing race and gender to class since the primacy of class most often means putting the fight against racism and sexism at the center of the struggle for socialism). That is to say, I stress the explanatory primacy of class for analyzing the structural determinants of race, gender, and class oppression (Meyerson, 2000). To reduce identity to the experience that people have of their race, class, and gender location is to fail to acknowledge the objective structures of inequality produced by specific historical forces that mediate the subjective understandings of both individuals and groups. It is similarly a failure to acknowledge that while relations of oppression on the basis of race, class, and gender invariably intersect, their causes can be effectively traced in capitalist societies to the social relations of production. It is necessary to acknowledge that most social relations constitutive of difference—including those of race, ethnicity, gender, etc.—are considerably shaped by the relations of production and that there is undoubtedly a racialized and gendered division of labor whose severity and function vary depending on where one is situated in the capitalist global economy.

That racism and sexism are necessary social relations of oppression for organizing contemporary capitalist formations (neocolonialist, fascist, imperialist, subimperialist) seems to escape the collective imaginations of those who theorize difference in a truncated and exclusively culturalist manner. (Of course, capitalism can also survive quite well in relations of relative gender and racial equality. Capitalism has, after all, been multiculturalized.) Indeed, we find it remarkable that so much of contemporary social theory, including strands of postcolonial theory (ostensibly concerned with marginalized peoples, i.e., the subaltern), have largely abandoned the problems of class, labor exploitation, and socialist struggle at a time when colonialism is reasserting itself in the form of global trade rules and structural adjustment programs.

The Birth Pangs of a New Social Movement

In the United States, an anti-immigration bill sponsored by Rep. James Sensenbrenner which criminalizes undocumented immigrants and makes living and working in the United States illegally a felony has outraged and angered many immigrant communities across the United States. A compromise bill, the Kennedy-McCain immigration bill, while an improvement, is little more than an echo of the "bracero" program of the 1940s, a binational temporary contract labor program initiated in 1942 by the United States and Mexico.

A Marxist analysis of race can be accused of ignoring, understating or even denigrating the importance of anti-racist struggle. In my recent work, I stress the *explanatory primacy* of class for analyzing the *structural determinants* of race, gender and class oppression. I attempt to highlight how class operates as a universal form of exploitation whose abolition is central to the abolition of all manifestations of oppression. One must abolish a class-defending state in order to make real headway in eliminating racism and patriarchy. I take the position that forms of oppression based on categories of difference do not possess relative autonomy from class relations but rather constitute the ways in which oppression is lived and experienced within a class-based system. It is important to specify how all forms of social oppression function within an overarching capitalist system. We must use a multipronged approach in our social struggle. We must choose to organize against racism, sexism, class oppression and white supremacy *simultaneously* as part of a larger anti-imperialist project directed towards the struggle for socialism. Forms of non-class domination such as racism must often be fought in advance of the class struggle. Certainly we cannot make headway in fighting class oppression without fighting racism and sexism. And clearly, racism and sexism must be fought against, despite whether or not we have traced their existence to capitalist relations of exploitation. In order for Euro-American workers to participate in their own class liberation, it's absolutely imperative that they reject in the strongest possible way the system of white-skin privilege. Marxists certainly shouldn't naturalize whiteness, nor should they simplify race by reducing it to class. At the same time, race is more than a social construct delinked from capitalist social relations of production.

At great personal risk, immigrants have taken part in a surge of protests against anti-immigration, transforming the political landscape in the United States. Millions are rallying against the government, asking important questions about the nature of this system and how they can participate in the fight for a better world. *Juntos en la lucha,* students and I marched together with over half a million immigrants, mostly from Mexico and other South and Central American countries during a day of protest that was billed "A Day Without Immigrants" and "The Great American Boycott." We walked four miles through Koreatown and the Mid-Wilshire district of downtown Los Angeles, to La Brea Avenue. We witnessed numerous signs that read "We are all immigrants" and "No human being is illegal." In a show of support, Seventh Street wholesale fruit stands, meatpacking plants, and garment factories closed down in order to allow their nondocumented employees to march. Elsewhere throughout the city, factories, restaurants, construction, landscaping, transportation, and many other industries and services ground to a halt. After noticing several signs that read, "Si por que soy Mexicano dicen que soy 'illegal' revisa la historia real pues estoy en mi tierra natal" ("If because I am Mexican they say that I am illegal, revisit the real history, I am in my native country"), we remembered the fact that for the past 156 years, the United States has occupied Mexico, and that even George W. Bush's ranch in Crawford, Texas, stands on stolen Mexican land. The Minutemen, a vigilante citizen group that hunts immigrants along the border with Mexico (which Mexicans call "la linea" or "the line"), have already set off on a cross-country trek through rural and ur-ban communities in Arizona, New Mexico, Texas, Arkansas, Tennessee, Georgia, Alabama, and Virginia. Some Minutemen have sported T-shirts with the emblem "Kill a Mexican today?" and others have organized "for profit" human safaris in the desert (Robinson, 2006). Jim Gilchrist, the pugnacious and brawny founder, wears a bulletproof vest in addition to having three or more bodyguards nearby at all times. Yet while clearly trying to inspire fear among undocumented workers, Minutemen are being challenged by crowds chanting: "¡Bush escucha! ¡Estamos en la lucha!" and "¡El pueblo unido jamás será vencido!" ("Bush listen up! We are in struggle!" and "The people united will never be defeated!").

While conservative politicians and the unprincipled pettifoggers who work for them no longer are speaking of conquering land, resources, and/or people adjacent to the southwest U.S. border, they nevertheless view themselves and the Anglo-American constituencies they represent as living at the cusp of an inevi-table "brown wave" of immigration that could wash over them inexorably and extinguish their identities. Consequently, there is a strong emphasis on national-ism and the acculturation and assimilation of Latina/os to the American Way of Life. The American way of life reinforces the self-validating attributes of gender, kinship or parentage, skin color, and the naturalizing markers demarcating them from the subjugated and subordinated peoples, thereby serving as a functioning principle of the imperial nation-state, one that seeks an "asymmetrical distribu-tion of social wealth and power" (San Juan, 2002, p. 93). According to E. San Juan, the object of nationalism signifies a community "just like us" which is in-extricably linked to the nation-state's formation of classes and social groups. San Juan elaborates on this position by unfolding the core roots of American national identity. He asserts that the development of American "patria" takes place along two primary dimensions: the systematic inclusion and exclusion of certain seg-ments of the population, and the political management of social life forms ac-cording to the hierarchization of morals and codes of conduct (p. 93). These identity formations are made manifest across multiple dimensions. The media, the electorate, pop culture, and education work symbiotically to sustain and pro-liferate hegemonic interpretations of what it means to be "American." Tensions do arise, however, when such formations are threatened by dramatic demographic shifts in the population that no longer are able to secure a static or unyielding social configuration. It is precisely when the geopolitical landscape becomes destabilized that we witness an inversion in dominant discourses. The "colonizers" claim to be the "colonized" and consequently, a spate of systematic and sustained political initiatives make their way into the legislative body as a necessary precaution or defense against the inclusion of "other" cultural arrangements.

We must work against neoliberal economic imperialism that, on the one hand, creates the need for cheap, exploitable, and deportable labor, and that on the other creates the conditions that cause the displacement of workers worldwide and which, in the context of the United States, encourages the formerly privileged sectors of the White working class to engage in the most repugnant forms of racism and to scapegoat immigrants of color. And we struggle against conditions that allow nondocumented immigrants to be deported, because the threat of deportation is the club that employers hold over the heads of nondocumented workers to keep them in a condition of dependency and helps to ensure their silence in the process of their superexploitation (Amoo-Adare, in press). An op-ed in the *Wall Street Journal* received widespread attention when Shelby Steele, an African American neoconservative scholar from Stanford University's Hoover Institute, lamented that the U.S. allows itself to be hampered in its foreign policy objectives by the paralysis of White guilt. Such guilt, claimed Steele, is the engine that drives anti-Americanism, which in turn is a "construct of Western sin." Steele described White guilt as a "vacuum of moral authority visited on the present by the shames of the past." He believes such guilt was spawned after the "collapse of white supremacy as a source of moral authority, political legitimacy and even sovereignty," which according to Steele occurred sometime after World War II. But a price was exacted—"a kind of secular penitence in which the slightest echo of past sins brings down withering condemnation." As "the greatest embodiment of Western power," the United States is, according to Steele, currently stigmatized as an ugly imperialist and racist regime because it cannot dissociate itself from its past sins.

Steele writes that "White guilt makes our Third World enemies into colored victims, people whose problems—even the tyrannies they live under—were created by the historical disruptions and injustices of the white West. We must 'understand' and pity our enemy even as we fight him." Consequently, White guilt forces us to fight Islamic extremism with "managerial minimalism" detached from the "passions of war." The argument that the United States fights its wars in a minimalist fashion and does not have "enough ferocity to win" is one that we find difficult to swallow, especially when you consider the brutal and sweeping ruthlessness of its military campaigns over the last half century. We suppose Steele would like the military to act with a type of dispassionate passion, a cold, calculated killing machine able to ratchet up the kill ratio of its troops without so much as a twinge of White guilt. Perhaps along with blasting limbs from bodies, the military could also blast away any of the coordinates of reason that might be holding back its troops, unhinging the gates of our White conscience for the sake of a morally frictionless annihilation of the enemy—murder with an excess of efficiency. Steele would like us not to have a second thought about why we are killing so many people of color and why we are attacking so many nations of non-Christians or those who might have a different opinion about the free market than American business leaders. Steele also uses his theory of White guilt to explain why we are so impotent in "truly regulating the southern border" against illegal immigrants.

Reflections on Educating Inside the Beast

Here, in the world's imperial heartland, education has become an epicenter of debate over the meaning of citizenship and the role and status of the United States in world history. Science is under attack in the high schools; theories of evolution are being challenged by those of creationism and intelligent design, and privatization is destroying what is left of public schools.

An emphasis on testing resulting in a teaching-to-the-test mania, strict accountability schemes, prepackaged and scripted teaching for students of color, and a frenetic push towards more standardized testing—what Kozol refers to as "desperation strategies that have come out of the acceptance of inequality" (2005, p. 51)—has been abundantly present since the mid-1990s. But what has this trend produced? As Jonathan Kozol points out, the achievement gap between Black and White children has substantially widened since the early 1990s, about the same time as we began to witness the growing resegregation of schools (when the courts began to disregard the mandates of the *Brown* decision). This has led to what Kozol calls "apartheid schooling." Kozol reports that in 48% of high schools in the country's largest districts (those that have the highest concentrations of Black and Latina/o students), less than half of the entering ninth graders graduate in 4 years. There was a 75% increase between 1993–2002 in the number of high schools graduating less than half of their ninth-grade class in 4 years. In the 94% of districts in New York State where the majority of the students are White, nearly 80% of students graduate from high school in 4 years. In the 6% of districts where Black and Latina/o students make up the majority, the percentage is considerably less—approximately 40%. There are 120 high schools in New York (enrolling nearly 200,000 minority students) where, Kozol notes, less than 60% of entering ninth graders make it to the twelfth grade. This statistic prompted Kozol to exclaim: "There is something deeply hypocritical about a society that holds an eight-year-old innercity child 'accountable' for her performance on a high-stakes standardized exam but does not hold the high officials of our government accountable for robbing her of what they gave their own kids six or seven years earlier" (p. 46).

Reflections on Our Providential History

The history of the United States is deeply providential. The increasing ranks of Americans who profess to serve no other king but Jesus see themselves as moral stewards of a country preordained by God to save humanity. Besotted with the White man's burden of uplifting the ignorant masses of the third world so that they might join the ranks of the civilized, evangelical Christians (including and perhaps especially those "power puritans" and "opportunistic ayatollahs" who serve at the helm of the Bush administration) betray a Messianic vision rooted in bad theology, rapture politics, and the covenant God has apparently made with consecutive White House administrations throughout history (no doubt more favourably rewarding Republican administrations).

With so many professed Christians braying about how important moral values are in the United States, it might come as a surprise that in 2004, as a share of our economy, we ranked second to last, after Italy, among developed countries in government foreign aid. Per capita we each provide fifteen cents a day to official development assistance to poor countries. And it's not because we were giving to private charities for relief work instead. Such funding increases our average daily donation by just six pennies, to twenty-one cents. It's also not because Americans were too busy taking care of their own, nearly 18 percent of American children lived in poverty (compared with, say, 8 percent in Sweden). In fact, by pretty much any measure of caring for the least among us you want to propose—we come in nearly last among the rich nations, and often by a wide margin. The point is that (as everyone already knows) the American nation trails badly in all these categories, categories to which Jesus paid particular attention. And it's not as if the numbers are getting better: the U.S. Department of Agriculture reported last year that the number of households that were "food insecure with hunger" had climbed more than 26 percent between 1999 and 2003. (McKibben, 2005, p. 32).

The attack by right-wing law makers on public schools is in part a condemnation of ungodly secular humanism that is seen as robbing the moral authority of the state of its imprimatur granted by God. The same callow calculus cloaked in a sacred rage has had a hand in defining what is to be considered unpatriotic and anti-American, especially after September 11, 2001. What we may see in so-called progressive, critical classrooms throughout the United States is not a pedagogy steeled in opposition to oppression, but rather an ersatz critical pedagogy, a domesticated approach to Freirean teaching that stresses the centrality of engaging student experiences and histories. This situation provokes the following sempiternal questions: Are these histories and experiences self-evident? If not, how are the histories of the oppressed written, and who writes them? How are experiences interpreted, and whose interpretation counts the most? What languages of critique are employed at understanding the formation of student subjectivities?

What languages of possibility? Experiences, after all, are the "effects" of discursive regimes which, in turn, are given birth in a vortex of contending social forces, cultural formations, linguistic fields, ideological structures, institutional formations, and which are overdetermined by social relations of production.

Those pedagogies that affirm (through dominant narratives and discourses that unproblematically valorize democracy and freedom) student experiences but fail to question how these experiences are produced conjecturally in the formation of subjectivity and agency, accept a priori the sovereignty of the market over the body politic; and this, in turn, helps to resecure a pliant submission to the capitalist law of value. And they are often the soft-focus pedagogies of the give-advantage-to-the-already-advantaged, self-empowerment variety. These dominant pedagogies systematically negate rather than make meaningful alternative understandings of the relationship between identity-formation and social relations of production. They are not only reflective but also productive and reproductive of antagonistic social relations, dependent hierarchies of power, and privilege and hegemonic strategies of containing dissent and opposition.

Reflections on a Pedagogy for Life: Paulo Freire in Urgent Times

Motivated by a desire to anchor their students in a coherent worldview and provide them with an enduring stability, teachers especially become an easily breached conduit for the official narratives of the state, whether these be providential, imperialist, triumphalist, capitalist, or a combination of all of these. The moral panic surrounding the meaning of patriotism in the post-9/11 United States has produced confusion among teachers and students alike—proclivities easily leveraged by the Bush administration through the corporate media that amplify, echo, mirror, and appease official government narratives at times of national crisis. Loyalty to the office of the President, to the troops fighting our imperialist wars, and to whatever laws have been put in to place to protect us from the hirsute terrorists has become the highest desideratum.

For over a century, the U.S. government has intervened both forcibly and covertly to topple the governments of numerous countries, including Nicaragua, Guatemala, the Philippines, Panama, South Vietnam, and Chile. For instance, to cite just one of dozens of examples, when the U.S. overthrew Jacobo Arbenz, the left-leaning president of Guatemala, and imposed a military regime, a 30-year civil war ensued in which hundreds of thousands died. One reason that you find some of the most open political rebellions against U.S. policies in Latin America is because this is a region where the U.S. has frequently intervened and where populations have been brutally victimized as a result. It should come as no surprise that South America has become the site from which some of the most prescient analyses of U.S. imperialism and capitalist exploitation have been developed.

At this moment in history, the work of Paulo Freire threatens to explode the culture of silence that informs our everyday life as educators in the world's greatest imperialist democracy, a key overarching saga of which has been the successful dismantling of public schooling by the juggernaut of neoliberal globalization and the corporatization of the public sphere. As critical pedagogy's conscience-in-exile, Freire sought through the pedagogical encounter to foist off the tyranny of authoritarianism and oppression and bring about an all-embracing and diverse fellowship of global citizens profoundly endowed with a fully claimed humanity. Yet instead of heeding a Freirean call for a multivocal public and international dialogue on our responsibility as the world's sole superpower, one that acknowledges that we as a nation are also changed by our relationship to the way we treat others, we have permitted a fanatical cabal of politicians to convince us that dialogue is weakness, an obstacle to peace, that probity is a trait that is secondary to achieving "results," and univocal assertion is a strength. I have taken inspiration for my work from Paulo Freire, and I, like many other educators, have spoken out—and continue to speak out—against acts of imperialist aggression by the United States government. I have done so in numerous books, articles, and speeches over the past 30 years. The broader context for these writings has been my work in critical pedagogy that involves, among other things, publishing critiques of mainstream educational policy and practice and revealing how such policy and practice are underwritten by the politics of neoliberal capitalist globalization. I have also engaged in anticapitalist, antiracist and antiimperialist activism as part of my ongoing struggle for a socialist alternative to capitalism.

Those who live and write a critical pedagogy are open to attack by both right-wing and liberal critics. I have been challenging the efforts of right-wing politicians and conservative social critics who are attempting to pass a bill in various state legislatures throughout the United States that, under the pretext of establishing political neutrality in the classroom, is designed to curtail the rights of professors in universities to speak out against social and political injustice. Right-wing critics charge that professors like me, who follow a Freirean example, "indoctrinate" students with left-wing propaganda. If passed, "The Academic Bill of Rights"will expressly forbid professors from using the classroom to supposedly "propagandize" their views. In other words, the classroom will become even more of a politically contested site than it is at present, with neoconservatives trying to shut down critical dialogue surrounding initiatives of right-wing politicians. There are many educators who have put themselves at greater risk in their attempts to resist injustice in various educational arenas, and that underscores the rabid intensity of the right in their assault on critical approaches to teaching and learning. Charges of indoctrinating students were addressed by Paulo Freire, specifically in his magisterial book, *Pedagogy of Hope* (1994), and they serve as an excellent resource for teachers, especially those in the United States who are being labeled as "traitors" and "supporters of terrorism" because they use the classroom as forums for critical dialogue about the war in Iraq and other controversial issues. It is important for teachers to return to the work of an educator who we still use as a compass for our pedagogical life, a life that does not end when the door to the classroom is closed for the day, but one which we have integrated into our hearts and minds, and adapted to the everyday rhythm of our lives. Freire observes that educational practice reveals a "helplessness to be 'neutral'" (1994, p. 77). There is, Freire argues, no "educational practice in zero space-time" (1994, p. 77); that is, there is no neutral practice. This is because educators are disposed to be ethical agents engaged in educative practice that is directive, political, and indeed has a preference. Freire writes that as an educator, he must "live a life full of consistency between my democratic option and my educational practice, which is likewise democratic" (1994, p. 79). He agrees that we find authoritarianism on both the right and the left of the political spectrum. Both groups can be reactionary in an "identical way" if they "judge themselves the proprietors of knowledge, the former, of revolutionary knowledge, the latter, of conservative knowledge" (1994, p. 79). Both forms of authoritarianism are elitist. Freire underscores the fact that we cannot "conscientize" students without at the same time being "conscientized" by them as well. Teaching should never, under any circumstances, be a form of imposition. On the other hand, we cannot shrink from our democratic duty and fear to teach because of manipulation. We always run this risk and must do so willingly, as a necessary act, as a leap across a dialectical divide that is necessary for any act of knowing to occur.

This is why critical educators stress the idea of the hidden curriculum as a way of self-examination, of remaining coherent, of remaining tolerant and at the same time of becoming critically disposed in their teaching. As Freire reminds us, tolerance breeds openness and critical disposition breeds curiosity and humility. Knowing is a type of dance—a movement but a self-conscious one. Criticality is not a line stretching into eternity; it is a circle. In other words, knowing can be the object of our knowing, it can be self-reflective, and it is something in which we can make an intervention. We inherit cognition as a species, but we acquire other skills along the way, and we need to grow integrally and with coherence. Freire reminds us that teaching cannot be reduced to the one-way transmission of the object of knowledge, or a two-way transaction between the teacher and the student but is rather a form of dialectical transformation of both the teacher and the student, and this occurs when a teacher knows the content of what is to be taught and a student learns how to learn. Teaching occurs when educators recognize their knowing in the knowing of the students. Freire argues that teachers must challenge students to move beyond their commonsense beliefs and assumptions regarding their self-in-the-world and their self-with-the-world, but must do so by respecting the commonsense knowledge that students bring into the classroom. Freire notes: "What is impermissible—I repeat myself, now—is disrespect for the knowledge of common sense. What is impermissible is the attempt to transcend it without starting with it and proceeding by way of it" (1994, p. 83). Yet at the same time we have a duty to challenge students' feelings of certainty about their own experiential knowledge. Freire asks:

> What kind of educator would I be if I did not feel moved by a powerful impulse to seek, without lying, convincing arguments in defense of the dreams for which I struggle, in defense of the "why" of the hope with which I act as an educator? What is not permissible to be doing is to conceal truths, deny information, impose principles, eviscerate the educands of their freedom, or punish them, no matter by what method, if, for various reasons, they fail to accept my discourse—reject my utopia. (1994, p. 83)

Freire makes it clear that we reject a "focalist" approach to students' experiential knowledge and approach a student's experiential knowledge contextually, inserting our respect for such knowledge "into the larger horizon against which it is generated—the horizon of cultural context, which cannot be understood apart from its class particularities, and this indeed in societies so complex that the characterization of those particularities is less easy to come by" (1994, p. 85). Students' experiences must be understood within the contextual and historical specificities in which such experiences are produced. They must be read dialectically against the larger totality in which they are generated. For Freire, the regional emerges from the local; the national emerges from the regional; the continental emerges from the national, and the worldwide emerges from the continental. He warns: "Just as it is a mistake to get stuck in the local, losing our vision of the whole, so also it is a mistake to waft above the whole, renouncing any reference to the local when the whole has emerged" (1994, p. 87). We are universalists, yes, because we struggle for universal human rights, for economic justice worldwide, but we begin from somewhere, from concrete spaces and places where subjectivities are forged and commodified (and, we hope, decommodified), and where critical agency is developed in particular and distinct ways. And when Freire speaks of struggling to build a utopia, he is speaking of a concrete as opposed to an abstract utopia, a utopia grounded in the present, always operating "from the tension between the *de*nunciation of a present becoming more and more intolerable, and the '*an*nunciation,' announcement, of a future to be created, built—politically, esthetically, and ethically—by us women and men" (1994, p. 91). Utopias are always in motion; they are never pregiven, they never exist as blueprints which would only ensure the "mechanical repetition of the present," but rather they exist within the movement of history itself, as opportunity and not as determinism. They are never guaranteed.

While it is vitally important that we, as educators, never underestimate knowledge produced from our daily, commonsense experience (since such a rejection of popular knowledge amounts to a form of nearsightedness that is sectarian, elitist, and that occasions epistemological error), by the same token it is important not to engage in the "mythification of popular knowledge, its superexaltation" (p. 84). And while it is important to dream of a better world—since dreaming is "a necessary political act, it is an integral part of the historico-social manner of being a person. . . part of human nature, which, within history, is in permanent process of becoming" (pp. 90–91)—we need to remember that "there is no dream without hope." Critical educators are in the process of creating their own dreams of a world that is arching towards social and economic justice and can see those dreams reflected in the mirror of Freire's pedagogical dream, one that is inspired by a hope born of political struggle and a belief in the ability of the oppressed to transform the world from "what is" to "what could be," to reimagine, re-enchant, and recreate the world rather than adapt to it. The reverse mirror image of this dream is the one that drives the "neutral" pedagogy that neoconservatives are struggling to bring about in the United States. Pressuring professors to be silent about politics in their classrooms by threat of legal action is itself an abridgement of academic freedom; it is an attempt to remove politics from the classroom by means of imposing politics—and a narrow politics, I might add—on the education process itself. Academic freedom means freedom from having my curriculum scrutinized by a political act of adjudication, by the establishment of some crude political scale from "liberal" to "conservative" that actually prevents critical knowledge from thriving.

Neoconservative educators in the United States defend the freedom to choose to be poor or rich, the freedom to be sick or healthy, the freedom to vote or not to vote—but truly free choice is a choice in which I do not merely choose between two or more options presented to me on a grid preapproved by legislative fiat. Rather, it is the freedom to change the very grid in which those choices are lodged. That is what the concept of freedom means in the practice of critical pedagogy, in the struggle for social justice. And that is what makes Freire's work so important, as important today as it ever was—perhaps even more. Possibly the greatest reproach that Freire addressed to the authoritarian culture of his time concerned the devitalization and devaluation of human life; the fragmentation and commodification of subjectivity; and the erection of barriers to freely associated labor, joyful participation in social relations, and the self-development of the subject—an indictment that we must extend to all of capitalist society. It would be difficult for progressive educators in the United States not to interpret Freire's message as a call to overthrow the political curates with whom most Americans took refuge after

9/11, priests of disorder who dragged the country deep into some sulfuric swamp-land populated by church-going elementals and hairy-knuckled demons clutch-ing Bibles—an inferno fit for politicians that even Dante could not imagine. It is surely striking how Freire's eviscerating pedagogical commentary, by planting the seed of catharsis and thereby placing in our hands the responsibility to overcome the political amnesia that has become the hallmark of contemporary teaching, cannot be officially welcomed into the classrooms of our nation by the guardians of the state. For they have witnessed the unnerving intimacy and camaraderie Freire was able to forge among his admirers worldwide and the extent to which they were challenged by the disseminating force of his liberatory language of hope and possibility. And while teacher education programs have not been able to root him out of the philosophy of teaching, they have cannily managed to domesticate his presence. They have done this by transforming the political revolutionary with Marxist ideas into a friendly sage who advocates a love of dialogue, separating this notion from that of a dialogue of love. Hence, the importance of reclaiming Paulo Freire for these urgent times. Freire was critical of teachers who, while turning their podiums in the direction of history, refused to leave their seminar rooms in order to shape it.

Of particular significance for teachers is Freire's last book, *Teachers as Cultural Workers: Letters to Those Who Dare Teach.* It is significant because it serves as an exhortation to a mindfulness of where we are going as educators, of what kind of world we are living in, of what kind of world we would like to see in its place. I would like to reflect upon some of the themes of this book as a way of addressing the challenge we face as citizens in a desperate and uncertain future. One of the central themes is the importance of a pedagogy powered by love. For Freire, love is preeminently and irrevocably dialogical. It is not an attachment or emotion isolated from the everyday world; it viscerally emerges from an act of daring, of courage, of critical reflection. Love is not only the fire that ignites the revolution-ary but also the creative action of the artist, wielding a palette of sinew and spirit on a canvas of thought and action, its explosion of meaning forever synchronized with the gasp of human freedom. Freire writes:

> We must dare in the full sense of the word, to speak of love without the fear of being called ridiculous, mawkish, or unscientific, if not antiscientific. We must dare in order to say scientifically, and not as mere blah-blah-blah, that we study, we learn, we teach, we know with our entire body. We do all of these things with feeling, with emotion, with wishes, with fear, with doubts, with passion, and also with critical reasoning. (1998, p. 3)

On the topic of love, Freire also writes:

To the humility with which teachers perform and relate to their students another quality needs to be added: *lovingness*, without which their work would lose its meaning. And here I mean lovingness not only toward the students but also toward the very process of teaching. I must confess, not meaning to cavil, that I do not believe educators can survive the negativities of their trade without some sort of "armed love," as the poet Tiago de Melo would say. Without it they could not survive all the injustice or the government's contempt, which is expressed in the shameful wages and the arbitrary treatment of teachers, not coddling mothers, who take a stand, who participate in protest activities through their union, who are punished, and who yet remain devoted to their work with students. It is indeed necessary, however, that this love be an "armed love," the fighting love of those convinced of the right and the duty to fight, to denounce, and to announce. It is this form of love that is indispensable to the progressive educator and that we must all learn. (1998, pp. 40–41)

In addition to the quality of lovingness, Freire adds to the characteristics of the progressive teacher those of humility, courage, tolerance, decisiveness, security, the tension between patience and impatience, joy of living, and verbal parsimony, often inflecting some of these terms with nuance and poetic meaning. For instance, Freire denotes humility as the characteristic of admitting that you don't know everything; for critical citizens it represents a "human duty" to listen to those considered less competent without condescension, a practice intimately identified with the struggle for democracy and a distain for elitism. Another example is that of tolerance. For Freire, tolerance is not understood as "acquiescing to the intolerable" or "coexistence with the intolerable" nor does it mean "coddling the oppressor" or "disguising aggression." Freire claims that tolerance "is the virtue that teaches us to live with the different. It teaches us to learn from and respect the different." Freire elaborates:

On an initial level, tolerance may almost seem to be a favor, as if being tolerant were a courteous, thoughtful way of accepting, of *tolerating,* the not-quite-desired presence of one's opposite, a civilized way of permitting a coexistence that might seem repugnant. That, however, is hypocrisy, not tolerance. Hypocrisy is a defect; it is degradation. Tolerance is a virtue. Thus if I live tolerance, I should embrace it. I must experience it as something that makes me coherent first with my historical being, inconclusive as that may sound, and second with my democratic political choice. I cannot see how one might be democratic without experiencing tolerance, coexistence with the different, as a fundamental principle. (1998, p. 42)

Freire's dialectics of the concrete (to borrow a phrase from Marxist philosopher Karil Kosik) is very unlike the methodology of the educational postmodernists who, in their artful counterposing of the familiar and the strange in order to deconstruct the unified subject of bourgeois humanism, mock the pieties of monologic authoritarianism with sportive saber slashes across the horizon of familiarity and consensus. Whereas postmodern "resistance" results in a playful hemorrhaging of certainty, a spilling forth of fixed meanings into the submerged grammars of bourgeois society, remixed in the sewers of the social as "resistance" and rematerialized in the art-house jargon of fashionable apostasy, Freire's work retains an unshakable modernist faith in human agency consequent upon language's ineradicable sociality and dialogical embeddedness. What Freire does have in common with the postmodernists, however, is a desire to break free of contemporary discourses that domesticate both the heart and mind. He is not content to remain with the postmodernists in the nocturnal world of the subconscious; rather, he is compelled to take his critical pedagogy to the streets of the real. Freire writes:

> To the extent that I become clearer about my choices and my dreams, which are substantively political and attributively pedagogical, and to the extent that I recognize that though an educator I am also a political agent, I can better understand why I fear and realize how far we still have to go to improve our democracy. I also understand that as we put into practice an education that critically provokes the learner's consciousness, we are necessarily working against myths that deform us. As we confront such myths, we also face the dominant power because those myths are nothing but the expression of this power, of its ideology. (1998, p. 41)

Ultimately, Freire's work is about establishing a critical relationship between pedagogy and politics, highlighting the political aspects of the pedagogical and drawing attention to the implicit and explicit domain of the pedagogical inscribed in the political. While Freire extolled the virtues of socialism and drew substantively from various Marxist traditions, he was also critical of dogmatic, doctrinaire Marxists whom he saw as intolerant and authoritarian. In fact, he chastised the practice of some "mechanistic Marxists" whom he claimed believed "that because it is part of society's superstructure, education has no role to play before the society is radically transformed in its infrastructure, in its material conditions" (1998, p. 67). In fact, Freire argues that by refusing to take education seriously as a site of political transformation and by opposing socialism to democracy, the mechanistic Marxists have, in effect, delayed the realization of socialism for our times. Political choices and ideological paths chosen by teachers are the fundamental stuff of Freirean pedagogy. Freire goes so far as to say that educators "are politicians" and that "we engage in politics when we educate" (1998, p. 68). And if it is the case that we must choose a political path, then let us, in Freire's words, "dream about democracy" while fighting "day and night, for a school in which we talk to and with the learners so that, hearing them, we can be heard by them as well" (1998, p. 68). This is the central challenge of Freire's work and one that, especially at this difficult time in world history, requires a dauntless courage, a hopeful vision, and a steadfast commitment as we struggle within and against these troubling times.

Reflections on a Revolutionary Socialist Pedagogy

On a recent trip to Caracas, Venezuela, to support the Bolivarian revolution, I had the opportunity to reflect upon what a socialist pedagogy might mean for the deepening development of a Freirean-based critical pedagogy. At Miraflores Palace, President Hugo Chavez offered me and my colleague some brief words of hope. Initially he cautioned us that a monster was living in Washington, a monster that has been a disaster for the entire world; in order to bring about a better world we must remain united in our attempts to defeat this monster. While thanking us for the pedagogical work we have been doing, he nevertheless implored us to work harder, and to be inspired by the example of the Bolivarian revolution. By enfranchising Venezuela's vast working class through an attack on neoliberalism and by channeling increased oil revenues into social projects aimed at increasing educational opportunities and medical treatment for the poor, Chavez is creating the conditions of possibility for a robust push towards socialism. Two thirds of the population of Venezuela who voted for Chavez did so with an understanding that he intends to build socialism of the 21st century. Chavez is working towards Latin American integration to defeat the Monroe Doctrine and he is getting more control of economic sectors. Chavez seeks an integration of the continent and a "complementation" of economies. A few days later we were present at a taping of *Aló Presidente*, Chavez's weekly television address to the people of Venezuela, and were sitting next to the great Nicaraguan poet of the revolution, Ernesto Cardenal. Responding to an attempt by President Chavez to imagine a new relationship of solidarity and anti-imperialist struggle between people of good will in the United States and those in Venezuela, Cardenal called President Chavez a prophet who was proclaiming a desire for a mystical union among people from opposing nations based on love:

> Mr. President, you have said some things that are very important and moreover are also prophetic . . . when I was a monk my teacher prophesized that one day the people of the United States and the people of Latin America were going to unite but not with an economic union, nor political, nor military, but a mystic union, of love, of two peoples (or nations) loving each other. I have now heard this from you and I want this to be revealed because it is something that hasn't been heard. I have heard it from my teacher and now you have made it a prophecy. [translated by Nathalia Jaramillo]

How Freirean, indeed!

We were impressed by the Bolivian Missions. These missions consist of anti-poverty and social welfare programs. We were fortunate to be able to visit many of them. In one year, the Chavez government was able to graduate 1.43 million Venezuelans from Mission Robinson, a program launched in June 2003. Volunteers who worked for Mission Robinson teach reading, writing, and arithmetic to illiterate adults using the Yo Si Puedo (Yes I Can) method developed in Cuba. This method uses a combination of video classes and texts which, in only seven weeks, brings students to a basic literacy level. Indigenous peoples are taught to read and write in Spanish and in their own languages, in line with the indigenous rights outlined in the 1999 Bolivian Constitution, Articles 199, 120 and 121 (Mission Robinson International has just been launched in Bolivia). Mission Robinson II provides basic education up to the sixth grade and Mission Robinson III teaches functional literacy and links these efforts to the creation of production units. Mission Ribas, a two-year remedial secondary school program (it teaches Spanish, mathematics, world geography, Venezuelan economics, world history, Venezuelan history, English, physics, chemistry, biology and computer science), targets five million Venezuelan dropouts. This program has a Community and Social-labor Component, where groups use their personal experience and their learning to develop practical proposals to solve community problems. I was fortunate enough to join in a group discussion of this component of the program in Barrio La Vega and was especially impressed with the efforts of students to design a day care center. Unemployed graduates of Mission Ribas (known as "lanceros") are encouraged to enroll in Mission Vuelvan Caras (About Face), where they receive training in endogenous development, and are eventually incorporated into the formal economy. Mission Sucre provides a scholarship program in higher education to the most impoverished sectors of Venezuela, graduating university professionals in three years as opposed to the traditional five years. Our work in an international think-tank based in Caracas, Centro International Miranda, has six areas of focus in helping to further the Bolivarian revolution. One of these areas is critical pedagogy. What is needed now are pedagogies that connect the language of students' everyday experiences to the larger struggle for autonomy and social justice carried out by groups in pursuit of genuine democracy and freedom outside of capital's law of value, organizations working towards building socialist communities of the future. That is something taught by Bolivarian educators who are struggling to build a socialist future in a country deeply divided by class antagonisms.

In our pursuit of locally rooted, self-reliant economies; in our struggles designed to defend the world from being forced to serve as a market for corporate globalists; in our attempts at decolonizing our cultural and political spaces and places of livelihood; in our fight for antitrust legislation for the media; in our challenges to replace indirect social labor (labor mediated by capital) with direct social labor; in our quest to live in balance with nature; and in our various efforts to replace our dominant culture of materialism with values integrated in a life economy, we need to develop a new vision of the future, but one that does not stray into abstract utopian hinterlands too far removed from our analysis of the present barbarism wrought by capital. Our vision of the future must go beyond the present but still be rooted in it; it must exist in the plane of immanence, and not some transcendent sphere where we engage in mystical union with the inhabitants of Mount Olympus. It must attempt to "speak the unspeakable" while remaining organically connected to the familiar and the mundane. We cannot deny the presence of the possible in the contradictions we live out daily in the messy realm of capital. We seek, therefore, a concrete utopia where the subjunctive world of the "ought to be" can be wrought within the imperfect, partial, defective, and finite world of the "what is" by the dialectical act of absolute negation. Not only must we understand our needs and our capacities—with the goal of satisfying the former and fully developing the latter—but we need to express them in ways that will encourage new cultural formations, institutional structures, and social relations of production that can best help meet those needs and nurture those capacities to the fullest through democratic participation. Equally important is realizing, through our self-activity and subjective self-awareness and formation, that socialism is a collective enterprise that recognizes humankind's global interdependence, that respects diversity while at the same time building unity and solidarity. These very principles underlay the ongoing work in Venezuela's literacy and educational programs taking place in the barrios. Meeting several of the leaders and coordinators of these programs in Barrio La Vega, Sector B, emphasized for me the importance of working towards socialism as an endpoint but not in some teleological sense. Rather, the struggle could best be animated by the words of Antonio Machado's (1962, p. 826) poem: "Caminante no hay camino, se hace el camino al andar" ("Traveler, there is no road. The road is made as one walks").

Michael Lebowitz (2005) talks about the possibility of "another kind of knowledge" that might exist in a world that is able to transcend capitalism—a socialist world. He urges us to think about what it would be like to operate in a world by means of a direct social knowledge that cannot be communicated through the indirect medium of money: a knowledge tacitly based upon recognition of our unity and solidarity:

> It is a different knowledge when we are aware of who produces for us and how, when we understand the conditions of life of others and the needs they have for what we can contribute. Knowledge of this type immediately places us as beings within society, provides an understanding of the basis of all our lives. It is immediately direct social knowledge because it cannot be communicated through the indirect medium of money. (p. 64)

This is a knowledge, affirms Lebowitz, "which differs qualitatively and quantitatively from the knowledge we have under dominant social relations" (p. 65). It is different precisely because knowledge is no longer treated as a scarce commodity; there is no longer a monopolization and restriction on knowledge as private gain. This type of knowledge, writes Lebowitz, has to be based on certain values; values that are, he notes, enshrined in the Constitution of the Bolivarian Republic of Venezuela, especially Article 299 that is based on "ensuring overall human development"; Article 20, which stipulates that "everyone has the right to the free development of his or her own personality"; and Article 102, where the focus is upon "developing the creative potential of every human being and the full exercise of his or her personality in a democratic society" (pp. 66–67). Such development can only occur through participation (as set out in Article 62) in democratic social formations that enable self-management, co-management, and cooperation in many forms (as set out in Article 70). Lebowitz's example of Venezuela and its Constitution is a good one, and one that critical educators everywhere would do well to consider for deepening their approach to their own particular struggles.

Reflections on Critical Pedagogy for a Better Society

We are currently living in what Antonio Gramsci called a "war of position"—a struggle to unify diverse social movements in our collective efforts to resist global capitalism—in order to wage what he called "a war of maneuver"; that is, a concerted effort to challenge and transform the state, to create an alternative matrix for society other than value. Part of our war of position is taking place in our schools. While there is much talk about labor today, and the decline of the labor movement, what is important for educators to keep in mind is the *social form that labor takes*. In capitalist societies, that social form is human capital. Schools are charged with educating a certain form of human capital, with socially producing labor power, and in doing so enhancing specific attributes of labor power that serve the interests of capital. In other words, schools educate the labor-power needs of capital—for capital in general, for the national capital, for fractions of capital (manufacturing, finance, services, etc.), for sectors of capital (particular industries, etc.), or for individual capital (specific companies and enterprises, etc.); they also educate for functions of capital that cut across these categories of capital. General education, for instance, is intentionally divorced from labor-power attributes required to work within individual capitals and is aimed at educating for capital in general. Practical education tries to shape labor-power attributes in the direction of skills needed within specific fractions or sectors of capital. Training, on the other hand, involves educating for labor-power attributes that will best serve specific or individual capitals (Rikowski, 2005).

It is important to note that Rikowski has described capital not only as the subsumption of concrete, living labor by abstract alienated labor but also as a mode of being, as a unified social force that flows through our subjectivities, our bodies, our meaning-making capacities. Schools educate labor power by serving as a medium for its constitution or its social production in the service of capital. But schools are more than this; they do more than nourish labor power because all of capitalist society accomplishes that. In addition to producing capital in general, schools additionally *condition* labor power in the varying interests of the market-place. But because labor power is a living commodity, and a highly contradictory one at that, it can be reeducated and shaped in the interests of building socialism; that is, in creating opportunities for the self-emancipation of the working class. Labor power, as the capacity or potential to labor, doesn't have to serve its current master—capital. It serves the master only when it engages in *the act of laboring for a wage.* Because individuals can refuse to labor in the interests of capital accumulation, labor power can therefore serve another cause—the cause of socialism. Critical pedagogy can be used as a means of finding ways of transcending the contradictory aspects of labor-power creation and creating different spaces where a dereification, decommodification, and decolonization of subjectivity can occur. Critical pedagogy is an agonistic arena where the development of a discerning political subjectivity can be fashioned (recognizing that there will always be socially and self-imposed constraints).

Revolutionary critical pedagogy is multifaceted in that it brings a Marxist humanist perspective to a wide range of policy and curriculum issues. The list of topics includes the globalization of capitalism, the marketization of education, neoliberalism and school reform, imperialism and capitalist schooling, and so on. Revolutionary critical pedagogy (as I am developing it) also offers an alternative interpretation of the history of capitalism and capitalist societies, with a particular emphasis on the United States. Revolutionary classrooms are prefigurative of socialism in the sense that they are connected to social relations that we want to create as revolutionary socialists. The organization of classrooms generally tries to mirror what students and teachers would collectively like to see in the world outside of schools—respect for everyone's ideas, tolerance of differences, a commitment to creativity and social and educational justice, the importance of working collectively, a willingness and desire to work hard for the betterment of humanity, and a commitment to antiracist, antisexist, and antihomophobic practices. If, within the social universe of capital, we are inevitably lashed to the very conditions we as critical educators hope to abolish, then there is no sense in trying to strike a delicate equipoise between capital and labor. The time has come to look beyond the value form of labor and seek alternatives to capitalism. Those of us who work in the field of education cannot afford to sit on the sidelines and watch this debate over the future of education as passive spectators. We need to take direct action, creating the conditions for students to become critical agents of social transformation. This means subjecting social relations of everyday life to a different social logic—transforming them in terms of criteria that have not already seeped in the logic of commodification. Students can—and should—become resolute and intransigent adversaries of the values that lie at the heart of commodity capitalism. This implies a new social culture, control of work by the associated producers, and also the very transformation of the nature of work itself.

Critical educators need to move beyond the struggle for a redistribution of value, because such a position ignores the social form of value and assumes a priori the vampirelike inevitability of the market. We need to transcend value, not redistribute it, since we can't build a socialist society on the principle of selling one's labor for a wage. Nor will it suffice to substitute collective capital for private capital. We are in a struggle to negate the value form of mediation, not to produce it in different degrees, scales, or registers. We need freedom, not to revert to some pristine substance or abstract essence prior to the point of production, but the freedom to learn how to appropriate the many social developments formed on the basis of alienated activity, to realize our human capacities to be free, to be a self-directed subject and not merely an instrument of capital for the self-expansion of value, and to be a conscious and purposeful human being with the freedom to determine the basis of our relationships. Here, subjectivity would not be locked into the requirements of capital's valorization process.

Revolutionary critical pedagogy operates from an understanding that the basis of education is political, and that spaces need to be created where students can imagine a different world outside of capitalism's law of value (i.e., social form of labor), where alternatives to capitalism and capitalist institutions can be discussed and debated, and where dialogue can occur about why so many revolutions in past history turned into their opposite. It looks to create a world where a new mode of distribution can prevail, not based on socially necessary labor time, but on actual labor time; where alienated human relations are subsumed by authentically transparent ones; where freely associated individuals can successfully work towards a permanent revolution; where the division between mental and manual labor can be abolished; where patriarchal relations and other privileging hierarchies of oppression and exploitation can be ended; where, to paraphrase Marx, we can truly exercise the principle "from each according to his or her ability and to each according to his or her need." It looks to create a world where we can traverse the terrain of universal rights unburdened by necessity, moving sensuously and fluidly within that ontological space where subjectivity is exercised as a form of capacity building and creative self-activity within and as a part of the social totality: a space where labor is no longer exploited and becomes a striving that will benefit all human beings, where labor refuses to be instrumentalized and commodified and ceases to be a compulsory activity, and where the full development of human capacity is encouraged (Hudis, 2005). It also builds upon forms of self-organization that are part of the history of liberation struggles worldwide, such as the 1871 Paris Commune, Cuba's *Consejos Populares* formed in 1989, those that developed during the civil rights, feminist, and worker movements, and those organizations of today that emphasize participatory democracy.

Critical pedagogy is by no means commensurate with the attention it excites in the academic literature, yet it continues to provide an important site of praxis-making which can be used to educate and agitate about crucial issues that affect our collective future. We need more than powerful exhortations; we need actions that can transform existing concrete situations into socialist solutions. We can't blithely conjure exploitation out of existence with benevolent abstractions—with words that are treated as revolutionary acts in themselves, no matter how universal their reach (Amoo-Adare, in press). Neither can we comfortably rest in our assurance that populism is the answer.

Reflections on Bad Faith Rebels

We would do well to avoid the pretentiousness and arrogance—not to mention competitiveness—that inflicts some educators with the disease of presenting themselves as a living litmus test for true radical praxis. Every so often these educators feel it necessary to announce their radical credentials to the world, marking their territory with stale ink from an acerbic pen. Such educators, often under the cover of "solidarity," attempt to set the boundaries of what counts as radical politics. Highlighting their closeness to grassroots communities, they ready themselves for a progressive purge of the field which, in their mind, is to dismiss the contributions of anyone who uses language that ruptures the accessible tropes of what counts as good journalism.

This type of grandstanding was not useful twenty years ago, and it is even less useful today. To minimize the contributions of critical theory to the project of educational transformation because its scholarly language appears too removed from everyday life is to slide into a reactionary form of populism or "basism" which Paulo Freire warned us against decades ago. Dismissing those who choose to engage in conceptual work that addresses issues of theory or philosophy as unworthy and unqualified to join the ranks of the "real" activists, these so-called "radicals" try to stigmatize critical theorists as failed revolutionaries hopelessly trapped in rhetorical paralysis (despite the nature of the grassroots work in which such theorists might be engaged outside of the academy), often as an attempt to inflate their own contributions to the field. Everything must have an immediate connection to people "on the ground," it must be laden with a workable strategy. Working out difficult issues that deal with philosophical principles and concepts is just, well, a form of elitism. According to the reactionary populists, writing about conceptual developments in critical social theory doesn't permit educators to feel transformed. In the words of one reactionary populist, such writing doesn't help teachers to feel "free" enough. These educators partake of a woeful misreading of the concept of freedom, at least from the standpoint of revolutionary critical pedagogy. To feel free is not to get yourself into a particular state of mind. It's not a characteristic of "affect." From the perspective of revolutionary critical pedagogy, to "feel free" actually requires human beings to "be free" from necessity, and this goal has many paths, and requires the participation of many educators, and the key task is the transformation of social relations of production.

For many reactionary populists, to be of service to the struggle for social justice mandates that first and foremost you must be all about sharing experiences and making affective connections with teachers and students and community members on the ground. Sharing experiences and making connections is all well and good, but doing so without understanding how such experiences are mediated and shaped by larger social relations is really missing the point. All too frequently, these "radical" educators dismiss the language of philosophy or theory because, they bloviate, it is too removed from everyday discourse. This, of course, ignores the insight of Marx that abstractions are often the best way to grasp the concrete. The so-called liberating language of the reactionary populist in many cases becomes a language filled with thoughts and ideas but looted of concepts and analysis. It's also an example of what Sartre called "bad faith." Critical educators strive for "another kind of knowledge" that might exist in a world that is able to transcend capitalism—a socialist world. What would it be like to operate in a world by means of a direct social knowledge that cannot be communicated through the indirect medium of money: a knowledge tacitly based upon recognition of our unity and solidarity? (Lebowitz, 2005) We need to take to the streets alongside those whose stolid persistence and arduous years of unmerited suffering have earned them the right to fight back. We need to find ways of fighting back together. For those who have ears, you can listen to the groans of Marx in his grave; he stubbornly refuses to die because his mission is not yet completed. The more his adversaries pronounce him dead, the more he bangs his fist against his crypt, reminding us that capitalism never sleeps, and neither should we until our job as its gravediggers is complete. For critical educators, Marx is no longer the backdrop on the shallow stage of history or a portent of failed worker states; nor is he heralded as the unsung savior of humankind, fulsomely celebrated by those who possess the correct interpretation of his texts. Rather, he offers to educators a way to move forward in the struggle to make classrooms spaces of social critique and social transformation, where teachers and students alike can exercise a dialectical pedagogy of critique and hope, grounded in an exploration of what it means to labor and to educate one's labor power for the future purpose of selling it for a wage, and understanding this process from the perspective of the larger totality of capitalist social relations. And further, to cultivate the necessary political agency to move from understanding the world to changing it.

Undoubtedly, critical pedagogy remains a source of hope and possibility for educators engaged in struggles against oppression in their classrooms. The time has come for teachers and educators to embrace critical pedagogy with a renewed interest and sense of urgency. While critical pedagogy comes under increasing attack by reactionary ideologies and ideologues, its message only becomes more urgent and important in these troubled and dangerous times.

Note

This chapter draws from several recent essays, including a chapter in the fifth edition of *Life in Schools* (2006), and an introduction to a special issue of the journal *Ethnicities,* edited by Peter McLaren and Nathalia E. Jaramillo (2006).

References

Amoo-Adare, A. (in press). An interview with the Dirty Thirty's Peter McLaren. *Chopbox Magazine.*

Arellano, G. (2006, May 3). The anti-immigrant all-stars. *LA Weekly,* p. 18.

Blum, W. (2005, July 14). The anti-empire report. Retrieved January 15, 2007 from http://www.killinghope.org

Blum, W. (2006, September 25). The anti-empire report. Retrieved January 15, 2007 from http://members.aol.com/bblum6/aer37.htm

Burgos, R. (2002). The Gramscian intervention in the theoretical and political production of the Latin American Left. *Latin American Perspectives, 29*(1), 9–37.

Craig, B. (2006, June 1). New Florida law tightens control over history in schools. *George Mason University's History News Network.* Retrieved January 15, 2007 from http://hnn.us/roundup/entries/26016.html

Freire, P. (1998). *Teachers as cultural workers: Letters to those who dare teach* (Expanded ed.). (D. Macedo, D. Koike, and A. Oliveira, Trans.). Boulder, CO: Westview Press.

Freire, P. (1994). *Pedagogy of hope: Reliving pedagogy of the oppressed.* (R. R. Barr, Trans.). New York: Continuum.

Gonzalez, M. (2004). Postmodernism, historical materialism and Chicana/o cultural studies. *Science & Society, 68*(2), 161–186,

Gramsci, A. (1971). *Selections from the Prison Notebooks.* New York: International Publishers.

Gulli, B. (2005). The folly of utopia. *Situations, 1*(1), 161–191.

Hudis, P. (2005, March). *Directly and indirectly social labor: What kind of human relations can transcend capitalism?* Paper presented at series "Beyond Capitalism," Chicago, IL.

Kincheloe, Joe. (2005). *Critical Pedagogy: A Primer.* New York: Peter Lang Publishing.

Kosik, K. (1976). *Dialectics of the concrete: A study on problems of man and world.* Boston: D. Reidel Publishing Company.

Kovel, J. (2002). *The enemy of nature: The end of capitalism or the end of the world?* New York: Zed Books.

Kozol, J. (2005, September). Still separate, still unequal: America's educational apartheid. *Harper's Magazine, 311*(1864), 41–54.

Lebowitz, M. A. (2005, July/August). The knowledge of a better world. *Monthly Review, 57*(3), 62–69.

Machado, A. (1962). *Manuel y Antonio Machado: Obras Completas.* Madrid: Editorial Plenitud.

Marx, K. (1992). *Capital: A critique of political economy,* (Vol. 1). (B. Fowkes, Trans.). New York: Penguin Classics. (Original work published 1887)

Mayo, P. (2004). *Liberating praxis: Paulo Freire's legacy for radical education and politics.* Westport, CT: Praeger.

McKibben, B. (2005, August). The Christian paradox: How a faithful nation gets Jesus wrong. *Harper's Magazine, 311*(1863), 31–37.

McLaren, P. & Jaramillo, N. (2006). Juntos en la lucha. *Ethnicities, 6*(3), 283–296.

McLaren, P. & Jaramillo, N. (2005). God's cowboy warrior: Christianity, globalization, and the false prophets of imperialism. In P. McLaren (Ed.), *Capitalists and conquerors: A critical pedagogy against empire* (pp. 261–333). Lanham, MD: Rowman and Littlefield.

Meyerson, G. (2000). Rethinking Black Marxism: Reflections on Cedric Robinson and others. *Cultural Logic, 3*(2). Retrieved January 15, 2007, from http://clogic.eserver.org/3–1&2/meyerson. html

Miller, J. (2006, May 15). Forget the Middle East: The U.S. Harbors the World's Most Dangerous Terrorists. *The Baltimore Chronicle & Sentinel.* Retrieved January 15, 2007, from http://baltimorechronicle.com/2006/042506Miller.shtml

Rikowski, G. (2005, February). "Distillation: Education in Karl Marx's social universe." Paper presented at lunchtime seminar at the School of Education, University of East London, Barking Campus.

Robinson, W. (2006). *"¡Aqui estamos y no nos vamos!: The struggle for immigrant rights in the U.S.* Unpublished paper.

San Juan, E. (2002). *Racism and cultural studies: Critiques of multiculturalist ideology and the politics of difference.* Durham, NC: Duke University Press.

Scatamburlo-D'Annibale, V. & McLaren, P. (2004). Class dismissed? Historical materialism and the politics of 'difference.' *Educational Philosophy and Theory, 36*(2), 183–199.

Scatamburlo-D'Annibale, V. & McLaren, P. (2003). The strategic centrality of class in the politics of race and 'difference.' *Cultural Studies/Critical Methodologies, 3*(2), 148–175

Somerville, J. (2005). The philosophy of Marxism: An exposition. [Special Issue]. *Nature, Society, and Thought, 18*(1).

Steele, S. (2006, May 2). White guilt and the Western past: Why is America so delicate with its enemy? *The Wall Street Journal.* Retrieved January 15, 2007, from http://www.opinionjournal. com/editorial/feature.html?id=110008318

Wood, E. M. (1995). *Democracy against capitalism: Renewing historical materialism.* Cambridge, UK: Cambridge University Press.

Zavarzadeh, Mas'ud. (2003). The pedagogy of totality. *Journal of Advanced Composition, 23*(1), 1–52.

Zimmerman, J. (2006, June 7). All history is revisionist. *Los Angeles Times.* Retrieved January 20, 2007 from http://www.latimes.com/news/opinion/commentary/la-oe-zimmerman-7jun07,0,5940045.story?coll=la-news-comment-opinions

Zunes, Stephen. (2006, December 31). Gerald Ford's foreign policy legacy. Retrieved January 20, 2007 at http://www.commondreams.org/views06/1231–20.htm

TEN

Poststructuralism, Difference, and Critical Pedagogy

Peter Trifonas and Effie Balomenos

OISE/UT

The material domain of discriminatory social practices is constituted by the cultural politics of an exclusionary agenda tending toward the disequalization of subjectivities, difference from the accepted "norm" being accorded a pejorative connotation vis-à-vis highly arbitrary criteria of judgment that are based on the problematic categories of race, ethnicity, class, gender, or sexuality. This conscious disenfranchisement of alternate subjectivities is therefore a societal production of the meaning of representation, which measures difference in relation to cultural ordinances of aspect, conceived as a narrowly defined and fixedly qualitative measure of personal or group "characteristics." Moreover, the question of difference elides with how the dominant ideology defines selfhood. And the transversal function of an amassing of diverse ideologies under the overarching structure of a single "controlling culture" has been a key factor for theories of subjectivity attempting to explain the social interpellation of the individual into "subject" (Althusser, 1971). Yet, there has also been reaction to this relative autonomy of ideology that posits the subjective manifestations of an unimpeded and, hence, automatic reproducibility of meaning reconstructions within the symbolic realms of consciousness. The emancipatory impetus of educational reform projects such as critical pedagogy has risen up to protect the agency of the subject against what is tantamount to a willful regimentation of "truth" within a concept of identity that only serves to bolster the already well-wrought fetters of social inequality

(Stanley, 1992). The liberating hope of theorizing a critical pedagogy has resided in enabling the subject to free itself of complicity with the onerous symptoms of a *false consciousness.* And by so doing, the selfhood of subjectivity would be allowed—or at least given the opportunity—to self-consciously reinscribe the meaning of itself in the difference of a newly achieved awareness of world structures. To realize such a thing as "a nascent disciplinary trajectory within education that has its roots in Marxian analyses of class" (McLaren, 1994, p. 319), critical pedagogy has crafted its methodological arsenal from a selective mixture of first-generation Frankfurt School critical theory, Antonio Gramsci's idea of hegemony (coupled with the intellectual application of a counterhegemonic resistance to ideology), and Paulo Freire's educational theory/action of conscientization. More recently, however, there have been attempts made by some of the major theorists subsumed under the rubric of critical pedagogy to co-opt specific principles of poststructuralism for use in the important operation of educational critique. This chapter will examine the epistemological overlap between poststructural theorizing and critical pedagogy as it relates to the concept of difference. A juxtaposition of theoretical perspectives of variations on the theme of difference will provide: 1) a stronger sense of the specific points at which the philosophical orientations that inform the epistemological presuppositions of both discourses intersect; and 2) a particular focus for organizing the discussion of the specificity of these points as they are brought to bear on the actual field of curricular studies.

The Critical Difference of Postmodern French Philosophy

If there is a principal connection to be made between poststructural theorizing and critical pedagogy, it lies in the all-but-sudden awakening of contemporary scholarship to the inherent limitations and the repressive inadequacies of the foundationalism of the modernist paradigm of empirical science. Poststructural theorizing aggressively refutes the methodical rationality of conceptual dualisms that articulate the certainty of either Cartesianist subjectivity or simply sense experience. On the whole, it rejects the modernist belief in the positive possibility of describing the determinate rules and systems of empirical reality, a posteriori perception—that is, the depiction of truth as a generalizable "universal," independent of bias, prejudice, or the ideological attributes of tradition (Lyotard, 1984). The critical groundwork for an opposition to the teleology of knowledge was arguably laid out in the latter half of the nineteenth century by the pre-postmodern German philosopher Friedrich Nietzsche (1844–1900) (Best & Kellner, 1991). Nietzsche was the first philosopher to vehemently dispute the legitimacy of Western metaphysics as claims to knowledge that amounted to nothing more than a correspondence theory of truth. He denied the univocality of meaning so crucial to establishing an epistemological prerequisite for the empiricality of science, or the inaugurating of self-explanatory systems of cause-effect relations resulting from an autotelic experiencing of real-world phenomena by the sensing subject. Attacking the absolutism of such an unyielding position to be illusory, Nietzsche established the precedence for looking beyond an ontotheology of signification and an ethnocentric mythologizing of philosophical discourse to explore how the confluence of ideological interests within a society or culture motivates knowledge constructions. Jacques Derrida (1976), Michel Foucault (1973), and Jean-François Lyotard (1984), to name but a few major figures of poststructuralism, have furthered the iconoclastic content of Nietzsche's brand of antihumanism by sustaining the radical flair of a critique of Western epistemology. The links between "Enlightenment" philosophy and the moral basis of social institutions have been addressed by these philosophers through a gauging of the complex problems related to the implications of the eternal return of history, the untimely death of God, the phenomenological passion of Western logocentrism, and so on. It is because the epistemological battlefields of contemporary French philosophy have, by and large, provided the principal influences upon what are the "politics" of poststructural thinking that an understanding of the theoretical precepts fueling the fire of these much celebrated debates is constituent to the lines of inquiry stated previously regarding critical pedagogy and the notion of difference.

The hierarchical schematization of densely prescriptive knowledge structures is promulgated by the conceptual dualism of an oppositional epistemological exemplar (i.e., presence/absence, nature/culture, right/wrong, etc.). The structuring of this model of binarism is conveyed in poststructural thinking as the product of a reductive interpretation of phenomena congealed within the medians of a transferable logic of culture. And the power of a cultural politics of knowledge, which is the ideological basis of sociohistorical meaning constructions, is inhered by the discursive *habitus* of the subject as the semiotic outworking of forces intrinsic to the communication of concepts through which a consciousness of self is induced (Bourdieu, 1984). Foucault (1980) conducted "archaeological" or "genealogical" research into the discursive niches of the historicity of Western epistemology. The synchronic and diachronic structuration of ideology was illuminated as a power/knowledge nexus formulized through cultural expropriations of the practicable elements of language. From the ordering of vague concepts in the mind to the work of language upon the cultures of society, the discursive nature of human existence is depicted by Foucault via an architectonic methodology defined by the expanding regions of an array of belief systems that function to inform subjectivity. The linguistic essence of subjective identity sets up the difference of being and of Being. The desire to "respect . . . differences, and even try to grasp them in their specificity" (Foucault, 1973, p. xii) of construction enabled Foucault to reflect upon the obvious ideological inconsistencies within the "macrology" of systems of thought and how readings of subjectivity may be conducted from the "microscopy" of an intensified querying of attitudes toward language. Even more radically antifoundationalist in scope than the de-archiving "methods" of Foucault, Derrida (1976) has reinforced Hegel's conception of difference only to reappropriate its principles in an ironic reversal of the laws of speculative idealism. In doing so, he has acknowledged what lies beyond the conceptual and practical reconciliation or synthesis of a binary opposition. In this instance, difference is an epistemological benchmark of "the Other" but moves beyond the idealization of identity to signify the (non)endedness of absolute knowledge or the self-effacement of dialectical totalities (Derrida, 1981). Derrida extends the Hegelian imperative for a strict negativity to the quasisemantics of meaning deferrals. This is an iterability articulated by the affective differences of repetition displacements, or *différance*. What Foucault and Derrida have clarified are the dangers of humanist arguments for the "singularity" and "particularity" of subjective identity intending to regularize the cognitive, the affective, or even the "pragmatic" behaviours of individuals within a society by promoting "the truth" of knowledge. They contend that the outcome of a dialectical symmetrization of subjective identity as either positive or negative in nature can no longer be condoned. To suggest that there is an equationing of perception propitiated by the presence of unchanging eidetic entities in the mechanisms of mind is a very simplistic hypothesis. The phenomenology of apperception and the communication of the consciousness of phenomena external to the subject are governed within the affective experiences generated from a teleological model of writing. There are differences within perception correlating to differences within subjectivities that must be taken into account (Derrida, 1981). Valorizing the fragmentation of subjectivity or acknowledging the multiplicity of difference warrants an appreciation for the plurality of discourses or alternative configurations of power/knowledge sources that embrace the contexts of society and culture that ground identity. In identifying the need to be open to a plethora of subject positions, what poststructural theorizing forthrightly challenges is the appropriation of otherness, an objectification of identity leading to an "exoticization" of the other. The abject differentiation of subjectivities reconstitutes a stereotypical metaphor of cultural authenticity.

Knowledge claims vis-à-vis the historicity of "Reason" grant primacy to epistemological "edicts" while suppressing the capacity to reinforce the "ideological" otherness of marginalized group identities insofar as a reliance upon an introspective normativity is entrenched within a monotheism of subjective consciousness. Poststructuralism provides the critical means for facilitating a hermeneutic shift in the power/knowledge references that would offer much-needed respect to the dissonance of voices kept at the borderlines of a "general culture." The unifying aspect of poststructuralism is the recognition of an originary difference. Or the acknowledgment of an ethic of heterogeneity that would foster an appreciation for otherness and difference by concentrating on the contextual dependency of human understandings relative to the multivariate nature of experience. An open dialogue questioning the nature of intersubjectivity is crucial to the recognition of differences for the enrichment of society overall. Acceding to differences of alternative domains within the communicative substrata of culture could lead to a sublimation of the axiomatics for upholding a hierarchy of privilege by defusing the institutionalized logic of an enforced unity of identity through either visible or invisible means of discipline, training, and correction to "normalize" subjectivity. What entitles the "subalterned" to a voice penultimately dislocates the logic calling for a reification of subjectivity. A radicalization of ethics beyond the oppositional schemata of binary thinking protects the inherent differences of subjective identity against the consensus and consistency of a dominant discourse (Spivak, 1992).

A corollary effect of recognizing the communicative "semiosphere of cultures" and its floating signifiers à la Yuri Lotman is the psychological necessity of coping with the lack of determinacy in meaning-making amid the aftermath of the fissuring of rigid "moral" standards due to an approbation of otherness or of difference. This relative type of social bonding requires a more "open" than "closed" interpretative matrix through which to renegotiate the cultural politics of a critical awareness of subjective differences. Poststructural theories of signification proffer such flexible critical tools for analyzing the cybernetics of institutional knowledge constructions. They show how the ideological presuppositions within the textualized forms of a discursive expression of content mediate to systemically neutralize the freedom of subjective conclusions by a reconstruction of the conceptual conditions of "truth" through writing. Sometimes described as needlessly cynical or just "playful," poststructuralism suspends the finality of an idiosyncratic reading by resisting the terminating values of signification within a text. Meaning is taken to a subjective plateau of situationally viable, but potentially variable interpretative choices that cannot appeal to objective measures or standards for a verification of "truthfulness" (Derrida, 1976). Poststructuralism destabilizes the disinterestedness of knowledge by grounding texts firmly within the contexts or the situations of their ideological constructions to expand the intersubjectivity of world to the variegated dimensions of "possible worlds" (Eco, 1979). Denying objectivity within perception and placing perception within the affectivity of discourse so as to account for the effectuation of consciousness from it, the validity of arguments is shown not to be self-evident. Rather it is contiguous to a presentation of contextually discerned phenomena that are both faithful and unfaithful to the constructions of their own logic (Derrida, 1976).

Simulations and Simulacra: Visual Differences and Cultural Realities

Lyotard (1984) and Baudrillard (1981) align the poststructural arena of information exchange as signification to the spectacle of computer-simulated graphics and the images of techno-pseudo presentation within the symbolic field of cultural production. The effects of these "new" visual-based media fetishize the sense of otherness or of difference within communities by imploding the conceptual limits of identity in a ready-made format for a globally disseminated intersubjective networking of fictional realities. The swift metastasis of available *technes* for simulating "real-world" phenomena has so permeated contemporary society through the proliferation of "virtual media" (e.g., television, video, computers, etc.) that the boundaries separating "the real" from "the fabricated" are no longer clarifiable, but are disguised in the glossed formulas of an idyllic *hyperreality* (Baudrillard, 1981). The transgressive inventions of these *simulacra* of the real, having refurbished and recoded the essential qualities of reality, consequently shape the understanding of knowledge by superimposing upon a manifold of subject positions a more intricate system of information de-archiving from which subjective identity is accessed and not realized in selfhood (Baudrillard, 1981). Seeking a transcendental referent or signified in technological dissimulations of reality limits what can or should be thought in the parameters of simulated realities. It is because the generic or normative archetypes of fictionalizations of phenomena are fed back into the real that "truth" therefore loses all plausibility within the infinite permutations of meaning-making propagated through the cross-mediality of a visual semiotics of cultural literacy. Lyotard (1984) echoes such a typical poststructural stance apropos representation and interpretation by refuting the commensurability of meaning across incompatible ideologies or competing epistemologies to separate modernist metanarratives from "postmodern" discourses:

> Consensus does violence to the heterogeneity of language games. And invention is always born of dissension. Postmodern knowledge is not simply a tool of the authorities; it refines our sensitivity to differences and reinforces our ability to tolerate the incommensurable. (p. 75)

The application of the Wittgensteinean phrase "language games" to discourse refers to, at least, a partial incommensurability of understandings among subjects or a nonpractical consensus of intersubjectivity: the reconcilability of meaning-making emanating less from genuine agreement than from the pragmatic suppression of differing ideological orientations maintained relative to individual belief systems. What Lyotard seems to suggest is that claims to knowledge can only be approached through a self-critical consciousness, whereby dissent is the questioning of the difference of concepts in a constantly malleable state of flux. It is a prototype of reading for broadening a subjective acquaintance of the likelihood of alternative semantic-stylistic prospects within expression. Scrutinizing the astructural "depths" of the interplay of these discursive potentialities fuses the interpretability of content with "textualizations" of experience by harnessing the critical power of the subject to unearth the ideological undertones that influence the recording of a perspective and the means to attempt to comprehend it.

The Lack of Closure and the End of History: An Abyss of Reason

The break of poststructural theorizing with the philosophical foundationalism has been much celebrated, but where this "epistemological rupture" leads remains a highly contested issue. On the one side, the more apophatic factions within the debate envision the presently confused critical condition as the result of an apocalyptic resignation looking forward in space and time to the end of history: All options will soon be exhausted in *toto*, leaving no "tangible" future from which to realize the human progression of a history of meaning. On the other side, more optimistic factions view the current condition of critical collage as an extension of interpretative differences denied modernism and portray the alterity of the re-representation of ideas by a linking of the cultural sphere of knowledge to an intertwining of discourses exhibiting an endless intertextuality of expressive forms of representation. The pluralism of our times has given rise to the need for a re-vitalization of theorizing and of expression—for example, forms of identity and representation that might successfully cohabitate with the ideological vicissitudes of a poststructural politics of knowledge. The critical subtlety of a poststructural consciousness of difference engenders an acceptance, if only a relative one, of the very belief systems it attempts to subjugate and to problematize by incorporating them within the boundless textuality of its pliant corpus. In this fashion, perspectival standards are immanently assessed to permit "aesthetic forms and social formations to be problematized by critical reflection" (Hutcheon, 1992, p. 77). Relating the dilemma of difference and representation more specifically to the growing discipline of cultural studies, Hall (1986) believes individuals can no longer subscribe to critical absolutes within such a magnitude of contradictory understandings of reality-pervading societies. Systematized traditions can offer insights for a critical consumption of their relative value as discourses of difference or examples of otherness so that the force of "old arguments" changes in light of more original and more radically open perspectives. Whereas theoretical absolutism has offered a "series of uneven developments that have emerged out of conflicts between traditional economic models and new cultural formations and modes of criticism" (Giroux, 1988c, pp. 10–11), a poststructural perspective would, more often than not, embrace an acceptance of plurality and of difference within hermeneutic frameworks. It would encourage a self-critical analysis of the discursive conceptual structures of arguments in order to bring to the surface any "blind spots" (i.e., contradictions of position, ideological hierarchies, etc.). Such a "deconstructive reading" would play the language or themes of a text against itself to test the solidity of the logic of its conceptual foundations (Derrida, 1976).

Deconstruction reveals the argumentative means organizing the authority of a subject position that is featured in a text by evaluating the preoccupations of discourse that follow the linguistic structuring of a perceived reality. However, Derrida (interviewed in Kearns & Newton, 1980) warns of the dangers of instrumental uses of deconstruction to unilaterally reject all claims to knowledge:

> I would never say that every interpretation is equal. . . . The hierarchy is between forces and not between true and false. . . . I would not say that some interpretations are truer than others. I would say that some are more powerful than others. The hierarchy is between forces and not between true and false. There are interpretations which account for more meaning and this is the criterion. (p. 21)

The external and internal interaction of the "system of forces" acting to generate meaning-making potential (to which Derrida has often referred as the outcome of the cumulative effects of psychologically motivated factors) are never identical for any two individuals (Derrida, 1976, 1981). Every individual brings to an act of reading the mental differences of a subjective identity drawn from experiences that have inculcated the (un)conscious formation of a personalized psychic reality. Derrida (also from Kearns & Newton, 1980) comments further upon the role of the subjectivity differences in deconstruction:

> No-one is free to read as he or she wants. The reader does not interpret freely, taking into account only his own reading, excluding the author, the historical period in which the text appeared and so on. . . . I think that one cannot read without trying to reconstruct the historical context but history is not the last word, the final key, of reading. (pp. 21–22)

Derrida's explanation, at odds with the hyperrelativism attributed to deconstruction by its critics, leaves open a hermeneutical space or "gap" in which to explore the significance of meaning (re)constructions derived from the reading, while simultaneously suggesting that such considerations are to be seen as but a single agent coloring the discursive mediation of experience resulting in the textualization of "reality." Perspectives may not be consciously "selected," but differences within the discursive conditions of experience are at the forefront of a variety of subject stances that therefore concede a surplus of positional definitions.

Poststructural theoretical discourses engage in criticism removed from nurturing the isolation of personal meaning-making by constantly searching for "the possible" in "the unlikely" or "the improbable." And the iconoclastic experimentalism of this epistemological adventurousness is valorized by the gravity of Jencks's (1992) postmetaphysical observations: "The uncontested dominance of the modern world view has definitely ended. Like it or not the West has become a plurality of competing subcultures where no one ideology and episteme dominates for long" (p. 11). Rather than helping to create an adversely competitive environment that would deny "subcultures" the right to be heard over the monologue of dominant metanarratives, accepting the heterogeneity of perspectives within contemporary societies requires legitimating the interplay among a variety of differing voices (Lyotard, 1984). It now remains to be seen how critical pedagogy will offer the possibility of an educational orientation sensitive to the imminent reality of the differences in such a postmodern cultural condition.

Critical Pedagogy and the Education of Difference

The term "critical pedagogy" relates to and originates from within the material conditions of the epistemological effects that poststructural theorizing has attempted to critique, by contextualizing the basis of the possibilities for social change to bring about a more equitable "new-world-picture" through the education of the subject. Because the term "critical pedagogy" possesses obvious semantic connotations associated with conceptual analysis, the early interpretations of it were taken to imply a method of pedagogy used to involve students in overtly critical exercises. The adjective "critical" within "critical pedagogy" refers to "critical theory," the Marxist philosophical tract upon which its theoretico-methodological ends are founded. Critical theorists, such as Theodor Adorno and Herbert Marcuse, have argued that subjects should strive for social and intellectual emancipation from the circumstance of political and economic domination enshrined by the powers-that-be (Stanley, 1992). Critical pedagogy emulates the urgency of this core Marxian tenet by maximizing the subject's capacity for a revolutionary move to such a state of freedom. It does so with deconstructive/reconstructive exercises that clarify ideology and exude the potential for an interpretative plurality within hegemonic discourses by illuminating the educational institution's oppressive power (Giroux, 1988d, 1987; McLaren, 1991). The idea of a de-reification of power through negative critique, or "negative dialectics," aims at de-subjectifying the "false consciousness" of the self. This estrangement of the incorporate shell of subjective identity is a fundamental step to the individual's emancipation from the hegemony of ideology infusing the site of unabashed exploitation. A counterhegemonic practice well-versed in the nuances of negative critique is the intellectual instrument for a sustained resistance to the imposition of meaning from ideologically overdetermined sources outside the self. To liberate subjectivity, in this sense, does not mean to deny self-identity but to assert independence and control over the homeostatic effects of ideology that enslave the subject to a living-through of the interests and desires of the system.

Much of the canon of critical pedagogy can also be traced to the writings of the Brazilian philosopher of education Paulo Freire (Kaplan, 1991). Freire (1970) maintained that educational systems should foster an ability for autonomous thought and independent action by encouraging students to actively take part in the development of their own personalized systems of logic to deal with the knowledge claims thrust upon them. Showing how the subordinated groups of a dominant cultural orientation become alienated within the educational system of the *status quo*, Freire advocated teaching-learning environments that would be conducive to critical reflection by teachers and students alike. These environments would enable individual subjects to fervently realize the legitimacy of honoring differences, especially ideological ones, by not subscribing a priori experience to the oppressive structural arrangements of institutions, often organized according to austere doctrines of manipulation. The necessity of developing in classrooms teaching-learning situations responsive to the essential reflexivity of such a "critical literacy" for self-liberation is then realized by encouraging students to relay personal experiences to one another. This exercise would incite thought and discussion upon their own discourse and those of others, through which provisional but intelligibly framed arguments—that are not governed solely by a dictated percipience—could be actualized (Freire & Faundez, 1989). For Freire (1970), reality is not "concrete" or "static" but a relentless enmeshing of the contextual factors reshaping its construction in the conscious and unconscious axiology of the subject's perception. Concomitantly, it is admitted that interpretations of experience are troublesome if they are qualified by the justifiability of each claim to knowledge as a contingent language of possibility and not as a dictatorial language of imposition (McLaren, 1991, 1994). Criticism is the resource to broaden knowledge through dialogic constructions of the differences of experience stemming from deconstructive/reconstructive exercises designed to synthesize the subject's return to self, or "conscientization" (Freire, 1970). By using critical discourse to question and to challenge the assumptions of the self and of the other, students can gravitate toward fresh understandings and can circumvent the need to reproduce institutionally endorsed ideologies. Students engage in critical activities to uncover more options for themselves as equal members of society and to develop the skill or breadth of a more penetrating insight into the cultural remnants of past myths, through which the knowledge gained from institutionalized systems of teaching-learning is augmented.

The Myriad of Culture and the Affluence of Difference

It may be said that critical pedagogy has risen from within a sociocultural milieu that has been insensitive to the reality of the global condition in which a torrent of differences simply exist (Stanley, 1992; Giroux, 1988c). On one level, the subjects of contemporary societies are characterized in terms of this "world of difference," where individuals are considered to be identities constructed from an unceasing exposure to a diverse array of images, discourses, codes, etc. (Spivak,

1992). On another level, the heterogeneity of identity is exemplified in communities of otherness in which people further embellish primary subjectivity differences through complex, integrated, and endless combinations of gender, class, race, ethnic or sexual orientations. This abundance of individuality, mapped both within and on the "fringes" of society, is not always given the freedom to organize and to assert a sense of personalizable or personalized identity within school systems. Moreover, educational institutions are inclined to enforce subscription to prefabricated norms and authorized policies. In this case, individual freedoms and rights are predisposed to the "governmentality" of prescriptive knowledge structures, regulated through the juridical strategies of supposedly democratic systems that exclude participants because of inherent or inherited differences to the common system.

This attitude is taken by a number of critical pedagogy theorists (i.e., McLaren, 1988, 1991; Kanpol, 1992; Giroux, 1988a; and Smyth, 1987), and critical educators who have questioned the "commonizing rituals" through which the arrangement of schooling structures or educational systems exculpate conformist intellectual or behavioral expectations without showing sensitivity to the knowledge students hold in relation to personalized subcodes of meaning-making and forms of discourse production (Giroux & McLaren, 1992). Students are seen as being forced to comply with the commodification of knowledge, an intellectual potential having to be re-aimed at the realization of a predesignated "cultural capital" so as to ensure success within the hegemony of the school order. Apple (1990) and Bourdieu (1984) have persuasively argued that a dominant culture both overtly and covertly transmits a code of value structures within the practical implementation of curriculums; educational programs that endorse certain knowledges and behaviors facilitate the reproduction of the mean by championing their superiority over other forms of understanding, thereby creating a hierarchy of identities based upon ideological conformity. Individuals from groups of lower social status entering the school systems are at an obvious disadvantage from the beginning of the educational process due to a relatively limited exposure to dominant forms of cultural knowledge (Apple, 1992). In short, the reasoning subordinated groups bring to the traditional school setting is not supported by the cultural hegemony of an ideological ordering of school syllabi and curricula. And an individual's class, gender, racial identity, ethnicity, or sexual preference can work against his or her ability to receive optimum educational benefits from a school system that does not embrace forms of knowledge that stem from non-dominant worldviews. Because societies are amalgams of differing populations and peoples, such a phenomenon in the educational enterprise is destructive because it fails to offer an effective form of pedagogy for a great portion of groups represented within society. School systems often exhibit little appreciation for and sensitivity to the potentially divergent interests of lower or marginalized status groups (Giroux & McLaren, 1992).

Kanpol (1992) stresses the importance of privileging the "ideals" of difference in educational contexts by bringing attention to the need to supersede pedagogical theories that locate knowledge within exclusionary totalizations of subjectivity. Individual differences are celebrated when the existence of subjective identities relative to group membership is critically engaged and whole-heartedly endorsed. As Kanpol (1992) states, "Of course what must be established within schools are personal struggles that are not only separate and different—by race, class, or gender—given their discursive nature, but also intimately connected by their commonalities" (p. 220). Critical pedagogy values an ethos of intersubjectivity within the diaspora of communities of difference. The mien of educational practices that pervade the intellectual and ethical environment of the subject should inculcate an empathy for and not a tolerance of otherness, using critical reflection upon the cultural sites of discourse production. To illuminate a rhizome of existing realities, critical educators facilitate this analytic exploration of differing perspectives by way of ongoing dialogues with the other. Through open and challenging dialogue, meanings of differences are more likely to be negotiated, apprehended, and then woven into interpersonal schemata or codes of meaning-making to stretch individual perceptions of "possible worlds." For the reconstructive phase of this genre of intercommunicative learning to take place, the subjective authorities of the student and of the teacher must be reinstated within the institutional scene of teaching-learning. The educational system must identify content that is relevant to the personal experiences of both and not encased in the educational agendas of modulated syllabi handed down through preplanned and prepackaged curricula (Stanley, 1992).

Toward this end, critical pedagogy, like poststructural theorizing, does not indicate "clear-cut" or "definitive" learning outcomes *per se*. Rather, it yields to the interpretative interests of individuals, for which, to realize the central logic of the structuring of concepts presented in areas of study supersedes the confines offered by a given "dominant group" reading. Apple (1990) has analyzed the indoctrinating power of the institution by citing the practice of schools using ready-made instructional packages that bypass any critical role the teacher or student might play in selecting materials for the teaching-learning process. This common practice makes teachers and students appear as monodimensional cogs lost in a tangled lattice of intrainstitutional paraphernalia and fit only to be governed by managerial organizers who are external to the reality of the classroom environment. The trend toward pedagogical accountability or excellence in education has reinstated standardized syllabi and measurable curricular outcomes of learning-teaching that enforce student and teacher conformity for meeting the technocratic goal of the commercial productivity of "sustainable economies." Such mainstream approaches to a "back-to-basics" education tend to undermine the sociopolitical interests of marginal groups because the competitive edge of the pedagogy secures the teaching-learning of knowledge as a form of "cultural capital" worth having by rewarding its reproduction (Bourdieu & Passeron, 1977). This drives the inequalities in education opportunities while claiming its reduction through the provisioning of an equal access to education provided to all. By using critical discourse to emancipate the self from the need to internalize such a "rote-learning" of the system's teachings, the "democratic" plight of critical pedagogy is not stultified but guided to help individuals actualize their natural potential to counter domination (Goodman, 1988).

Henry Giroux, a theorist who has offered the most systematic theoretical and practicable outline of the parameters and merits of critical pedagogy after Freire (i.e., Giroux, 1988a, 1988b, 1988d, 1992), accents the educational importance of unveiling the oppressive element of institutional knowledge. He, too, advocates a pedagogical sense of reflexivity in experiential frameworks for an education more suited to introspections of subjectivity. Teachers can draw upon these reflections to heighten students' awareness of self as a vital source of informational logic and to motivate critical thinking in direct relation to the communicative act of teaching-learning. Giroux envisions a more equitable institutionalization of education that crosses the boundaries of culture, helps all students form truly original ideas, and protects their democratic right to voice opinions without having to hide under a veil of commonality to suppress tacit knowledge. This process of "applied reasoning" or "critical thinking" can be, as Blatz (1989) notes, "understood as the deliberate pursuit of well-supported beliefs, decisions, plans, and actions" (p. 107). The "genuineness" of these pursuits is displayed in the accountability of actions to the train of logic constructing one's own subjective understandings as influenced by race, ethnicity, class, gender, or sexuality. By expanding the capability to elaborate upon or to amplify a unique critical voice or analytic perspective to add to the classroom presentation, previously "subordinated" group understandings and perceptions are given the opportunity to be realized in full. Critical pedagogy, as a result, teaches students to be open-minded to accepting a variety of differing viewpoints, including their own, by affirming knowledge through a problematizing of its discursive possibilities.

The Difference of Critical Pedagogy

As McLaren (1988) suggests, "Critical pedagogy is positioned irreverently against a pedantic cult of singularity in which moral authority and theoretical assurance are arrived at unproblematically without regard to the repressed narratives and suffering of the historically disenfranchised" (p. 73). Critical educators are not interested in using "effective methods" for the efficient and manageable consumption of a content of self-mirroring knowledges. Knowledge does not reside in the materiality of "real-world" resources or commodities to be given out, "consumed," and verily reproduced for the sociocultural or political-economic benefit of the subject but is an entity requiring the painstaking rigors of involved intellection—an understanding that stems from a highly personalized grounding of experience and interpretation (Giroux, 1987, 1992).

The summative goal of critical pedagogy is to empower students with the ability to think and act reflectively as individual subjects of a society or a culture. It helps them form self-awareness of the meanings of their multiple affiliations and the significance of their worldly transactions with the other. That a platform for the creative exchange of student experiences must be maintained within the practicable components of a theory of learning is vital to critical educators. Giroux (1988d) correctly explains:

> Students have experiences and you can't deny that these experiences are relevant to the learning process even though you might say that these experiences are limited, raw, unfruitful or whatever. Students have memories, families, religions, feelings, languages and cultures that give them a distinctive voice. We can critically engage that experience and we can move beyond it. But we can't deny it. (p. 53)

The unevenness of experience alters subjectivity through the repetition of difference and of changes in how subjects relate to it. This, in turn, influences the modality of the subject's ascribed "rational" stances. Subjectivity changes just as the experience of the subject changes over space and time. Critical educators aspire to elevate the consciousness of students to the translatability of these "living changes" so as to inspire the self-confidence to actively question concepts and themes set in relation to an ever-expanding difference of understandings (Kaplan, 1991). This does not imply that teachers are stripped of the right to voice and to convey the experience of their own understandings, for as Giroux and Simon (1988) put it:

> Indeed, the pedagogical struggle is lessened without such resources. However, teachers and students must find forms within which a single discourse does not become the locus of certainty and certification. Rather, teachers must find ways of creating a space for mutual engagement of lived difference that does not require the silencing of a multiplicity of voices by a single dominant discourse; at the same time, teachers must develop forms of pedagogy informed by a substantive ethic that contests racism, sexism, and class exploitation as ideologies and social practices that disrupt and devalue public life. (p. 16)

Discourse serves as the medium from which students practice the critical power to interrogate concepts for the sake of learning more about the self while keeping in mind the exploitation or alienation that may arise when knowledge claims are taken to be absolute and not interpretations to be enriched by creatively considering experiential difference as a rational possibility. To this end, teachers and students work together to appreciate otherness and to simultaneously bridge the discursive abyss of an untranslatability of difference through patient rereading and self-critical rationality. Critical pedagogy, as it engages the need to develop a sensitivity for otherness over a willful submission to the castigation of cultural metanarratives, structures educational programs within the difference of everyday conditions that house the living ethical realm of student aspirations.

References

Althusser, L. (1971). *Lenin and philosophy and other essays*. (B. Brewster, Trans.). London, England: New Left Books.

Apple, M.W. (1990). *Ideology and curriculum*. New York, NY: Routledge.

Apple, M. W. (1992). Education, culture, and class power: Basil Bernstein and the neo-marxist sociology of education. *Educational Theory, 42*(2), 1–27.

Baudrillard, J. (1981). *Simulcres et simulation*. Paris, France: Galilée.

Baudrillard, J. (1983). *For a critique of the political economy of the sign*. St. Louis, MO: Telos Press.

Bennington, G. (1986). Postmodernism. In L. Appignanesi (Ed.), *Postmodernism* (p. 5). London, England: Institute of Contemporary Arts.

Best, S., & Kellner, D. (1991). *Postmodern theory*. New York, New York: The Guilford Press.

Blatz, C. V. (1989). Contextualism and critical thinking: Programmatic investigations. *Educational Theory, 39*(2), 107–119.

Bourdieu, P. (1984). *Distinction: A social critique of the judgement of taste*. (R. Nice, Trans.). Cambridge, MA: Harvard University Press. Original work published 1979.

Bourdieu, P., & Passeron, J.C. (1977). *Reproduction in education, society and culture*. (R. Nice, Trans.). London, England: Sage.

Bromley, H. (1989). Identity politics and critical pedagogy. *Educational Theory, 39*(3), 207–223.

Cherryholmes, C. H. (1988). *Power and criticism: Poststructural investigations in education*. New York, NY: Teachers College Press.

Cherryholmes, C. H. (1993). Reading research. *Curriculum Studies, 25*(1), 1–32.

Corson, J. D. (1992). Social justice and minority language policy. *Educational Theory, 42*(2), 201–216.

Derrida, J. (1976). *Of grammatology*. (G. C. Spivak, Trans.). Baltimore, MD: Johns Hopkins University Press. Original work published 1967.

Derrida, J. (1981). *Dissemination*. (B. Johnson, Trans.). University of Chicago Press. Original work published 1972.

Doll, W. E. (1989). Foundations for a postmodern curriculum. *Journal of Curriculum Studies, 21*(1), 243–253.

Eco, U. (1979). *The role of the reader: Explorations in the semiotics of text*. Bloomington, IN: University of Indiana Press.

Foster, H. (1983). Postmodernism. In H. Foster (Ed.), *The anti-esthetic* (pp. ix–xvi). Port Townsend, WA: Bay Press.

Foucault, M. (1973), *The order of things*. New York, NY: Vintage.

Foucault, M. (1979). *Discipline and punish: The birth of the prison*. (A. Sheridan, Trans.). New York, NY: Vintage. Original work published 1975.

Foucault, M. (1980). *Knowledge/power*. (C. Gordon, Trans.). New York, NY: Pantheon.

Freire, P. (1970). *Pedagogy of the oppressed*. (M. B. Ramos, Trans.). New York, NY: Seabury Press. Original work published 1970.

Freire, P., & Faundez, A. (1989). *Learning to question: A pedagogy of liberation*. New York, NY: Continuum.

Giroux, H. A. (1987). Critical literacy and student experience: Donald Graves' approach to literacy. *Language Arts, 64*(2), 175–181.

Giroux, H. A. (1988a). *Schooling and the struggle for public life*. Minneapolis, MN: University of Minnesota Press.

Giroux, H. A. (1988b). Postmodernism and the discourse of educational criticism. *Journal of Education, 170*(3), 5–30.

Giroux, H. A. (1988c). Border pedagogy in the age of postmodernism. *Journal of Education, 170*(3), 162–181.

Giroux, H. A. (1988d). The hope of radical education: A conversation with Henry Giroux. *Journal of Education, 170*(2), 91–101.

Giroux, H. A. (1990). The politics of postmodernism. *Journal of Urban and Cultural Studies, 1*(1), 5–38.

Giroux, H. A. (1992). *Border crossings: Cultural workers and the politics of education*. New York, NY: Routledge.

Giroux, H. A., & McLaren, P. (1992). Writing from the margins: Geographies of identity, pedagogy, and power. *Journal of Education, 174*(1), 7–29.

Giroux, H. A., & Simon, R. I. (1988). Schooling, popular culture, and a pedagogy of possibility. *Journal of Education, 170*(1), 9–26.

Goodman, J. (1988). Teachers as intellectuals: Toward a critical pedagogy of learning. *Journal of Education, 170*(2), 143–149.

Guba, E. G. (1992). Relativism. *Curriculum Inquiry, 22*(1), 17–23.

Hall, S. (1986). On postmodernism and articulation: An interview. *Journal of Communication Inquiry, 10*(2), 45–60.

Harvey, D. (1990). *The condition of postmodernity*. Cambridge, MA: Blackwell.

Hutcheon, L. (1992). Theorizing the postmodern. In C. Jencks (Ed.), *The post-modern reader* (pp. 76–93). New York, NY: St. Martin's Press.

Jameson, F. (1989). *Postmodernism, or, the cultural logic of late capitalism*. Durham, NC: Duke University Press.

Jencks, C. (1986). *What is post-modernism?* New York, NY: St. Martin's Press.

Jencks, C. (1987). *Post-modernism: New classicism in art and architecture*. New York, NY: Rizzoli.

Jencks, C. (1992). The postmodern agenda. In C. Jencks (Ed.), *The post-modern reader* (pp. 19–39). New York, NY: St. Martin's Press.

Kanpol, B. (1992). Postmodernism in education revisited: Similarities within differences and the democratic imaginary. *Educational Theory, 42*(2), 217–230.

Kaplan, L. D. (1991). Teaching intellectual autonomy: The failure of the critical thinking movement. *Educational Theory, 41*(4), 361–370.

Kearns, J., & Newton, K. (1980). An interview with Jacques Derrida. *Literary Review, 14*, 21–22.

Kellner, D. (1988). Reading images critically: Toward a postmodern pedagogy. *Journal of Education, 170*(3), 31–52.

Kellner, D. (1989). *Critical theory, marxism and modernity*. Baltimore, MD: Johns Hopkins University Press.

Lather, P. (1989). Ideology and methodological attitude. *JCT, 9*(2), 7–26.

Lather, P. (1991). *Getting smart: Feminist research and pedagogy within the postmodern*. New York, NY: Routledge.

Luke, C., & Gore, J. (Eds.). (1992). *Feminisms and critical pedagogy*. New York, NY: Routledge.

Lyotard, J. F. (1984). *The postmodern condition: A report on knowledge*. (G. Bennington & B. Massumi, Trans.). Minneapolis. MN: University of Minnesota Press.

Lyotard, J. F. (1986). Defining the postmodern. In L. Appignanesi (Ed.), *Postmodernism* (pp. 6–7). London, England: Institute of Contemporary Arts.

Lyotard, J. F. (1992). What is postmodernism? In C. Jencks (Ed.), *The post-modern reader* (pp. 138–150). New York, NY: St. Martin's Press.

Martusewicz, R. A. (1992). Mapping the terrain of the post-modern subject: Post-structuralism and the educated woman. In W.F. Pinar & Reynolds (Eds.), *Understanding curriculum as phenomenological and deconstructed text* (pp. 131–158). New York, NY: Teachers College Press.

McLaren, P. (1988). Schooling the postmodern body: Critical pedagogy and the politics of enfleshment. *Journal of Education, 170*(3), 53–83.

McLaren, P. (1991). Critical pedagogy, postcolonial politics and redemptive remembrance. In J. Zutell & S. McCormick (Eds.), *Fortieth yearbook of the National Reading Conference* (pp. 33–48).Chicago, IL: The National Reading Conference, Inc.

McLaren, P. (1994). Critical pedagogy, political agency, and the pragmatics of justice: The case of Lyotard. *Educational Theory, 44*(3), 319–340.

Siegel, H. (1988). *Educating reason.* New York, NY: Routledge.

Smyth, J. W. (1987). *A rationale for teachers' critical pedagogy: A handbook.* Victoria, Australia: Deakin University.

Spivak, G. C. (1992). Acting bits/identity talk. *Critical Inquiry, 18*(4), 770–803.

Stanley, W. B. (1992). *Curriculum for utopia.* Albany: State University of New York Press.

Von Glassersfeld, E. (1989). Cognition, construction of knowledge, and teaching. *Synthese, 80,* 121–140.

Wittgenstein, L. (1953). *Philosophical investigations.* (G. E. M. Anscombe, Trans.). New York, NY: Macmillan.

ELEVEN

Critical Pedagogy and Cultural Studies Research

Bricolage in Action

Shirley R. Steinberg

In the contemporary information environment of the twenty-first century—so aptly named hyperreality by Jean Baudrillard—knowledge takes on a different shape and quality. What appears to be common sense dissipates slowly into the ether, as electronic media refract the world in ways that benefit the purveyors of power. We have never seen anything like this before, a new world—new forms of social regulation, new forms of disinformation, and new modes of hegemony and ideology. In such a cyber/mediated jungle, new modes of research are absolutely necessary. This chapter proposes a form of critical cultural studies research that explores what I refer to as cultural pedagogy. Cultural pedagogy is a branch of critical pedagogy and is the educational dimension of hyperreality, as learning migrates into new sociocultural and political spaces. In these pages, I will focus my attention on my research with film, specifically on *doing educational research* with a bricolage of methods leading to tentative interpretations.

Cultural Studies

Observing that the study of culture can be fragmented among the disciplines, those who advocate cultural studies look at an interdisciplinary approach, that which transcends any one field. Additionally, a critical cultural study does not commit a qualitative evaluation of culture by a definition of "high" or "low" culture, and culture may be the most ambiguous and complex term to define in the domain of the social sciences and humanities. Arthur Asa Berger (1995) estimates that anthropologists alone have offered more than 100 definitions of culture. At the risk of great reductionism, I use the term in this chapter to signify behavior patterns socially acquired and transmitted by the use of social symbols such as language, art, science, morals, values, belief systems, politics, and many more. Educators are directly implicated in the analysis of culture (or should be) in that culture is transmitted by processes of teaching and learning, whether formally (schools) or informally (by wider social processes, e.g., popular culture). This pedagogical dynamic within all culture is a central concern of this chapter. Indeed, culture is inseparable from the human ability to be acculturated, to learn, and to employ language and symbols.

Culture, in this chapter, specifically involves its deployment in connection with the arts. This is where we move into the social territories traditionally referred to as elite or high culture and popular culture. Individuals who attend symphonies, read the "great books," and enjoy the ballet are steeped in elite culture—or as it is often phrased, "are cultured." Referring to "low" culture, many scholars assert that the artifacts that grew within a local or regional movement are indeed low. Fitting neither into a category of low or high culture is mass culture. Cultural theorists do not agree on any one definition for each type of culture. However, MacDonald (1957, p. 60) summarizes the difference between the three, and the propensity of all types of culture to become political:

> Folk art grew from below. It was a spontaneous, autochthonous expression of the people, shaped by themselves, pretty much without the benefit of high culture, to suit their own needs. Mass culture is imposed from above. It is fabricated by technicians hired by businessmen; its audiences are passive consumers, their participation limited to the choice between buying and not buying. . . . Folk art was the people's own institution, their private little garden walled off from the great formal park of their masters' high culture. But mass culture breaks down the wall, integrating the masses into a debased form of high culture and thus becoming an instrument of political domination.

Within critical cultural studies, it is maintained that the boundary between elite/high culture and popular/low culture is blurring. Such occurrence holds important ramifications for those interested in pedagogy (Berger, 1995). The study of culture, for the purpose of this chapter, is not to delineate the "level" or "type" of culture invoked by popular films but to discuss the pedagogical, sociological, and political themes within the films. Consequently, a debate as to the "quality" of popular culture or its place in light of elite culture will not be undertaken. I will use the term popular culture to define that which is readily available to the American public as a form of enjoyment and consumption.

Popular culture defies easy definition. It can be defined as the culture of ordinary people—TV shows, movies, records, radio, foods, fashions, magazines, and other artifacts that figure in our everyday lives (Berger, 1995; Hebdige, 1988). Often analysts maintain that such artifacts are mass mediated and consumed by large numbers of individuals on a continuing basis. Academicians often viewed such phenomena condescendingly—unworthy of scholarly analysis. As addressed in this chapter, the aesthetic dynamics of popular culture are not the focus; rather the social, political, and pedagogical messages contained in popular culture and their effects are viewed as some of the most important influences in the contemporary era. In this context the study of popular culture is connected with the sociology of everyday life and the interaction and interconnection of this microdomain with macrosociopolitical and structural forces. Thus, the popular domain—as ambiguous and ever-shifting as it may be—takes on unprecedented importance in the electronically saturated contemporary era.

Cultural Studies and Pedagogy

Cultural studies and pedagogy involve education and acculturation that take place at a variety of cultural locations, including but not limited to formal educational institutions. Cultural studies scholars extend our notion of cultural pedagogy, focusing their attention on the complex interactions of power, knowledge, identity, and politics. Issues of cultural pedagogy that arise in this context include:

1.   the complex relationship between power and knowledge.

2.   the ways knowledge is produced, accepted, and rejected.

3.   what individuals claim to know and the process by which they come to know it.

4.   the nature of cultural/political authority and its relation to the dialectic of empowerment and domination.

5.   the way individuals receive dominant representations and encodings of the world—are they assimilated, internalized, resisted, or transformed?

6.   the manner in which individuals negotiate their relationship with the "official story," the legitimate canon.

7.   the means by which the official and legitimated narrative positions students and citizens to make sense of their personal experience.

8.   the process by which pleasure is derived from engagement with the dominant culture—an investment that produces meaning and formulates affect.

9. the methods by which cultural differences along the lines of race, class, gender, national origin, religion, and geographical place are encoded in consciousness and processed by individuals.

10. the ways that scientific rationality shapes consciousness in schools and the culture at large.

It is with the above definitions in mind that I create my bricolage.

The attempt to delineate a universal research method for the study of the cultural curriculum and cultural pedagogy is a futile quest. The critical research of cultural studies and cultural pedagogy can make no guarantees about which questions will be important in different contexts; thus, no one method should be promoted over others. At the same time, none can be eliminated without examination. Ethnography, textual analysis, semiotics, deconstruction, critical hermeneutics, interviews, psychoanalysis, content analysis, survey research, and phenomenology simply initiate a list of research methods an educational scholar might bring to the table (Kincheloe & Berry, 2004; Nelson, Treichler, & Grossberg, 1992). Such an eclectic view of research has been labeled *bricolage* by several scholars (Kincheloe & Berry, 2004; Kincheloe, 2001; Levi-Strauss, 1966; Denzin & Lincoln, 2005, 2000; Becker, 1989). Bricolage involves taking research strategies from a variety of scholarly disciplines and traditions as they are needed in the unfolding context of the research situation. Such an action is pragmatic and strategic, demanding a self-consciousness and an awareness of context from the researcher. The researcher who employs bricolage, the *bricoleur,* must be able to orchestrate a plethora of diverse tasks, including interviewing and observing, historiographical analysis, self-monitoring, and intrapersonal understanding.

The text produced by this research process of bricolage should be a complex collage, as it weaves together the scholar's images, insights, and interpretations of the relationship between the popular cultural text, critical questions of justice, the social context that produced it, and its effect on youth and the cultural curriculum (Kincheloe & Berry, 2004; Kincheloe, 2005, 2001; Denzin & Lincoln, 2005, 2000). Using theoretical and conceptual frames drawn from critical theory, poststructuralism, postmodern epistemologies, feminism, psychoanalysis, hermeneutics, recovery theory, and other traditions, bricolage interprets, critiques, and deconstructs the text in question. Because scientific research has traditionally offered only a partial vision of the reality it seeks to explore, pedagogical bricoleurs attempt to widen their perspectives through methodological diversity. In no way, however, do they claim that as the result of the multiperspective bricolage they have gained "the grand view." From their poststructuralist perspective they understand that all inquiry is limited and incomplete. Humble in this knowledge, the bricoleur attempts to gain expanded insight via historical contextualization, multiple theoretical groundings, and a diversity of knowledge by collecting and interpreting methodologies (Kincheloe, 2005, 2001; Kellner, 1995).

Theoretical bricolage compensates for the blindness of relying on one model of reading a cultural text. Bricolage does not draw upon diverse theoretical/methodological traditions simply for the sake of diversity. Rather, it uses the different approaches to inform and critique each other. A critical theoretical analysis of popular culture that is informed by psychoanalysis, for example, will be different than one that relies only on the sociological dimension of the text under analysis. Such an interpretive process subverts the tendency of knowledge producers to slip into the position that their interpretation is the "right one" (Kincheloe, 2005, 2001; Kellner, 1995). As we study the pedagogy of film, we are able to position it not only in historical, sociopolitical, and economic contexts, but in relation to other films on a particular topic, with similar themes, or identified with a particular genre—for example, the films of John Hughes concerning middle-class male misbehavior. Expanding our ways of seeing with diverse perspectives, we begin to grasp the ideological dimensions of films that often fall through the cracks. A more specific focus on how particular methodologies may be used in this popular cultural/film context may be in order.

Critical Ethnography

Critical ethnography is an example of a critical research methodology that can be used within the bricolage. Ethnography is often described as the most basic form of social research: the analysis of events as they evolve in their natural setting. While ethnographers disagree about the relative importance of each purpose, ethnography attempts to gain knowledge about a cultural setting, to identify patterns of social interaction, and to develop holistic interpretations of societies and social institutions. Thus, typical educational ethnographies attempt to understand the nature of schools and other educational agencies in these ways, seeking to appreciate the social processes that move educational events. Ethnography attempts to make explicit the social processes one takes for granted as a culture member. The culture could be as broad as the study of an ethnic culture or as narrow as the middle-class white male culture of misbehavior. The critical ethnographer of education seeks to describe the concrete experiences of everyday school/educational life and its social patterns, the deep structures that support it (Hammersley & Atkinson, 1983; Smith, 1989; Clough, 1992). In a bricolage, ethnography can be used in a variety of ways to gain insight into film. The most traditional involves audience studies in which ethnographers observe and interview film audiences. John Fiske (1993) began his book *Power Plays, Power Works* using such a methodology, as he observed and interviewed a group of homeless men in a shelter as they watched the movie *Die Hard*. What was the nature of the interrelationship between the viewers and the text? What did the men's responses to the film tell us about their self-images? What did the men's responses tell us about film viewing in general and its ideological effects? Fiske's answers to these questions—to interpret his data—constitutes much of the content of the book.

In addition to such "audiencing" ethnographies, scholars can use ethnographic methods to explore the characters and cultures portrayed within the film and their relation to social dynamics outside the texts. Gaining knowledge about the "film culture" provides insight into the ideological orientations of filmmakers and entertainment corporations. Through the identification of patterns of cultural expression and social interaction, researchers can begin to specify the ideological dynamics at work. As sociopolitical processes are exposed, hidden agendas and tacit assumptions can be highlighted so as to provide new appreciations of the power of film to both reflect and shape culture. Poststructuralist forms of ethnography have focused on the discontinuities, contradictions, and inconsistencies of cultural expression and human action. As opposed to more modernist forms of ethnography, poststructuralist methods refuse to reconcile the asymmetries once and for all. The poststructuralist dimension of ethnography highlights the tendency of classical ethnography to privilege a dominant narrative and a unitary, privileged vantage point. In the effort to connect knower and known, the poststructuralist ethnographer proposes a dialogue between researcher and researched that attempts to smash traditional hierarchical relations between them (Atkinson & Hammersley, 1994).

In this critical process, the modernist notion of ethnography as an instrument of enlightenment and civilization of the "native" *objects* of study is overthrown. Poststructuralist ethnographies are texts to be argued over, texts whose meaning is never "natural" but are constructed by circumstance and inscribed by context (Aronowitz, 1993). Thus, a film never stands alone as an object of study in poststructuralist ethnography. Seen as a living part of culture and history, the film takes on new meaning and circumstances and contexts change. How different the movie *The Green Berets* (1968) looked to the young audience that viewed it in the late 1960s and early 1970s than it does to young people viewing it in the post-Gulf War 1990s. More young people of the present era may positively resonate with the ideological intentions of the filmmakers than did young antiwar viewers of the era in which it was produced. Circumstance and context must always be accounted for in critical poststructuralist ethnography. In this context poststructuralist ethnography informs and is informed by feminist and minority researchers concerned with the status quo of apologetics of film and traditional ethnography itself (Nelson, Treichler, & Grossberg, 1992; Willis, 1977; Marcus & Fischer, 1986; Griffin, 1985; Clifford, 1992; Taussig, 1987).

Content Analysis

Traditionally a content analysis could be considered methodical and quantitative in nature. The important issue about literally analyzing text is to allow the text to open and present themes for the researcher. The following is a method I have used with success in first, analyzing text, and second, in letting the textual analysis speak to me and suggest the themes that can be included. The content analysis then becomes an authentic interpretive analysis that precludes preliminary hypothesis and instead waits to allow the data to speak for itself in mulilayered ways. The analysis especially lends itself to research in film, written text, visual text (comics, photography, etc.). It then becomes ready for the critical hermeneutic interpretation, which is my tentative research goal.

In addition to such ethnographic analysis, critical educational scholars use other methods of studying the social dynamics and effects of film. Douglas Kellner (1995) performs content analyses of film reviews and criticisms, in the process gaining new vantage points out of the ways that film texts become embedded in popular discourses. This "mode of reception" study was promoted by the Frankfurt School critical theorist Walter Benjamin (Kellner, 1995). Appropriating Benjamin's methodology, literary critics and theorists developed literary reception research that continues to contribute innovative ways of exploring textual effects. Distributed throughout Aaron Gresson's analysis of *Forrest Gump* is the discussion of the film by various critics and the news media. Beginning with the traditional "thumbs up" or "thumbs down" types of articles and moving to more esoteric and scholarly discussion, Gresson (1996) is able to trace themes relating back to his original suggestion of the recovery of whiteness and maleness in film. In this context, various research methodologies can be added to the bricolage, in the process providing ever more nuanced forms of insight into popular cultural texts.

Semiotics plays an invaluable role in the methodological pantheon with its focus on codes and signs that contribute to individuals' attempts to derive meaning from their surroundings. Educational researchers can use semiotic methods to gain insight into the social dynamics moving classroom events. Classrooms are full of codes calling out for semiotic analysis. Not only are classrooms saturated with codes and signs, but they are characterized by rituals and conventions that are rarely questioned. The ways that teachers, students, and administrators dress; pupils' language when speaking to teachers compared to conversations with classmates; graffiti in a middle school restroom; systems of rules of behavior; the use of bells and the intercom in schools; memos sent to parents; and the nature of the local community's conversation about school athletics are only a few of the topics an educational semiotician could study.

Observation Methods

Contrary to notions that qualitative research dealing with popular culture is vacuous and without rigor, I submit my methodology in the spirit of academic scholarship and indeed, a poststructuralist, feminist, pedagogical research in which I am not seeking answers, but seeking questions, questions, and more questions in which to make sense of the world of youth and of education. In their *Handbook of Qualitative Research,* Norm Denzin and Yvonna Lincoln (2005; 2000; 1994) discuss their union of poststructural/postmodernist cultural research (Denzin) and constructivist/pedagogical research (Lincoln). They contend that traditional research stops short of boundary crossing within interpretation. Observing that "over the past two decades, a quiet methodological revolution has been taking place in the social sciences" (Denzin & Lincoln, 1994, p. ix), Denzin and Lincoln define this revolution as the "blurring" of the boundaries within disciplinary research. As I discuss my methods and objectives in my research, keep in mind that I want to make "noise" in this so-called "quiet" revolution. In fact, I question whether or not it has ever been quiet. Certainly there have been attempts to silence the noise caused by radical qualitative research—silence in the denial of the politicization of the research of pedagogy; however, my qualitative predecessors have worked long and hard in the legitimization of the discipline. The word *rigor* seems to rear its ugly head at methodological junctures. I assert here that my research is indeed rigorous, challenging, and constantly changing. Unlike those who use a statistical formula, an organized hypothesis, and a proven theorem, I am not beginning with any assumptions other than the one that popular culture must be studied. My thoughts about my subjects and my expectations in my observations changed each time I analyzed and recorded (for lack of a better word) *data*. It was within this discovery and rediscovery that I found rigor and challenge. It is within this context that I present my *literal method of interpretation*. I assert that rigorous scripting, recording, and viewing/reviewing (or consuming/reconsuming) are essential for critical hermeneutical research, and it is this process I delineate here.

The postmodern condition has also redetermined and redefined the actual research methods and practices that we use. No longer, as in earlier cultural research, do we view a film at the theater, go to the typewriter, and write a response and review. We have the tools of hyperreality, the video recorder and the pause/stop/reverse/forward components of the remote that allow us to interpret, reinterpret, and then problematize our own interpretations as we attempt to make meaning from the text of film. Unlike viewer/historians of the past, we are able to revisit an event, a text, and look for the tacit assumptions that reside within each signifier, floating signifier, code, and ideology presented within the film.

Materials and Process

In order to be able to revisit and review text, I found it essential to have access to videotapes of the films I wished to discuss. Wherever possible, I have avoided even alluding to films still in the theater as I feel they are available for a shallow interpretation at best (unless, of course, one owns his or her own theater). Along with the videotapes, I needed a video recorder, television and a good remote control. Other "equipment" I needed included an unlimited amount of colored pencils, ruled notebooks, and a pen. However, on review of these methods, I feel that the use of a laptop computer while viewing could have or would have enhanced and possibly quickened the recording method.

In the manner of traditional ethnography, I used scripting as my form of recording. I wrote constantly through each film, usually filling up my notebooks after two films. I wrote quickly and intuitively. I cannot delineate *what* to record. I can only describe that I recorded *everything* that made me think. Consequently I relied on my own pedagogical intuition in my records. The use of the remote was essential in being able to rewind and record exact dialogue or to view a scene closely. In some films, I recorded no dialogue, only impressions of the scenery or music or cinematography. In most films I did record dialogue, discerning it as the salient data that would eventually be entered into my hermeneutical interpretations and discussions.

Each film took many hours to watch and rewatch. When I felt comfortable that I had scripted enough to begin my transcriptions, I transcribed the notebooks into word-processed form. Using phrases, I typed my entries going down each page as I had originally written them. After completing the transcription of all of the films, I read through the entire set of data. As I examined this completed set of scripting, themes and motifs started to emerge. As they began to repeat themselves, I wrote down my impressions of their emergence and *named* them as separate entities. After my first reading of the data, I used the colored pencils to code each theme/motif that I wanted to pursue. Underlining each item with a different color, I began to see macrothemes emerge, as the microthemes seemed coalesced under the auspices of larger themes. Analyzing all the pages of scripting, I discovered additional themes each time. In many instances there would be three or four different colors under a certain situation or dialogue indicating an overlap among the themes.

Both visually and intuitively, I began the task of arranging microthemes and placing them within the macrothemes. Given the thematic crossover, it was important to not essentialize any situation or dialogue and limit it to only one "category." I kept in mind that through my choice of bricolage, I was not adhering to one method of interpretation. Consequently it was important to record and underline each microtheme every time it emerged in all macrocategories.

Viewing and Naming Films

As this is a chapter discussing critical pedagogical research methods, I chose not to use traditional methods of film theory and criticism. I will delineate three terms that I used within my bricolage. As a bricoleur, I cut and pasted what I felt was significant and examined the multiple meanings that emerged. Traditional film criticism, as in any form of sociological research, has categories and philosophies attached to methods of interpretation of audiences and of text. And, as in traditional research, this criticism essentializes and closes itself off to the boundary crossing to which Denzin and Lincoln have chosen to blur. By taking each interpretative method and applying it to a film bricolage, I was able to use film criticism and theory to my advantage in my critical hermeneutical readings.

Traditional film criticism "reads" film in many ways. The most compelling methods and classifications involve concepts of 1) *auteurism* 2) *montage* and 3) *genre*. Each term has value in critical hermeneutics; however, using them in a unilateral deconstruction would limit interpretation to a dogmatic ideological framework established by the original researcher.

Auteurism

As the name suggests, auteurism refers to the authorship of the text. As in a Derridian deconstruction, the text becomes the only artifact examined, and unlike a Derridian deconstruction, the text in relationship to the author/creator is the essential interpretation. The entire act of meaning-making in auteurism is restricted to who the author is, his or her positionality, and his or her tacit and overt agendas in regard to the text. While I would be unable to discount the inclusion of auteurism in interpreting film text, in no way would I be comfortable limiting the interpretation to this narrow theory. In the case of the writer/director John Hughes—whose films I rely on heavily in my research—I cannot discount the fact that he is a white, middle-class male and a baby boomer from Chicago. Further discovery of his own background and education *can* inform me about him and "where he comes from." However, to allow auteurism to define the purpose of his films, for example: Ferris Bueller *is* John Hughes or Hughes's plotlines revolve around his own personal agenda for humiliating adults would direct and possibly limit my interpretation(s). Robin Wood (1995) insists that limiting film theory to auteurism adds to the propensity of inconclusive, inaccurate research that insists "on its own particular polarization" (p. 59).

Montage

Like auteurism, montage relies on one lens through which to view a text. Unlike auteurism, montage examines the intent of the editor in the analysis of the "essential creative act" of filmmaking (Wood, 1995). While auteur theory exclusively reads the act of the author as the textual interpretation, montage theory introduces the notion that the cutting-room floor becomes the site for the decisive interpretative act. Once again, one cannot ignore the possible intent of the film editor and/or cinematographer. However, to limit interpretation to montage at the expense of any other aspect of film criticism and theory would once again limit the thickness of the interpretation.

Genre

In the traditional literary manner, the concept of genre is used to define and classify texts into manageable categories which immediately allow the interpreter to draw conclusions and make expected observations. For instance, when we refer to the western as a genre, it is easy to imagine horses, Indians, pioneers, and a white cowboy on a majestic horse. Within genre theory, we are able to find familiar western themes of patriarchy, white supremacy, and colonialism without much effort. If we refer to *film noir*, we easily picture the frames of shadowy figures, a femme fatale, and a Bogartesque antihero engaged in questionable activities. Once again, a prevailing theme of patriarchy emerges without question. Consider the 1950s sci-fi genre—a white, upper-middle-class scientist who goes against the odds to defeat an alien invader—back to patriarchy, colonialism, and so forth. Exclusive reliance on genre theory determines in advance which themes will be analyzed and which will not—again the possibility of new interpretations is truncated. Categorizing texts aids us in the ability to place videos on the shelf, to place books in the library, and to choose different genres in which to research. However, the discussion of genre should be used only in the general sense to name the macrocategory of film that the researcher chooses to interpret. The catch is that the genre must be determined and defined by each researcher in the context of his or her own research. Consequently, what I view as a western may indeed be viewed as a political satire by one researcher and a classic by another.

With the use of auteurism, montage and genre, I have combined the qualitative method of bricolage using critical ethnography, semiotics, feminist theory, and critical hermeneutics to interpret my research.

Feminist Research

Another important aspect of the bricolage involves feminist research with its subversion of the principle of neutral, hierarchical, and estranged interaction between the researcher and the researched (Fee, 1982; Mies, 1982; Olesen, 1994; Hekman, 1990; Flax, 1990; Ferguson, 1993; Collins, 1990; Clough, 1992; Butler, 1990). It is important that no one body of feminist theory exists. Three forms of feminist analysis have dominated the feminist critique:

1. Liberal feminism has focused on gender stereotyping and bias. While such analyses have provided valuable insights, liberal feminism in general has failed to engage issues of power. As a result, the position has been hard-pressed to make sense of social reality with its subtle interactions of power, ideology, and culture—an interaction that needs to be analyzed in the larger effort to understand both the oppression of women and male privilege (Weiler, 1988; Rosenau, 1992);

2. Radical feminism has maintained that the subjugation of women is the most important form of oppression in that it is grounded on specific biological differences between men and women. In radical feminism, concerns with race and class are more rejected than ignored, as radical feminists maintain the irrelevance of such categories in the study of women's oppression;

3. The form of feminist theory privileged in my research is critical poststructuralist feminism. This articulation of feminism asserts that feminism is the quintessential postmodern discourse. As feminists focus on and affirm that which is absent and/or peripheral in modernist ways of seeing, they ground the poststructuralist critique in lived reality, in the material world (Kipnis, 1989; Jagger, 1983). As critical poststructuralist feminists challenge modernist patriarchal exclusions, they analyze the connections between an unjust class structure and the oppression of women (Weiler, 1988; Rosenau, 1992). Often, they contend, male domination of women is concretized on the terrain of class, e.g., the feminization of poverty and the growth in the number of women who are homeless over the last 15 years (Kincheloe & Steinberg, 1997).

In this poststructuralist feminist context, research can no longer be seen as a cold, rational process. Feminist research injects feeling, empathy, and the body into the act of inquiry, blurring the distinction between knower and known, viewer and viewed—looking at truth as a *process* of construction in which knowers and viewers play an active role, and embedding passion into the bricolage. Researchers in this context see themselves as passionate scholars who connect themselves emotionally to what they are seeking to know and understand. Modernist researchers often weeded out the self, denying their intuitions and inner voices, in the process producing restricted and object-like interpretations of socioeducational events. Using the traditional definitions, these object-like interpretations were certain and scientific; feminist self-grounded inquiries were inferior, merely impressionistic, and journalistic (Reinharz, 1979, 1992). Rejecting the authority of the certainty of science, feminist researchers charged that the so-called objectivity of modernist science was nothing more than a signifier for the denial of social and ethical responsibility, ideological passivity, and the acceptance of the privileged sociopolitical position of the researcher. Thus, feminist theorists argued that modernist pseudo-objectivity demands the separation of thought and feeling, the devaluation of any perspective maintained with emotional conviction. Feeling is designated as an inferior form of human consciousness—those who rely on thought or logic operating within this framework can justify their repression of those associated with emotion or feeling. Feminist theorists have pointed out that the thought-feeling hierarchy is one of the structures historically used by men to oppress women (Walby, 1990). In intimate heterosexual relationships, if a man is able to present his position in an argument as the rational viewpoint and the woman's position as an emotional perspective, then he has won the argument—his is the voice worth hearing.

Drawing from feminist researchers, critical poststructuralists have learned that inquiry should be informed by our "humanness," that we can use the human as a research instrument. From this perspective, inquiry begins with researchers drawing upon their own experience. Such an educational researcher is a human being studying other human beings, focusing on their inner world of experience. Utilizing his or her own empathetic understandings, the observer can watch educational phenomena from within—that is, the observer can know directly; he or she can watch and experience. In the process, the private is made public. Not only do we get closer to the private experience of students, teachers, and administrators and the effect of these experiences on the public domain, but we also gain access to the private experience of the researcher and the effect of that experience on the public description that the researcher presents of the phenomena observed (Reinharz, 1979, 1982, 1992). Thus not only do we learn about the educational world which surrounds us, but we gain new insights into the private world within us—the world of our constructed subjectivity. By revealing what can be learned from the everyday and the mundane, feminist scholars have opened a whole new area of inquiry and insight. They have uncovered the existence of silences and absences where traditional scholars had seen only "what was there." When the feminist critique is deployed within the methodological diversity of the bricolage, new forms of insight into educational and social affairs as well as the cultural curriculum emerge.

Connecting to Social Theory

In examining social dynamics of media/popular culture via the research methodologies of ethnography and semiotics and the political and epistemological concerns of poststructuralist feminism, an effort is made to connect research to the domain of social theory. Indeed, theory is very important in the bricolage of critical poststructuralist research. Theory involves the conceptual matrix analysts use to make sense of the world. Theory, whether it is held consciously or unconsciously, works as a filter through which researchers approach information, designate facts, identify problems, and devise solutions to their problems. Different theoretical frameworks, therefore, privilege different ways of seeing the world in general or the domain of popular culture in particular (Kincheloe, 2001; Aronowitz, 1993; Giroux, 1988). The theory behind a critical poststructuralist way of seeing recognizes these theoretical dynamics, especially the potential tyranny that accompanies theoretical speculation. The problem that has undermined the traditional critical project of understanding and changing the inequality plaguing modernist societies has involved the production of a theory that was too totalizing (all encompassing) and rigid to grasp the *complexity* described here. Critical poststructuralist theory is committed to a theoretical stance that guarantees the individual or community the capacity to make meaning and to act independently. Any theory acceptable to critical poststructuralists, thus, must take into account local divergence. This is not to adopt a position that insists researchers allow phenomena to speak for themselves. Theory in this context is a resource that can be used to generate a dialogue with a phenomenon. It is always contingent, and it never whispers the answers to the researcher in advance (Rosenau, 1992; Dickens & Fontana, 1994; Grossberg, 1995; During, 1994). Theory does not travel well from one context to another. Indeed, theory's usefulness is always mitigated by context.

Such a locally sensitive theoretical position allows bricolage research a space from which to view movies and popular cultural phenomena that maintains an oppositional but not a totalizing and deterministic interpretive strategy (Smith, 1989). Such a strategy searches for manifestations of domination and resistance in popular texts in light of larger questions of democracy (Kellner, 1995). Drawing upon the theoretical work of the Frankfurt School of Critical Theory, the concept of immanent critique helps us understand this oppositional dynamic. Critical theory, according to Max Horkheimer, attempts to expose and assess the breach between reality and ideas of "what is" and "what could be." Within capitalist society, Horkheimer maintained, there is an inherent contradiction between the bourgeois order's words and deeds. The more the power bloc speaks of justice, equality, and freedom, the more it fails under its own standards. Immanent critique, therefore, attempts to evaluate cultural production "from within," on the basis of the standards of its producers. In this way it hopes to avoid the accusation that its concepts inflict superfluous criteria of evaluation on those it investigates. Employing such a theoretical critique, critical theorists hope to generate a new understanding of the cultural phenomenon in question—an understanding that is able to articulate both the contradictions and possibilities contained with it (Held, 1980).

Critical Hermeneutics and the Process of Interpretation

I ground my research in the hermeneutical tradition and its concern with both the process of understanding the meaning of various texts and the production of strategies for textual interpretation. Traditionally concerned with the interpretation of religious texts and canonical scriptures within their social and historical context, hermeneutics, after the scientific revolution of the European Enlightenment, emerged as the tradition that challenged the increasingly powerful shibboleths of the empirical scientific tradition. One of the central assertions of hermeneutics is that research and analysis of any variety involve an awareness of one's own consciousness and the values residing tacitly within it. Such values and the predispositions they support, hermeneuts maintained, unconsciously shape the nature of any project of inquiry. Such profound arguments, unfortunately, exerted little influence on their scientific contemporaries, as they held fast to their science of verification, the notion of objectivity, and the absurdity of the need for self-analysis on the part of the researcher (Kincheloe, 2005; Peters & Lankshear, 1994).

Central to the hermeneutic method is an appreciation of the complexity and ambiguity of human life in general and the pedagogical process in particular. Hermeneutics attempts to return lived experience and meaning-making to their original difficulty. In this context, words and images are relegated to the realm of the living with all the possibility for change such a state implies. Words and images to the hermeneutical analyst are not dead and static but alive and dynamic. Such a reality, of course, complicates the process of interpretation but concurrently provides a far more textured picture of human experience. The Greek root of hermeneutics, *hermeneuenin,* refers to the messenger god Hermes. Such an etymology well fits hermeneutics' ambiguous inscription, as Hermes was often a trickster in his official role of translator of divine messages to human beings. Interpretation is never simple and straightforward—humans in the Greek myths learned this lesson frequently at the hands of their deceptive messenger. This lesson is not lost in 20th century hermeneutics, as analysts focus their attention on the sediments of meaning and the variety of intentions that surround social, political, and educational artifacts. Transcending the scientific empirical need for final proof and certainty, hermeneuts celebrate the irony of interpretation in the ambiguous lived world. Framing the methods of such interpretation as both analytic and intuitive, hermeneutics pushes the boundaries of human understanding in a manner more consonant with the contradictory nature of the world around us.

The Nature of Hermeneutic Interpretation

Hermeneutics insists that in social/educational science there is only interpretation, no matter how vociferously empirical scientists may argue that the facts speak for themselves. The hermeneutic act of interpretation involves in its most elemental articulation making sense of what has been observed in a way that com-municates understanding. Not only is human science merely an act of interpreta-tion, but hermeneutics contends that perception itself is an act of interpretation. Thus, the quest for understanding is a fundamental feature of human existence, as encounter with the unfamiliar always demands the attempt to make meaning, to make sense—but such is also the case with the familiar. Indeed, as in the study of commonly known popular movies, we come to find that sometimes the familiar may be seen as the most strange. Thus, it should not be surprising that even the so-called objective writings of qualitative research are interpretations, not value-free descriptions (Denzin, 1994; Gallagher, 1992).

Learning from the hermeneutic tradition and the postmodern critique, criti-cal researchers have begun to reexamine textual claims to authority. No pristine interpretation exists—indeed, no methodology, social or educational theory, and discursive form can claim a privileged position that enables the production of authoritative knowledge. Researchers must always speak/write about the world in terms of something else in the world. As creatures of the world, we are oriented to it in a way that prevents us from grounding our theories and perspectives outside of it. Thus, whether we like it or not we are all destined as interpreters to analyze from within its boundaries and blinders. Within these limitations, however, the interpretations emerging from the hermeneutic process can still move us to new levels of understanding, appreciations that allow us to "live our way" into an experience described to us. Despite the impediments of context, hermeneutical researchers can transcend the inadequacies of thin descriptions of decontextual-ized facts and produce thick descriptions of social/pedagogical texts characterized by the context of its production, the intentions of its producers, and the meanings mobilized in the process of its construction. The production of such thick descrip-tions/interpretations follows no step-by-step blueprint or mechanical formula. As with any art form, hermeneutical analysis can be learned only in the Deweyan sense—by doing it. Researchers in this context practice the art by grappling with the text to be understood, telling its story in relation to its contextual dynam-ics and other texts first to themselves and then to a public audience (Kincheloe, 2005; Denzin, 1994; Gallagher, 1992).

Thoughts about Hermeneutical Methods of Interpretation

These concerns with the nature of hermeneutical interpretation come under the category of philosophical hermeneutics. Working in this domain, hermeneuti-cal scholars attempt to think through and clarify the conditions in which in-terpretation and understanding take place. The following analysis moves more in the direction of normative hermeneutics in that it raises questions about the purposes and procedures of interpretation. In its critical-theory-driven cultural-studies context, the purpose of hermeneutical analysis employed in this research is to provide understanding of particular cultural and educational phenomena of contemporary American life. Drawing upon the Frankfurt School's goal of theorizing the driving forces of the present moment, critical hermeneutics is used to develop a form of cultural criticism that sets the stage for a future politics/pedagogy of emancipation. Hermeneutical researchers operating with these objectives build bridges between reader and text, text and its producer, historical context and present, and one particular social circumstance and another. Accomplishing such interpretive tasks is a difficult endeavor, and scholars interested in normative hermeneutics push aspiring hermeneuts to trace the bridge-building process employed by successful interpreters of culture and pedagogy (Kincheloe, 2005; Kellner, 1995).

Grounded by this hermeneutical bridge-building, critical social analysts in a hermeneutical circle (a process of analysis in which interpreters seek the historical and social dynamics that shape textual interpretation) engage in the back and forth of studying parts in relation to the whole and the whole in relation to parts. No final interpretation is sought in this context, as the activity of the circle proceeds with no need for closure (Kincheloe, 2005; Gallagher, 1992; Peters & Lankshear, 1994). This movement of whole to parts is combined with an analytical flow between abstract and concrete. Such dynamics often tie interpretation to the interplay of larger social forces (the general) to the everyday lives of individuals (the particular). A critical hermeneutics brings the concrete, the parts, the particular into focus, but in a manner that grounds it (them) contextually in a larger understanding of the social forces, the whole, the abstract (the general) that grounds it (them). Focus on the parts is the dynamic that brings the particular into focus, sharpening our understanding of the individual in light of the social and psychological forces that shape him or her. The parts and the unique places they occupy ground hermeneutical ways of seeing by providing the contextualization of the particular—a perspective often erased in modernist science's search for abstract generalizations (Kincheloe, 2005; Kellner, 1995; Gallagher, 1992; Peters & Lankshear, 1994).

The give and take of the hermeneutical circle induces analysts to review existing conceptual matrixes in light of new understandings. Here, preconceptions are reconsidered and reconceptualized to provide a new way of exploring a particular text. Making use of an author's insights hermeneutically does not mean replicating his or her response to his or her original question. In the hermeneutical process, the author's answer is valuable only if it catalyzes the production of a new question for our consideration in the effort to make sense of a particular textual phenomenon (Gallagher, 1992). In this context, participants in the hermeneutical circle must be wary of critical techniques of textual defamiliarization that have become clichéd. For example, feminist criticisms of Barbie's figure and its construction of the image of the ideal woman became such conventions in popular cultural analysis that other readings of Barbie were suppressed (Steinberg, 1997). Critical hermeneutical analysts in this and many other cases have to introduce new forms of analysis to the hermeneutical circle—to defamiliarize conventional defamiliarizations—in order to achieve deeper levels of understanding (Berger, 1995).

Within the hermeneutical circle, we may develop new metaphors to shape our analysis in ways that break us out of familiar modes. For example, thinking of movies as mass-mediated dreams may help us reconceptualize the interpretive act as a psychoanalytic form of dream study. In this way, educational scholars could examine psychoanalytical work in the analysis of dream symbolization for insights into their studies of the pedagogy of popular culture and the meanings it helps individuals make via its visual images and narratives. As researchers apply these new metaphors in the hermeneutic circle, they must be aware of the implicit metaphors analysts continuously bring to the interpretive process (Berger, 1995). Such metaphors are shaped by the sociohistorical era, the culture, and the linguistic context in which the interpreter operates. Such awarenesses are important features that must be introduced into the give and take of the hermeneutical circle. As John Dewey wrote almost a century ago, individuals adopt the values and perspectives of their social groups in a manner that such factors come to shape their views of the world. Indeed, the values and perspectives of the group help determine what is deemed important and what is not, what is granted attention and what is ignored. Hermeneutical analysts are aware of such interpretational dynamics and make sure they are included in the search for understanding (Berger, 1995; Gallagher, 1992).

Situating Interpretation

Researchers who fail to take Dewey's point into account operate at the mercy of unexamined assumptions. Since all interpretation is historically and culturally situated, it befalls the lot of the hermeneutical analyst to study the ways both interpreters (often the analysts themselves) and the object of interpretation are constructed by their time and place. In this context the importance of social theory emerges. In this research critical social theory is injected into the hermeneutic circle to facilitate an understanding of the hidden structures and tacit cultural dynamics that insidiously inscribe social meanings and values (Gallagher, 1992; Kellner, 1995). This social and historical situating of interpreter and text is an extremely complex enterprise that demands a nuanced analysis of the impact of hegemonic and ideological forces that connect the microdynamics of everyday life with the macrodynamics of structures of white supremacy, patriarchy, and class elitism. The central hermeneutic of this work will involve the interaction between the cultural curriculum and these situating sociohistorical structures.

When these aspects of the interpretation process are taken into account, analysts begin to understand Hans-Georg Gadamer's contention that social frames of reference influence researchers' questions, which, in turn, shape the nature of interpretation itself. In light of this situating process, the modernist notion that a social text has one valid interpretation evaporates into thin air. Researchers, whether they admit it or not, always have a point of view, a disciplinary orientation, a social or political group with which they identify (Kincheloe, 2005, 2001, 1991). Thus, the point, critical hermeneuts argue, is not for researchers to shed all worldly affiliations but to identify them and understand their impact on the ways they approach a social and educational phenomenon. Gadamer labels these worldly affiliations of researchers their "horizons" and deems the hermeneutic act of interpretation the "fusion of horizons." When researchers engage in the fusion of horizons, they enter the tradition of the text. Here, they study the conditions of its production and the circle of previous interpretations. In this manner they begin to uncover the ways the text has attempted to represent truth (Berger, 1995).

In the critical hermeneutical tradition these analyses of the ways interpretation is situated are considered central to the critical project. Researchers, like all human beings, argue critical analysts, make history and live their lives within structures of meaning they have not necessarily chosen for themselves. Understanding this, critical hermeneuts realize that a central aspect of their cultural pedagogical analysis involves dissecting the ways people connect their everyday experiences to the cultural representations of such experiences. Such work involves the unraveling of the ideological codings embedded in these cultural representations. This unraveling is complicated by the taken-for-grantedness of the meanings promoted in these representations and the typically undetected ways these meanings are circulated into everyday life (Denzin, 1992). The better the analyst, the better he or she can expose these meanings in the domain of the "what-goes-without-saying"—in this research those features of the media curriculum that are not addressed, that don't elicit comment.

At this historical juncture—the postmodern condition or hyperreality, as it has been labeled—electronic modes of communication become extremely important to the production of meanings and representations that culturally situate human beings in general and textual interpretations in particular. In many ways it can be argued that the postmodern condition produces a second-hand culture, filtered and preformed in the marketplace and constantly communicated via popular cultural and mass media. Critical analysts understand that the pedagogical effects of such a *media*ted culture can range from the political/ideological to the cognitive/epistemological. For example, the situating effects of print media tend to promote a form of linearity that encourages rationality, continuity, and uniformity. On the other hand, electronic media promote a nonlinear immediacy that may encourage more emotional responses that lead individuals in very different directions. Thus, the situating influence and pedagogical impact of electronic media of the postmodern condition must be assessed by those who study the pedagogical process and, most importantly in this context, the research process itself (Kincheloe, 2005; Kellner, 1995; Berger, 1995; Denzin, 1992).

Critical Hermeneutics

Understanding the forces that situate interpretation, critical hermeneutics is suspicious of any model of interpretation that claims to reveal the final truth, the essence of a text, or any form of experience. Critical hermeneutics is more comfortable with interpretive approaches that assume that the meaning of human experience can never be fully disclosed—neither to the researcher nor even to the human who experienced it. Since language is always slippery with its meanings ever "in process," critical hermeneuts understand that interpretations will never be linguistically unproblematic and will never be direct representations. Critical hermeneutics seeks to understand how textual practices such as scientific research and classical theory work to maintain existing power relations and to support extant power structures (Denzin, 1992). This research draws, of course, on the latter model of interpretation with its treatment of the personal as political. Critical hermeneutics grounds a critical pedagogy that attempts to connect the everyday troubles individuals face to public issues of power, justice, and democracy. Typically, within the realm of the cultural curriculum, critical hermeneutics has deconstructed popular cultural texts that promote demeaning stereotypes of the disempowered (Denzin, 1992). In this research, critical hermeneutics will be deployed differently in relation to popular cultural texts, as it examines popular movies that reinforce an ideology of privilege and entitlement for empowered members of the society—in this case, white, middle- or upper-class males.

In its ability to render the personal political, critical hermeneutics provides a methodology for arousing a critical consciousness through the analysis of the generative themes of the present era. Such generative themes form the basis of the cultural curriculum of popular culture (Peters & Lankshear, 1994). Within the academy, there is still resistance to the idea that movies, TV, and popular music are intricately involved in the most important political, economic, and cultural battles of the contemporary epoch. Critical hermeneutics recognizes this centrality of popular culture in the postmodern condition and seeks to uncover the ways it impedes and advances the struggle for a democratic society (Kincheloe, 2005; Kellner, 1995). Appreciating the material effects of media culture, critical hermeneutics traces the ways movies position audiences politically in ways that not only shape their political beliefs but formulate their identities. In this context, Paulo Freire's contribution to the development of a critical hermeneutics is especially valuable. Understanding that the generative themes of a culture are central features in a critical social analysis, Freire assumes that the interpretive process is both an ontological and an epistemological act. It is ontological on the level that our vocation as humans, the foundation of our being, is grounded on the hermeneutical task of interpreting the world so we can become more fully human. It is epistemological in the sense that critical hermeneutics offers us a method for investigating the conditions of our existence and the generative themes that shape it. In this context we gain the prowess to both live with a purpose and operate with the ability to perform evaluative acts in naming the culture around us. In the postmodern condition the pedagogical effects of popular culture have often been left unnamed, allowing our exploration of the shaping of our own humanness to go unexplored in this strange new social context. Critical hermeneutics addresses this vacuum (Kincheloe, 2005; Peters & Lankshear, 1994).

Critical hermeneutics names the world as a part of a larger effort to evaluate it and make it better. Knowing this, we can find it easy to understand why critical hermeneutics focuses on domination and its negation, emancipation. Domination limits self-direction and democratic community-building while emancipation enables it. Domination, legitimated as it is by ideology, is decoded by critical hermeneuts who help individuals discover the ways they have been entangled in the ideological process. The exposé and critique of ideology are two of critical hermeneutics' main objectives in its effort to make the world better. As long as our vision is obstructed by the various purveyors of ideology, our effort to live in democratic communities will be thwarted (Gallagher, 1992). Power wielders with race, class, and gender privilege have access to the resources that allow them to promote ideologies and representations in a way individuals without such privilege cannot. Resources such as entertainment and communication industries are used to shape consciousness and construct subjectivity (Kincheloe, 2005; Peters & Lankshear, 1994; Denzin, 1992).

Critical Hermeneutics, the Production of Subjectivity, and Cultural Pedagogy

Those who operate outside the critical tradition often fail to understand that the critical hermeneutical concern with popular culture in the postmodern condition is not a matter of aesthetics but an issue of sociopolitical impact. In light of the focus of this research on the cultural curriculum and cultural pedagogy, a key aspect of this socio-political impact involves the socialization of youth. Those same outsiders sometimes look down their noses at the popular texts chosen for interpretation in the critical context, arguing that cultural productions such as *Fast Times at Ridgemont High,* for example, doesn't deserve the attention critical scholarship might devote to it. Critical hermeneuts maintain that all popular culture that is consumed and makes an impact on an audience is worthy of study regardless of the aesthetic judgments elite cultural scholars might offer (Berger, 1995). A movie like *Fast Times at Ridgemont High* is important to critical analysts because it is both inscribed with profound cultural meanings and so many people have watched it. Because popular texts like movies can explore oppression and emancipation, self-direction, personal freedom, and democratic community-building, critical hermeneuts know that they shape the production of subjectivity; they also understand that such a process can be understood only with an appreciation of the sociohistorical and political context that supports it (Ellis & Flaherty, 1992).

Norm Denzin (1992) is extremely helpful in developing this articulation of critical hermeneutics, drawing on the sociological genius of C. Wright Mills and his "sociological imagination." A key interest of this tradition, which Denzin carries into the contemporary era, involves unearthing the connections among material existence, communications processes, cultural patterns, and the formation of human consciousness. This articulation of a critical hermeneutics has much to learn from Denzin and Mills and their concern with subjectivity/consciousness, their understanding that cultural productions of various types hold compelling consequences for humans. Denzin is obsessed with the way individuals make sense of their everyday lives in particular cultural contexts by constructing stories (narratives) that, in turn, help define their identities. Employing a careful reading of Denzin, critical hermeneuts can gain insight into how cultural texts help create a human subject. How, Denzin wants to know, do individuals connect their lived experiences to the cultural representations of these same experiences (Berger, 1995; Denzin, 1992)?

Following this line of thought, critical hermeneutics concerned with the pedagogical issue of identity formation seeks cultural experiences that induce crises of consciousness when an individual's identity is profoundly challenged. Such moments are extremely important to any pedagogy, for it is in such instants of urgency that dramatic transformations occur (Denzin, 1992). In this research it is argued that such moments are not uncommon in individual interaction with popular texts and that the results of such experiences can be either oppressive or liberating in nature. Indeed, some pedagogical experiences may be characterized as rational processes, but they almost always involve a strong emotional component. Too often in mainstream research, this emotional dynamic has been to some degree neglected by logocentric social science (Ellis & Flaherty, 1992). Critical hermeneutics that is aware of such cultural pedagogical dynamics will empower individuals to make sense of their popular cultural experiences and provide them with specific tools of social interpretation. Such abilities will allow them to avoid the manipulative ideologies of popular cultural texts in an emancipatory manner that helps them consciously construct their own identities. Critical social and educational analysis demands such abilities in its efforts to provide transformative insights into the many meanings produced and deployed in the media-saturated postmodern landscape (Ellis & Flaherty, 1992; Berger, 1995; Kellner, 1995).

Conclusion

To conclude with my interpretation of the themes that emerged through my bricolaged content analysis by way of critical cultural studies, ethnography, semiotics, hermeneutics, and feminist theory would, of course, extend this chapter far too long and give away the dénouement from the book I am working on reflecting this research. This chapter, I hope, described the way that cultural studies can be used with a bricolaged approach in combining critical research methods in order to critically interpret film, in this case, for a cultural pedagogical reading. As one who self-defines herself as abstract random, with a strange penchant for organization, I believe that cultural studies is best read through an approach that does not limit itself to one research method.

References

Aronowitz, S. (1993). *Roll over Beethoven: The return of cultural strife.* Hanover, NH: Wesleyan University Press.

Atkinson, P., & Hammersley, M. (1994). Ethnography and participant observation. In N. Denzin & Y. Lincoln (Eds.), *Handbook of qualitative research.* Thousand Oaks, CA: Sage.

Becker, H. (1989). Tricks of the trade. *Studies in Symbolic Interaction, 10,* pp. 481–490.

Berger, A. (1995). *Cultural criticism: A primer of key concepts.* Thousand Oaks, CA: Sage.

Butler, J. (1990). *Gender trouble.* London, England: Routledge.

Clifford, J. (1992). Traveling cultures. In C. Nelson, P. Treichler & L. Grossberg (Eds.), *Cultural studies* (pp. 96–117). New York, NY: Routledge.

Clough, P. (1992). *The end(s) of ethnography: From realism to social criticism.* Newbury Park, CA: Sage.

Collins, J. (1990). *Architectures of excess: Cultural life in the information age.* New York, NY: Routledge.

Denzin, N. (1992). *Symbolic interactionism and cultural studies: The politics of interpretation.* Cambridge, MA: Blackwell.

Denzin, N. (1994). The art and politics of interpretation. In N. Denzin & Y. Lincoln (Eds.), *Handbook of qualitative research* (pp. 1–25). Thousand Oaks, CA: Sage.

Dickens, D., & Fontana, A. (1994). Postmodernism in the social sciences. In D. Dickens & A. Fontana (Eds.), *Postmodernism and social inquiry.* New York, NY: Guilford.

During, S. (1994). Introduction. In S. During (Ed.), *The cultural studies reader* (pp. 1–28). New York, NY: Routledge.

Ellis, C., & Flaherty, M. (1992). An agenda for the interpretation of lived experience. In C. Ellis & M. Flaherty (Eds.), *Investigating subjectivity: Research on lived experience.* Newbury Park, CA: Sage.

Fee, E. (1982). Is feminism a threat to scientific objectivity? *International Journal of Women's Studies, 4*(4), 378–392.

Ferguson, K. (1993). *The man question: Visions of subjectivity in feminist theory.* Berkeley, CA: University of California Press.

Fiske, J. (1993). *Power plays, power works.* New York, NY: Verso.

Flax, J. (1990). *Thinking fragments: Psychoanalysis, feminism, and postmodernism in the contemporary West.* Berkeley, CA: University of California Press.

Freire, P. (1985). *The politics of education: Culture, power, and liberation.* South Hadley, MA: Bergin & Garvey.

Gallagher, S. (1992). *Hermeneutics and education.* Albany, NY: SUNY Press.

Giroux, H. (1988). *Teachers as intellectuals: Toward a critical pedagogy of learning.* South Hadley, MA: Bergin & Garvey.

Gresson, A. (1996). Postmodern America and the multicultural crisis: Reading *Forrest Gump* as the call back to whiteness. *Taboo: The Journal of Culture and Education,* Spring, 1–34.

Griffin, C. (1985). *Typical girls? Young women from school to the job market.* London, England: Routledge & Kegan Paul.

Grossberg, L. (1995). What's in a name (one more time)? *Taboo: The Journal of Culture and Education,* Spring, 1–37.

Hammersley, M., & Atkinson, P. (1983). *Ethnography: Principles in practice.* New York, NY: Tavistock Publications.

Hebdige, D. (1988). *Hiding in the light.* New York, NY: Routledge.

Hekman, S. (1990). *Gender and knowledge: Elements of a postmodern feminism.* Boston, MA: Northeastern University Press.

Held, D. (1980). *Introduction to critical theory.* Berkeley, CA: University of California Press.

Jagger, A. (1983). *Feminist politics and human nature.* Totowa, NJ: Rowman & Allanheld.

Kellner, D. (1995). *Media culture: Cultural studies, identity and politics between the modern and the postmodern.* New York, NY: Routledge.

Kincheloe, J. (1991). *Teachers as researchers: Qualitative paths to empowerment.* New York. NY: Falmer Press.

Kincheloe, J. (2001). Describing the bricolage: Conceptualizing a new rigour in qualitative research. *Qualitative Inquiry, 7*(6), 679–692.

Kincheloe, J., & Berry, K. (2004). *Rigour and complexity in educational research: Conceptualizing the bricolage.* London, England: Open University Press.

Kipnis, L. (1989). Feminism: The political conscience of postmodernism. In A. Ross (Ed.), *Universal abandon? The politics of postmodernism* (pp. 149–168). Minneapolis, MN: University of Minnesota Press.

Levi-Strauss, C. (1966). *The savage mind.* Chicago: University of Chicago Press.

MacDonald, D. (1957). A theory of mass culture. In B. Rosenberg & D. White (Eds.), *Mass culture.* Glencoe, IL: Free Press.

Marcus, G., & Fischer, M. (1986). *Anthropology as cultural critique: An experimental moment in the human sciences.* University of Chicago Press.

Mies, M. (1982). Toward a methodology for feminist research. In G. Bowles & R. Klein (Eds.), *Theories of women's studies.* Boston, MA: Routledge & Kegan Paul.

Nelson, C., Treichler, P., & Grossberg, L. (1992). Cultural studies: An introduction. In C. Nelson, P. Treichler, & L. Grossberg (Eds.), *Cultural studies.* New York, NY: Routledge.

Olesen, V. (1994). Feminisms and models of qualitative research. In N. Denzin & Y. Lincoln (Eds.), *Handbook of qualitative research.* Thousand Oaks, CA: Sage.

Peters, M., & Lankshear, C. (1994). Education and hermeneutics: A Freirean interpretation. In P. McLaren & C. Lankshear (Eds.), *Politics of liberation: Paths from Freire.* New York, NY: Routledge.

Reinharz, S. (1979). *On becoming a social scientist.* San Francisco, CA: Jossey-Bass.

Reinharz, S. (1982). Experimental analysis: A contribution to feminist research. In G. Bowles & R. Klein (Eds.), *Theories of women's studies.* Boston, MA: Routledge & Kegan Paul.

Reinharz, S. (1992). *Feminist methods in social research.* New York, NY: Oxford University Press.

Rosenau, P. (1992). *Postmodernism and the social sciences: Insights, inroads, and intrusion.* Princeton: Princeton University Press.

Smith, P. (1989). Pedagogy and the popular-cultural-commodity text. In H. Giroux & R. Simon (Eds.), *Popular culture: Schooling and everyday life.* Granby, MA: Bergin & Garvey.

Steinberg, S. (1997). The bitch who has everything. In S. Steinberg & J. Kincheloe (Eds.), *Kinderculture: The corporate construction of childhood.* Boulder, CO: Westview Press.

Taussig, M. (1987). *Shamanism, colonialism, and the wildman: A study in terror and healing.* Chicago: University of Chicago Press.

Walby, S. (1990). Theorizing patriarchy. *Utne Reader, 64,* 63–66.

Weiler, K. (1988). *Women teaching for change.* South Hadley, MA: Bergin & Garvey.

Willis, P. (1977). *Learning to labour: How working class kids get working class jobs.* Famborough, England: Saxon House.

Wood, R. (1995). Ideology, genre, auteur. In B. Grant (Ed.), *Film genre reader II.* Austin, TX: University of Texas Press.

Filmography

Die Hard, 1988. John McTiernan, Director.

Fast Times at Ridgemont High, 1982. Amy Heckerling, Director.

Forrest Gump, 1994. Robert Zemeckis, Director.

Ferris Bueller's Day Off, 1986. John Hughes, Director.

The Green Berets, 1968. Ray Kellogg and John Wayne, Directors.

Critical Pedagogy in the Classroom

TWELVE

Paulo Freire's Radical Democratic Humanism

The Fetish of Method

Stanley Aronowitz

The name of Paulo Freire has reached near iconic proportions in the United States, Latin America, and, indeed, in many parts of Europe. Like the cover comment by Jonathan Kozol on the U.S. edition of Freire's major statement *Pedagogy of the Oppressed* (1990), his work has been typically received as a "brilliant methodology of a highly charged political character." Freire's ideas have been assimilated to the prevailing obsession of North American education, following a tendency in all the human and social sciences, with methods of verifying knowledge and, in schools, of teaching—that is, transmitting knowledge to otherwise unprepared students. Within the United States it is not uncommon for teachers and administrators to say that they are "using" the Freirean method in classrooms. What they mean by this is indeterminate. Sometimes it merely connotes that teachers try to be "interactive" with students; sometimes it signifies an attempt to structure classtime as, in part, a dialogue between the teacher and students; some even mean to "empower" students by permitting them to talk in class without being ritualistically corrected as to the accuracy of their information, their grammar, or their formal mode of presentation—or to be punished for dissenting knowledge. All of these are commendable practices, but they hardly require Freire as a cover. Consequently, Freire is named a master teacher, a kind of Brazilian progressive educator with a unique way of helping students, especially those from impoverished families and communities.

The term he employs to summarize his approach to education, "pedagogy," is often interpreted as a "teaching" method rather than a philosophy or a social theory. Few who invoke his name make the distinction. To be sure, neither does the *Oxford English Dictionary.* Yet a careful reading of Freire's work, combined with familiarity with the social and historical context within which it functions obliges the distinction: nothing can be further from Freire's intention than to conflate his use of the term pedagogy with the traditional notion of teaching. For he means to offer a system in which the locus of the learning process is shifted from the teacher to the student. And this shift overtly signifies an altered power relationship, not only in the classroom but in the broader social canvas as well. This type of extrapolation is fairly typical of the U.S. reception of European philosophy and cultural criticism. For example, after more than a decade during which many in the humanities, especially literature, made a career out of working with the concept of "deconstruction" as formulated by Jacques Derrida, treating the French philosopher as a methodologist of literary criticism, one or two books finally appeared that reminded the American audience that Derrida is, after all, a philosopher, and that his categories constituted an alternative to the collective systems of Western thought.

Some writers have even begun to grasp that Derrida may be considered as an ethicist. Similarly, another philosopher, Jürgen Habermas, has been taken up by sociology as well as by a small fraction of younger philosophers and literary theorists, and read in terms of their respective disciplines. What escapes many who have appropriated Habermas's categories is his project: to reconstruct historical materialism in a manner that takes into account the problem of communication, and especially the nonrevolutionary prospect of the contemporary world (Habermas, 1979). Whether one agrees or disagrees with this judgment, the political configuration of his theoretical intervention ought to be inescapable, except for those bound by professional contexts. None of these appropriations should be especially surprising. We are prone to metonymic readings, carving out our subjects to suit our own needs. In all of these cases, including that of Freire, there are elective affinities that make plausible the ways in which these philosophers and critics are read. For example, with the progressive education tradition, Freire rejects the "banking" approach to pedagogy, according to which teachers, working within the limits imposed by their academic discipline and training, open students' heads to the treasures of civilized knowledge. He insists that no genuine learning can occur unless students are actively involved, through praxis, in controlling their own education (here "praxis" is understood in the sense employed by several strains of Marxism—political practices informed by reflection). He is firmly on the side of a pedagogy that begins with helping students achieve a grasp of the concrete conditions of their daily lives, of the limits imposed by their situation on their ability to acquire what is sometimes called "literacy," of the meaning of the truism "knowledge is power." Freire emphasizes "reflection," in which the student assimilates knowledge in accordance with his or her own needs, rather than rote learning; he is dedicated, like some elements of the progressive tradition, to helping the learner become a subject of his or her own education rather than an object of the system's educational agenda. Like many progressives, Freire assails education that focuses on individual mobility chances while eschewing collective self-transformation. There are enough resemblances here to validate the reduction of Freire to the Latin John Dewey. Accordingly, if one adopts this analogy, his frequent allusions to revolutionary left-wing politics can be explained as a local phenomenon connected to the events of the 1960s and early 1970s, especially the advent in Brazil of the military dictatorship in 1964, the resistance to it, and the powerful popular social movements, particularly in Chile, with which he worked. Presumably, given a more thoroughly democratic context such as that which marks the political systems of North America and Western Europe, the core of Freire's teaching, the Method, would become apparent.

Similarly, while Dewey wrote on science, ethics, logic, and politics, among a host of other topics, outside the tiny band of Dewey specialists within schools of education, educational theory and practice routinely ignores the relationship between his general philosophical position and his education writings. And until very recently he was virtually unread by professional philosophers. Once at the center of American philosophy, his ideas have been deployed (in the military sense) by an insistent minority in full-scale revolt against the prevailing analytic school. Needless to say, just as Freire's revolutionary politics are all but dismissed in the countries where he has been elevated to a teacher-saint, Dewey's engaged political liberalism is generally viewed as a (surpassed) expression of the outmoded stance of public intellectuals at the turn of the century until the immediate postwar period. What can professional Dewey scholars say about his role in the founding of the American Federation of Teachers in 1916, or his role as chair of the commission that investigated the murder of Leon Trotsky?

Since American education has been thoroughly integrated into the middle-class cultural ideal that holds out the promise of individual mobility to those who acquiesce to the curriculum, engaged intellectuals like Dewey and Freire remain "relevant" to the extent that they can be portrayed within the dominant paradigms of the social sciences upon which educational theory rests. It is not surprising that Kozol can refer to Freire's "methodology," given the depoliticization of educational theory and practice in the United States—that is, the relative isolation of education issues, at least until recently, from the wider economic, political, and cultural scenes. Seen this way, his characterization of Freire as a "highly charged politically provocative character" seems almost an afterthought, or more to the point, a personal tribute not crucially intertwined with the "brilliant methodology."

Ivan Illich's statement on the same cover that Freire's "is a truly revolutionary pedagogy" comes closer to capturing what is at stake in his writing. The modifier "revolutionary" rather than "progressive" signifies an intention that is carefully elided by many of Freire's followers and admirers in schools. Or the term must be instrumentalized to mean that the pedagogy itself, as a methodological proto-col, represents a radical departure from banking or rote methods of instruction. Therefore it is possible, if not legitimate, to interpret the significance of Freire's work not in the broader connotation of a pedagogy for life, but as a series of tools of effective teaching, techniques that the democratic and humanist teacher may employ to motivate students to imbibe the curriculum with enthusiasm instead of turning their hacks on schooling.

True, Freire speaks of "method," especially in chapter 2 of *Pedagogy of the Oppressed*. In the early pages of this chapter, Freire seems to focus, in the narrow sense, on the "teacher-pupil" relationship as if to valorize the tendency of much educational theory toward microanalysis. For example, he provides a detailed "list" of characteristics of the banking method. Aside from obvious choices, such as who speaks and who listens, Freire makes his central point: "the teacher confuses the authority of knowledge with his own professional authority, which he sets in op-position to the freedom of the student." From this and the other specifications issues the conclusion that in the banking method "the teacher is the Subject of the learning process, while the pupils are the mere objects" (Freire, 1990, p. 59).

To this "method" Freire counterposes "problem-posing education" where "men [sic] develop their power to perceive critically *the way they exist* in the world with which and in which they find themselves; they come to see the world not as a static reality but as a reality in the process of transformation" (Freire, 1990, p. 71). This is where most American educators stop. Taken alone, the tacit thesis according to which Freire, not withstanding his political provocation, is essen-tially a phenomenological progressive who uses language not too distant from that of psychologists working in this tradition, such as, say, Rollo May, seems to be justifiable. There is reference here to seeing life not as a static state of being but as a process of *becoming*. This spiritually laced education talk might be found as well in the writing of George Leonard and other American educators. American educators influenced by phenomenology are, typically, concerned with saving in-dividuals from the dehumanizing effects of what they perceive to be an alienating culture. With few exceptions, they have adopted the implicit pessimism of most of their forebears, which, despairing of fundamental social transformation, fo-cuses on individual salvation.

But I want to argue that the task of this revolutionary pedagogy is not to fos-ter critical self-consciousness in order to improve cognitive learning, the student's self-esteem, or even to assist in "his" aspiration to fulfill his human "potential." Rather, according to Freire, problem-posing education is revolutionary futurity.

Hence it is prophetic. . . . Hence it corresponds to the historical nature of man. Hence it affirms men as beings who transcend themselves. . . . Hence it identifies with the movement which engages men as beings aware of their incompletion—an historical movement which has its point of departure, its subjects and its objective. (Freire, 1990, p. 72)

It is to the liberation of the oppressed as historical subjects within the framework of revolutionary objectives that Freire's pedagogy is directed. The "method" is developed within a praxis, meaning here the link between knowledge and power through self-directed action. And contrary to the narrow, specialized, methodologically oriented practices of most American education, Freire's pedagogy is grounded in a fully developed philosophical anthropology, that is, a theory of human nature, one might say a secular liberation theology, containing its own categories that are irreducible to virtually any other philosophy. What follows is an account of this philosophical intervention and its educational implications.

Freire's Humanism

To speak of a philosophical anthropology in the era of the postmodern condition, and a poststructuralism which condemns any discourse that betrays even a hint of essentialism, seems anachronistic. Indeed, any superficial reading of Freire's work can easily dismiss its theoretical scaffolding as quaint, however much it may be sincere. For example, we read:

The Pedagogy of the Oppressed animated by authentic humanism (and not humanitarian) generosity presents itself as a pedagogy of man. Pedagogy which begins with the egoistic interests of the oppressors (an egoism cloaked in the false generosity of paternalism) and makes of the oppressed the objects of its humanitarianism, itself maintains and embodies oppression. It is an instrument of dehumanization. (Freire, 1990, p. 39)

Now, we have already learned about the "fallacy of humanism" from the structuralists, especially Althusser and Levi-Strauss. In Althusser's critique, humanism defines the object of knowledge, "man," as an essential being, subject to, but not constituted by, the multiplicity of relations of a given social formation (Althusser, 1970). In adopting the language of humanism, Freire's debt to the early Marx and to Sartre is all too evident. He relies heavily on Marx, the Feuerbachian, whose materialism is severely tempered and reconfigured by a heavy dose of philosophical idealism. Recall Feuerbach's critique of religion, in which human suffering is displaced to God's will (Feuerbach, 1957). Feuerbach argues that religion is made by humans and the problems to which it refers can only be addressed here, on earth. As if to underscore his own formation by this "flawed" tradition, Freire goes on to argue that the pedagogy he advocates addresses the problem of the authentication of humans by means of their self-transformation into a universal species:

> The truth is. . . that the oppressed are not "marginals," are not men living "outside" society. They have always been "inside"—inside the structure that made them "beings for others." The solution is not to "integrate" them into the structure of oppression but to transform the structure so they can become "beings for themselves". . . . They may discover through existential experience that their present way of life is irreconcilable with their vocation to become fully human. . . . If men are searchers and their ontological vocation is humanization, sooner or later they may perceive the contradiction in which banking education seeks to maintain them and then engage themselves in the struggle for their liberation. (Freire, 1990, pp. 61–62)

Echoes of Hegelianism here. Freire invokes the familiar humanistic Marxian project: the revolution's aim is to transform what Frantz Fanon terms "the wretched of the earth" from "beings for others" to "beings for themselves," a transformation that entails changing the conditions of material existence, such as relations of ownership and control of labor, and the lordship-bondage relation which is the psychosocial expression of the same thing. Freire invokes the notion of the "ontological vocation" to become human. In a brief dialogue with Lukács, who, in his tribute to Lenin (Lukács, 1970), endorses the role of the political vanguard to "explain" the nature of the oppression to the masses, since their consciousness has been victimized by commodity fetishism. Freire emphasizes the idea of self-liberation, proposing a pedagogy whose task is to unlock the intrinsic humanity of the oppressed. Here the notion of ontological vocation is identical with the universal, humanizing praxis of and by the most oppressed rather than "for" them. For a genuine liberatory praxis does not cease, even with the revolutionary act of self-liberation. The true vocation of humanization is to liberate humanity, including the oppressors and those, like teachers, who are frequently recruited from among the elite classes to work with the oppressed, but who unwittingly perpetuate domination through teaching.

Note here that Freire theorizes the class struggle, not as a zero-sum game in which the victory of the oppressed constitutes a defeat for the oppressor, but as a praxis with universal significance and, more to the point, universal gain. For, as Freire argues, as oppressors of their fellow humans, the "dominant elites" lose their humanity, are no longer capable of representing the general will to complete the project of humanization. This is the significance of working with the most oppressed, who in Brazil and the rest of Latin America are poor agricultural laborers and the unemployed huddled in the city's *favellas,* shantytowns, which in Sao Paulo, for instance, harbor a million and a half people. Many of these are migrants from forest and agricultural regions that are in the process of being leveled for wood processing, mining and "modern" corporate farming. As we can see in the citation above, Freire plays ambiguously with Marx's notion that the working class is in "radical chains." Where Marx sees the working class "in" but not "of" society, Freire insists they are "inside the structure" that oppresses them. As we shall see, this phrase signifies Freire's move toward psychoanalytic theory as a sufficient explanation of which material circumstances are the necessary conditions for accounting for the reproduction of class domination.

In the light of this admittedly humanistic discourse, what can be said about Freire's philosophy that rescues it from the dread charge of essentialism, and thereby relegates the entire underpinning of Freire's pedagogy to its own historicity? A closer examination of the crucial category of the "unfinished" shows the tension between his secular theology of liberation and the open futurity of the pedagogy. Taken at face value "liberation," "emancipation," and "self-transcendence" are teleologically wrought categories that presuppose an outcome already present in the "project." In this aspect of the question, the goal, liberation, has the status of a *dens (deus) ex machina* of revolutionary action. For some critics, intellectuals, not the oppressed themselves, have designated the telos. It is intellectuals who have nominated themselves to deliver the subaltern from the yoke of material deprivation and spiritual domination. The oppressed must be the agent of universal humanization which, for Freire, is the real object of praxis. Taken at the surface of discourse, Freire can be indicted for reproducing the Leninist dictum according to which the task of the avant-garde intellectuals—in this case teachers—is to lead the masses into liberation. But as we shall see, this judgment, however plausible, turns out to be misleading. I want to show that Freire's specific deployment of both psychoanalytic theory and phenomenological Marxism leads in exactly opposite directions. Moreover, Freire is aware that his rhetorical moves may easily be interpreted as another kind of elitism and takes up this issue. Freire's overt debt to Erich Fromm's psychological equivalent of material oppression, *the fear of freedom,* comes into play (Fromm 1940). Freire takes from Freud, Reich, and especially Fromm the insistence that oppression is not only externally imposed but that the oppressed introject, at the psychological level, domination. This introjection takes the form of the fear by members of the oppressed classes that learning and the praxis to which it is ineluctably linked will alter their life's situation. The implication is that the oppressed have an investment in their oppression because it represents the already-known, however grim are the conditions of everyday existence.

In fact, Freire's pedagogy seems crucially directed to breaking the cycle of psychological oppression by engaging students in confronting their own lives, that is, to engage in a dialogue with their own fear as the representation within themselves of the power of the oppressor. Freire's pedagogy is directed, then, to the project of assisting the oppressed not only to overcome material oppression but also to attain freedom from the sado-masochism that these relationships em-

264   *Stanley Aronowitz*

body. For Freire, profits and accumulation may account for exploitation of labor, but are insufficient explanations in the face of brutal domination. The dominating elites have a collective sadistic character corresponding to the masochism of the dominated. Freire quotes Fromm:

> The pleasure in complete domination over another person (or other animate creature) is the very essence of the sadistic drive. Another way of formulating the same thought is to say that the aim of sadism is to transform man into a thing, something animate into something inanimate since by complete and absolute control the living loses one essential quality of life—freedom. (Freire, 1990, p. 45)

Freire goes on to say that "sadism is a perverted love—a love of death, not of life." The specific form of masochism is the "colonized man," a category developed by Frantz Fanon and Albert Memmi. Memmi (1973) argues that the colonized both hate and are fatally attracted to the colonizer. In the educational situation this takes the form of deference to the "professor"; the students may begin to generate themes but suddenly stop and say, "We ought to keep quiet and let you talk. You are the one who knows. We don't know anything" (Freire, 1990, p. 50). Although Freire does not mention the term "masochism," that in this context manifests itself as the will to be dominated through introjecting the master's image of the oppressed, psychoanalysis insists that it is the dialectical inverse of sadism and that the two are inextricably linked. This introjection is, of course, the condition of consent, without which sadism could not exist without resorting to utter force to impose its will. Or, to be more precise, it would be met by resistance and a violence directed not horizontally among the oppressed but vertically against the master.

It is not at all excessive to claim that the presuppositions of psychoanalytic theory are as fundamental to Freire's pedagogy as the existential Marxism that appears, on the surface, as the political and theological motivation of his discourse. For by positing the absolute necessity that the oppressed be self-emancipated rather than "led," on the basis of struggles around their immediate interests, by an avant-garde of revolutionary intellectuals, Freire has turned back upon his own teleological starting point. For the achievement of freedom, defined here as material, that is, economic and political as well as spiritual liberation, is a kind of *permanent* revolution in which the achievement of political power is merely a preliminary step. Freire posits the absolute necessity of the oppressed to take charge of their own liberation, including the revolutionary process which, in the first place, is educational. In fact, despite occasional and approving references to Lenin, Freire enters a closely reasoned argument against vanguardism which typically takes the form of populism. In contrast to the ordinary meaning of this term in American political science and historiography, Freire shows that populism arises as a "style of political action" marked by mediation (he calls this "shuttling back and forth between the people and the dominant oligarchies" [Freire, 1990, p. 147]). Moreover, he makes a similar criticism of some elements of the "left" which, tempted by a "quick return to power," enter into a "dialogue with the dominant elites." Freire makes a sharp distinction between political strategies that "use" the movement to achieve political power (a charge often leveled against the Bolsheviks as well as the Communist parties) and "fighting for an authentic popular organization" in which the people themselves are the autonomous sources of political decisions.

Freire's political philosophy, in the context of the historical debates within the revolutionary left, is neither populist, Leninist, nor, indeed, social-democratic in the contemporary sense, but libertarian in the tradition of Rosa Luxemburg and the anarchists. Recall Luxemburg's sharp critique of Lenin's conception of the party as a vanguard organization, particularly his uncritical appropriation of Kautsky's claim that the working class, by its own efforts, could achieve merely trade union but not revolutionary consciousness. Inspired, in part, by Mao's conception of the cultural revolution, in which the masses are, ideologically and practically, the crucial force or the movement is nothing, Freire's pedagogy can be seen as a set of practices that attempts to specify, in greater concreteness than Mao did, the conditions for the fulfillment of this orientation. Having proclaimed the aim of pedagogy to be the development of *revolutionary initiative from below,* Freire nonetheless rejects what he views as the two erroneous alternatives that have plagued the left since the founding of the modern socialist movements: on the one hand, leaders "limit their action to stimulating. . . one demand," such as salary increases, or they "overrule this popular aspiration and substitute something more far reaching—but something which has not yet come to the forefront of the people's attention." Freire's solution to this antinomy of populism and vanguardism is to find a "synthesis" in which the demand for salaries is supported, but posed as a "problem" that on one level becomes an obstacle to the achievement of full "humanization" through workers' ownership of their own labor. Again, workers pose wage increases as a solution to their felt oppression because they have internalized the oppressor's image of themselves and have not (yet) posed self-determination over the conditions of their lives as an object of their political practice. They have not yet seen themselves *subjectively* (Marx, 1975).

Freire's philosophy constitutes a tacit critique of poststructuralism's displacement of questions concerning class, gender, and race to "subject-positions" determined by discursive formations. The oppressed are situated within an economic and social structure, and tied to it not only by their labor but also by the conditions of their psychological being. The task of his pedagogy is to encourage the emergence of a specific kind of discourse which presupposes a project for the formation of subjectivities that is increasingly separate from that of the structure.

Freire's construction does not *necessarily* repudiate the theoretical principle that the world and its divisions are constituted as a series of discursive formations into which subjects pour themselves. But he is addressing himself not to the bourgeois subject to which the old humanism refers—an individual "consciousness" seeking the truth through reason, including science—but to the possibility of working with a new problematic of the subject. Unlike twentieth-century Marxism, especially in Third World contexts, which accepts the ineluctability of domination based upon its position that underdevelopment breeds more or less permanent dependency (just as Lukács and the Frankfurt School essentially hold to reification as a permanent barrier to self-emancipation) in all of its aspects, Freire's is a philosophy of *hope*.

Recall Freire's statement, "problem posing education is revolutionary futurity." Its prophetic character crucially depends on specific interventions rather than declarations of faith. The teacher-intellectual becomes a vehicle for liberation only by advancing a pedagogy that decisively transfers control of the educational enterprise from her or himself as subject to the subaltern student. The mediation between the dependent present and the independent future is *dialogic* education:

> Dialogue is the encounter between men [sic], mediated by the world, in order to name the world. Hence dialogue cannot occur between those who want to name the world and those who do not wish this naming-between those who deny other men [sic] the right to speak their word and those whose right to speak has been denied to them. Those who have been denied their primordial right to speak their word must first reclaim and prevent the continuation of this dehumanizing aggression. (Freire, 1990, p. 76)

Thus, Freire's deployment of psychoanalysis is not directed toward *personal* liberation but instead to new forms of social praxis. The basis of this praxis is, clearly, the overriding notion that humans are an unfinished project. This project, for Freire, is grounded in his conception that to be fully human, in contrast to other species of animals, is to shed the image according to which only the "dominant elites," including leftist intellectuals, can be self-directed. His pedagogy, which posits the central category of dialogue, entails that recovering the voice of the oppressed is the fundamental condition for human emancipation.

From Revolution to Radical Democracy

I have deliberately abstracted Freire's social, psychological, and political philosophy from the social context in which it emerged in order to reveal its intellectual content. However, one cannot leave matters here. Without completely historicizing the significance of this intervention, we are compelled to interrogate this revolutionary pedagogy in the light of the sweeping transformations in world economic, political, and cultural relations, to re-place Freire's philosophy and pedagogy in the emerging contemporary world political situation.

Of course, I need not rehearse in detail here the extent of the changes that have overtaken revolutionary Marxism since, say, the fall of the Berlin Wall in December 1989. It is enough for our purposes to invoke the world-transforming events in Eastern Europe. They were simultaneously liberating—the Soviet Union and the nations of that region may be entering a new epoch of democratic renewal—and disturbing. We are witnessing the collapse of bureaucratic and authoritarian state rule in favor of liberal democracy, the emergence of capitalism, or at least radically mixed economies, but also nationalism, accompanied by a burgeoning anti-Semitism and racism, even signs of resurgent monarchism.

In Latin America, the site of Freire's crucial educational practice, not only in his native Brazil but also in pre-Pinochet Chile, revolutionary perspectives have, to say the least, suffered a palpable decline, not only after the defeat of the Sandinistas in the Nicaraguan election, but also in the choice by much of the erstwhile revolutionary Marxist left to place the struggle for democracy ahead of the class struggle and the struggle for socialism. Some have even theorized that, despite deepening poverty and despair for much of the population, socialism is no longer on the immediate agenda of Latin American societies in the wake of the world shifts that have decimated their economies, shifts that also encourage the formation of totalitarian military dictatorships.

In this environment, recent political liberalizations have shown themselves to be fragile. For example, presidential democratic regimes in Argentina and Chile had hardly taken root before the military threatened to resume power to restore "law and order." Some political theorists of the left, notably Norberto Bobbio, have forcefully and influentially argued that parliamentary democracy within the framework of a mixed economy dedicated to social justice is the farthest horizon of socialist objectives (Bobbio, 1987a and 1987b). Following him, many leaders of the Brazilian left have acknowledged the limits of political transformation under conditions of underdevelopment. Others, while agreeing with the judgment according to which the revolutionary insurgencies of the 1960s and 1970s were profoundly misdirected, dispute Bobbio's thesis that radical democratic perspectives suffer from romantic nostalgia and would inevitably fail. What is important here is, in either case, a decisive skepticism concerning the prospects for revolutionary socialism, at least for the present. Which raises the question of whether there can be a revolutionary pedagogy in nonrevolutionary societies. Is it not the case that Freire's philosophy has been historically surpassed even if, in the context of its formation, it possessed the virtues of perspicacity?

Under present circumstances, is it not enough to preserve Freire's work in a more modest form, as a teaching method? To be sure, Freire himself is excruciatingly aware of the changed circumstances of the late 1980s and the 1990s. On the occasion of his appointment to the post of secretary of education for the newly elected Workers' Party (PT) municipal administration in São Paulo, Freire told an interviewer that he saw in this unexpected victory "a fantastic possibility for at least changing a little bit of our reality" (Williams 1990). The prospect for this radical left democratic administration was to achieve some reforms in health, transportation, and education. His perspective in accepting the post was to "start the process of change" during the PT's four years of elective office. Even before assuming office, Freire was aware of the severe limits to change posed by the economic and political situation. But he was also facing schools in which sixty to seventy percent of students dropped out and had barely four years of schooling, the majority of whom will be day laborers working for minimum wages. He was responsible for thirty thousand teachers in the city's school system, many of whom lacked training for the awesome task of helping students break from the fatalism of Brazilian society.

In 1990, after a year of reform, Freire and his associates were speaking about democracy—social democracy—rather than "revolution" in the strict political sense. The term "popular democratic school" is counterposed to the "capitalist" school. The capitalist school "measures quality by the quantity of information it transmits to people," says Freire's associate, Gadotti (Williams, 1990). The popular school, on the other hand, measures quality by "the class solidarity it succeeds in establishing in the school." In order to achieve this objective the school must be "deformalized," debureaucratized, a measure that entails democratizing schools so that "the community" elects the school director, and there is direct accountability. This means the director can be removed at any time by the base, but also that curriculum and other decisions are broadly shared. Freire uses the term "accountability" to describe this desired relationship. In the postdictatorship period, one might say in the postcolonial situation, the popular-democratic philosophy has not changed, but the discourse is now eminently practical: as a schools' administrator Freire speaks the language of praxis, rather than merely invoking it. The PT and its education secretary must address issues of teacher training, school-based decision-making, administration and curriculum, but from the base of a working-class-oriented political formation that holds radical democratic reform toward popular power as its core ideology. Freire is still trying to transfer power to the oppressed through education, now framed in the context of state-financed and controlled schooling.

Sharing Power

In his "spoken" book with Antonio Faundez, *Learning to Question* (1989), prepared before the PT victory, Freire had already altered his discursive practice. Throughout the text, Freire returns to the vexing relation between theory, ideological commitment, and political practice. Here I want to give just one example of the degree to which his fundamental framework remains constant, even in the wake of the shift from revolutionary to democratic discourse. In one section Faundez and Freire engage in a fascinating dialogue on intellectuals. Faundez begins by reiterating a fairly well-known Marxist idea: that there is a social "science," a body of knowledge which is not merely descriptive of the present state of affairs, but "guides all action for social change, how can we ensure that this scientific knowledge. . . actually coincides with the knowledge of the people" (Freire and Faundez, 1989, pp. 55–56). At this point Faundez contrasts the science possessed by intellectuals with the "ideology" of the dominant classes that suffuses the people's knowledge, as well as the diverse elements of practical knowledge, inconsistency between theory and practice, and so forth. The intellectuals as bearers of science find themselves caught in an excruciating paradox. On the one hand, they are bearers of scientific knowledge, owing not so much to their talent, as to their social position which gives them access to it. On the other hand, only by merging their science with the internalized knowledge of the people and, more particularly, by fusing their vision of the future with popular imagined futures can the elitism of the various political vanguards be avoided.

As in most leftist discussions of intellectuals, Faundez draws from Gramsci's undeniably pioneering writings, especially themes which Mao and Foucault are later to elaborate and develop: that all knowledge is specific, and that it is situated in a national context. Freire responds by objecting to the view that the future is only particular. He wants to preserve the universal in the particular, and argues that we already have, in outline, a vision. But the nub of the problem remains: are the radical intellectuals prepared to share in the "origination" of new visions with the masses, or are these fixed so that the problem of coincidence is confined to strategy and tactics? Freire presses Faundez here to clarify the role of intellectuals in relation to the popular movements. Freire is plainly uneasy with the formulation that intellectuals are the chief bearers of scientific knowledge, and wants to assert that, to achieve radical democratic futures, a fundamental shift in the relationship between intellectuals, especially their monopoly over scientific knowledge, and the movements must take place. Moreover, he is concerned to remove the curse, "bourgeois," from the concepts of democracy. A radical democracy would recognize that there are no fixed visions. And if visions are fashioned from knowledge of the concrete situations gained through practice, there can be no science that provides certitude, in its categories, its descriptions, much less its previsions.

Reporting on a conversation with workers' leaders in São Paulo, Freire *defines* class consciousness as the power and the will by workers and other oppressed and exploited strata to share in the formulation of the conditions of knowledge and futurity. This demand inevitably alters the situation of power: intellectuals must be consistent in the translation of their democratic visions to practice. In other words, they must share the power over knowledge, share the power to shape the future. This exchange is a meditation on Latin American revolutionary history and current political reality, most especially the failure of Leninist versions of revolutionary Marxism and socialism. Explicitly, Freire warns against defining the goal of radical movements exclusively in terms of social justice and a more equitable society, since these objectives can conceivably be partially achieved without shared decision-making, especially over knowledge and political futures. The key move away from the old elitist conception in which the intellectuals play a dominant role is to challenge the identity of power with the state. Faundez sets the stage for this shift: I think that the power and the struggle for power have to be rediscovered on the basis of resistance which makes up the power of the people, the semiological, linguistic, emotional, political and cultural expressions which the people use to resist the power of domination. And it is beginning from the power which I would call primary power, that power and the struggle for power have to be rediscovered. (Freire and Faundez, 1989, p. 64)

Freire's reply sets a new ground for that rediscovery. Having focused traditionally on workers' and peasant movements, he now enters significantly into the debates about the relationship between class and social movements. He names movements of the urban and rural poor who, with the assistance of priests from the liberationist wing of the Catholic Church, began in the 1970s to redefine power as the power of resistance. But he goes on to speak of movements of "environmentalists, organized women and homosexuals," as "new" social movements whose effectivity must inexorably influence the strategies of the revolutionary parties: It is my opinion today that either the revolutionary parties will work more closely with these movements and so prove their authenticity within them—and to do that they must rethink their own understanding of their party, which is tied up with their traditional practice—or they will be lost. Being lost would mean becoming more and more rigid and increasingly behaving in an elitist and authoritarian way vis-à-vis the masses, of whom they claim to be the salvation. (Freire and Faundez 1989, p. 66) With these remarks, Freire distances himself from elements of his own revolutionary Marxist past but not from a kind of open Marxism represented by Gramsci's work. For there can be no doubt that this comment is directed towards those in the revolutionary left for whom class defines the boundaries of political discourse.

Without in any way renouncing class as a fundamental category of political struggle, Freire places himself in the company of those theorists, some of whom are situated in the social movements and not within the parties, who have challenged the priority of class over other social categories of oppression, resistance, and liberation. His intervention is also postmodern when he puts into question the claim of political parties to "speak in behalf of a particular section of society." In his latest work Freire takes a global view, integrating the democratic ideology of the Guinea-Bissauan leader Amilcar Cabral, with whom he had forged a close relationship. Freire is sympathetic to Faundez's reminder that knowledge and its bearers are always specific, that historical agency is always situated in a national context. Yet, with Cabral, he reiterates the need to "overcome" some features of culture. This overcoming means that tendencies towards the valorization of "localism" which frequently are merely masks for anti-intellectualism among populist-minded leaders, should be rejected. So Freire's postcolonial, postmodern discourse does not sink into the rigidities that have frequently afflicted these perspectives. Finally, at the end of the day, we can see that to appreciate difference does not resolve the knotty issues of judgment. Freire is an implacable opponent of bureaucracy that throttles popular initiative but suggests that workers for social change must retain their "overall vision" (Freire and Faundez, 1989, p. 123).

Redefining power democratically entails, at its core, interrogating the concept of "representation." The claim of revolutionary parties to represent workers, the masses, the popular majority, rests in the final analysis on the status, not of the demand for social justice, for liberal parties may, under specific conditions, also make such claims. Instead, it rests on the rock of scientific certainty, at least as to the descriptive and prescriptive propositions of a body of knowledge whose bearers, the intellectuals, thereby legitimate their own right to leadership. Freire's call for sharing recognizes the unique position of intellectuals in the social and technical division of labor, and thereby disclaims the stance of populism that almost always renounces the role of intellectuals in social movements, and with that renunciation is left with a vision of the future in the images of the present. But, by breaking with the "state," that is, coercion and representation as its key features, it also rejects the notion that liberation means the hegemony of intellectuals—political, scientific, cultural—over the movements. In this way, any attempt to interpret Freire's recent positions as a *retreat* from the revolutionary pedagogy of his earlier work is entirely unjustified.

On the contrary, Freire reveals his undogmatic, open thought in his most recent work. In fact, it may be argued that the Christian liberation theology of the past two decades is a kind of vindication of his own secular theology, with its categories of authenticity, humanization, and self-emancipation. The paradoxes in his political thought are not apparent; they are real. For like the rest of us, Freire is obliged to work within his own historicity, an "overall vision" that is at once in global crisis, and remains the only emancipatory vision of a democratic, libertarian future we have.

Notes

1. "Pedagogy—the work or occupation of teaching. . . the science or art of teaching." *Oxford English Dictionary* (complete edition) (New York: Oxford University Press, 1971), p. 604.

2. See, especially, Stephen W. Melville, *Philosophy Beside Itself: On Deconstruction and Modernism* (Minneapolis: University of Minnesota Press, 1986).
3. John Dewey himself is a model for the idea of *collective* self-transformation; see his *Democracy in Education* (Glencoe, Illinois: Free Press, 1959).

References

Althusser, Louis. 1970. *For Marx.* New York: Vintage.

———. 1971. "Ideology and Ideological Apparatuses." In *Lenin and Philosophy.* New York: Monthly Review Press.

Anderson, Perry. 1976. *Considerations on Western Marxism.* London: New Left Books.

Arendt, Hannah. 1958. *The Human Condition.* Chicago: University of Chicago Press.

———. 1961. "The Crisis in Education." In *Between Past and Future.* New York: Penguin Books.

Aronowitz, Stanley. 1973. *False Promises: The Shaping of American Working Class Consciousness.* New York: McGraw-Hill.

———. 1984. "When the New Left Was New:" In *60s Without Apology,* ed. By Sonhya Sayres, Anders Stephanson, Stanley Aronowitz, and Fredric Jameson. Minneapolis: University of Minnesota Press.

———. 1996. *Death and Rebirth of American Radicalism.* New York: Routledge.

———. 2000. *The Knowledge Factory: Dismantling the Corporate University and Creating True Higher Education.* Boston: Beacon Press.

Aronowitz, Stanley, and William DiFazio. 1994. *The Jobless Future.* Minneapolis: University of Minnesota Press.

Aronowitz, Stanley, and Henry Giroux. 1985. *Education Under Siege.* South Hadley, MA: Bergin and Garvey.

Bazin, André. 1989 [1961]. *What Is Cinema?* Berkeley: University of California Press.

Berube, Michael, and Cary Nelson. 1994. *Higher Education Under Fire.* New York: Routledge.

Blum, Linda. 1991. *Between Feminism and Labor: The Significance of Comparable Worth.* Berkeley: University of California Press.

Bobbio, N. 1987a: *Future of Democracy.* Minneapolis: University of Minnesota Press.

———. 1987b. *Which Socialism?* Minneapolis: University of Minnesota Press.

Bourdieu, Pierre, and Jean-Claude Passeron. 1977. *Reproduction in Education, Culture and Society.* London: Sage Publications.

Brint, Steven, and Jerome Karabel. 1989. *The Diverted Dream: Community Colleges and the Promise of Educational Opportunity in America.* New York: Oxford University Press.

Christgau, Robert. 2001. *Any Old Way You Choose It.* Cambridge, MA: Harvard University Press.

Cicourel, Aaron, and John Kitrae. 1963. *The Education Decision-Makers.* New York: Bobbs-Merrill.

Dewey, John. 1980 [1916]. *Democracy and Education.* Carbondale: Southern Illinois University Press.

Du Bois, William Edward Burkhardt. 1903. *The Souls of Black Folk.* Chicago: A. C. McClung.

Elman, Richard M. 1966. *The Poorhouse State: The American Way of Life on Public Assistance.* New York: Pantheon Books.

Feuer, Lewis. 1969. *The Conflict of Generations: The Character and Significance of Student Movements.* New York: Basic Books.

Feuerbach, L. 1957. *The Essence of Christianity.* New York: Harper Torchbooks.

Fink, Leon, and Brian Greenberg. 1989. *Upheaval in the Quiet Zone: A History of Local 1199.* Urbana: University of Illinois Press.

Fisher, Donald. 1993. *Fundamental Development of the Social Sciences: Rockefeller Philanthropy and the United States Social Science Research Council.* Ann Arbor: University of Michigan Press.

Fitch, Robert. 2006. *Solidarity for Sale: How Corruption Destroyed the Labor Movement and Undermined America's Promise.* New York: Public Affairs.

Freire, P. 1990. *Pedagogy of the Oppressed.* New York: Continuum.

Freire, P., and Faundez, A. 1989. *Learning to Question: A Pedagogy of Liberation.* New York: Continuum.

Friedman, Thomas. 2005. *The World Is Flat: A Brief History of the Twenty-first Century.* New York: Farrar, Straus, and Giroux.

Fromm, E. 1940. *Escape from Freedom.* New York: Holt, Rinehart and Winston.

Fukuyama, Francis. 1992. *The End of the History and the Last Man.* New York: Free Press.

Giroux, Henry. 2000. *Stealing Innocence: Youth, Corporate Power, and the Politics of Culture.* New York: St. Martin's Press.

Gompers, Samuel. 1924. *Seventy Years of Life and Labor: An Autobiography.* New York: E. P. Dutton.

Goodman, Paul. 1959. *Growing Up Absurd.* New York: Random House.

Gramsci, Antonio. 1971. *Selections from the Prison Notebooks,* ed. And trans. with an introduction by Quintin Hoare. New York: International Publishers.

Habermas, J. 1979. "The Reconstruction of Historical Materialism." In *Communication and the Evolution of Society.* Boston: Beacon Press.

Hardt, Michael, and Antonio Negri. 1994 [1890]. *Labor of Dionysus.* Minneapolis: University of Minnesota Press.

Heidegger, Martin. 1968. *What Is Called Thinking?* New York: Harper and Row.

Horkheimer, Max, and Theodor Adorno. 2002. *Dialectic of the Enlightenment,* trans. by Edmund Jephcott. Palo Alto, CA: Stanford University Press.

James, William. 1890. *Principles of Psychology.* New York: H. Holt.

Kael, Pauline. 1994. *I Lost It at the Movies.* New York: Marion Boyers.

Katz, Michael B. 1970. *The Irony of Early School Reform: Educational Innovation in Mid-Nineteenth-Century Massachusetts.* Boston: Beacon Press.

Kenney, Martin. 1986. *The University/Industrial Complex.* New Haven: Yale University Press.

Kerr, Clark. 1972. *The Use of the University.* New York: Harper and Row.

Kracauer, Siegfried. 1995. *The Mass Ornament.* Cambridge, MA: Harvard University Press.

Krause, Paul. 1992. *The Battle for Homestead.* Pittsburgh: University of Pittsburgh Press.

Lichtenstein, Nelson. 1996. *The Most Dangerous Man in Detroit: Walter Reuther and the Fate of American Labor.* New York: Basic Books.

Locke, John. 1954. *An Essay Concerning the Human Understanding.* New York: Dover.

Lucas, Christopher J. 1994. *American Higher Education: A History.* New York: Saint Martin's Press.

Lukács, G. 1970. *Lenin.* London: New Left Books.

Lynd, Robert S. 1964 [1939]. *Knowledge for What? The Place of Social Science in American Culture.* New York: Evergreen.

Macdonald, Dwight. 1983. *Against the American Grain.* New York: Da Capo Press.

Marcus, Greil. 1975. *Mystery Train.* New York: Random House.

Marcuse, Herbert. 1964. *One-Dimensional Man.* Boston: Beacon Press.

Marx, K. 1975. "Thesis on Feuerbach." In *Early Writings,* ed. D. Fernbach. New York: Vintage.

McLaren, Peter. 1999. *Schooling as a Ritual Performance.* Lanham, MD: Rowman and Littlefield.

McLuhan, Marshall. 1964. *Understanding Media.* New York: McGraw-Hill.

Memmi, A. 1973. *The Colonizer and the Colonized.* New York: Holt, Rinehart and Winston.

Metz, Christian. 1991. *Film Language: A Semiotics of the Cinema.* Chicago: University of Chicago Press.

Mills, C. Wright. 1956. *The Power Elite.* New York: Oxford University Press.

Postman, Neil. 1986. *Amusing Ourselves to Death.* New York: Viking.

Powdermaker, Hortense. 1950. *Hollywood: The Dream Factory.* Boston: Little, Brown.

Ross, Andrew. 2004. *No Collar: The Humane Workplace and Its Hidden Costs.* Philadelphia: Temple University Press.

Sennett, Richard, and Jonathan Cobb. 1973. *The Hidden Injuries of Class.* New York: Vintage.

Slaughter, Sheila, and Larry Leslie. 1997. *Academic Capitalism: Politics, Policies, and the Entrepreneurial University.* Baltimore, MD: The Johns Hopkins University Press.

Spivak, Gayatri. 1988. "Can the Subaltern Speak?" *Marxism and the Interpretation of Culture,* ed. by Cary Nelson and Larry Grossberg. Urbana: University of Illinois Press.

Teitelbaum, Kenneth. 1995. *Schooling for "Good Rebels": Socialism, American Education, and the Search for Radical Curriculum.* New York: Teachers College Press.

Trachtenberg, Alan. 1988. *The Incorporation of America.* New York: Hill and Wang.

Veblen, Thorstein. 1993 [1918]. *The Higher Learning in America.* New Brunswick, NJ: Transaction Books.

Walsh, Sharon. 1994. "Berkeley Denies Tenure to Scientist Who Criticized Ties to Industry." *Chronicle of Higher Education* 50, 18 (January).

Williams, E. 1990. Interview with Paulo Freire, Sao Paulo.

Willis, Paul. 1981. *Learning to Labor: How Working Class Kids Get Working Class Jobs.* New York: Columbia University Press.

THIRTEEN

Creating the Conditions for Cultural Democracy in the Classroom

Antónia Darder

> But democracy, by definition, cannot mean merely that an unskilled worker can become skilled. It must mean that every "citizen" can "govern" and that society places him [or her] in a general condition to achieve this.
> —Antonio Gramsci, *Selections from the Prison Notebooks*

Cultural democracy in the classroom cannot be discussed within the context of a critical bicultural pedagogy, outside of the theoretical dimensions that function to position teachers with respect to their educational practice. Antonio Gramsci's words support a theory of cultural democracy that not only locates bicultural students[1] within a historical and cultural context but also addresses questions related to moral and political agency within the process of their schooling and the course of their everyday lives. In short, this critical view suggests that prior to any engagement with instrumental questions of practice, educators must delve rigorously into those specific theoretical issues that are fundamental to the establishment of a culturally democratic foundation for a critical bicultural pedagogy in the classroom.

This view is also consistent with that of Freire (1970) and other critical educational theorists who emphatically express that any liberatory pedagogy cannot represent a recipe for classroom practice. Rather, it is meant to provide a set of critical educational principles that can guide and support teachers' critical engagement with the forces determining the reality of classroom life. Informed by this tradition, a critical foundation for bicultural education must not be presented in the form of models for duplication or how-to instruction manuals. One of the most important reasons for this thinking is expressed by Simon (1988), who speaks eloquently to the notion that all educational practice must emerge from the contextual relationships defined by the very conditions existing at any given moment within the classroom. Such a practice "is at root contextual and conditional. A critical pedagogy can only be concretely discussed from within a particular 'point of practice,' from within a specific time and place, and within a particular theme" (p. 1).

Hence, efforts to instrumentalize or operationalize a critical perspective outside the context in which it is to function fails to engage with the historical, cultural, and dialogical principles that are essential to a critical learning environment. In addition, this approach also ignores that prior to the development of practice, there are cultural and ideological assumptions at work determining how educators define the purpose of education, their role, and the role of their students in the process of schooling. The belief that teachers must be provided with "canned" curriculum to ensure their success fails to acknowledge the creative potential of educators to grapple effectively with the multiplicity of contexts that they find in their classrooms and to shape environments according to the lived experiences and actual educational needs of their students.

Teacher education programs are notorious for reducing the role of teachers to that of technicians. Instead of empowering teachers by assisting them to develop a critical understanding of their purpose as educators, most programs foster a dependency on predefined curriculum, outdated classroom strategies and techniques, and traditionally rigid classroom environments that position not only students but teachers as well into physically and intellectually oppressive situations. This occurs to such a degree that few public school teachers are able to envision their practice outside the scope of barren classroom settings, lifeless instructional packages, bland textbooks, standardized tests, and the use of meritocratic systems for student performance evaluation. Educators of bicultural students must recognize the manner in which these conditions work to disempower both teachers and students in American public schools. Teachers can then begin to refuse the role of technicians in their practice as educators as they struggle together to abandon their dependency on traditional classroom artifacts. This represents an essential step if teachers are to educate students of color to discover themselves and their potential within an environment that permits them to interact with what they know to be their world. This is particularly important, given the fact that values supporting cultural diversity, social struggle, and human rights are so often absent from the curricular materials teachers are forced to use in most public schools.

A critical bicultural pedagogy that is built on a foundation of cultural democracy represents a missing educational discourse in the preparation and practice of most public school teachers. The many different forms, in which the bicultural experience manifests itself in American life, seldom find their way into traditional classroom settings. Instead, bicultural experiences remain, for the most part, hidden within the reinforced silence of students of color. If the voices of difference are to find a place in the everyday interactions of public schools, educators of bicultural students must create the conditions for all students to experience an ongoing process of culturally democratic life. With this in mind, this chapter will address the major questions and issues that educators face in their efforts to pave the way for a critical bicultural pedagogy.

The Question of Language

It is impossible to consider any form of education—or even human existence—without first considering the impact of language on our lives. Language must be recognized as one of the most significant human resources; it functions in a multitude of ways to affirm, contradict, negotiate, challenge, transform, and empower particular cultural and ideological beliefs and practices. Language constitutes one of the most powerful media for transmitting our personal histories and social realities as well as for thinking and shaping the world (Cole & Scribner, 1974). Language is essential to the process of dialogue, to the development of meaning, and to the production of knowledge. From the context of its emancipatory potential, language must be understood as a dialectical phenomenon that links its very existence and meaning to the lived experiences of the language community and constitutes a major cornerstone for the development of voice.

The question of language must also be addressed within the context of a terrain of struggle that is central to our efforts to transform traditional educational structures that historically have failed bicultural students. In doing so, it is essential that we do not fall into totalizing theoretical traps—ignoring that human beings are in fact able to appropriate a multitude of linguistic forms and utilize them in critical and emancipatory ways. It is simplistic and to our detriment as educators of bicultural students to accept the notion that any one particular form of language (i.e., "standard" English), in and of itself, constitutes a totalizing dominant or subordinate force, as it is unrealistic to believe that simply utilizing a student's primary language (e.g., Spanish, Ebonics, etc.) guarantees that a student's emancipatory interests are being addressed. Consequently, the question of language in the classroom constitutes one of the most complex and multifaceted issues that educators of bicultural students must be prepared to address in the course of their practice.

The complexity of language and its relationship not only to how students produce knowledge but also to how language shapes their world represent a major pedagogical concern for all educational settings. In public schools, teachers can begin to address this complexity by incorporating activities based on the languages their students bring into the classroom. In this way, the familiar language can function as a significant starting point from which bicultural students can engage with the foreign and unknown elements that comprise significant portions of the required curriculum. An example of how teachers might do this with younger students is to develop language instruction and activities with their students, activities that give them the opportunity to bring the home language into the context of the classroom. This can be done by having students and parents introduce their languages through songs, stories, games, and other such activities. Giving attention to the home language raises it to a place of dignity and respect, rather than permitting it to become a source of humiliation and shame for bicultural students. It should be noted that the introduction of different languages must also be accompanied by critical dialogues that help students examine prevailing social attitudes and biases about language differences. These discussions can assist students to consider typical discriminatory responses to such situations as when people speak with "foreign" accents, or when people do not understand the language being spoken. In addition, students from similar cultural and language communities can be encouraged and made to feel comfortable when they converse together in their primary language as part of the classroom experience. Such opportunities support the development of voice, as well as affirm the bicultural experience of students of color. bell hooks (1989) addresses this point:

> Learning to listen to different voices, hearing different speech challenges the notion that we must all assimilate—share a single similar talk—in educational institutions. Language reflects the culture from which we emerge. To deny ourselves daily use of speech patterns that are common and familiar, that embody the unique and distinctive aspect of our self is one of the ways we become estranged and alienated from our past. It is important for us to have as many languages on hand as we can know or learn. It is important for those of us who are Black, who speak in particular patois as well as standard English, to express ourselves in both ways. (pp. 79–80)

With older students, the issue of language can be addressed in more complex terms. As mentioned previously, bicultural students must find opportunities to engage in classroom dialogues and activities that permit them to explore the meaning of their lived experiences through the familiarity of their own language. But also important to their development of social consciousness and their process of concretization is the awareness of how language and power intersect in ways that include or exclude students of color from particular social relationships. Although it is paramount that bicultural students fully develop and strengthen their bicultural voices (as Puerto Ricans, Chicanos, African Americans, etc.) through their interactions with others in their own communities, it is also imperative that, in order to understand more fully the impact of language on social structures and practices, students of color enter into critical dialogues with those outside their cultural communities. Through the process of these cross-cultural dialogues, students come to better recognize for themselves the manner in which language works to define who they are, and how language as a tool can assist them to explore critically those possibilities that have remained hidden and out of their reach.

It is significant for teachers to recognize that it is more common for bicultural students to reflect on these issues and to express themselves predominantly through a *language of practice*—a highly pragmatic language that is primarily rooted in notions of common sense and concrete experiences. Although this process represents a necessary step in the empowerment of bicultural students, their transformative potential can only be extended when they are able to unite practice with theory, or when they are able to recognize themselves as critical beings who are constantly moving between concrete and abstract representations of experiences that influence how they make decisions about their actions in the world.

In order to create the conditions for students to determine their own lives genuinely within a multiplicity of discourses, teachers must introduce their students to *the language of theory*. The language of theory constitutes a critical language of social analysis that is produced through human efforts to understand how individuals reflect and interpret their experiences and, as a result, how they shape and are shaped by their world. Although it is a language generally connected to the realm of abstract thinking, its fundamental function of praxis cannot be fulfilled unless it is linked to the concrete experiences and practices of everyday life. Such language also encourages the use of more precise and specific linguistic representations of experience than is generally expected—or even necessary—in the course of everyday practice. Challenging bicultural students to engage openly with the language of theory and to understand better its impact on their lives can awaken them to the tremendous potential available to them as social agents.

At this point it is significant to note that what has been traditionally considered theoretical language has also been—almost exclusively—controlled and governed by those who have held power in academic circles: namely, elite, White males. As a result, the greatest number of formal theoretical texts considered as legitimate knowledge, reflect conservative, Eurocentric, patriarchal notions of the world. Generally speaking, these texts uniformly support assumptions that reinforce racism, classism and sexism, while written in such a way as to justify claims of neutrality and objectivity.

In their efforts to resist conservative forms of language domination, many educators disengage from all forms of theoretical language, thereby relegating the language of theory exclusively to a sphere of domination. Not surprisingly, this uncritical view comes dangerously close to being little more than a less recognized form of anti-intellectualism. The greatest danger is that it abandons the struggle for a liberatory language of theory by its refusal to challenge academic work that perpetuates all forms of domination and to assert the need for multiple forms of theoretical language rooted in culturally diverse perspectives and a variety of styles (hooks, 1989).

From another standpoint, efforts to resist the inequality and alienation reinforced by traditional uses of theoretical language can result in protective mechanisms of resistance among students of color, and this too can give rise to unintentional forms of anti-intellectualism. Given the nature of such responses, it is not unusual for bicultural students, who have suffered the negative impact of domination in their lives, to reject indiscriminately those cultural forms and social institutions that they come to associate with hostility and alienation. As a consequence, it is no simple task to challenge attitudes of anti-intellectualism in the classroom. To do so requires that teachers recognize that attitudes of resistance manifested by students of color are very often rooted in legitimate fears and subsequent responses to support community survival. In addition, these fears and responses are strongly fostered by a legacy of resistance, which is reinforced daily through their personal and institutional relationships. These relationships include interactions with their parents, who often harbor unspoken fears that they may lose their children forever if they should become educated. In her writings, hooks (1989) describes this parental fear:

> They feared what college education might do to their children's minds even as they unenthusiastically acknowledged its importance. . . . No wonder our working class parents from poor backgrounds feared our entry into such a world, intuiting perhaps that we might learn to be ashamed of where we had come from, that we might never return home, or come back only to lord it over them. (1989, pp. 74–75)

Also included among these interactions are relationships with many of their teachers, who themselves have never successfully moved beyond the language of practice. Consequently, it is not unusual for many teachers, when asked to engage with the language of theory, to respond by feeling almost as fearful, intimidated, and disempowered as their students. Simon (1988) addresses this *fear of theory* among teachers who are graduate students in his classes:

> A fear of theory [is] more often expressed by students who have had to struggle for acceptance and recognition within the dominant institutions which define the terrain of everyday life. These are students whose lives have been lived within the prescriptive and marginalizing effects of power inscribed in relations of class, gender, ethnicity, race and sexual preference. (p. 7)

These responses by teachers are often used by teacher preparation programs around the country to justify astute arguments against the widespread use of theoretical language. More often than not, these arguments are shaped by a lack of critical engagement with the emancipatory potential of language and by a reproductive ideology that reduces students to simple objects who are somehow mystically stripped of all dignity and voice by expecting them to engage in disciplined critical thought and to address abstract concepts related to practice in more precise ways. These complaints are generally accompanied by a call for more visual language, more anecdotal accounts, or more how-to discussions. In essence, such requests for the predominant use of a language of practice inadvertently perpetuate a nondialectical and dichotomized view of theory and erode the teacher's potential for creative social action. If one listens carefully between the lines of this pragmatic educational discourse, it echoes a "false generosity of paternalism" (Freire, 1970) built on assumptions that arise from a lack of faith in the ability of oppressed groups to appropriate, transform, and utilize the language of theory in a liberatory fashion.

Educators in bicultural communities must grapple with their own language biases and prejudices beyond the simple issue of language differences and work to encounter the deep frustrations and anxieties related to their fear of theory. This significant area of concern also needs to be adequately addressed by teacher preparation programs. This is particularly true for those programs that have traditionally neglected or ignored altogether this fundamental issue, as evidenced by curricula that place a greater emphasis on numerous predefined ways to teach the standard subjects rather than on exploring the complexity inherent in the human dynamics of creating meaning and producing knowledge in the classroom.

Language represents one of the most significant educational tools in our struggle for cultural democracy in the public schools. It is intimately linked to the struggle for voice and so is essential to our struggle for liberation. Through language we not only define our position in society, but we also use that language to define ourselves as subjects in our world. Herein lies one of the most important goals for a critical bicultural pedagogy: creating the conditions for the voices of difference to find their way to the center of the dialogical process rather than to remain forever silent or at the fringes of American classroom life.

The Question of Authority

The question of authority represents one of the most heated areas of contention among major educational theorists in this country. This should not be surprising, for the manner in which we conceptualize authority truly represents a necessary precondition for the manner in which we define ourselves, our work, and our very lives—so much so that it is impossible to discuss cultural democracy in the classroom without addressing the issues that directly stem from this question.

In order to engage critically with the notion of authority, it is vital that teachers come to understand that authority does not automatically equal authoritarianism. Authority, within the context of a critical bicultural pedagogy, is intimately linked to the manner in which teachers exercise control, direct, influence, and make decisions about what is actually to take place in their classrooms. To engage with the question of authority in a liberatory fashion clearly requires an understanding of power and how power is used to construct relationships, define truth, and create social conditions that can potentially either subordinate or empower bicultural students. Hence, authority must be understood as a dialectical "terrain of legitimation and struggle," rather than simply as an absolute, hierarchical, and totalizing force (Giroux, 1988).

Efforts to examine the question of authority in the classroom also require teachers to address their personal contradictions related to how they formulate ideas of control, power, and authority in their own lives. This is particularly necessary given the manner in which teachers in public schools are consistently subject to administrative dictates and school conditions that undermine their power and authority. As teachers struggle together to challenge their conflicts and contradictions in this area, they are more able to build environments that support an emancipatory view of authority, stimulating their students to rethink critically their values, ideas, and actions in relation to the consequences these might have on themselves and others.

Although the question of authority is seldom discussed in liberatory terms by either conservative or liberal educators, it is essential that it be critically addressed in teacher preparation programs. As mentioned above, it is difficult for teachers to address the issue of authority if they themselves hold uncritical, conflicting, and contradictory attitudes about power and its relationship to human organization. Such attitudes are apparent in prevailing commonsense beliefs about the nature of power. While conservative educators are more likely to see power as a positive force that works to maintain order, earn respect, and "get the job done," liberals—and even many radical educators—are more prone to believe that "power corrupts" and that, despite human efforts, power ultimately leads to destruction. As a consequence, power is commonly perceived either as an absolute force for good, or else as an evil or negative force that dehumanizes and divests the individual's capacity for justice and solidarity with others. Understanding how these views of power are enmeshed in the contradictory thinking of teachers can help to shed light on the inadequacy and helplessness that so many educators express. This is of particular concern, given the fact that so many liberal and radical educators who hold negative assumptions related to power also speak to the necessity of *empowering* students, communities, and teachers alike.

The contradictory assumptions that underscore the question of authority also function to perpetuate the status quo, through the manner in which they sabotage, limit, and distort teachers' perceptions of classroom authority and their ability to alter the conditions they find in public schools. Such teachers, who do not possess a dialectical view of authority, generally lack the critical criteria to challenge attitudes, beliefs, and actions that perpetuate social injustice. In light of this, authority can be more readily understood in terms of its potential to uphold those emancipatory categories essential to the foundation of critical democratic life.

In our efforts to address this dimension, it must be explained that contradictory assumptions of authority cannot be deconstructed by simply utilizing a language of practice. The task of challenging society's contradictions requires educators to delve fearlessly into both the abstract and concrete experiences that unite to inform the theoretical realm. Through uniting their critical reflections of practice with theory, teachers come to discover the manner in which distorted views of power inform those classroom practices that reinforce undercurrents of oppression, perpetuating conditions that marginalize and alienate students of color.

The authoritarian nature of a conservative view of teacher authority is often hidden beneath the guise of traditional notions of respect, which can incorporate objective, instrumental, and hierarchical relationships that support various forms of oppressive educational practices at the expense of student voice. On the other hand, the oppressive impact of the liberal view of teacher authority, which all but disengages with questions of authority, often functions in an equally perverse manner. Hidden under the values of subjectivity, individualism, and intentionality, this view easily deteriorates into a crass relativism, asserting that all expressed values and ideas are deserving of equal time (Giroux, 1981). This is put into practice to the extent that some teachers proudly proclaim that they always consider all ideas generated by their students as equal, irrespective of personal histories, ideologies, or cultural differences—thus professing a specious notion of shared power. Although this perspective may ring true when entertained exclusively in the language of practice, theoretically it reflects an uncritical disengagement with issues related to social forms of domination and the manner in which ideas are generated and informed by particular interests that silence and oppress students from subordinate groups. Therefore, it is fraudulent to pretend that a teacher does not possess the authority and power over students to determine how the classroom will be governed, and it is an act of irresponsibility for teachers to abdicate their duty to challenge critically the oppressive nature of student ideas when these ideas constitute acts of racism, sexism, classism, or other forms of psychological violence that attack the dignity and self-worth of students of color.

Unlike traditional views on teacher authority, an emancipatory view of authority suggests that, although teachers hold knowledge that is considered to render them prepared to enter the classroom, they must come to recognize that knowledge as a historical and cultural product is forever in a creative state of partiality. And, as a consequence, all forms of discourse represent only one small piece of the larger puzzle that constitutes all possible knowledge at any given moment in time. Hence, all forms of knowledge must be open for question, examination, and critique by and with students in the process of learning. In this way, teachers actively use their authority to create the conditions for a critical transformation of consciousness that takes place in the process of the interaction of teacher, students, and the knowledge they produce together. Grounded in criteria informed by a liberatory vision of life, teachers embrace the notion of authority in the interest of cultural democracy, rather than against it.

Redefining Fairness and Equality

If American public schools are to establish classroom environments that are culturally democratic, teachers will have to undertake a critical analysis of what has been traditionally defined as *fair and equal.* Just as the principles of democracy have so often been reduced to numerical head-counts and majority rule, concepts of fairness and equality have also been reduced to such quantifiable forms. Therefore, it is not unusual to hear teachers across the country express the belief that fair and equal is equivalent to providing the same quantity and quality of goods to all students across the board, irrespective of differences in social privilege and economic entitlement.

Clearly inherent in this perspective of fair and equal is the elimination of any transformative impact that these principles might have on the lives of disenfranchised students. The consequence in public schools is that students from the dominant culture who enter with major social and economic advantages receive as much—and at times even more—than students from subordinate cultures who arrive with far fewer social advantages. In an analysis of resource distribution among students in public schools, it is unquestionably apparent that poor children, who receive the least at home, receive the least from public education (Kozol, 1990). This painfully reminds us that the American educational system has little to do with cultivating equality. For if equality were, in fact, a part of the philosophical vision of education, the educational system would prioritize its resources in such a manner as to ensure that the majority of students were placed in settings where they could achieve successfully. Under such conditions, students from disenfranchised communities who require more educational opportunities by way of teacher contact, educational materials, nutritional support, and health care would receive more, while those students who arrive with greater privileges and with many more resources already in place would receive less.

Instead, what we find in most schools is the opposite. Students from the dominant culture who excel because they have been raised in homes that can provide them with the social, economic, and cultural capital necessary to meet the elitist and ethnocentric standards of American schools enjoy greater advantages and more positive regard than those from disenfranchised communities who must consistently struggle to succeed under social conditions working to their detriment. For decades it has been well documented that students from the dominant culture, who are raised in environments of privilege, score higher on standardized examinations. Hence, these students are perceived as superior when compared to most bicultural students. In addition, many of these superior students are also considered by public schools to be exhibiting mentally gifted abilities, while the majority of students of color are stigmatized and shamed by assignments into basic and remedial classes. This mentally gifted status has then been used as a justifiable rationale for appropriating additional resources to the already privileged—a group that just happens to include very few working-class students of color.

The consequence here is that the majority of bicultural students who are in need of greater school resources and educational opportunities find themselves in less challenging and less stimulating environments—environments that operate under the assumption that the students themselves, their parents, and their culture are to blame for their deficiency, while ignoring the deficiencies of a larger social caste system that replicates itself in public schools. Efforts by the White House in the past decade have merely functioned to make the situation worse. Plans that had been made to equalize school funding among districts have been replaced by a major reduction of funding to educational programs and an emphasis on building student motivation and self-control. Jonathan Kozol suggests that the consequences of tougher conservative rhetoric and more severe demands have led to further discrimination toward disenfranchised students:

> Higher standards, in the absence of authentic educative opportunities in early years, function as a punitive attack on those who have been cheated since their infancy. Effectively, we now ask more of those to whom we now give less. Earlier testing for schoolchildren is prescribed. Those who fail are penalized by being held back from promotion and by being slotted into lower tracks where they cannot impede the progress of more privileged children. Those who disrupt classroom discipline are not placed in smaller classes with more patient teachers; instead, at a certain point, they are expelled—even if this means expulsion of a quarter of all pupils in school. (Kozol, 1990, p. 52)

Buried deep within traditional institutional views of fairness and equality is a stubborn refusal to engage with the reality of social conditions that marginalize students of color in this country. As a consequence, not only are bicultural students perceived as somehow less intelligent and therefore less deserving than middle-class students from the dominant culture, but also they are taught through their interactions with the system to perceive themselves in this way. If conditions in public schools are to change, teachers must openly challenge traditional views of fairness and equality and expose how these have functioned to reinforce notions of entitlement and privilege based on a doctrine of Social Darwinism that has proven to be incompatible with any emancipatory vision of social justice and equality.

The Use of Multicultural Curriculum

When educators first begin to think about how they can meet the needs of students of color, one of the most common places to begin is by bringing traditional cultural objects and symbols into the classroom. In fact, most multicultural curricula place a major emphasis on such cultural artifacts because they can be easily seen, manipulated, and quantified, although they ignore the more complex subjectivities of cultural values, belief systems, and traditions that inform the production of such cultural forms. Also problematic are depictions of cultural images and symbols that promote Eurocentric interpretations of cultural groups—depictions that function to dissolve cultural differences and reinforce mainstream expectations of assimilation. As a consequence, these traditional multicultural approaches operate to the detriment of students of color because they fail to respect and affirm their cultural differences and to help them understand the social and political implications of growing up bicultural in American society.

This is not to imply that bicultural students should not be exposed to a curriculum that seeks to present cultural artifacts affirming their cultural traditions and experiences but rather to emphasize that such multicultural materials and activities do not, in and of themselves, ensure that a culturally democratic process is at work. As mentioned above, this is in fact the case with most traditional efforts to promote cultural diversity. And many situations exist in which students are presented with games, food, stories, language, music, and other cultural forms in such a way as to strip these expressions of intent by reducing them to mere objects disembodied from their cultural meaning.

In order to prevent such an outcome, educators must become more critical not only of the actual curriculum they bring into the classroom but also of the philosophical beliefs that inform their practice. First, they can begin to assess carefully their personal assumptions, prejudices, and biases related to issues of culture. Since it is far more common for teachers to think of themselves as neutral and unbiased toward all students, many racist, classist, and sexist attitudes and behaviors are most often disguised by faulty common-sense assumptions utilized extensively to assess student academic performance or classroom behavior. For example, most teachers still retain notions of culture that reflect colorblind or melting-pot assumptions and a bootstrap mentality. Simply put, these teachers believe that all people are the same in spite of race or culture, that the United States is a place where all cultures have (or should have) melted together to form one culture, and that anyone who wants to succeed *can* succeed, irrespective of social or economic circumstances.

Unfortunately these assumptions work to undermine the emancipatory potential of multicultural curricula. This is primarily because, when educators engage with issues related to cultural diversity based on these beliefs, they are unable accurately to address cultural issues related to power and dominance, as well as the impact that these forces have on the lives of bicultural students. For instance, in situations where students of color act out their resistance to cultural domination by passively refusing to participate in classroom activities or by actively disrupting the process, these student behaviors are interpreted by the majority of teachers as simply a classroom management problem—or, at most, as cause for concern about the emotional stability or well-being of the student. Seldom does it occur to most teachers who are faced with such behaviors to consider the manner in which cultural subordination and prevailing social hostility toward differences might represent the genesis of classroom resistance. Consequently, despite well-meaning efforts by teachers to intervene, their faulty assumptions generally hinder their effectiveness with bicultural students through unintentional acts of cultural invasion and further cultural subordination of students of color.

Second, in order to approach effectively the need for culturally relevant curriculum in the classroom, educators must be willing to acknowledge their limitations with respect to the cultural systems from which bicultural students make sense of their world. This requires teachers to recognize that students and their families bring to the classroom knowledge about their cultures, their communities, and their educational needs. This can best be accomplished by creating conditions for students to voice more clearly what constitutes the cultural differences they experience and to unfurl the conflicts as they struggle together to understand their own histories and their relationships with others. In addition, teachers must take the time to learn about the communities in which their students live. As teachers gain a greater understanding of students' lives outside of school, they are more able to create opportunities for classroom dialogue, which assists bicultural students to affirm, challenge, and transform the many conflicts and contradictions that they face as members of an oppressed group.

Third, educators also need to become more critical in their assessment of multicultural curricula and activities with respect to the consequences of their use in the classroom. For example, many teachers believe that making feathered headbands and teaching students about the Indians' contributions to the first Thanksgiving are effective activities for the study of Native Americans. In reality, these types of activities constitute forms of cultural invasion that reinforce stereotypical images of American Indians and grossly distort the history of a people. Although this is a deeply problematic representation of culture for all students, it has a particularly perverse effect on students who have had little or no exposure to Native Americans other than what they have seen on television and in films and a destructive impact on the self-esteem and identity of Native American students who are victimized by such distorted depictions of their cultural histories.

And fourth, teachers must come to realize that no multicultural curriculum, in and of itself, can replace the dialogical participation of bicultural students in the process of schooling. This is to say that even the most ideologically correct curriculum is in danger of objectifying students if it is utilized in such a way as to detach them from their everyday lives. Gramsci (1971) observes,

> Thus, we come back to the truly active participation of the pupil in the school, which can only exist if the school is related to life. The more the new curricula nominally affirm and theorize the pupil's activity and working collaboration with the teacher, the more they are actually designed as if the pupil were purely passive. (p. 37)

Gramsci's words support the notion that a genuine affirmation of cultural diversity in the classroom requires the restructuring of power relations and classroom structures in such a manner as to promote the *active* voice and participation of bicultural students. Through the creation of culturally democratic classroom conditions that also place bicultural voices at the center of the discourse, all students can come together to speak out about their lives and engage in dialogues that permit them to examine their cultural values and social realities. In this way, students can learn to make problematic their views of life, search for different ways to think about themselves, challenge their self-imposed as well as institutionally defined limitations, affirm their cultural and individual strengths, and embrace the possibilities for a better world through a growing sense of solidarity built on love, respect, and compassion for one another and a commitment to the liberation of all people.

Challenging Racism in the Classroom

No matter how much a teacher might feel committed to the notion of cultural diversity, it is impossible to create a culturally democratic environment that can effectively meet the educational needs of bicultural students if that teacher is ill equipped to challenge incidences of racism when they surface in the curriculum or in student relationships. As described earlier, racism results from institutionalized prejudices and biases that perpetuate discrimination based on racial and cultural differences. When educators fail to criticize discriminatory attitudes and behaviors, they permit bicultural students to suffer needless humiliation and psychological violence that negatively reinforce feelings of disentitlement and marginalization in society.

Despite attitudes to the contrary, cultural differences do not constitute the problem in public schools; rather, the problem is directly related to the responses of the dominant culture to these differences—responses that function to perpetuate social, political, and economic inequality. Instead of adopting the neutral position of most multicultural approaches, Carol Phillips (1988) suggests that educators teach students

> how to recognize when cultural and racially different groups are being victimized by the racist and biased attitudes of the larger society; how these behaviors are institutionalized in the policies and procedures of [schools] and programs; how these practices of excluding people are so mystified that well-meaning advocates for change fail to see them operating; [and] how to act against prevailing forces that perpetuate racism. (p. 45)

The inability to address racism, as suggested by Phillips, is commonly observed in the failure of educators to address even racial slurs when they occur. A common scenario may find two or more students in a disagreement, and one or more may yell out at the other, "You nigger!" or "You greaser!" More times than not, educators who overhear such comments—unable to deal with their own discomfort—let them go by altogether, or they may tell the students to stop fighting, or that it is against the rules to call each other names. Unfortunately, despite good intentions, these approaches ignore the social circumstances that inform such behavior and the consequences for all students involved. In addition, it does nothing to assist these students and their peers to understand their actions critically nor will it transform their relationships in any way.

Educators who strive for culturally democratic environments will need to call on their courage and inner strength to challenge the tension and discomfort they experience when confronting issues of discrimination in the classroom. Instead of looking for quick-fix methods to restore a false sense of harmony at such moments of confrontation, educators must seek to unveil the tensions, conflicts, and contradictions that perpetuate discriminatory attitudes and behaviors among their students. In a situation such as the one described above, the teacher can bring students together into a critical dialogue about racial epithets and their role in perpetuating injustice. This may begin with questions about the feelings that precipitate these words: Where did they learn the words? What is the intent behind their use? What are the effects of these epithets on the victim? On the victimizer? How does this behavior relate to other forms of racism in the community? How could students engage in resolving their differences in other ways?

Dialogues such as this should be consistently introduced and encouraged among students within the context of the classroom, so that they may come to understand how their attitudes and behaviors affect others and, more importantly, so that they may come to act on behalf of all who are oppressed. Through their participation in this process, students have the opportunity to speak their feelings about race and how it relates to their lived experiences and to become conscious of their own investment in racist attitudes and behaviors. In addition, they also learn to analyze how racism affects the conditions that exist in their communities and to develop strategies for countering racism when they encounter it in their own lives (Giroux, 1990). For bicultural students, the dialogue must extend further. It must also assist them to identify the different ways in which their relationships with the dominant culture have conditioned them to take on contradictory attitudes and beliefs about themselves that cause them to participate unintentionally in the perpetuation of their own oppression.

The Culture of the Teacher

Whenever educators begin seriously to confront the complexity of teaching in bicultural communities, they also begin to question what impact the teacher's cultural background has on her or his ability to educate successfully students of color. It is an important question to consider within the context of a critical bicultural pedagogical discourse—particularly because of the profound nature of cultural belief systems and their relationship to issues of identity and social power. In addition, it brings into the arena of discussion notions of cultural differences with respect to the roles that teachers play if they are from the dominant culture versus those who come from subordinate cultures.

As suggested earlier, in their efforts to learn about different cultural communities, teachers generally pursue materials that address the more visible or tangible aspects of cultural experience, while neglecting the deep structural values that inform the cultural worldviews of subordinate groups. In conjunction with this, teachers have been socialized to believe that by simply gathering or obtaining information on any particular subject they can come to know that subject. From a critical bicultural perspective, learning about a culture from a book or a few seminars does not constitute knowing that culture. This is particularly true with respect to understanding the daily lived experiences of the group and the historicity of social forces that work to shape and shift how its members interact in the world. For example, someone who is not Hopi might read many books or articles about the Hopi people and yet still not know what it means to grow up as a Hopi in American society.

To even begin to comprehend the bicultural experience requires that teachers from the dominant culture invest time and energy into establishing critical dialogues with people of color if they wish to understand their communities better. Even then, these teachers must recognize and respect that their process of learning and knowing is inherently situated *outside* that cultural context and is therefore different from the knowledge obtained from living *within* a particular cultural community. This is an essential understanding for teachers who have been raised in the dominant culture and whose cultural reference point is based on white Euro-American values—which are the predominant values informing most American institutions. This is not to say that all Anglo-Americans conform to these values but rather to suggest that, even in states of nonconformity, Euro-American values represent the central reference point that individuals of the dominant culture move toward or move away from in the course of their personal and institutional relationships. This reference point also dictates the multitude of subject positions that individuals from the dominant culture assume in their lives with respect to class, gender, sexual orientation, spirituality, politics, and other ideological categories related to worldview.

The biculturation process represents an attempt to describe the dynamics by which people of color interact with the conflicts and contradictions arising when growing up in a primary culture that dictates a reference point and subject positions in conflict with those of the dominant culture. As a consequence, members from subordinate groups must find ways to cope and function within institutional environments that on the one hand generally undermine and curtail their rights to equality and on the other hand push them to assimilate the values of the dominant culture. The different ways in which bicultural people attempt to resolve the tension created by such forces are reflected in the predominant response patterns they utilize to survive. What complicates this process further is the manner in which Euro-American values are perpetuated through hegemonic forces of social control, while the primary values of African Americans, Latinos, Native Americans, Asians, and other subordinate groups are relegated to subordinate positions in American society.

The consequence is that very often people of color whose bicultural voices and experiences have been systematically silenced and negated are not necessarily conscious of the manner in which racism and classism have influenced their individual development, nor how they have functioned to distort perceptions of their cultural group within an Anglo-centric world. Therefore, the fact that a person is bicultural does not guarantee that she or he occupies a position of resistance to such domination. In fact, under current social conditions, it is not unusual to find people of color in positions of power who ignore issues of social power and perpetuate ideas and beliefs that function to the detriment of their own people. Such prominent figures include the likes of Senator Samuel Hayakawa, who was an outspoken advocate for a national English-only initiative; Linda Chavez, a former member of the National Human Relations Commission; and Shelby Steele, the author of *The Content of Our Character*. This is also the case with the many teachers of color who have naively made attempts to assimilate into the dominant culture without critically engaging with the impact of their beliefs on their lives and work.

This perspective is offered here because it represents a reality that must be understood if educators are honestly to consider questions related to the cultural background of the teachers who educate bicultural students. It is a reality that must be acknowledged if we are to prevent falling into the trap of essentialist arguments, such as those proclaiming that only teachers of color can effectively educate students of color. Instead, what is needed is the courage, willingness, and desire to speak honestly to those issues that relate directly to how individuals define their cultural identity and how this influences their work with bicultural students. How teachers perceive the notion of cultural identity is especially important, given that the majority of educators in the United States are members of the dominant culture and that most educators—of all cultures—have been schooled in traditional pedagogical models. Hence, the teacher's cultural background, espoused ideology, and academic preparation embody equally important areas of concern in our efforts to create conditions that are conducive to a culturally democratic life in the classroom.

If public schools are to provide successfully for the educational needs of bicultural students, they must work in collaboration with bicultural educators, students, parents, and their communities. Anything short of this effort suggests an educational process that is in danger of oppressing and disempowering students of color. This is not to imply that all teachers in bicultural communities must necessarily be teachers of color, but rather to emphasize that it is an arrogant and patronizing gesture for educators from the dominant culture to think that they can meet the needs of a culturally different community when they fail to work in solidarity with educators and other members of that community.

Efforts to establish solidarity among culturally diverse groups require relationships based on mutual respect and equality. White teachers need to abandon, willingly, unfair notions of entitlement and privilege so they may enter into relationships with people of color that support the struggle for freedom and a better world. This requires that white educators acknowledge the manner in which people of color have been historically discriminated against and subordinated to inferior positions in the society at large and the manner in which public education has perpetuated this process. They must come to see how these injustices actually exist in their own profession by the very nature of the assumptions that inform their practice. For example, it is not unusual to find bicultural/bilingual instructional aides with ten or more years of experience in the classroom working under inexperienced white middle-class teachers who know very little about the actual needs of bicultural students. Yet, when such conditions are challenged as part of a wider struggle for more bilingual/bicultural teachers, it is interesting to note the manner in which questions of social control ultimately inform the responses of many public school districts. Rather than create the conditions for well-experienced instructional aides to complete their education and receive certification, many large urban school districts have decided to import teachers from Spain. These are teachers who, in fact, are less knowledgeable of the American bicultural experience than Euro-American educators. This illustrates only one of the ways in which a process of hegemony operates in public schools to sabotage the transformative struggles of oppressed communities and to ensure the perpetuation of the status quo. Such forms of hegemony can be understood by teachers and challenged in the course of their work.

Further, in order for bicultural students to develop both an individual and a social sense of empowerment in their lives, they need to establish relationships with both white and bicultural teachers who are genuinely committed to a democratic vision of community life. When students actually experience the process of white teachers and bicultural teachers working together to address issues related to cultural differences and conflicts, they also come to better understand cultural democracy and learn to participate in cross-cultural dialogues in ways that truly respect and honor the emancipatory rights of all people.

Critical educators from the dominant culture demonstrate a spirit of solidarity and possibility when they willingly challenge both cultural values and institutional conditions of inequity despite the fact that these potentially function to their material benefit. Their refusal to accept social conditions of entitlement and privilege for themselves at the expense of oppressed groups helps to lay the groundwork for relations with people of color based on a solidarity and commitment to social justice and equality. Such educators truly recognize the need to create conditions in the classroom that empower students of color and to open opportunities that historically have remained closed to these students. Operating from this perspective, programs developed under such mandates as affirmative action and equal educational opportunity are given support as beginning efforts toward social equality, rather than seen as somehow taking away from members of the dominant culture. The way in which teachers themselves address these issues in the larger world is significant, because it usually also reflects how they relate with students of color in the course of their daily interactions with them in the classroom.

It is also essential that students of color experience a variety of teachers of color during the course of their schooling. Bicultural educators who are socially conscious bring a wealth of knowledge and experience that often resonates with the realities that students of color experience in their own lives. Many of these teachers are bilingual, understand the complexity of their students' cultural worldviews, are knowledgeable about their history and literature, are cognizant of the different styles in which students learn and communicate, are conscious of the rules of appropriate relationships and interactions among people, and know the communities from which their students come. As a consequence, bicultural teachers are generally more able to use their own learning experiences and knowledge of their cultural values to develop effective curricula that engage with issues related to cultural diversity. In addition, through their knowledge of community, they are able to find ways in which to integrate the students' lived culture into classroom relationships. They are also more genuinely able to affirm and support the development of the bicultural voice, given their ability to engage with the lived conditions of cultural domination and resistance. Hence, it must be recognized that bicultural teachers serve vital roles as models for students of color—many of whom have seldom witnessed people of color in positions of power and influence. Most importantly, through their experiences with critical bicultural educators, bicultural students are more concretely challenged and supported as they come to redefine their possibilities within the context of American society.

Restructuring Public Schools

Critical educators of bicultural students must consider creative ways in which they can work to restructure public school environments that support experiences of culturally democratic life. The manner in which this is done must take into account not only the specific needs that bicultural students bring into the classroom, but also the needs that teachers have in order to be more effective educators. Through gaining a better understanding of the lived histories and daily lives of both students of color and their teachers, classroom structures can be transformed to reflect meaningful social relationships and critical pedagogical approaches that are built on the principles of cultural democracy. Just as students are critically challenged to redefine the possibilities for transforming the world, their teachers should be actively involved in such a process within the context of their own profession. First of all, efforts by teachers to promote the development of voice, participation, social responsibility, and solidarity are strongly reflected in the way they physically structure and situate the learning environment in their classrooms. A few classroom changes that would address this concern include these examples:

- The furniture, and in particular the seating in the room, is arranged so as to permit free physical movement of students about the classroom.

- Classroom spaces promote working in groups and on collaborative projects.

- Classroom bulletin boards are generated in conjunction with the participation of students, who are encouraged to utilize materials that are meaningful to them. These forms of cultural expression are then used to stimulate dialogues about their relationship to the context of students' lives and communities.

- Curricular activities are created for students to have opportunities to converse in their home languages with each other and to introduce various aspects of their language experience to other students.

- Students are actively involved in the development of classroom rules and in making decisions about classroom activities whenever possible. In addition, they are involved in dialogues designed to help them consider the consequences of rules and decisions made with respect to themselves as individuals and the class as a whole.

It is important to note that none of these suggestions, in and of itself, constitutes the way to incorporate a critical bicultural pedagogy, for the manner in which a critical pedagogy evolves in any particular classroom environment must be based on the contextual conditions present. No lesson plan or curriculum should ever supersede the actual learning needs expressed by students or identified by the teacher. Learning is a contextual experience by which knowledge and meaning are produced within the complexity of a multitude of potential responses generated by students and teacher alike.

The few suggestions mentioned above focus on what teachers can do to transform the structures and relationships within their own classrooms. But outside the classroom, there is also much to be done related to the general restructuring of the working conditions that teachers find in public schools. Critical educators must explore some possible ways in which to transform these conditions so that schools may function to support their own empowerment as well as an emancipatory vision for education. Some suggestions to consider with respect to this concern are as follows:

- The development of cross-cultural teaching teams in schools with large bicultural student populations.

- The initiation of professional development opportunities for all teachers to become knowledgeable in the principles of a critical bicultural pedagogy. This would provide teachers the opportunity to better understand the bicultural experience of students and to examine together their own prejudices and biases related to issues of cultural diversity.

- A greater involvement of teachers in the development, evaluation, and selection of texts, films, and other instructional materials.

- An ongoing collaborative effort with parents and community members to transform the educational environments of public schools.

- Establishment of regular public forums within schools to discuss issues related to bicultural students, such as bilingualism, the bicultural process, the academic needs of students, parent involvement in the classroom, and so forth.

In addition, teachers must also struggle to transform the structural conditions related to both out-of-class work and class size. Much of the demoralization teachers experience is not, for the most part, a consequence of low pay; rather, it is more closely linked to the powerlessness generated by working in an environment that is fundamentally incompatible with engaging in the complexities of teaching a culturally diverse student population. In order to address this issue, public school teachers might begin by demanding that the number of students in their classrooms be limited to approximately twenty. It is not unusual to find public schools in large urban settings where teachers are assigned up to forty students, with limited assistance from an instructional aide. One of the most revolutionary actions that public school teachers can take, at this point in time, is to assume an uncompromising posture with respect to the issue of class size. It is well documented that students are more successful when they receive more individualized attention from the teacher. So completely conscious of this fact are private schools that they use as a major selling point their policy of small class size. Teacher unions and other teacher organizations need to become advocates for themselves as well as for disenfranchised students by asserting the entitlement of the latter to the rights enjoyed by students from privileged classes. Most importantly, teachers who are less burdened by the tremendous demands placed on them by large class size are more able to engage consistently and critically with the actual needs of bicultural students and issues related to cultural diversity.

Also of major importance is the struggle for the redefinition of the teacher's workday. Seldom are teachers afforded opportunities to come together on an ongoing basis to reflect and dialogue critically about the concerns they experience in their efforts to meet the needs of their students. And even more seldom do they have the time to maintain some consistent form of personal contact with parents, despite the fact that studies clearly indicate this to be a significant factor in the achievement of bicultural students (Rashid, 1981; Goldenberg, 1987; Cummins, 1986). Teachers require institutional support in their efforts to develop working relationships with their colleagues, students, parents, and the communities in which they work. This can only take place when the teacher's work is redefined more realistically to include both what teachers are required to implement daily in their classrooms and those important functions they must perform outside the classroom setting to be effective educators. But this redefinition can only take place when teachers struggle to transform the conditions of their labor within the context of a critical process that is generated by working together for a better life—not only as educators, but as workers and free democratic citizens.

Beyond Despair

Much frustration is evident in the attitudes and responses of many educators to the conditions they find in public schools. Many teachers blame the problems they experience on the increasing number of students of color. Others are acutely aware that they were insufficiently prepared by teacher education programs to meet the needs of a culturally diverse student population. Still others experience a deep feeling of personal frustration, which they attribute to their own individual failure as teachers. Whatever the manner in which teachers define the cause of their frustration, it is clear that their perceptions echo a great sense of despair and powerlessness.

It is important to note that those teachers who find themselves within public school conditions—where their voices are silenced and their opportunities to decide on curricula, texts, and other classroom requirements are limited—are most in danger of experiencing a sense of despair. Public school teachers in these environments must work together to challenge themselves and each other to move beyond the limitations that they find in these schools. In addition, they must also move beyond their own dependency on traditional classroom structures and the artifacts that support the perpetuation of their disempowerment.

For example, under such conditions as described above, teachers must initially cultivate their creative abilities to utilize commonplace materials and natural environments that can serve as ideal conditions for students to investigate the ordinary, and through acting on it discover their potential power to create and change their world. Given this approach, any classroom situation can potentially be converted into a critical environment as educators discover the multitude of pedagogical possibilities at their disposal. But this can only take place when educators courageously abandon old and disempowering notions of what is necessary and certain and move beyond the boundaries of prescribed educational practice and into the realm of creativity and discovery.

As emphasized earlier, fundamental to creating the conditions for cultural democracy is a political commitment to a liberatory vision. A critical bicultural pedagogy can only emerge within a social context where teachers are grounded in a commitment to both individual and social empowerment. Hence, the smaller political endeavor of the classroom is not seen as simply an encapsulated moment in time, but rather it is consistently connected to a greater democratic political project. From this vantage point, teachers function as empowered social agents of history, who are firmly committed to collaborative struggles for transformation as they seek to change and redefine the conditions that threaten the opportunities for voice, participation, and solidarity in their schools. As teachers work in solidarity with their colleagues, parents, students, and the community, they discover their tremendous collective power, and through this process of affirmation move beyond despair. It is, in part, this critical commitment to act on behalf of freedom and social justice that also serves as a model for their students to discover their own personal power, social transformative potential, and spirit of hope.

Embodied in this emancipatory spirit of hope is also a faith in the capacity of human beings to transform the oppressive and dehumanizing conditions that disconnect, fragment, and alienate us from one another. Grounded in this struggle by a collective vision of liberation, critical educators search out creative ways to expand the opportunities for students of color to become authentic beings for themselves, in spite of the limitations of traditional curricula and prevailing social conditions. Students are encouraged to question the conflicts, contradictions, disjunctions, and partiality of standardized knowledge forms—in their own lives as well. Consistently, liberatory educators support and challenge bicultural students to struggle together so that they may come to know all the possibilities that might be available to them as free citizens. For it is through this critical process of discovery and empowerment that teachers and students move in solidarity across the terrain of cultural differences to arrive at the knowledge that hidden in the complexity of these differences are many ways to be human, and many ways to struggle for a world in which we can all be free.

Note

1. The term "bicultural" is utilized in this article as associated with a larger project of bicultural development that refers to the identity development of individuals who are considerate subordinate cultural subjects in a society. Given particular historical conditions of colonization and slavery, bicultural populations are forced to contend with what Frantz Fanon terms a double-consciousness—that is, the necessity to survive within a dominant society that is fundamentally different in cultural values, norms, and customs. Hence, biculturalism here not only refers to the notion of growing up in two cultures but, more importantly, to the fact that there is a considerable power differential at work that marginalizes and oppresses members of the so-called minority group.

References

Cole, M., and Scribner, S. (1974). *Culture and Thought*. New York: John Wiley & Sons.

Cummins, J. (1986). "Empowering Minority Students: A Framework for Intervention." *Harvard Educational Review 56*: pp. 18–36.

Freire, P. (1970). *Pedagogy of the Oppressed*. New York: Seabury Press.

Giroux, H. (1981). *Ideology, Culture, and the Process of Schooling*. Philadelphia: Temple University Press.

———. (1988). *Schooling and the Struggle for Public Life*. Minneapolis: University of Minnesota Press.

———. (1990). "The Politics of Postmodernism: Rethinking the Boundaries of Race and Ethnicity." *Journal of Urban and Cultural Studio* 1: pp. 5–38.

Goldenberg, A. (1987). "Low-income Hispanic Parents' Contribution to Their First Grader Children Word Recognition Skills." *Anthropology and Education Quarterly* 18: pp. 149–77.

Gramsci, A. (1971). *Selections from the Prison Notebooks*. New York: International Publications.

hooks, b. (1989). *Talking Back*. Boston: South End Press.

Kozol, J. (1990). "The New Untouchables." *Newsweek, Special Issue*, pp. 48–53.

Phillips, C. (1988). "Nurturing Diversity for Today's Children and Tomorrow's Leaders." *Young Children* 43: pp. 42–47.

Rashid, H. (1981). "Early Childhood Education as a Cultural Transition for African-American Children." *Educational Research Quarterly* 6: pp. 55–63.

Simon, R. (1988). "For a Pedagogy of Possibility." *Critical Pedagogy Networker* 1: pp. 1–4.

FOURTEEN

The Struggles to Eliminate the Tenacious Four-Letter "F" Word in Education

Vivian García López

Existing in a Dehumanizing World

As technology flourishes with smaller and more prevailing devices to integrate the world into its *web*, it is fascinating to see how relationships between individuals begin to transform into different communication modes, (un)meaningful connections, different levels of intimacy, and (in)humane associations or interactions with people. As I visit friends who have young children and teenagers in their homes, it is typical to see a young person connected to a gadget, who if allowed, will spend hours, days, or weeks connected to that electronic device. As an example, several faculty and staff recently attended a small informal gathering at a colleague's home. The meeting took place in a dining room where most individuals sat at the table, but there was also a young European American adult in the home who sat on a nearby couch and was spellbound with some type of digital device with an earpiece.

This informal gathering transpired all day, and the young adult stayed in the same seat the entire time with minimal physical movement or without any verbal interaction or salutation to at least acknowledge family members or guests arriving and leaving the home or individuals who sat beside the young adult and attempted to make conversation. It must be noted that after a year of occasional gatherings at this colleague's home, the (none) responsive characteristic this young adult displayed was typical throughout the year.

It was remarkable to observe an individual so intensely attached to an object seemingly unable to display any interest in acknowledging anyone who arrived and left their home, or to even grant them a slight gesture of acknowledgment or a glance, much less a "hi or hello." Symbolically, I imagined this young adult to be representative of other individuals who eventually become educators and remain disinterested in establishing any relationships with students they may work with or students' families, almost as if intentionally detached from any sense of community in general, but more specifically, from communities who are different from her/his own as described by Douglas, et al. (2008), Gibson (2004), Kohli (2008), Takei & Shouse (2008), and others.

In addition, this young adult represented, in my view, other individuals who express challenges to establishing a rapport with people in general, or an inability to read their world as described in Paulo Freire and Donaldo Macedo's (1987) *Literacy: Reading the Word and the World.* Or perhaps as a former European American pre-service student indicated, "these issues (regarding relationship building) are pretty much important to you and people like you. . .you know. . .(people) who have different needs. . .you know. . .some people need to be needed and others don't" (personal conversation, fall 2009). This statement not only illustrates a form of racism, Othering and privilege, it also creates a concern about how teachers may view the importance or lack of significance for genuine relationships between teachers and students. These missed opportunities and challenges frequently create learning environments in which students feel frustrated regarding their educators' schooling practices and inability to relate to them as individuals, their families, and communities (Milner, 2007; Pollock, 2008).

When teachers no longer believe interconnections with students and their families are important, or who believe relationship-building is a "cultural" thing for people of color and dismiss partnerships with students and families as insignificant in education or life, the dehumanization of individuals is reproduced. I had met with a group of Indigenous and Latina women, who are mothers of school-aged children, who expressed their concerns regarding educators' behaviors, practices, and language. I witnessed the tears streaming from the faces of women when they spoke about their frustrations and experiences with school personnel and others in the local and surrounding communities. When the women commented about speaking and not being heard by educational practitioners, specifically when discussing their children's lack of education, it illustrated the social realities of these women and families. One particular woman discussed how her child experienced three retentions in elementary school, none of which had been beneficial for him academically, socially, or psychologically. The child was going to be 14 years of age in 6th grade and continued to struggle academically.

She indicated she had recently been informed by his teacher that he was reading at a 2nd grade level and was taller and more mature than his peers, and beginning to demonstrate low self-esteem and confidence. The woman claimed retentions with early childhood students was the norm, which demonstrated for this particular mother and child that the retentions were not the best decisions made for her son and he was now displaying rebellious behaviors, demonstrating his detestation for school and anything associated with academics; he seemed as though he hated life, she explained as tears rolled down her face.

This woman, a mother of a young adolescent and two younger children, believed her son had lost hope in life. She commented he no longer had that spark in his eye or enthusiasm he did when he first started school. She stated that she felt she had lost the most valuable part of her life and person worth living for, her son. She continued to explain that she approached the school for assistance but felt as if the teachers and the principal had also given up on him when they told her that her parenting skills, home environment, and lack of English skills were to blame for his academic failure and misbehaviors. She was reminded that she had signed all the necessary documents giving the school permission to retain her child. She was devastated. She expressed feeling helplessness because she did not know what to do; she felt guilty because perhaps, as these educational practitioners indicated, she didn't do exactly what was needed to *correctly* raise a child; she also felt deceived because she trusted the school experts by signing the retention documents informing her it was in the best interest of her child; and she expressed feeling hopeless because her son was no longer the same child she gave birth to; he had lost his spark in life and would never be the same.

The idea of relationship-building is not presented as a "reductionist" perspective as noted by Omi & Winant (1994) but rather as an intricate human component in which students and families regularly feel marginalized, invisible, thus often influencing their views about themselves in a way that makes them feel less valued in schools and the larger society. As an example, k-12 students with whom I have worked discussed lived-experiences that seemed to reflect educational disparities that Angela Valenzuela (1999) referred to in her theory of *subtractive schooling* as similar to behaviors and values modeled by the student(s) described herein.

While facilitating classes with pre-service teachers, I emphasize how school practices can nurture and enhance students' *beingness* rather than their *schooling-ness*, as required by No Child Left Behind {NCLB} (U.S. Department, 2002), in order to avoid further colonization through measuring-standards, fostering racially hegemonic educational environments, and reproducing unequal educational practices. As I continue to grow within the academy, I find that the emphasis I promote in teacher education courses addresses only a minuscule concern within our society. This glimpse of reality is specifically what Winant (2006) describes as a current "racial crisis" that includes "enormous discrepancies and contradictions. . . between official racial rhetoric and the actual dilemmas of racial experience and social organization. . . [which] shapes identities and life-chances" (pp. 4, 20).

As I reflected on the young European American adult and what appeared to be social disengagement, it moved me to question how relationships are severed and continue to be severed through the widespread and frequent use of socio-political and racialized colonial efforts, including educational structures and ideologies. I wondered about the pre-service teachers of European ancestry with whom I work and whether they believe in the importance of building school communities and relationships with their students or if the giant four-letter "F" word becomes apparent, paralyzing and depriving them of healthy professional relationships with students and families. Particularly, I thought about whether pre-service educators held a genuine interest in building relationships and establishing connections with culturally and linguistically diverse students and families, especially if there have been few or no personal experiences with individuals of color, especially those who attended a Eurocentric post-secondary education program that typically did not support building and nurturing relationships as a focal point in the educational process, ultimately sustaining and actively reproducing racialized positionalities and fear.

All too often teacher education programs do not focus on relationship building between students, families, and teachers; or foster individuals' abilities to work with diverse realities faced in society, therefore creating socially constructed forms of anesthetization designed *not* to impact people's consciousness or humanity, especially marginalized communities (Bourdieu, 1991; Kivel, 2002). Pre-service teachers many times express their feelings of not wanting to see the "negative" in our society or believe that utilizing a critical lens is too depressing because the "isms" are directly in view for their analysis. For some individuals it is easier to stick their head in the sand, so to speak, by not acknowledging the lived-realities students in schools face daily, thus foregoing an opportunity to really get to know their students.

While there are those who will stand by and hegemonically observe oppressive conditions, there are others who involve themselves in counter-hegemonic struggles to support communities. Although bystanders are not directly involved in the act, the unrecognized repressive actions of individuals from the dominant society make them by default, active participants in racism, classism, sexism, ageism, ableism and other "isms" that are linked to individuals' cultural, linguistic, and socio-political identities. In addition, Audre Lorde (1984) describes this unrecognized treatment as a form of "depersonalization" through the use of "isms," leading individuals and communities toward social invisibility and imposing an ideology of non-existence, hence leading to the politics of not seeing.

The existence of social color-blindness, race neutrality, and an inability to recognize "isms" may be explained in experiences of normalization and standardization of power relationships, which include a history of how hegemony has been adapted to social and political structures in society (Bonilla-Silva, 2003; Dei, 1999; Villalpando, 2003). Power and "isms" remain to be included in social, cultural, and economic structures of the world; it is acknowledged that oppressive behaviors, practices, language and ideologies exist through power relationships and systems. Michel Foucault (2000) explained that his work regarding power was not intended to discuss a methodology or a theory but rather to discuss the history of power and how systems have been organized to spin human beings into subjects, similar to how human beings and humanity have become de-centered within structures of education, particularly in marginalized communities. He proclaimed that the processes of systems or institutions of power are those that compartmentalize individuals into categories of humanness, otherness or difference.

In addition, there is a seemingly hidden curriculum of epistemological consequence in the United States which strongly argues for folks to eradicate their identities, especially those who are not of European descent. As Leonardo (2005) points out, "humanity meant male, white, and propertied" (p. 39). These differences are viewed with deficit, creating a sub-culture of individuals not valued as a people or are not perceived as contributing members of society; moreover, their humanness is altogether amputated from their existence, particularly when demonized for their differences. These kinds of power relationships frequently internalize privilege and dominant ideologies which commonly create sorted social spaces and locations, unexamined behaviors, and ultimately elitist hierarchies. Kumashiro (2002) describes how individuals are placed in a hierarchical system that creates a space for the Other. He explained the Other as individuals who are:

> Traditionally marginalized, denigrated, or violated in society, including (people) of color, (people) from under- or unemployed families, (individuals) who are female, or male but not stereotypically "masculine" and (individuals) who are or are perceived to be queer. They are often defined in opposition to groups traditionally favored, normalized, or privileged in society, and as such are defined as other than the idealized norm. (2002, p. 32)

The types of violations in society that Kumashiro (2002) described are commonly considered to be different forms of hegemony. The hierarchies he discussed are supported through the use of language, ideology, and practice, ultimately reinforcing discriminating and racializing systems in society (Bonilla-Silva, 2003, 2005; Macedo, 2006; Mohanty, 2003; Torres, 2003). Bourdieu (1991) contended that power is intertwined with language and the inequalities produced by power structures become normalized by society and exercised without consciousness, as if living in a state of anesthesia or paralysis. In addition, Foucault (1979, 2000) proposed that different forms of powers exist from the diverse relationships and structures in society; structures that create a sophisticated mechanism that transforms, elaborates, organizes and adjusts according to the circumstances which, in turn, may help explain why ethnic groups who have been marginalized or excluded in society have historically altered themselves to accommodate the dominant society.

Lastly, there are individuals who identify white racial hegemony, such as Bonilla-Silva (2005); Brayboy, Castagno, & Maughan (2007); Huber, et al. (2008); Leonardo (2005); and others, as white supremacy that has historically and currently utilizes the practice of law and other policies as protection to the continued development of colonization, thus controlling social structures authoritatively and openly benefit from these reproductive privileges. As noted by Brayboy, Castagno & Maughan (2007), "white supremacy leads to entitlement among those who are privileged and, all too often, tacit acceptance by those who are not, in such a way that we come to expect certain social conditions and view those expectations (and conditions) as natural and normal" (p. 177).

The impact of dehumanizing practices and systematic structures that lead people to believe they are the *Other* is influential in transforming individuals and in framing how persons are viewed as either knowledgeable or imbeciles. According to Cornel West (1999), there have been people, such as Africans and Indigenous communities whose humanity has been questioned legally and socially in the United States. He as well as Grande (2004) suggested that the relationship between knowledge and power is complex, yet there are social structures that will grant or take individuals' political and economic capital, their resources and social position in society. Acceptance into the status quo halls has always been a white-male appropriation bestowed by the social and economic rulers.

West (1999) also claims humanity and power are interconnected and when people lose their understanding and appreciation of their existence, their ability to critically analyze their condition is unsatisfactory in their "freedom fight" (p. 222). The feelings of hopelessness and despair among individuals who have been marginalized may suggest that the loss of "freedom fight," as proposed by West (1999), is the result of losing one's dignity, humanity, and value in life. The relationship between hegemony and humanity in American history is illustrated throughout cultural imperialism and colonization periods, particularly with slavery, including the creation of public policy in which communities were exterminated, people were forced to migrate, and where objectification occurred, even when people were dehumanized and ultimately, when their spirit, *being*, and their dignity were abolished.

> Imagine no longer having your dignity, no longer living, but rather only existing
> Imagine Experiencing The killing Of your spirit Each day Imagine the death

of Your being Imagine No longer Being—Vivian García López, personal communication, 2009

Humanizing Education

"Education is ultimately about social justice and humanizing. If we are unable to recognize the humanity in others, we shall never recognize it in ourselves." According to Macedo (2008), this statement by Paulo Freire promotes the humanization in educational institutions, specifically by educators. Thus it appears that there is a need to relearn and unlearn how to live differently from historical colonial traditions. The connections between humanization and education, Freire stated, often promote and encourage individuals to redefine themselves as human beings, recognize, and include in one's practice and praxis, that all individuals are human.

Several of the theoretical frameworks utilized to deconstruct socio-political complexities within society typically include perceptions about power but rarely include language about being human; thus, the following will offer a space to view diverse ontologies. From an Indigenous perspective, Stewart-Harawira (2005) envisions people as living beings, *beings* that are interconnected to all life forms and are constantly engaged in the transformations of their lives. She adds, the inter-relationships with all forms of life that illustrate the continuous transformations of a "creation as a process of continuous action or coming into being, the impetus for which emanates from the world of potential being" (p. 155). She suggests being human is not only the existence of inter-relationships with all matters of life, but also the spirit world.

An emphasis by Four Arrows' (2008) acknowledgment regarding life transformations also involve the heart and the spirit, not just the memory or thinking with one's head, but being human also includes thinking with one's heart and spirit. Thus, the valued Indigenous traditions and cultural ontologies that help understand the interconnections of human beings, provide a basis for the context of becoming human. These references to being human are introduced to challenge Eurocentric ideologies that have been an intricate component of schooling within education and other social contexts.

Perhaps the concept of leaving the whole human being completely out of dialogues and discourses pertaining to education is a cultural difference from my understanding regarding living and learning as a Hiaki/Chicana. Typically, perspectives that involve human beings holistically are absent from most Eurocentric educational institutions and frameworks, therefore, creating structures that perform emotional, cultural, psychological, and spiritual genocide. In contrast, according to Cajete (2005), Indigenous ways of teaching and learning have occurred in a holistic social context that nurtures and promotes a sense of importance in each individual and acknowledges her/him as an essential member of the social group. Stewart-Harawira (2005) conveys that Vine Deloria described Indigenous ontologies as "intrinsically connected to the lives and experiences of human beings, individuals, communities" (p. 155). The focus according to these views lessens the possibility that people will not be reduced to objectivity. It is not the actual measuring of a person's head and what specific tools are utilized to provide one with this knowledge; instead, it is the understanding that actually takes place with relationships that matters as avowed by LaDuke (2005).

As a result, relationship-building is the most important process necessary to humanize pedagogies and research as declared by Cajete (2005). Alternative views about education and educational research and the manner in which it is carried out will determine a more humane dimension in schools and in the academy. In addition, Stewart-Harawira (2003) suggests relationships are intricately woven into the dynamism of life which reinvents "new understandings of being in the world and the development of radical pedagogies of hope," thus situated in meaning-making processes.

By utilizing Tribal and Latina/o Critical Race Theory frameworks to facilitate courses for pre-service education majors, they will help guide our (students' and my own) self-reflections and reflective processes that de-construct power, language, self-identity as well as externally imposed identities, ontologies and epistemologies, and "isms" that are consistently integrated and mirrored within our socio-political contexts and ideologies (Brayboy, 2005; Choi, 2008; Ladson-Billings & Tate, 1995; Parker & Stovall, 2005; Delgado & Stephancic, 2001). It is from my individual experiences and counter-hegemonic positionality that my stories originate and are utilized to challenge the racialized structures, particularly education, and as Solórzano & Yosso (2003) suggest, apply stories as a "tool for exposing, analyzing, and challenging the majoritarian stories of racial privilege" (p. 32). As noted in Grande (2004), Four Arrows (2008), and Mihesuah & Wilson (2004), curriculum and pedagogy have been employed as an instrument to civilize individuals into Eurocentric American hierarchical practices that include culture, values, and understandings; thus, as educators and cultural workers, reflection is imperative to recreate oneself and the practices utilized in education. Reflections offer individuals opportunities to reach deep within one's own understandings and challenge the contributions one makes as an educator but more importantly as a human being. By exercising reflections, individuals have opportunities to dialogue, encourage, and to take action, a process that Paulo Freire (1974) includes in the language of hope and possibility. These types of reflections may be a form of consciousness-building in which one reviews her/his reason for existence and choices for living. Reflections may also be utilized to reinvent one's self and effectively use cultural work to transform hegemonic and racist ideologies and practices in the direction of social justice, equity and respectful relationships with human beings.

My observation of the young adult reinforced my need to ask a predominant group of European American pre-service teachers who were required to take my course about their preparation within their educational programs which focused on building relationships with students, families, colleagues, and community members. It was almost standard to see blank faces, while a few of them explained that one or two classes "touched" on the importance of parent involvement or discussed professors who *stressed* the significance of establishing relationships with the students; yet, the majority of pre-service teachers articulated feelings of lack of confidence, anger and frustration with the notion of building relationships, or distressed feelings when challenged about misperceptions they had of culturally, linguistically diverse (CLD) communities, which resulted in the surfacing of the big four-letter "F" word, FEAR.

The discussions by pre-service teachers and their fear in how to build relationships and partnerships with school communities, particularly individuals from CLD populations, have been exacerbated by education along with other sociopolitical contexts in society. The big four-letter "F" word took several forms with regard to the pre-service teachers who were queried about their interest and belief in the importance of establishing professional student-teacher relationships that included knowing their students' dreams, families, communities, and histories. Most of the pre-service teachers expressed they would be working with communities in which they currently live, which are predominantly white, middle to upper class, and English language dominant. Thus, many of the students seemed disinterested in learning about the historicities of people of color within the U.S. and how to critically view the reoccurring threads of colonial structures, including racist ideologies in education and contexts within the larger society.

One student asked, "Why should I treat minority students differently from my other students? I am there to be their teacher, not their friend. And I will teach *all* my students the same" (personal conversation, spring 2009). In addition, a couple of other students openly displayed their anger when presented the histories of CLD communities in the U.S. with examples of classism, racism, sexism, culturally unresponsive practices identified in the curricula in which CLD students were presented. A European American female pre-service teacher claimed that "the most discriminated against person in our society today is the white male" (personal conversation, fall 2009), whereas another European American student expressed an outburst during an open classroom activity when he yelled, "why are we doing all this crap!?" (personal conversation, fall 2009). In comparison, Aveling's (2006) student indicated, "I am sick of people throwing it in my face. I didn't do anything!!! Some heathen bastards from the 1700s who didn't know any better are responsible. Let's move on, stop wasting energy looking for apologies and throwing history in the faces of non-aboriginal [sic] Australians" (p. 267).

Interestingly, I found similar responses to Aveling's experiences in another country, among the students enrolled in my sections of required education courses. As displayed in these discussions as well as others, many students of European ancestry have not acquired the social consciousness to be able to recognize their own privilege or account for their actions against people who differ from them (McIntosh, 1989; Moreton-Robinson, 2006). Additionally, many of the students enrolled in these courses were graduating and soon to be employed as educators. These university students would shortly be recognized by government standards, as licensed and "highly qualified teachers," by meeting their degree requirements which included one diversity course to help them prepare to work with cultural diversity in schools. I found several pre-service teachers I worked with in class to have pre-determined false notions about working *with* students and their communities that were not only troubling and problematic but also ethically questionable.

A normalization of these privileges usually leads to subconscious acts correlated with discrimination and mistreatment of people who are different from the prevailing community as described by Peggy McIntosh (1989). She claims there is a white privilege influenced by socio-political literacies that create a subconscious condition and unearned cultural capital that, by design, promote oppression by those in power against marginalized groups. Cultural capital and supremacy are correlated with privileged white communities in this country, explaining the standards and dominant social, political, and spiritual structures in the U.S. which, in turn, create a social order that is dominated by one population (Delgado & Stefancic, 2001). Wise (2008) expressed that "it is precisely the collision between the rhetoric of equality and the crushing evidence of inequality and injustice that has in other words, necessitated white denial" (p. 64). He explains that European American individuals have now taken a more aggressive role in claiming they are the new victims to racism, oftentimes centered on the notion of declaring being "good decent people," but rarely acknowledging their families owned other human beings. They committed various forms of genocide and were thieves of properties and land in the U.S. (Wise, 2008, pp. 64–68).

Also, Jean Anyon's (1980) article, "Social Class and the Hidden Curriculum of Work," includes descriptions of educators' practices for low and high income level students. Although Anyon's (1980) article may be considered dated, the illustrated "isms" presented in her discussion are those that can typically be seen in schools today. For instance, some of the lower economic class practices that continue to exist are yelling at students to "shut-up," an emotionally and psychologically damaging, humiliating, isolating and hostile practice to control students in a learning environment. In the courses I have facilitated, I learned from the students that they had not experienced any of the discussed dehumanizing practices in their own schooling, thus reinforcing a privilege of "not knowing what they don't know" as a way of life. In other words for these students, reading their world with their lens automatically assumed a universal reality. Interestingly, many of these pre-service teachers remain unaware that these emotional and psychological blows by educators have the potential to damage individuals for a lifetime, as noted by Adams (1995), Alfred (1999), Anzaldúa (1999), and Torres (2003), among others.

> Eventually, if the colonizers' system functions as intended, the colonized "do not even need to be exterminated any more. No, the most urgent thing. . .is to humiliate them, to wipe out the pride in their hearts, to reduce them to the level of animals. The body will be allowed to live on, but the spirit will be destroyed. Tame, train, punish: those are the words that obsess the colonizer. (Churchill, 2004, p. 77)

In turn, language and actions among educators to deliberately and intentionally strip children's human dignity continue to happen. It is not uncommon to see, hear, or read about violent acts against humanity in our society, including schools, that continue unabated daily. Accordingly, when observing the history of curriculum and pedagogies utilized as an instrument of manipulation through hierarchical practices of Eurocentric culture, values, and understandings, it invents a pedagogy of indignation as described by Paulo Freire (2004). These forms of injustices, a la Vine Deloria (1991), are those that *one may misunderstand but will not misexperience* (p. 31).

Personal and professional experiences in schools have created memories of what could be considered as malpractice or human rights violations by "highly qualified" educators. For instance, in 2007 a principal arranged to have a local sheriff arrest a student who was five or six years old in a school building early in the morning while everyone was starting the school day. This young student was physically dragged out of the school, as bystanders of the school community watched in horror and while others, astonishingly, laughed. The student, clearly traumatized by this incident, kicked, screamed and cried as his little body was forcibly pulled by his handcuffed hands through the crowded front door of the school. I later found out that the principal had decided this child needed to learn a lesson and the public display of this unbecoming act would send a message to all students and educators.

Other dehumanizing school incidents stamped in my memory include students' experiences in which students were punished for speaking their heritage language, displaying cultural traits, such as American Indian traditions on school grounds. While other displays of educators' aggression were meant to humiliate and degrade students and their families with racist or patronizing language, such as students who were members of a particular ethnic group or identified as living in the U.S. as an undocumented citizen. Other forms of institutional racism included educators involved in intentional mis-diagnosis of English Language Learners (ELL) or people of color who were enrolled in special education services as a result of strategically moving students out of general education classrooms. Along with the utilization of deficit language as a weapon that reinforced racist ideologies and practices, these acts were permitted and supported within hegemonic structures and school policy as described by Kohli (2008), Lomawaima & McCarty (2006), Reyhner (2007), Russell (2002) and others.

In presenting critical multicultural perspectives in education courses, it was evident among pre-service teachers that the notion to establish relationships with students, especially CLD individuals, was problematic for them, leading me to revisit the image of the young adult who was interconnected to the electronic device. When educational institutions recycle socially detached, controlling, disturbing, and emotionally and critically disengaging frameworks to prepare educators to work with diverse communities, white supremacy ideologies persist in dominating intellectual as well as socio-political contexts, ultimately benefiting white communities. As Kendell (2001) suggests, white privilege allows individuals to choose to "listen to others, hear them or neither. . . or silence (ultimately don't include) the reality of others" (p. 5).

Pinterits, Poteat & Spanierman (2009) conducted a study on white privilege attitudes and suggested, "with regard to fear or apprehension, scholars have noted several variations. For example, fear might be linked to potential loss of material benefits, likely downward mobility in the absence of race-based advantages, and fear of losing power" (p. 417). Their study provided qualitative results that suggested some European American students fear an up-rising by "racial minority" individuals against the dominant population due to the injustices that have taken place historically in the U.S. They claim that "fear can be associated with ambivalence to engage in behavioral changes that entails risks in challenging white privilege" (p. 427).

These beliefs, mores, values and ideals are intricately related to issues of race, language, cultural traditions, and economic power and can thus be deliberately internalized by people's attitudes and beliefs, sustaining a culture of fear and paralysis that is stimulated by hegemony. For instance, some pre-service students identified their feelings to advocate for a European American student who received special education services and who had been bullied by a teacher; whereas on the contrary, they had little or no feelings of indignation for a student who was an English language learner who had been bullied by a teacher, suggesting differences in their ideologies as to who is considered a human being and who is not. As Jackson (2008) indicates, "the blatant hostility and fear of the early days of the nation have diminished, whereas the more subtle forms of discrimination have continued, spawning new fears. Race still matters and remains the center of the United States' dilemma to achieve equality and equity" (p.148).

As history illustrates, there are so many acts that dehumanize individuals because of differences from the dominant group via their citizenship, ethnicity, language, age, gender, ability, economic status, spiritual beliefs, or other identified differences. However, history also portrays those who resisted oppressive conditions, behaviors, and ideologies as individuals who consciously acted to transform the social and human conditions, a form of praxis. Praxis is a term that has been used to describe action. Cornel West (1999) explained praxis as a "tragic action with revolutionary intent, usually reformist consequences and always visionary outlook" (p. 167). For instance, praxis as described by West (1999), was observed during the social struggles that took place in this country involving social movements imperative to political, economic, educational, and social change. Many of the current conflicts occurring in communities these days, resemble those that happened over 60 years ago. As Anyon (2005), Blackwell (2003), Freire (2000), and Martinez (2002) discussed, hope and possibility utilizes a common thread for transformation in society which includes the need to acknowledge the injustices, the investigations, the naming, and the implementation of political/social praxis. Although there are many injustices that continue to take place in society, there have been many insights, epistemologies, and spaces created for diversity in communities that had historically been excluded from mainstream society. Hope has been influenced by revolutionary frameworks not usually seen in education, but rather in other fields such as social work, history, anthropology, political science, and sociology. The revolutionary actions in the U.S. have usually related to political and social movements, such as the era of the civil rights movement during the 1960s.

Praxis that transpires with the aim of regaining one's freedom and emancipation in which sacrifices and risks were taken to become human again was part of yesteryear's social movements. These revolutionary actions were an attempt to never forget one's humanity, liberation, and spiritual freedom. In this way, praxis is shaped by the historical revelations, reflections, understandings, and further inquiries. Thus, praxis may be identified as an epistemological dialogue between the oppressed and oppressor and as political positioning that is intended as acts of reflection, theoretical connections, and revolutionary proceedings that created or transformed people, one's environment, or the relationships in one's world as noted by Freire (2002) and McLaren (2007). For instance, during the 1960s in the US, the voices of Dolores Huerta and Cesar Chávez carried the struggle for human and civil rights of *campesinos* (farm workers). Other struggles by human and civil rights' advocates influenced social movements, such as the work of Wilma Mankiller, Russell Means, Vine Deloria, and Dennis Banks in the American Indian Movement (AIM); or Elizabeth "Betita" Martinez' and Luis Valdez' mobilization efforts in the Chicano Movement; or those who utilized spiritual spaces, such as Gustavo Gutierrez' work in Liberation Theology (1990), or Malcolm X's organized efforts in the Black freedom movement. This era was rich with forms of praxis in which individuals were involved in activism of collaboration, organization, implementation in a struggle to transform societal inequities. The efforts to mobilize, as seen from a civil rights movement lens, included individuals deeply involved as participants in the course of a transformative process. Many transformations included celebrations of identity, culture and language. Civil rights workers' praxis within social movements included working for *la gente* (the people), and their actions were honorable and effective. Their lives were significant in making change en route to equality and social justice, particularly in education. They were also first-hand, everyday-life cultural workers. They were seen as struggling within a people's movement in which they too went to jail and similarly were harassed and threatened, beaten and tortured, and some individuals were even killed, murdered, and silenced for speaking out and applying their praxis.

Social movements are another form of praxis designed to secure the human and civil rights of people, especially those who have been historically and systematically oppressed and marginalized. Forms of revolutionary activism include identifying injustices and creating resolutions through protests against authoritarianism, exploitation and cruel treatment of people through a sociopolitical movement that provides a voice for individuals who are victims of injustices. It can be a powerful vehicle that uses praxis for understanding and formulating truth through first-hand knowledge, and participation in the struggle for justice. Social movements can "ultimately change federal and state laws, American mores of acceptability, institutional practices, and U.S. culture" as noted by Anyon (2005, p. 152).

Although praxis may be described as engaged activism by individuals or groups, as previously mentioned, I utilize the term praxis as a concept that includes distinct acts for incorporating relationship-building, dialog, identification of issues, reflections, conscientization, theory and action toward individual, community or societal transformation. There are many instances in which social and political activism demonstrate actions to improve the lives of individuals; however, many times the theories do not incorporate a framework inclusive of relationships, diversity, cultures, or ideologies to being human. It appears that theory is a separate entity of academia which merely manufactures ideas, scientifically based research and non-political contributions to society. Gadotti (1996), Gramsci (1971) and Freire (1974, 2000, 2004) also view praxis as a basis for theoretical connections to a critical consciousness regarding inequities in society and the struggle it takes to end inequities and injustices. There is a historical awareness and understanding of oppressive conditions in society, but there are also revolutionary counterpositions that have been initiated and acted upon.

Research as Praxis

Research is another type of praxis among academicians. Historically, research standards have required the researcher to be disengaged from participants. According to Gumport (1997) the researcher takes the role of a "prescribed persona" instead of being her/his "authentic self" in trying to meet the traditional research-er's role of reporting even though she suggests also utilizing a disjointed procedure while conducting interviews. "Treading on dangerous scholarly ground or at least a ground far from the objectivity ideals of social science" when individuals devi-ate from the standards for traditional research is common (Gumport, 1997, p. 188). She stated she experienced the big four-letter "F" word, fear, and backlash from colleagues for providing personal reflections in her report when presenting "deeper human experience" (Gumport, 1997, p. 189). Trepidation of not meet-ing the standards for publication or achieving notable research is common among researchers. Thus, Gumport's (1997) example of peer pressure to comply with traditional research paradigms appears to reign in the academy, claiming a "cost [for] trading approval for understanding" (p. 191) and living in co-optation.

Reflecting upon Bateson's (1997), Bensimon et al.'s (2004) and Gumport's (1997) experiences as researchers, the academy creates spaces where particular forms of knowledge are constructed and valued by higher education institutions, policy makers and others who may be perceived as promoting another form of capitalism. Academia is identified by Gumport (1997) as a factory for publica-tion, creating a "currency for career development," which implies the objective for research is production of cultural, economical, and social capital as described by Bourdieu (Calhoun et al., 1993). Information provided by folks for research is organized and produced through meaning-making by researchers primarily for the purpose of publishing, which Gumport (1997) asserts is "at once a powerful privilege with the potential for exploitation" (p. 190).

In employing a critical theoretical lens, I ask why and for whom does research exist and who determines what information should be disseminated? These ques-tions and other inquiries about research are also presented by Porsanger (2004), Pualani (2007) and Smith (1999/2006). In the struggle to engage in social trans-formation where self-determination and autonomy are indispensable, research must become more than just a tool to collect data and produce publications for the sake of surviving a career in higher education. In considering a researcher's socio-political responsibility to act only as an observer and reporter, she or he must introspectively find civic courage and rid her/himself of the big four letter "F" word, when children's emotional and psychological well-being is abused. When communities' identities, their heritage language and culture, their self-esteem and a host of other ways of life are forcefully stripped from them, genocide may be con-sidered as suggested by Card (2003), Churchill (2004), Moore (2003), and Smith (1999/2006). Thus, when social, cultural and emotional genocide are occurring right before the eyes of the researcher, does she/he have the social responsibility to take corrective action? This is a question eternally debated in academia but must continue to be asked as a way of revealing the moral, ethical, social and political responsibilities of the researcher to create transformative changes for social justice.

It is often suggested that researchers enter communities utilizing a traditional research paradigm, collect data, interpret and report the information, and never return to discuss the final publication with the community that was researched. Also, the traditional Eurocentric research process does not appear to consider or value communities enough to co-construct knowledge, expertise, and recommendations but instead maintains a structure of hegemony. In addition, Reason (1998) adds, the practice of co-constructing knowledge "demands that we look radically at our ontological and epistemological principles, and at the whole purpose of inquiry" (p. 5).

How can a researcher believe her/his work is complete after learning the lived-realities of a community are the same or actually worse than they were 50 years ago? Also, how can researchers simply walk away from a community after learning from the research process about the social and academic horrors occurring in the community? And how can a researcher consider herself/himself as moral and ethical when the research participants are left behind in the same conditions as they were found when the research project began? Another research model is greatly needed to defend (not rescue) and promote communities' rights to be human—that is, to be whole in one's mind, heart, cultural, and spiritual being. Indigenous Research challenges the social and ethical responsibility of the academy to work *with* communities who seek autonomy and self-determination, assist to improve conditions with historically marginalized communities, and to seek transformative action(s) that nurture, as Champagne (2007) describes, a "cultural and political continuity" and community ownership of the knowledge produced by the research.

It is time for change within the academy in order to create global opportunities and new understandings toward meeting the social transformations taking place in the world. A search for a more human approach to research is currently taking place within the academy. Linda Tuhiwai Smith (1999/2006) claimed,

> To be able to share, to have something worth sharing gives dignity to the giver. To accept a gift and to reciprocate gives dignity to the receiver. To create something new through that process of sharing is to recreate the old, to reconnect relationships and to recreate our humanness. (p. 105)

It seems to me there is a social hierarchy in the academy in which people in power control the paradigm of research standards mentioned by Huck (2004) and pre-determine the objective of the research, which usually discourages relationship-building between researchers and communities and transformational praxis. In looking at the traditional research paradigms and how "representational knowledge" is produced by researchers' definitions, interpretations, methodology and reporting, Bensimon et al. (2004) stated that "what is needed is another model for research production in higher education—a model that will at least supplement the traditional model if not replace it" (p. 106). To move this idea further, I agree with Waziyatawin Angela Wilson and Michael Yellow Bird (2005), who suggested there is a need for decolonizing methodologies,

> Decolonization is the intelligent, calculated, and active resistance to the forces of colonialism that perpetuate the subjugation and/or exploitation of our minds, bodies, and lands, and it is engaged for the ultimate purpose of overturning the colonial structure and realizing Indigenous liberation. . . .It is not about tweaking the existing colonial system to make it more Indigenous-friendly or a little less oppressive.

At this time, there is a mere binary system of knowledge production whether it is within a qualitative or quantitative perspective; however, Smylie et al. (2003) provide a description between Indigenous and Western scientific ways of knowing. They claim that Indigenous knowledge is "holistic, relational, ecologic, pluralistic, experiential, timeless, infinite, communal, oral, and narrative-based" and indicate that Western science is "reductionist, linear, objective, hierarchical, empirical, static, temporal, singular, specialized, and written" (p. 141). There are several discussions regarding a need for research that provides opportunities for inclusive and creative transformative work *with* communities by using worldview perspectives, those that are community born and not subjugated by Eurocentric ideologies (Champagne, 2007; Grande, 2004; López, 2006; Smith, 1999/2006). More specifically, Indigenous research offers opportunities to work *with* Indigenous communities through emancipatory and *conscientización* processes such as acknowledging, understanding the past, naming the past in current conditions, dialoging, and supporting the emergence of transformative achievements with regard to healing, reconnection, recovery, reinvention, mobilization, survival, decolonization, and self-determination aspirations (Champagne, 2007; Porsanger, 2004; Smith, 1999/2006; Stewart-Harawira, 2005).

A more humanistic approach to research is sought. Thus, a proposal to implement diverse theoretical, ideologies, epistemologies and ontology to utilize worldview perspectives with regard to knowledge has been presented by Four Arrows (2006). He points out that knowledge is like traditional stories in which it "takes a thousand voices to tell a story" and emphasizes a Native Hawaiian proverb that advocates "not all knowledge comes from the same school" (p. 260). Like Four Arrows (2006), I do not imply that Indigenous perceptions offer supremacy epistemologies but rather that the academy must be inclusive of worldviews and avoid a skewed predisposition of a limited understanding of all life forms, while discriminatingly implementing a Eurocentric view about knowledge (p. 260).

As the previous authors suggest, Eurocentric-based research is notorious for providing data that frequently appears to misinform the public by categorizing, measuring, marginalizing and reducing the complexity of people under the auspices of a "representational knowledge." Such traditional research has included published reports about Indigenous peoples often romanticizing the culture, traditions, and history. Eurocentric-based research is also accused of publishing misinterpretated or partial histories without the consent or voice of Indigenous peoples as noted by Mihesuah (2003):

> the majorities of writings are devoid of Native voices and are thereby only partial histories. In addition, most do not connect the past to the present. . .others have been written only for "entertainment" and to further the careers of the authors. (p. 4)

In addition, Bateson (1997) indicated that a traditional Western research paradigm in the academy prevents and discourages individuals from employing a humanistic research design or model. For example, personal involvement is strictly viewed as non-objective in traditional research paradigms believed to contaminate the findings. There are also requirements in academia for diverse ways of viewing and conducting studies, which commonly suppress or prohibit certain revelations of the research according to Gumport (1997). She discussed several areas of concern regarding the traditional requirements obligatory to conduct research. One of the requirements of working as a researcher in traditional Eurocentric paradigms includes taking a "scholarly stance" and becoming a "detached observer" from the "informants," thus creating a dehumanizing process by reinforcing the big four-letter "F" word by supporting non-relationship processes—yet, contradictorily, all are considered to be participants in the research (Gumport, 1997).

Indigenous research, on the other hand, creates opportunities to overcome the big four-letter "F" word, fear, and give birth to the voices and perspectives represented in the research. This research is for the people, by the people, and of the people as suggested by Champagne (2007) and Smith (1999/2006). Indigenous research is a an opportunity that challenges the academy to allow all participants in the research process to create a space for dialogue, identity, and reflection of their history, so as to experience transformative healing, decolonization, and *conscientización* and thus generate visions and analyses for organizing transformative activities in their community. Indigenous research can utilize collective knowledge and experience transformative actions, but more importantly as Fals-Borda & Rahman (1991) stated, "honor their (individual) dignity and the meaning of their own history" (p. 155). This involves Indigenous traditions commonly excluded in research as signified by Anzaldúa (1999), Torres (2003), Mihesuah & Wilson (2004) and others.

> Radicals cannot passively accept a situation in which the excessive power of a few leads to the dehumanization of all. (Freire, 1974, p. 9)

In conclusion, there is a call for research to be utilized and viewed as a socially and ethically responsible activity among academicians to respect and promote human rights, to value and build upon communities' strengths and knowledge, and to create new ways of knowing and transforming for the benefit of social justice and self-determination. Currently, most research paradigms do not include relationship building, listening, and healing as a process leading toward *conscientización* and transformative praxis, which are significant human components essential to working *with* communities rather than *on* communities as declared by Cajete (2005), LaDuke (2005), and Smith (1999/2006).

Thus, research, when used as a praxis tool of hope and possibility, carries within it the potential to co-construct epistemologies, practices, and lived realities in communities. In addition, the terms social justice and emancipation continually surface in discussions in relation to civil and human rights, yet these terms are noted in generalities with consideration to the well-being of individuals (Prilleltensky, 2001). Like so many disenfranchised groups, children and young adults in the U.S. also share the need to be acknowledged as humans so they can become human again. Thus, communities, social movements or activists should not dismiss children and young adults but rather recognize them as those who also seek justice, liberation, and the affirmation of being human.

The revolutionary praxis described by scholars such as Gadotti (1996), McLaren (2007), Reitz (2000) and others is necessary to create change starting with oneself and then moving to society at large; however, praxis is contingent upon one's growth and development (conicientization), otherwise the practices become domesticated and reduced to technocratic activities that do not necessarily lead to revolutionary transformation or the remaking of society as suggested by McLaren (2000, 2007). A case could be made in which educational institutions continue the cycle of upholding oppressive educational practices as a way to institutionalize knowledge and thus colonize educators to become a *patrón* (owner who controls all) or a *peone* (dominated, controlled, or imprisoned individual) in the academy. Contributions to communities by academicians and educators have historically been humanitarian-type practices, specifically when communities have been politicized into dependency upon academicians and their research to generate humanitarian aid for the communities by ways of projects and programs as presented by Reason (1998, 2004) and Bradbury (2006, 2004, 1998) to understand the world, but not necessarily change it.

Today's War in Education

If we don't do anything now, what is going to happen to our children? These are our children and we need to make sure they get everything they need because the teachers and the principals really don't care about our kids. . .they don't know our kids, they don't live here and soon they retire and never come back to "Esperanza." (Conversation with Angelita, April 4, 2007)

Estamos en una guerra, tenemos que tener los ojos viendo a todos lados. . .you know. . .en nuestras espaldas pero tambien en frente y a todos lados, protecting our children. (It's like we're in a war where we have to be watching all angles, including our backs, but we need to protect our children.) In addition she explained, no mas tenemos una chancita con nuestros niños, if we don't fight for them, they'll [educators] kill them and we'll lose them to gangs or drugs o algo" (Angelita, a mother of three children enrolled in a U.S. elementary school, personal conversation, September 11, 2007).

It appears that another era has emerged wherein civil and human rights violations have increased in the twenty first century, and where systematic racism, sexism and classism, as well as other "isms," have emerged as new ways of creating a need for educators to become activists at work and in their communities. Globalization has created a new dimension of abhorrence against marginalized communities through economic, political, and social means, and where women and children of color seem to have even more negative impacts (Wilson & Whitmore, 2000). As Torres (2003) declared, researchers have also allowed "the global economy to change the university from a place of learning into a knowledge factory, with students as both consumers and products" (p. 7). Perhaps it is time to reflect on the role of researchers and advocates of learning and to reconfigure the benefit of research in communities.

This neoliberal world has been forced to dismiss reports and research findings that address injustices no longer satisfactory to individuals and communities. Often, the reports inform and describe detailed accounts of related "isms"; however, these accounts may not actually reflect the abuses that have taken place for generations. Globalization, capitalism, and neoliberalism are common themes in today's discussions, thus among researchers there is a call to include global perspectives, including the use of transformative research, such as Indigenous research. One component of Indigenous research is *conscientización*, or what Smith (1999/2006) refers to as self-determination, which includes social, historical, psychological, cultural and economic landscapes (p. 116). The *conscientización* process awakens the individuals into action so as to remove oneself from the social anesthesia one has to breathe, as Foucault (1979, 2000) described. Researchers that not only report, but are also intricately involved in counter hegemonic actions could address social anesthesia, which is noted as a form of symbolic violence that strips from individuals their dignity, identity, culture, spirituality, humanity, while simultaneously molding individuals into obedient servants (Foucault, 2000).

As Angelita indicated, "*It's like we're in a war where we have to be watching all angles, including our backs, but we need to protect our children*" from the disconnected and dehumanizing practices and language by educators. In the struggle to create a more equitable society, there is a need for *conscientización* to assist individuals in dismantling racial hegemonic societal ideologies and racialized systems prominent in today's world, particularly within teacher education programs. These forms of praxis are necessary to create a more humane society in which educators will no longer stand by and claim a neutral position opting to be blind or recognize discriminatory and dehumanizing practices prevalent in schools and communities today. Educators can no longer afford being apolitical while at the same time observing the daily atrocities that impact and dehumanize children and youth. Academicians can no longer be irresponsible by only reporting the academic mayhem against children and youth in their schools and communities. The time for action is now for individuals to take an ethical and moral stand by using a praxis that Paulo Freire (2004) defined as authentic humanism instead of humanitarianism. Relationship building is imperative to being human. It is time to eliminate the tenacious four-letter "F" word in education from the vocabularies of children, youth, parents, teachers, administrators, and faculty. More importantly, it is time to eliminate FEAR in an attempt to break down institutional boundaries and racialized structures that prevent and stifle relationships and; ultimately, the celebration of humanity.

References

Adams, D.W. (1995). *Education for extinction. American Indians and the boarding school experience 1875–1928.* Lawrence, KS: University Press of Kansas.

Alfred, T. (1999). *Peace, power, righteousness: An Indigenous manifesto.* Ontario, Canada: Oxford University Press.

Anyon, J. (1980). Social class and the hidden curriculum of work. [Electronic version]. *Journal of education*, 162, 1, fall, np. Retrieved June 3, 2007 from http://cuip.uchicago.edu/~cac/nlu/fnd504/anyon.htm.

Anyon, J. (2005). *Radical possibilities: Public policy, urban education, and a new social movement.* New York: Routledge.

Anzaldúa, G. (1999). *Borderlands/la frontera: The new Mestiza* (2nd ed.). San Francisco, CA: Aunt Lute Books.

Aveling, N. (2006). "Hacking at our very roots": rearticulating White racial identity within the context of teacher education. *Race Ethnicity and Education.* [Electronic version], 9, 3, pp. 261–74. Retrieved from Wilson select database.

Bateson, M. C. (1997). Foreword. In A. Neumann & P. L. Peterson (Eds.). *Learning from our lives: Women, research, and autobiography in education* (pp. vii–viii). New York: Teachers College Press.

Bensimon, E. M., Polkinghorne, D. E., Bauman, G. L., & Vallejo, E. (2004). Doing research that makes a difference. *The Journal of Higher Education, 75,* 104–26.

Blackwell, M. (2003). Contested histories: Las hijas de Cuauhtemoc, Chicana feminisms, and print culture in the Chicano movement, 1968–1973. In G. F. Arredondo, A. Hurtado, N. Klahn, O. Najera-Ramirez & P. Zavella (Eds.), *A critical reader: Chicana feminisms* (pp. 59–89). Durham, NC: Duke University Press.

Bonilla-Silva, E. (2003). *Racism without racists: Color-blind racism and the persistence of racial inequality in the United States.* Lanham, MD: Rowman & Littlefield Publishers.

Bonilla-Silva, E. (2005). "Racism" and "new racism": The contours of racial dynamics in contemporary America. In Z. Leonardo (Ed.), *Critical pedagogy and race* (pp. 1–35). Malden, MA: Blackwell Publishing.

Bourdieu, P. (1991). *Language and symbolic power.* Edited and introduced by J. B. Thompson, English translation by G. Raymond & M. Adamson. Cambridge, MA: Harvard University Press.

Brayboy, B.M.J. (2005). Toward a tribal critical race theory in education. *The Urban Review,* 37(5), pp. 425–446. (Published online, March 14, 2006).

Brayboy, B.M.J., Castagno, A.E., & Maughan, E. (2007). Equality and justice for all? Examining race in education scholarship. *Review of Research in Education,* 31, pp. 159–94. Retrieved October 3, 2009 from http://rre.aera.net.

Cajete, G. (2005). American Indian epistemologies. *New Directions for Student Services, 109,* 69–78.

Calhoun, C., Lipuma, E., & Postone, M. (Eds.). (1993). *Bourdieu: Critical perspectives.* Chicago, IL: University of Chicago Press.

Card, C. (2003). Genocide and social death. [Electronic version]. *Hypatia, 18,* 63–79. Retrieved February 2, 2006, from the WilsonSelect database.

Champagne, D. (2007, Summer). In search of theory and method in American Indian studies [Electronic version]. *The American Indian Quarterly, 31,* 353–72. Retrieved February 12, 2008, from the WilsonSelect data base.

Choi, J. (2008). Unlearning colorblind ideologies in education class. [Electronic version]. *Educational foundations.* Retrieved November 1, 2009 from the JSTOR data base.

Churchill, W. (2004). *Kill the Indian, save the man: The genocidal impact of American Indian residential schools.* San Francisco, CA: City Lights Books.

Dei, G.J.S. (1999). Knowledge and politics of social change: the implication of anti-racism. [Electronic version]. *British Journal of Sociology of Education.* 20, 3, pp. 395–409. Retrieved October 13, 2009 from http://www.jstor.org/stable/1393254.

Delgado, R., & Stefancic, J. (2001). *Critical race theory: An introduction.* New York: New York University Press.

Deloria, V. (1991). Quote. In N. Hill (Ed.), *Words of power: Voices from Indian America.* p. 31. Golden, CO: Fulcrum Publishing.

Douglas, B., Lewis, C.W., Douglas, A., Scott, M.E., & Garrison-Wade, D. (2008). The impact of white teachers on the academic achievement of black students: An exploratory qualitative analysis. *Educational Foundations.* Winter-Spring, pp. 47–62.

Fals-Borda, O., & Rahman, M. A. (Eds.). (1991). *Action and knowledge: Breaking the monopoly with participatory action-research.* New York: The Apex Press.

Foucault, M. (1979). *Discipline and punish: The birth of the prison.* New York: Random House.

Foucault, M. (2000). *P ower: Essential works of Foucault 1954–1984.* Edited by J. D. Faubion. English translation by R. Hurley and others. Paul Rabinow, series ed. (Vol. 3). New York: The New Press.

Four Arrows (2008). Indigenous pedagogy. In D. Gabbard (Ed.), *Knowledge & power in the global economy. The effects of school reform in a neoliberal/neoconservative age* (pp. 493–500). Mahwah, NJ: Lawrence Erlbaum Associates.

Freire, P. (1974). *Freire: Education for critical consciousness.* New York: Continuum International Publishing Group, Inc.

Freire, P. (2004). *Pedagogy of indignation.* Boulder, CO: Paradigm Publishers.

Freire, P., & Macedo, D. (1987). *Literacy: Reading the word and the world.* Westport, CT: Bergin & Garvey.

Gadotti, M. (1996). *Pedagogy of praxis: A dialectical philosophy of education.* (Translated by J. Milton, Preface by P. Freire). Albany, NY: SUNY Press.

Gibson, C. (2004). Multicultural pre-service education: promising multicultural pre-service teacher education initiatives. [Electronic version]. *Radical Pedagogy.* Retrieved October 15, 2009 from http://radicalpedagogy.icaap.org/content/issue6_1/gibson.html.

Gramsci, A. (1971). *The prison notebooks.* Edited and translated by Q. Hoare & G. Nowell-Smith. New York: International Publishers.

Grande, S. (2004). *Red pedagogy: Native American social and political thought.* Lanham, MD: Rowman & Littlefield.

Gumport, P. J. (1997). First words: Still words. In A. Neumann & P. L. Peterson (Eds.), *Learning from our lives: Women, research, and autobiography in education* (pp. 183–193). New York: Teachers College Press.

Gutierrez, G. (1990). *A theology of liberation: History, politics, and salvation.* Maryknoll, NY: Orbis.

Huber, L.P., Lopez, C.B., Malagon, M.C., Velez, V., & Solórzano, D.G. (2008). Getting beyond the "symptom," acknowledging the "disease": theorizing racist nativism. [Electronic version]. *Contemporary Justice Review,* 11, 1, pp. 39–51. Retrieved October 12, 2009 from http://www.infomaworld.com.

Huck, S. W. (2004). *Reading statistics and research.* Boston, MA: Allyn & Bacon/Pearson Education.

Jackson, B.L. (2008). Race, education, and the politics of fear. [Electronic version]. *Educational Policy,* 22(1), 130–154. Retrieved October 23, 2009, from http://epx.sagepub.com.

Kendell, F. (2001). *Understanding white privilege: Creating pathways to authentic relationships across race.* New York: Routledge.

Kivel, P. (2002). *Uprooting racism. How white people can work for racial justice.* Gabriola Island, Canada: New Society Publishers.

Kohli, R. (2008). Breaking the cycle of racism in the classroom: Critical race reflections from future teachers of color. *Teacher Education Quarterly,* fall, 177–188.

Kumashiro, K. (2002). *Troubling education: Queer activism and antioppressive pedagogy.* New York: RoutledgeFalmer.

Ladson-Billings, G. & Tate, W. (1995). Toward a critical race theory of education. *Teachers College Record,* 97(1), pp. 47–68.

LaDuke, W. (2005). *Recovering the sacred: The power of naming and claiming.* Cambridge, MA: South End Press.

Leonardo, Z. (Ed.). (2005). *Critical pedagogy and race.* Malden, MA: Blackwell Publishing.

Lomawaima, K.T. & McCarty, T.L. (2006). *To remain an Indian: Lessons in democracy from a century of Native American education.* New York, NY: Teachers College Press.

López, V. G. (2006). *Challenging the fish-bowl tradition: Research As Praxis (RAP), a liberating research paradigm for a doctoral student.* Paper presented at the Third International Conference on Education, Labor and Emancipation, El Paso, TX, September 28, 2006.

Lorde, A. (1984). *Sister outsider. Essays and speeches by Audre Lorde.* Berkeley, CA: Crossing Press.

Macedo, D. (2006). *Literacies of power: What Americans are not allowed to know* (Expanded ed.). Boulder, CO: Westview Press.

Macedo, D. (2008, January 17–18). *SPARK Conference: Transnational pedagogies, bilingualism, biliteracy, and multicultural education.* The Encanto Hotel, Las Cruces, NM.

McIntosh, P. (1989, July/August). White privilege: Unpacking the invisible knapsack. *Peace and freedom.* Article provided by Peggy McIntosh at New Mexico State University, Fall 2007.

McLaren, P. (2000). Paulo Freire's pedagogy of possibility. In S. F. Steiner, H. M. Krank, P. McLaren, & R. E. Bahruth (Eds.), *Freirean pedagogy, praxis, and possibilities: Projects for the new millennium* (pp. 1–22). New York: Falmer Press.

McLaren, P. (2007). *Life in schools: An introduction to critical pedagogy in the foundations of education* (5th ed.). Boston, MA: Allyn and Bacon.

Mihesuah, D. A. (2003). *Indigenous American women: Decolonization, empowerment, activism.* Lincoln, NE: University of Nebraska Press.

Mihesuah, D. A., & Wilson, A. C. (Eds.). (2004). *Indigenizing the academy: Transforming scholarship and empowering communities.* Lincoln, NE: University of Nebraska Press.

Milner, H.R. (2007). Race, culture, and researcher positionality: working through dangers seen, unseen, and unforeseen. [Electronic version]. *Educational researcher,* 36 (pp. 388–400). Retrieved March 15, 2009 from http://edr.sagepub.com/cgi/content/abstract/36/7/388.

Mohanty, C. T. (2003). *Feminism without borders: Decolonizing theory, practicing solidarity.* Durham, NC: Duke University Press.

Moore, M. (Ed.). (2003). *Genocide of the mind: New Native American writing.* New York: Nation Books.

Moreton-Robinson, A. (2006). Whiteness, epistemology and Indigenous representation. Retrieved January 12, 2008, from http://www.aiatsis.gov.au/_data/assets/pdf_file/588/wrace_samplechapter.pdf

Omi, M., & Winant, H. (1994). *Racial formation in the United States from the 1960s to the 1990s.* (2nd ed.). New York, NY: Routledge.

Parker, L., & Stovall, D. (2005). Actions following words: Critical race theory connects to critical pedagogy. In Z. Leonardo (Ed.). *Critical pedagogy and race* (pp. 159–174). Malden, MA: Blackwell Publishing.

Pinterits, E.J., & Poteat, V.P., & Spanierman, L.B. (2009). The white privilege attitudes scale: Development and initial validation. *Journal of Counseling Psychology,* 56: 3, 417–429.

Pollock, M. (2008). From shallow to deep: toward a thorough cultural analysis of school achievement patterns. *Anthropology & Education Quarterly,* 39: 4, (pp. 369–80).

Porsanger, J. (2004). *An essay about Indigenous methodology.* [Electronic version]. Retrieved March 14, 2008, from http://uit.no/getfile.php?PageId=977&FileId=188.

Prilleltensky, I. (2001). Value-based praxis in community psychology: Moving toward social justice and social action [Electronic version]. *American Journal of Community Psychology, 39,* 747–778. Retrieved January 2, 2008, from the WilsonSelect database.

Pualani, Louis, R. (2007, June). Can you hear us now? Voices from the margin: Using Indigenous methodologies in geographic research [Electronic version]. *Geographical Research, 45*(2), 130–139. Retrieved January 19, 2008, from WilsonSelect database.

Reason, P. (1998). Co-operative inquiry as a discipline of professional practice. [Electronic version]. *Journal of Interprofessional Care, 12,* 419–436. Retrieved July 5, 2006, from WilsonSelect database.

Reason, P. (2004). Critical design ethnography as action research. *Anthropology and Education Quarterly, 35,* 269–76.

Reason, P., & Bradbury, H. (Eds.). (2006). *Handbook of action research.* Thousand Oaks, CA: Sage.

Reitz, C. (2000). Liberating the critical in critical theory: Marcuse, Marx, and a pedagogy of the oppressed: alienation, art, and the humanities. In S. F. Steiner, H. M. Krank, P. McLaren & R. E. Bahruth (Eds.), *Freirean pedagogy, praxis, and possibilities: Projects for the new millennium* (pp. 41–66). New York: Falmer Press.

Reyhner, J. (2007). Linguicism in America. [Electronic version]. *Teaching Indigenous languages.* Article published in the September/October 2007 issue 20(1), *National Association for Bilingual Education* (NABE) *News,* pp. 12–15. Retrieved January 21, 2009 from http://jan.ucc.nau.edu/%7Ejar/LIA.html.

Russell, C. (2002). Language, violence, and Indian mis-education. [Electronic version]. *American Indian Culture and Research Journal, 26*(4), 97–112. Retrieved December 17, 2007 from WilsonSelect database.

Smith, L. T. (1999). *Decolonizing methodologies: Research and Indigenous peoples.* London, UK: Zed Books. (Reprinted 2006).

Smylie, J., Martin, C. M., Kaplan-Myrth, N., Steele, L., Tait, C., & Hogg, W. (2003). Knowledge translation and Indigenous knowledge. [Electronic version]. *Circumpolar Health-Nuuk,* pp. 139–142. Retrieved May 17, 2008 from http://socserv.socsci.mcmaster.ca/ihrktn/ihrkt-images/Knowledge%20Translation%20&%20Indigenous%20Knowledge%20Smylie.pdf

Solórzano, D., & Yosso, T. (2005). Maintaining social justice hopes within academic realities: A Freirean approach to critical race/Latcrit pedagogy. In Z. Leonardo (Ed.). *Critical pedagogy and race* (pp. 69–91). Malden, MA: Blackwell Publishing.

Stewart-Harawira (2005). Cultural studies, Indigenous knowledge and pedagogies of hope. [Electronic version]. *Policy Futures in Education, 3*(2), 153–163. Retrieved December 21, 2006, from WilsonSelect database.

Takei, Y., & Shouse, R. (2008). Ratings in black and white: Does racial symmetry or asymmetry influence teacher assessment? *Soc Psychol Educ,* 11, pp. 367–87. DOI: 10.1007/s11218–008–0964–0.

Torres, E. E. (2003). *Chicana without apology: The new Chicana cultural studies.* New York: Routledge.

U.S. Department of Education. (2002). No Child Left Behind Act of 2001. Title I: Improving the Academic Achievement of the Disadvantaged, Public Law 107–110, January 8, 2002. Retrieved August 18, 2006 from http://www.ed.gov/policy/elsec/leg/esea02/pg2.html

Valenzuela, A. (1999). *Subtractive schooling: U.S.-Mexican youth and the politics of caring.* Albany: State University of New York Press.

Villalpando, O. (2003). Self-segregation or self-preservation? A critical race theory and Latina/o critical theory analysis of a study of Chicana/o college students. [Electronic version]. *International Journal of Qualitative Studies in Education,* 16, 5, pp. 619–46. Retrieved October 7, 2009 from http://www.tandf.co.uk/journals.

Waziyatawin, A.W. & Yellow Bird, M. (Eds.). (2005). *For Indigenous eyes only: A decolonization handbook.* Santa Fe, NM: School of American Research.

West, C. (1999). *The Cornel West reader.* New York: Basic Civitas Books.

Wilson, M. G., & Whitmore, E. (2000). *Seeds of fire: Social development in an era of globalism.* Croton-on-Hudson, NY: Apex Press.

Winant, H. (2006). Race and racism: Towards a global future. [Electronic version]. *Ethnic and racial studies,* 29, 5, pp. 986–1003. Retrieved October 7, 2009 from http://repositories.cdlib.org/postprints/2610.

Wise, T. (2008). *White like me.* Berkeley, CA: Soft Skull Press.

Critical Pedagogy and Higher Education

FIFTEEN

Higher Education Under Siege

Rethinking the Politics of Critical Pedagogy

Henry A. Giroux

What is the task of educators at a time when mainstream American culture is increasingly characterized by a declining interest in and misgiving about national politics? How one answers this question will have a grave impact not only on higher education but on the future of democratic public life. There are no simple solutions. Hence it becomes crucial for educators at all levels of schooling to provide alternative democratic conceptions of the meaning and purpose of both politics and education. In what follows, I want to argue that one of the primary tasks facing educators, students, community activists, and others in the 21st century should center around developing political projects that can challenge the ascendancy of cynicism and antidemocratic tendencies in the U.S. by defending the institutions and mechanisms that provide the pedagogical conditions for critical and engaged citizenship. Crucial to such a challenge is the role that higher education can play in reclaiming the links between education and democracy; knowledge and public service; and learning and democratic social change.

While the demand for college education is swelling among the nation's youth, schooling as an avenue for social and economic advancement is declining. In fact, "no more than 30% of jobs in the United States currently and for the foreseeable future, will require a college degree."[1] Moreover, as college costs and tuition skyrocket along with student debt, the poor and working classes are less likely to attend college while those students who are getting a college education are less likely to choose careers dedicated to public service.[2] But if higher education increasingly fails as the major mechanism for economic and social mobility as well as for preparing students to confront "the needs of a troubled world,"[3] then it is all the more crucial to consider the role of higher education as a democratic public sphere and as a public good.

Given the current assault on critical education by various right-wing groups, the increasing corporatization of the university, and the growing influence of the national security state, it becomes all the more necessary that higher education be defended as a democratic public sphere and that academics be seen and see themselves as public intellectuals who provide an indispensable service to the nation. Such a view must be based not on a recycled conception of professionalism but on the civic obligations and duties performed by such intellectuals. Unfortunately, too many academics retreat into narrow specialisms, allow themselves to become adjuncts of the corporation, or align themselves with dominant interests that serve largely to consolidate authority rather than to critique its abuses. Refusing to take positions on controversial issues or to examine the role they might play in lessening human suffering, such academics become models of moral indifference and examples of what it means to disconnect learning from public life. This is a form of education, as Howard Zinn notes, in which scholars "publish while others perish."[4] Even many leftist and liberal academics have retreated into arcane discourses that offer them the safe ground of the professional recluse. Such academics seem unconcerned about writing for a larger public and inhabit a world populated by concepts that both remove them from public access and subject them to the dictates of a narrow theoretical fetishism.[5] Making almost no connections to audiences outside of the academy or to the issues that bear down on their lives, such academics have become largely irrelevant. This is not to suggest that they do not publish or speak at symposiums, but that they often do so to very limited audiences and in a language that is overly abstract and highly aestheticized, rarely take an overt political position, and seem mostly indifferent to broader public issues. Theory increasingly seems to be "measured by the degree with which responsibilities can be escaped."[6] Treated less as a resource to inform public debate, address the demands of civic engagement, and expand the critical capacities of students to become social agents, theory increasingly degenerates into a performance for a small coterie of academics happily ensconced in a professionalized, gated community marked by linguistic privatization, indifference to translating private issues into public concerns, and a refusal to connect the acquisition of theoretical skills to the exercise of social power.[7] This retreat from public engagement on the part of many academics is increasingly lamentable as the space of official politics seems to grow more and more corrupt, inhabited by ideologues such as David Horowitz and Lynne Cheney, and groups such as Campus Watch, which exhibits both Taliban-like political orthodoxy and a deep disdain for debate, dialogue, and democracy itself.

The crisis in American democracy has been heralded and exacerbated by the nation's increasing skepticism—or even overt hostility—towards the educational system, if not critical thought itself, a view that fewer and fewer academics seem willing to oppose by either challenging the right-wing assault or offering positive alternatives. Prepackaged knowledge produced by the dominant media along with the Bush administration's Orwellian newspeak works aggressively to usurp critical consciousness and impede democratic critique and social engagement. Cynicism about politics and skepticism about education have become mutually reinforcing tendencies that, in order to be understood, must be analyzed in tandem. Many educators, if not the public itself, seem to have lost the language for linking schooling to democracy, convinced that education is now about job training and competitive market advantage. With democracy emptied of any substantial content, individuals are unable to translate their privately suffered misery into broadly shared public concerns and collective action. Needless to say, as Frank Furedi points out, "The devaluation of the status of the intellectual and the authority of knowledge has important implications for the conduct of public life."[8]

Against this cynicism, we need to pay attention to engaged intellectuals such as Arundhati Roy, Noam Chomsky, Toni Morrison, Zygmunt Bauman, Stanley Aronowitz, and Cornel West as well as the late Pierre Bourdieu, Jacques Derrida, and Edward Said, all of whom have offered models for academics as committed public intellectuals. Zinn, for instance, mocking those professional intellectuals for whom irony, cleverness, and a disdain for political engagement appear to be the last refuge, defends the link between scholarship and commitment and has written eloquently about the kind of work that scholars can do "in deliberate unneutral pursuit of a more livable world [who] reconsider the rules by which they have worked, and begin to turn their intellectual energies to the urgent problems of our time."[9] Similarly, Noam Chomsky argues that "the social and intellectual role of the university should be subversive in a healthy society . . . [and that] individuals and society at large benefit to the extent that these liberatory ideals extend throughout the educational system—in fact, far beyond."[10] Edward Said took a similar position and argued that academics should engage in ongoing forms of permanent critique of all abuses of power and authority, "to enter into sustained and vigorous exchange with the outside world," as part of a larger project of helping "to create the social conditions for the collective production of realist utopias."[11]

After outlining some of the major challenges facing educators in this age of diminishing freedoms under the administration of George W. Bush, I will argue that it is imperative that public intellectuals within and outside of the university defend higher education as a democratic public sphere, connect academic work to public life, and advance a notion of pedagogy that provides students with modes of individual and social agency that enable them to be both engaged citizens and active participants in the struggle for global democracy. Much of this discussion will draw on a line of argument extending from John Dewey to Cornelius Castoriadis to Jacques Derrida, in which higher education is tied to the cultivation of an informed, critical citizenry capable of ameliorating and governing a global democracy. I will conclude by considering the role that academics might assume as public intellectuals and the related emphasis on the importance of critical pedagogy in the service of a socially responsible and critically engaged citizenry.

Following Howard Zinn, Zygmunt Bauman, and others, I believe that intellectuals who inhabit our nation's universities should represent the conscience of American society not only because they shape the conditions under which future generations learn about themselves and their relations to others and the outside world, but also because they engage pedagogical practices that are by their very nature moral and political rather than simply technical. Pedagogy in this instance works to shift how students think about the issues affecting their lives and the world at large, potentially energizing them to seize such moments as possibilities for acting on the world and for engaging it as a matter of politics, power, and social justice. The appeal here is not merely to an individual's sense of ethics; it is also an appeal to collectively address material inequities involving resources, accessibility, and power in both education and the broader global society while viewing the struggle for power as generative and crucial to any viable notion of individual and social agency.

If the liberal Left seems particularly disheveled and ineffectual at this point in history, then the conservatives, by contrast, appear to be masters of persuasion and organization. Working for decades at grassroots organizing, they have taken both pedagogy and politics deadly seriously. The conservative assault on education at all levels began in the 1970s, following the white working- and middle-class backlash against Civil Rights-era programs such as affirmative action and busing. Schooling was increasingly reconfigured as a private rather than a public good. And with the shift away from public considerations to private concerns, "privatization" and "choice" became the catchphrases dominating educational reform for the next few decades. The attack on all things public was accompanied by attempts to empty the public treasury, and education became one of the first targets of neoliberals, neoconservatives, religious extremists, and fundamentalists advocating market interests over social needs and democratic values. With the publication of *A Nation at Risk*, the Reagan administration gave the green light to pass spending cuts in education—cuts that have been obligatory for each administration to follow. Reconceived as a "big government monopoly," public schooling was derided as bureaucratic, inefficient, and ineffectual, generating a product (dim-witted students) that was singularly incapable of competing in the global marketplace. In short, schools had committed "an act of unthinking, unilateral educational disarmament," the report accused.[12] Schools were to blame for increased joblessness and insecurity—not the rapacious greed of corporations eager to circumvent U.S. minimum wage laws, federal taxes, and environmental regulations, while breaking the back of unions at home.

Similarly, higher education was accused of harboring a hotbed of leftist academics and promoting culture wars that derided Western civilization. Higher education was portrayed as the center of a class and race war in which the dreams of the white working class were under attack because of the ideological residue of professors tainted by the legacy of radical '60s politics. The division and distrust between "elitist liberals" and a white working class were now complete and utterly secure. Employing a mobile army of metaphors drawn from Cold War rhetoric, the Right succeeded in a propaganda campaign to turn the popular tide against higher education. After 9/11, the trend continued at an accelerated rate as any academics and educators who had voiced dissent against government policies increasingly faced retaliatory accusations that equated their views with treason. The most important casualty of this attack on education was democracy itself.

In a like manner, universities are now accused of being soft on terrorism; dissident artists are increasingly branded as un-American because of their critiques of the Bush administration; homophobia has become the poster-ideology of the Republican Party; and a full-fledged assault on women's reproductive rights is being championed by Bush's evangelical supporters—most evident in Bush's Supreme Court appointments. An incessant assault on critical thinking itself and a rising bigotry have undercut the possibility for providing a language in which vital social institutions can be defended as a public good. Moreover, as social visions of equity recede from public memory, unfettered brutal self-interest and greed combine with retrograde social policies to make security and safety a top domestic priority. As the spaces for producing engaged citizens are either commercialized or militarized, the crushing effects of domination spread out to all aspects of society, and war increasingly becomes the primary organizing principle of politics.[13]

Unfortunately, the university offers no escape and little resistance. As theorists as diverse as W.E.B. Du Bois, John Dewey, Hannah Arendt, Václav Havel, and Cornelius Castoriadis have pointed out, a substantive democracy simply cannot exist without educated citizens. But today, the humanistic knowledge and values of the university are being excised as higher education becomes increasingly corporatized and stripped of its democratic functions. As market ideals take precedence over democratic values, and individual rights outweigh collective concerns, the university is increasingly being transformed into a training ground for the corporate workforce. Anyone who spends any time on a college campus in the U.S. these days cannot miss how higher education is changing. Strapped for money and increasingly defined in the language of corporate culture, many universities seem less interested in higher learning than in becoming licensed storefronts for brand name corporations—selling off space, buildings, and endowed chairs to rich corporate donors. College presidents are now called "CEOs" and are known less for their intellectual leadership than for their role as fund-raisers and their ability to bridge the world of academe and business. The appeal to excellence by university CEOs functions like a corporate logo, hyping efficiency while denuding critical thought and scholarship of any intellectual and political substance. In the corporate university, academics are now valued according to the grant money they attract rather than the quality of education they offer to students.[14] As the university is annexed by defense, corporate, and national security interests, critical scholarship is replaced by research for either weapons technology or commercial profits, just as the private intellectual now replaces the public intellectual, and the public relations intellectual supplants the engaged intellectual in the wider culture.

Venture capitalists now scour colleges and universities in search of big profits made through licensing agreements, the control of intellectual property rights, and investments in university spinoff companies. In the age of money and profit, academic subjects gain stature almost exclusively through their exchange value on the market. This is all the more so as the Bush Administration attempts to weigh more control over higher education, cut student aid, plunder public services, and push states to the brink of financial disaster. As higher education increasingly becomes a privilege rather than a right, many working-class students either find it impossible financially to enter college or, because of increased costs, have to drop out. Those students who have the resources to stay in school are feeling the tight pressures of the job market and rush to take courses and receive professional credentials in business and the bio-sciences as the humanities lose majors and downsize. Not surprisingly, students are now referred to as "customers," while some university presidents even argue that professors be labeled as "academic entrepreneurs."[15] As higher education is corporatized, young people find themselves on campuses that look more like malls, and they are increasingly taught by professors who are hired on a contractual basis, have obscene workloads, and can barely make enough money to pay the loans for their cars. Tenured faculty are now called upon to generate grants, establish close partnerships with corporations, and teach courses that have practical value in the marketplace. There is little in this vision of the university that imagines young people as anything other than fodder for the corporation or an appendage of the national security state. What was once the hidden curriculum of many universities—the subordination of higher education to capital—has now become an open and much-celebrated policy of both public and private higher education.[16]

The language of market fundamentalism and the emerging corporate university radically alter the vocabulary available for appraising the meaning of citizenship, agency, and civic virtue. Within this discourse, everything is for sale, and what is not has no value as a public good or practice. The traditional academic imperative to publish or perish is now supplemented with the neoliberal mantra "privatize or perish" as everyone in the university is transformed into an entrepreneur, customer, or client, and every relationship is ultimately judged in bottom-line, cost-effective terms. It is in the spirit of such a critique and act of resistance that educators, according to Pierre Bourdieu, need to break with the "new faith in the historical inevitability professed by the theorists of [neo]liberalism [in order] to invent new forms of collective political work" capable of confronting the march of corporate power.[17] At stake here is the need to question and reject those economic models so fashionable among the academic managers that emancipate economic activity from any activity except the dictates of profitability and the bottom line.

It is important to note that such attacks on higher education in the U.S. come not only from a market-based ideology that reduces education to training and redefines schools as investment opportunities; they also come from conservative Christian organizations such as the American Family Association, conservative politicians, and right-wing think tanks, all of whom have launched an insidious attack on peace studies, women's studies, Middle Eastern studies, critical pedagogy, and any field that "generates critical inquiry and thought often in opposition to the aims of the United States" and the Bush regime.[18] This is the same regime that believes gay married couples are terrorists, while it says nothing about U.S. involvement in the torture and abuse at Abu Ghraib prison (or any of the other secret prisons run by the CIA) or the U.S. policy of "extraordinary rendition" that allows the CIA to kidnap people and send them to authoritarian countries to be tortured.[19]

The frontal nature of such attacks against both dissent and critical education can also be seen in attempts by conservative legislators in Ohio and a number of other states to pass bills such as the "Academic Bill of Rights," which argues that academics should be hired on the basis of their ideology in order not only to balance out faculties dominated by left-wing professors but also to control what students are taught with the purpose of protecting conservative students against ideas that might challenge or offend their ideological comfort zones. The board of trustees at Utah Valley State College went so far as to insist that the faculty take into consideration conservative political ideologies for a newly required general education requirement for students.[20] Professors who address in their classrooms critical issues that unsettle and hold accountable any commonsense assumption that favors right-wing ideology are condemned for teaching propaganda. For instance, U.S. Congressman Anthony Weiner from New York called for the firing of Joseph Massad, a Columbia University professor, who has been critical of Israeli policies against Palestinians. Under the guise of patriotic correctness, conservatives want to fire prominent academics such as Massad because of their opposition to U.S. foreign policy, while completely ignoring the quality of their intellectual scholarship. Of course, such attacks are not limited to academics. *New York Times* columnist Thomas Friedman called upon the State Department to draw up a blacklist of those critics he calls "excuse makers," which included those who believe that U.S. actions are at the root cause of violence. According to Friedman, "These excuse makers are just one notch less despicable than the terrorists and also deserve to be exposed."[21] This kind of McCarthyite babble has become so commonplace in the U.S. that it is championed by a famous columnist in one of the world's leading newspapers. Challenging the current conservative wisdom—that is, holding views at odds with official orthodoxy—has now become grounds for being either labeled un-American, dismissed from one's job, or put on a government blacklist. As if to prove the point, some universities in Ohio are bringing back the McCarthy-like loyalty oath, requiring that faculty "fill out a form declaring that [they] have no ties (as described in six broad questions) to any terrorist groups as defined by the U.S. State Department."[22]

Higher education has also been attacked by right-wing ideologues such as David Horowitz and Lynne Cheney, who view it as the "weak link" in the war against terror and a potential fifth column.[23] Horowitz, in particular, acts as the figurehead for various well-funded and orchestrated conservative student groups such as the Young Americans and College Republicans, which perform the groundwork for his "Academic Bill of Rights" policy efforts that seek out juicy but rare instances of "political bias"—whatever that is or however it might be defined—in college classrooms.[24] These efforts have resulted in considerable sums of public money being devoted to hearings in multiple state legislatures, in addition to helping impose, as the *Chronicle of Higher Education* put it, a "chilly climate" of self-policing in the academy and in the classroom.[25] At the University of California, Los Angeles, the Bruin Alumni Association has posted on its website an article called "The Dirty Thirty," in which it targets what it calls the university's "most radical professors" and states as its mission the task of exposing and combating "an exploding crisis of political radicalism on campus."[26] The Bruin Alumni Association does more than promote "McCarthy-like smears," intolerance, and anti-intellectualism through a vapid appeal for "balance"; it also offers $100 prizes to any students willing to provide information on their teachers' political views.[27] Of course, this has less to do with protesting genuine demagoguery than it does with attacking any professor who might raise critical questions about the status quo or hold the narratives of power accountable.

In spite of their present embattled status and the inroads made by corporate power, the defense industries, and the neoconservative Right, universities and colleges remain uniquely placed to prepare students both to understand and to influence the larger educational forces that shape their lives. As Edward Said observes, "It is still very fortunately the case, however, that the American university remains the one public space available to real alternative intellectual practices: No institution like it on such a scale exists anywhere else in the world today."[28] Such institutions, by virtue of their privileged position, division of labor, and alleged dedication to freedom and democracy, have an obligation to draw upon those traditions and resources capable of providing a critical, liberal, and humanistic education to all students in order to prepare them not only for a society in which information and power have taken on new and potent dimensions but also for confronting the rise of a disturbing number of antidemocratic tendencies in the most powerful country in the world and elsewhere across the globe.

Part of a such a challenge means that educators, artists, students, and others need to rethink and affirm the important presuppositions that higher education is integral to fostering the imperatives of an inclusive democracy and that the crisis of higher education must be understood as part of the wider crisis of politics, power, and culture. Jacques Derrida argued that democracy contains a promise of what is to come and that it is precisely in the tension between the dream and the reality of democracy that a space of agency, critique, and education opens up and signals both the normative and political character of democracy.[29] But democracy also demands a pedagogical intervention organized around the need to create the conditions for educating citizens who have the knowledge and skills to participate in public life, question institutional authority, and engage the contradiction be-tween the reality and promise of a global democracy. Democracy must do more than contain the structure of a promise; it must also be nurtured in those public spaces in which "the unconditional freedom to question" becomes central to any viable definition of individual and social agency.[30] At stake here is the recognition that if democracy is to become vital, then it needs to create citizens who are criti-cal, interrogate authority, hold existing institutions accountable for their actions, and are able to assume public responsibility through the very process of govern-ing.[31] What I am suggesting is that higher education is one of the few public spaces left in which unconditional resistance can be both produced and subjected to critical analysis. That is, the university should be "a place in which nothing is beyond question, not even the current and determined figure of democracy, and not even the traditional idea of critique."[32] The role of the university in this instance, and particularly the humanities, should be to create a culture of ques-tioning and resistance aimed at those ideologies, institutions, social practices, and "powers that limit democracy to come."[33] The idea of the university as democratic public sphere raises important questions about not only the purpose of higher education but also the kinds of strategies needed for academics to address what sociologist Zygmunt Bauman calls "taking responsibility for our responsibility."[34]

Part of the struggle for the university as a democratic public sphere and as a site of resistance against the growing forces of militarism, corporatism, neocon-servatism, and the religious fundamentalism of the Christian Right demands a new understanding of what it means to be a public intellectual, which in turn

suggests a new language for politics itself. Central to such a challenge is the necessity to define intellectual practice "as part of an intricate web of morality, rigor
and responsibility" that enables academics to speak with conviction, enter the
public sphere in order to address important social problems, and demonstrate
alternative models for what it means to bridge the gap between higher education
and the broader society.[35] This is a notion of intellectual practice that refuses the
instrumentality and privileged isolation of the academy while affirming a broader
vision of learning that links knowledge to the power of self-definition and to the
capacities of administrators, academics, students, and artists to expand the scope
of democratic freedoms, particularly as they address the crisis of the social as part
and parcel of the crisis of democracy itself. This is the kind of intellectual practice
that is attentive to the suffering of others and "will not allow conscience to look
away or fall asleep."[36]

Given the seriousness of the current attack on higher education by an alliance
of diverse right-wing forces, it is difficult to understand why liberals, progressives,
and left-oriented educators have been relatively silent in the face of this assault.
There is much more at stake in this current attack on the university than the issue
of academic freedom. First and foremost is the concerted attempt by right-wing
extremists and corporate interests to strip the professoriate of any authority, render critical pedagogy as merely an instrumental task, eliminate tenure as a protection for teacher authority, and remove critical reason from any vestige of civic
courage, engaged citizenship, and social responsibility. The three academic unions
have a combined membership of almost 200,000, including graduate students
and adjuncts, and yet they have barely stirred. In part, they are quiet because they
are under the illusion that tenure will protect them, or they believe the assault
on higher education has little to do with how they perform their academic labor.
They are wrong on both counts, and unless the unions and progressives mobilize
to protect the institutionalized relationships between democracy and pedagogy as
well as teacher authority and classroom autonomy, they will be at the mercy of a
right-wing revolution that views democracy as an excess and the university as a
threat. Democracy demands the most concrete urgency. Of course, urgency entails not only responding to the crisis of the present—increasingly shaped by the
anonymous presence of neoliberal capitalism and a number of other antidemocratic tendencies—but also connecting to the future that we make available to the
next generation of young people. How much longer can we allow the promise of
democracy to be tainted by its reality? Making pedagogy and education central
to the political tasks of reclaiming public space, rekindling the importance of
public connectedness, and infusing civic life with the importance of a democratic
worldly vision are at the heart of opposing the new authoritarianism.

Democracy cannot work if citizens are not autonomous, self-judging, and
independent—qualities that are indispensable for students if they are going to

make vital judgments and choices about participating in and shaping decisions that affect everyday life, institutional reform, and governmental policy. Pedagogy, in this instance, is put in the service of providing the conditions for students to invest in a robust and critical form of agency, one that takes seriously their responsibility to others, public life, and global democracy. Hence, pedagogy becomes the cornerstone of democracy in that it provides the very foundation for students to learn not merely how to be governed but also how to be capable of governing. Cornel West has argued that we need to analyze the ominous forces shutting down democracy yet "we also need to be very clear about the vision that lures us toward hope and the sources of that vision."[37] In taking up this challenge, engaged public intellectuals need to emerge as central players in a wide range of social and educational institutions. If higher education is to be a crucial sphere for creating citizens equipped to understand others, exercise their freedoms, and ask questions regarding the basic assumptions that govern democratic political life, academics will have to assume their responsibility as citizen-scholars, take critical positions, relate their work to larger social issues, offer students knowledge, debate, and dialogue about pressing social problems, and provide the conditions for students to have hope and believe that civic life not only matters but that they can make a difference in shaping it. The engaged public intellectual, according to Edward Said, must function within institutions, in part, as an exile, "whose place it is publicly to raise embarrassing questions, to confront orthodoxy and dogma (rather than to produce them), to refuse to be easily co-opted by governments or corporations."[38] This politically charged notion of the oppositional intellectual as homeless—in exile and living on the border, occupying an unsutured, shifting, and fractured social space in which critique, difference, and a utopian potentiality can endure—provides the conceptual framework for educators to fight against the deadly instrumentalism and reactionary ideologies that shape dominant educational models.[39] Public intellectuals need to resist the seductions of a narrow understanding of academic labor with its specialized languages, its neutralization of ideology and politics through a bogus claim to objectivism, and its sham elitism and expertise rooted in all the obvious gender, racial, and class-specific hierarchies. Falsely secure in their professed status as specialists and experts, many full-time academics retreat into narrow modes of scholarship that display little interest in how power is used in institutions and social life to include and exclude, provide the narratives of the past and present, and secure the authority to define the future.[40] Higher education is one of the few places where scholars can be educated for life in a global democracy by becoming multiliterate in ways that not only allow them access to new information and technologies but also enable them to be border crossers capable of engaging, learning from, understanding, and being tolerant of and responsible for matters of inclusiveness, meaningful difference, and otherness.

Two of the most challenging issues facing the academy today are grasping what we mean by the political and what we mean by theorizing a politics of and for the 21st century. Academics should enter into a dialogue with colleagues and students about politics and the knowledge we seek to produce together and connect such knowledge to broader public spheres and issues while heeding Hannah Arendt's warning that "without a politically guaranteed public realm, freedom lacks the worldly space to make its appearance."[41] The role of engaged intellectuals is not to consolidate authority but to understand, interpret, and question it.[42] Social criticism has to be coupled with a vibrant self-criticism and the willingness to take up critical positions without becoming dogmatic or intractable. Critical education links knowledge and learning to the performative and worldly space of action and engagement, energizing people not only to think critically about the world around them but also to use their capacities as social agents to intervene in the larger social order and confront the myriad forms of symbolic, institutional, and material relations of power that shape their lives. These connections between pedagogy and agency, knowledge and power, and thought and action must be mobilized in order to confront the current crisis of authoritarianism looming so large in the U.S. and elsewhere around the globe today.

Individuals and collectivities have to be regarded as potential agents and not simply as victims or ineffectual dreamers. It is this legacy of critique and possibility, of resistance and agency, that infuses intellectual work with concrete hope and offers a wealth of resources to people within the academy and other public spheres who struggle on multiple fronts against the rising forces of authoritarianism. Hannah Arendt recognized that any viable democratic politics must address the totality of public life and refuse to withdraw from such a challenge in the face of totalitarian violence that legitimates itself through appeals to safety, fear, and the threat of terrorism.[43] Against this stripped-down legitimization of authority is the promise of public spheres that in their diverse forms, sites, and content offer pedagogical and political possibilities. Such inquiries can strengthen the social bonds of democracy and cultivate both critical modes of individual and social agency and crucial opportunities to form alliances in the collective struggle for a biopolitics that affirms life, hopeful vision, the operations of democracy, and a range of democratic institutions—that is, a biopolitics that fights against the terror of totalitarianism.

In a complex and rapidly changing global world, public intellectuals are confronted with the important task of taking back control over the conditions of intellectual production in a variety of venues in which the educational force of the culture takes root and holds a powerful grip over the stories, images, and sounds that shape people's lives throughout the globe. Such sites constitute what I call "new spheres of public pedagogy." They represent crucial locations for a cultural politics designed to wrest the arena of public debate within the field of global power away from those dangerous forces that endlessly commodify intellectual autonomy and critical thought while appropriating or undercutting any viable work done through the collective action of critical intellectuals. Such spheres are about more than legal rights guaranteeing freedom of speech; they are also sites that demand a certain kind of citizen informed by particular forms of education, a citizen whose education provides the essential conditions for democratic public spheres to flourish. Cornelius Castoriadis, the great philosopher of democracy, argues that if public space is not to be experienced as a private affair but instead as a vibrant sphere in which people experience and learn how to participate in and shape public life, then it must be shaped through an education that provides the decisive traits of courage, responsibility, and shame—all of which connects the fate of each individual to the fate of others, the planet, and global democracy.[44] Artists, cultural workers, youth, and educators need to not only create new discourses of understanding and criticism but also offer up a vision of hope that fosters the conditions for multiple collective and global struggles that refuse to use politics as an act of war or markets as the measure of democracy. The challenge posed by the current regime of religious extremism, market fundamentalism, state-sponsored terrorism, and the incursion of corporate power into higher education presents difficult problems for educators and demands a profoundly committed sense of individual and collective resistance if all of those who believe in a vibrant democracy are going to fight for a future that does not endlessly repeat the present. At the current moment, higher education faces a legitimization crisis—one that opens a political and theoretical space for educators to redefine the relationship among higher education, the public good, and democracy. Higher education represents one of the most important sites over which the battle for democracy is being waged. It is the site where the promise of a better future emerges out of those visions and pedagogical practices that combine hope and moral responsibility as part of a broader emancipatory discourse. Far from hopelessly utopian, such a task echoes an insight by the French philosopher Alain Badiou that famously captures a starting point for reclaiming higher education as a democratic public sphere: "In fact, it's an immense task to try to propose a few possibles, in the plural—a few possibilities other than what we are told is possible. It is a matter of showing how the space of the possible is larger than the one assigned—that something else is possible, but not that everything is possible."[45]

Notes

1. Tannock, S. (2006). Higher education, inequality, and the public good. *Dissent, 53*(2), 45.
2. Williams, J. (2006) Debt education: Bad for the young, bad for America. *Dissent, 53*(3), 53–59.
3. Zinn, H. (2001). *On history.* New York, NY: Seven Stories Press.
4. Ibid.

5. I have taken up this issue in Henry A. Giroux, *Impure Acts: The Practical Politics of Cultural Studies* (New York: Routledge, 2000) and in Henry A. Giroux and Susan Searls Giroux, *Take Back Higher Education* (New York: Palgrave, 2006).
6. Zygmunt Bauman cited in Fearn, N. (2006). Profile: Zygmunt Bauman. *New Statesman*, 32.
7. Buck-Morss, S. (2003). *Thinking past terror: Islamism and critical theory on the Left*. New York, NY: Verso; I have taken up this issue in a number of books: Henry A. Giroux, *Impure Acts* (New York: Routledge, 2000); Henry A. Giroux, *Public Spaces/Private Lives: Democracy Beyond 9/11* (Lanham, MD: Rowman and Littlefield, 2003); Henry A. Giroux and Susan Searls Giroux, *Take Back Higher Education: Race, Youth, and the Crisis of Democracy in the Post Civil Rights Era* (New York: Palgrave, 2006).
8. Furedi, F. (2004). *Where have all the intellectuals gone?* New York, NY: Continuum.
9. Zinn, H., ibid., *On history*, p. 186.
10. Chomsky, N. (2000). Paths taken, tasks ahead. *Profession, 35*.
11. Said, E. (2001). The Public Role of Writers and Intellectuals. *The Nation, 4*.
12. National Commission on Excellence in Education. (1983). A nation at risk. Retrieved from http://www.ed.gov/pubs/NatAtRisk/index.html
13. Hardt, M., & Negri, A. (2004). *Multitude: War and democracy in the age of empire*. New York, NY: The Penguin Press.
14. Giroux, H. A., & Giroux, S. S. (2005). *Take back higher education*. New York, NY: Palgrave.
15. Giroux, H. A. (2005). Academic entrepreneurs: The corporate takeover of higher education. *Tikkun, 20*(2), 18–22, 28.
16. Aronowitz, S. (1998). The new corporate university. *Dollars and Sense, (218)*, 32.
17. Bourdieu, P. (1999). *Acts of resistance*. New York, NY: New Press.
18. Paik, A. N. (2005). *Education and empire, old and new*. Unpublished manuscript.
19. Giroux, H. A. (2005). *Against the new authoritarianism*. Winnipeg, Manitoba: Arbeiter Ring.
20. Capriccioso, R. (2006). Walking on eggshells. Retrieved from http://insidehighered.com/news/2006/08/15/utah
21. Friedman, T. (2005). Giving the hatemongers no place to hide. *New York Times, 4*(41). Retrieved from http://www.nytimes.com/2005/07/22/opinion/22friedman.html?ex=1279684800&en=17fb5beb19b09d86&ei=5090&partner=rssuserland&emc=rss
22. Jaschik, S. (2006). Are you now or have you ever . . . . Retrieved from http://insidehighered.com/news/2006/08/15/oath
23. This charge comes from a report issued by the conservative group American Council of Trustees and Alumni (ACTA), founded by Lynne Cheney (spouse of Vice President Dick Cheney) and Joseph Lieberman (Democratic senator). See Jerry L. Martin and Anne D. Neal, *Defending Civilization: How Our Universities Are Failing America and What Can Be Done about It* (November 2001), p. 1. Available online: http://www.la.utexas.edu/~chenry/2001LynnCheneyjsg01ax1.pdf. This statement was deleted from the revised February 2002 version of the report available on the ACTA website: http://www.goacta.org/publications/Reports/defciv.pdf. ACTA also posted on its website a list of 115 statements made by allegedly "un-American professors."
24. David Horowitz's books trade in racist accusations, the ongoing claim that almost anyone who criticizes the Bush administration hates America and accuses critics of the Iraq war of getting Americans killed in Iraq. His latest book, *The Professors: The 101 Most Dangerous Academics in America* (New York: Regnery, 2006), purports to name and expose those left-wing professors who hate America, the military, and give comfort to terrorists.
25. Forum: A chilly climate on the campuses. (2005). *Chronicle of Higher Education, 52*(3), B7–B13.
26. Bruin Alumni Association. (n.d.). The dirty thirty. Retrieved from http://www.uclaprofs.com/articles/dirtythirty.html
27. Fogg, P. (2005). Independent alumni group offers $100 bounties to UCLA Students who ferret out classroom bias. *Chronicle of Higher Education, 51*(19). Retrieved from http://chronicle.com/daily/2006/01/2006011904n.htm

28. Said, E. (2004). *Humanism and democratic criticism*. New York, NY: Columbia University Press.
29. Derrida, J. (2001). The future of the profession or the unconditional university. In L. Simmons & H. Worth (Eds.), *Derrida down under* (pp. 253). Auckland, New Zealand: Dunmarra Press.
30. Ibid., p. 233.
31. Castoriadis, C. (1997). Democracy as procedure and democracy as regime. *Constellations, 4*(1), 10.
32. Derrida, J., ibid. *The future of the profession or the unconditional university.* p. 253.
33. Ibid., p. 253.
34. Bunting, M. (2003). Passion and pessimism. *The Guardian*. Retrieved from http:/books.guardian.co.uk/print/0,3858,4640858,00.html
35. Roy, A. (2001). *Power politics*. Cambridge, MA: South End Press.
36. Said, E. (2004). *Humanism and democratic criticism*. New York, NY: Columbia University Press.
37. West, C. (2004). Finding hope in dark times. *Tikkun, 19*(4), 18.
38. Said, E. (1994). *Representations of the intellectual: The 1993 Reith lectures*. New York, NY: Pantheon Books.
39. Giroux, H. A. (2005). *Border crossings: Cultural workers and the politics of education*, second edition. New York, NY: Routledge.
40. Aronowitz, S. (2003). *How class works: Power and social movement*. New Haven, CT: Yale University Press.
41. Arendt, H. (1977). *Between past and future: Eight exercises in political thought*. New York, NY: Penguin Books.
42. Said, E. (1994). *Representations of the intellectual: The 1993 Reith lectures*. New York, NY: Pantheon Books.
43. Arendt, H. (1976). *Totalitarianism: Part three of the origins of totalitarianism*. New York, NY: Harcourt.
44. See, especially, Castoriadis, C. (1991). The Greek polis and the creation of democracy. *Philosophy, politics, autonomy: Essays in political philosophy*. New York, NY: Oxford University Press.
45. Badiou, A. (1998). *Ethics: An essay on the understanding of evil*. London, England: Verso.

SIXTEEN

Understanding Academic Discourses

Lilia I. Bartolomé

The education of low-status linguistic-minority students in the United States can be generally characterized as a form of miseducation that continues to produce an unacceptably high rate of failure. The miseducation of linguistic-minority students is particularly noticeable among Latinos in general and Mexican Americans in particular. Although the majority of all students begin their schooling with more or less the same hopes, aspirations, and dreams, a high percentage of linguistic-minority students who enter high school never graduate, compared to 17 percent of Anglo students. Approximately 45 percent of Mexican American students drop out of school, and in some communities the dropout rate is ever higher. Because of the schools' failure to educate the largest Latino subgroup, Mexican Americans, and because of this subgroup's historical, pervasive and disproportionate academic underachievement, it is particularly urgent to better understand the multiple variables that influence the poor academic performance of the students. In addition to the intolerably high rate of academic failure, the projected increases for the Mexican American population dramatically illustrate the need for immediate academic intervention for these students as early as elementary school. Given the complexity of this problem, the high dropout rate and the academic failure of Mexican Americanss have directly and indirectly generated numerous research studies examining the underachievement phenomenon from a variety of perspectives.

This chapter was originally published in Bartolome, L. (1998). *The Misteaching of Academic Discourses: The Politics of Language.* Toronto: Harper.

From a linguistic perspective the academic failure of Mexican American students has historically been attributed to their lack of English-language proficiency. However, recent research shows that proficiency in English in and of itself is not sufficient for academic success. Although common perception suggests that the English proficiency of most Mexican American students is limited, a significant number of these students are bilingual in English and Spanish. Nevertheless, many English-proficient bilingual Mexican American students continue to experience difficulties and failure in school. In fact studies suggest that U.S.-born English-dominant Mexican American students may actually experience more academic failure than their foreign-born Spanish-dominant peers who have recently arrived in the United States; the latter may not have mastered English, but they are literate in their first language and have learned to communicate their knowledge via the academic discourse of their native language.

The concept of "academic discourses" refers to more than just the student's ability to produce Standard English by using the correct phonology (sound system), lexicon (vocabulary), and syntax (sentence structure). In addition to these three language dimensions, less easily measured language components such as cultural knowledge about rhetorical structure (the ability to create text whose logic and structure reflect academic and mainstream ways of organizing text) are equally important. For example, one valued academic discourse strategy involves the ability to produce text that reflect a unidimensional and linear line of argument.

James Gee, Sarah Michaels, and other researchers have shown that working-class African American students often produce utterances in English that are difficult for their middle-class white teachers to understand. The communication difference often lies in the manner in which the students organize their text and utilize contextual cues. For example, Sarah Michaels reported that middle-class white teachers often evaluated the narratives their African American students offered during sharing time as unwieldy, illogical, and confusing because the children (1) produced oral text structures that did not follow a linear line of thought, (2) assumed the audience shared their background knowledge, and (3)utilized culturally specific intonation cues to signal emphasis.

In the case of Mexican American students, the research suggests that older, recently arrived students who received their previous education in Mexican schools often come to U.S. classrooms already possessing knowledge about academic rhetorical structures and communication practices that are valued in school contexts and necessary for success, particularly if they come from middle-class backgrounds. These students may be temporarily handicapped because of their limited proficiency in English; however, once they acquire a threshold level of proficiency in English, they eventually are able to transfer their Spanish academic discourse skills to English, thus guaranteeing some degree of success in the classroom.

Ironically, Mexican American students born and bred in the United States often are not similarly skilled. This is because unlike their Mexican peers they usually have not had the opportunity to develop academic discourse skills in primary language in a school context that supports their full linguistic development. The sad irony that schools often require from these linguistic minority students precisely those academic discourse skills and knowledge that they often do not teach. This is what Donaldo Macedo has called a "pedagogy of entrapment" in that teachers require of students what they do not explicitly teach them. In other words, even well-intentioned teachers often fail to overtly teach the academic discourses necessary for school success.

Even in bilingual education classrooms designed to help students with limited English proficiency make the transition into English-only classrooms, teachers often make false assumptions concerning the level of the linguistic-minority students' ability to use English academic discourses; moreover, they seldom teach these discourses explicitly to these students. Teachers often fail to understand that the academic discourse prerequisites are not inherently part of these students' working-class, native-language competency. For example, most Mexican American students I have worked with come from a working-class reality and speak a variety of Spanish different from the Spanish academic discourse generally taught in bilingual programs. Thus, they are often confronted with two major linguistic problems: a lack of proficiency in the academic discourse in their second language, English, and a similar lack in their native language, Spanish. Hence, to assume that these students will automatically transfer a presumed academic metalinguistic awareness in the first language to the second represents a form of entrapment. That is, teachers require these students to have linguistic competency in the academic discourse that they were never taught in either language. One unfortunate result is that many linguistic-minority students in either English-only or bilingual settings are not being explicitly prepared to comprehend and produce more formal academic speech and writing in any language.

The Myth of "De-Contextualized" Language

The very real pedagogical entrapment experienced by the linguistic community and other working class students contradicts many of the common sense presumptions that in school settings teachers actually employ more "academic" ways of communicating, and students simply fail to acquire these more advanced communication skills. It is commonly accepted that an academic discourse that relies on linguistic cues such as precise vocabulary and unilaterally structured syntactic and rhetorical structures is more communicatively efficient in an academic setting. Unfortunately the reality is that academic discourse conventions are seldom explicitly taught to working-class, linguistic-minority students. Furthermore, there is also a tendency to glorify and romanticize a particular type of academic language discourse that is inaccurately referred to in the literature as de-contextualized "language." I say "inaccurately" because language production for meaningful communication cannot be achieved outside the cultural context that gives the produced language meaning in the first place. In other words, all language is context bound in one manner or another.

A variety of terms have been used to identify the so-called de-contextualized language. It has been referred to by researchers as literate or autonomous language, school language, disembedded language, less contextualized language and situation-independent language. These terms all attempt to capture the numerous language features related to a text over levels of precision, explicitness, and clarity. However, the use of these apparently innocuous and "objective" terms hides the reality that demand ideology often devalues language varieties that do not conform to the prescribed rules of the standard academic discourse.

For instance, it is assumed that a standard academic discourse has a general meaning outside of context, conveying explicit and precise messages that would be universally understood without relying on the specificity of context to access meaning. The assumption here is that the working class dialect is context borne, whereas the standard academic discourse transcends social and cultural locations and is therefore more universal, less localized and more autonomous. The very use of the term dialect to refer to the working-class language variety signals the devaluation of this variety and its speakers. By using the standard academic discourse as a yardstick against which all other varieties are measured, one begins to view nonstandard discourse negatively, for they "lack" the features attributed to the standard discourse (which is, coincidentally, also the dominant variety). This valuation process hides the asymmetrical power relation between the dominant standard discourse and all other, nonstandard varieties. For example, rarely do we refer to the standard discourse as a dialect, even though, linguistically speaking it is just that. The term of preference for the dominant standard discourse is usually language. Thus middle- and upper-class students, particularly whites, speak a language whereas lower-class racial and ethnic groups speak a dialect which amongst other features is characterized by its lack of autonomy from its social and cultural contexts.

Researchers who, in the name of science, create (or sustain) a false dichotomy between de-contextualized and contextualized discourse fail to realize that their coinage of these terms is false and that no discourse exists outside context; they also fail to realize that they play a key role in reproducing the dominant ideology, which is often hidden by language they use to describe different linguistic varieties. The so called de-contextualized discourse implies linguistic superiority while making its context invisible. How does one explain the fact that middle- and upper-class white students can answer questions on scholastic achievement tests (SATs) without having to actually read the accompanying passages? James Gee, for example, gave his students in an honors program (mostly populated by middle- and upper-class whites) at the University of Southern California the following SAT questions.

1. The main idea of the passage is that
   A. a constricted view of [this novel] is natural and acceptable
   B. a novel should not depict a vanished society
   C. a good novel is an intellectual rather than an emotional experience
   D. many readers have seen only the comedy [in this novel]
   E. [this novel] should be read with sensitivity and an open mind

2. The author's attitude toward someone who enjoys [this novel] and then remarks "but of course it has no relevance today" (lines 21–22) can best be described as one of
   A. amusement
   B. astonishment
   C. disapproval
   D. resignation
   E. ambivalence

3. The author [of this passage] implies that a work of art is properly judged on the basis of its
   A. universality of human experience truthfully recorded
   B. popularity and critical acclaim in its own age
   C. openness to varied interpretations, including seemingly contradictory ones
   D. avoidance of political and social issues of minor importance
   E. continued popularity through different eras and with different societies

Nearly 100 students who answered these questions answered them correctly 80 percent of the time without reading the accompanying passages. In fact, Gee noted "virtually no student has missed the answer to question 3 (which is A). However, when he gave the same questions to his "regular" undergraduate students (among whom there was more diversity along class, race, and ethnicity lines) a great many more students answered them incorrectly.

What guided the students in the honors program to answer the question correctly without reading the passage? Gee explained:

Avant garde literary critics certainly do not believe that a work of art is properly judged on the basis of its universality of human experience truthfully recorded. In fact, they believe something much closer to answer C; a work of art is properly judged on the basis of its openness to varied interpretations, including seemingly contradictory ones. And my honors students do not, in fact, believe that a work of arts is properly judged on the basis of its universality of human experience truthfully recorded, either. They are prone to believe something much closer to answer E: A work of art is properly judged on the basis of continued popularity through different eras and with different societies.

Why do not my honors students answer A to question 3? They do because they immediately recognize, in this question and the others, a certain set of values. They recognize a value like "truth and beauty transcend cultures"so they know that the answer to question 3 is A. They recognize a value like "truth and beauty transcend time," so they know that the answer to question 2 is C. And they recognize values like truth and beauty are open (and only open) to people who are appropriately sensitive and open minded (that is, people who are not "ideological") thus they know that the answer to question 1 is E.

As this SAT test experiment exemplified, students socialized in a particular set of vaues that correspond to those values held by the dominant institutions (such as schools and testing centers) had no difficulty answering the test questions correctly even when they did not read the questions' accompanying passages. They did not because they were guided by a set of values required through their class and culture socialization rather than by any innate intelligence.

As Gee also correctly argued, these students even betrayed their own beliefs so as to adhere to what they believe was a dominant consensus—a set of values shared by the dominant sector of the society. I would point out that the set of values that guided these students to the correct answers without reading the question represented a contextual point of reference for meaning-making similar to the visible, context-bound signposts used by working-class racial and ethnic students in their own meaning-making. The difference is that in the so-called de-contextualized discourse, the point of reference is often made invisible in keeping with the inner working of ideology. What is at work in the nomenclature of "de-contextualized discourse" is how students "respond appropriately to a specific hegemonic or displaced consensus centered on the values of dominant Discourses, a consensus achievement among persons (in the dominant groups or not) whose paths through life have for a time and place fallen together with the members of these dominant Discourses."

Hence the teaching and acquisition of the dominant academic discourse requires more than linguistic knowledge. It requires knowledge about "ways of being in the world, ways of acting, thinking, interacting, valuing, believing, speaking and sometimes writing and reading connected to particular identities and social roles." If a teacher fails to acknowledge that certain groups of students who come from subordinated and cultural and racial groups do not have access to and membership in the dominant discourse, he or she makes the power of the dominant discourse invisible and also reproduces the distinction (often invisible) that is inherent in the dominant discourse and that serves as a measure in society as a whole. Thus, teaching and the acquisition of the dominant discourse would inevitably involve democratizing social structures so that the dominant academic discourse and the social, economic, and political structures it sustains become more accessible to subordinated students. Despite the ideological nature of this type of discourse, the operationalization of so-called contextualized language in the literature has tended to focus on solely linguistic features that render written and oral text overtly explicit, such as using precise vocabulary and syntax.

Operationalizing "De-contextualized" Language

Much of the current educational research identifies numerous linguistic features, all related to a text's overt levels of explicitness and implicitness in its operationalization of "de-contextualized" language. Researchers' foci range from the use of lexical and prosodic cues to the complexity of sentence structure and the use of pronouns as well as the text's overall cohesiveness.

These researchers recognize that, in reality, so-called de-contextualized language is not truly de-contextualized (that is, devoid of all context) but rather is contextualized using chiefly linguistic cues and strategies restricted to the text to render a message explicit. Instead of relying on extralinguistic cues or cues located outside the sentence (such as use of body language, varying intonation and assumption of shared knowledge with interlocutors). However, the researchers stop short of recognizing that these linguistic cues and strategies rely on values that became the contextual point of reference.

Nonetheless, linguists such as James Gee are quick to point out that all language is contextualized, and they remind us of the culture-specific nature of using and valuing language that is linguistically contextualized. In fact, Gee has specifically linked children's ability to speak in "school-like"ways with their socialization in "school-like" home cultures:

> Certain cultures, as well as unschooled people in our culture, simply do not have, and thus do not use, the conventions prevalent in our schools that in certain contrived situations (like "show and tell time"), one pretends that people do not know or see what they obviously do know and see. . . . Such assumptions—
> that one should ignore what the hearer knows and explicitly say it anyway—are
> . . .the hallmark of many middle-class home-based practices with children (e.g., having the child repeat back an often-read book or rehearse at the dinner table daily events that one already knows about). In other social groups. . . such explicitness may be seen as rude because it is distancing, blunt or condescending to the hearer's intelligence.

As Gee suggested, certain cultural and social groups place value on producing texts that are overtly explicit and do not require interlocutor negotiation. That is, more middle-class and schooled ways of contextualizing text require distance between interlocutors so that the only visible cues for making meaning are linguistic ones.

I use the more specific descriptor linguistically contextualized, rather than the more conventional de-contextualized language, because, as discussed, the latter term erroneously contests that language can, indeed, be de-contextualized, that is, free of all context. The use of this popular term obfuscates the fact that de-contextualized language actually refers to language that utilizes the mainstream or dominant culture's preferred ways of contextualizing. I believe that the term linguistically contextualized constitutes a more accurate and objective descriptor of the type of language strategies we value in schools; it also does not perpetuate the erroneous and almost mystical air surrounding the term de-contextualized language. For example, the use of text-organized strategies such as the "topic-centered" organization of narratives that middle-class white children use (presenting a main point or thesis and elaborating about only that point or thesis) and the use of specific linguistic cues (such as introductory sentences that inform the listener of the speaker's main point as well as his or her plans for organizing and presenting the text) are treated in the literature not as culturally specific ways of contextualizing oral and written massages but as text that is de-contextualized. Described as de-contextualized text, it is thus believed to be capable of transmitting meaning on its own, irrespective of the context in which the communicative effort takes place.

Despite the linguistic reality that so-called de-contextualized language really is not free of all contextual information and cues, the social reality is that not all contextualizing conventions or strategies are perceived as equally valuable by the dominant culture. The use of linguistic cueing is perceived as more desirable and cognitively superior than relying on subordinate cultural cues (body language, the use of prosodic cues such as changing intimation, and so forth). Here, we begin to see how the dominant valuation system operates through distinction so as to asymmetrically distribute cultural goods. In fact, as argued earlier, even so-called de-contextualized discourse relies on extralinguistic structure such as a value system to generate meaning. To a great extent, especially in classroom situations in which students manage to communicate their intent, their preference for form over content reflects social and cultural preference rather than purely linguistic value.

I believe that as an educator committed to improving the academic achievement of linguistic minority students we need to investigate how and why the language and literacy practices and contextualizing strategies utilized by the schooled and socially powerful have come to be touted as inherently superior and desirable in comparison to those practiced by lower-status cultural groups. It is important to understand that the practice of contextualizing language by relying chiefly on linguistic cues reflects Western European essaying or essay-text tradition. Historically, oral language that resembles this type of written text organization has been heralded as more "logical" and describes less formal ways of structuring linguistic messages. Instead of recording the appropriateness of overtly explicit language (as well as its inappropriateness in certain situations the tendency has been to glorify this type of text organization. In the process ideological claims are made about the essay-text superior value, whether in speech or in writing, and these, in turn, become part of "an armory of concepts, conventions and practices" that privilege one's social formation as if it were natural, universal, or, at least, the end point of a normal developmental progression of cognitive skills.

Thus, we strip so-called de-contextualized language of the almost magical properties attributed to it when we understand that, in reality, it refers to a speaker's and writer's ability to rely on dominant cultural knowledge and linguistic cues to render language overtly explicit and precise. As I have noted researchers employ a variety of terms to describe oral and written language that relies primarily on linguistic cues for conveying meaning because shared meaning between interlocutors cannot be assumed. Consequently, linguistic messages must be elaborated on in an overtly precise and explicit manner and in an almost metacognitive fashion so that the risk of misinterpretation is minimized.

It is useful to dissect the concept of linguistically contextualized language (or "de-contextualized language" as it is more commonly referred to in the literature) to understand that its high value in part reflects dominant culture's preference for structuring and contextualizing language in ways that minimize the interlocutors' joint creation and negotiation of meaning. In an academic setting, high value is placed on producing text that is linguistically contexualized, thus reducing the importance of and need for human interaction and negotiation of meaning, especially when the interlocutors come from different class and ethnic groups.

Linguistically contextualized language therefore becomes a kind of lingua franca in academic domains. Certainly, the ability to contextualize language by relying chiefly on textual features, especially in academic domains where individuals are expected to communicate with distant and unknown audiences is a desired one. A set of agreed-upon contextualized conventions becomes necessary for successful communication to take place. Ana Maria Rodino accurately describes the types of skills and conceptions of language that students must possess in order to produce this academic lingua franca.

> Being removed from the face-to-face setting, and assuming no prior knowledge on the part of an unsupportive interlocutor (linguistically) contextualized language requires anticipating a recipient's needs/expectation; filling in background

information; assessing message effectiveness on-line; self monitoring and self repair; careful planning to achieve a coherent whole; using precise lexical reference; controlling the complex syntax necessary to make explicit all relationships between ideas, and to sustain lexicalized cohesion across the whole text.

It is important to recognize the value of lingua franca in formal academic settings. However, I argue that instead of imbuing linguistically contextualized language with almost magical properties and denigrating students from cultural and social groups that generally do not rely on these types of contextualizing cues, it is important for educators of linguistic-minority students to clearly comprehend the sociopolitical dimensions of language and literacy teaching, By doing so, these educators can resist viewing the dominant group's uses of language as inherently superior and desirable, and they can begin to identify ways for helping linguistic-minority students in the critical appropriation of academic discourses.

Language Devaluation and Resistance

In addition to this tendency to render the contextualizing strategies of the mainstream "invisible" (hence the term de-contextualized), there is also a tendency to make value judgments that adversely affect what is labeled contextualized language or language that is contextualized in paralinguistic ways and generally spoken by non-mainstream populations. In other words, nonlinguistically contextualized language is often associated with the language variety spoken by groups that are generally relegated to the margins of the society. Thus, their linguistic production is not only devalued but also perceived as needing a "metamorphosis" of sorts into the standard discourse and text organization style, which is identified as de-contextualized.

The shift from a so-called context-bound to a seemingly de-contextualized discourse often involves psychological ramifications that can be far-reaching and yet are largely ignored by most teachers. For instance, the shift from a context-bound to de-contextualized discourse can often be accompanied by the development or exacerbation of linguistic insecurity, to the degree that students are encouraged to abandon or repress their so-called context-bound language (which is usually devalued by the standard middle-class oriented curriculum). This form of linguistic coercion can produce linguistic resistance in students who begin to experience antagonism toward the academic discourses they are often cajoled into learning. If teachers do not fully understand these psychological processes, which are generally shaped by competing ideologies, they often fall into a binary position that does not bode well for a psychologically healthy pedagogy conducive to learning academic discourses. This lack of understanding about student resistance often eclipses any possibility that teachers may detect linguistic resistance so they can mediate it and effectively teach the academic discourses while honoring the home discourse of their students.

I am reminded of a story told by Dell Hymes, a respected anthropologist and educator, that illustrates my point. During the early sixties, while he was a professor at the Harvard Graduate School of Education, Hymes was recruited to help solve educational problems experienced by students in a Boston, public elementary school located next to what was then the poorest and most danger-ous housing project in Boston, populated primarily by African Americans. The school's student population was almost 100 percent African American, but over 95 percent of the teachers and administrators were middle-class whites.

Hymes put into place mechanisms that encouraged and facilitated African American parents' involvement in the schools. These mechanisms also enable teachers to familiarize themselves with the cultural backgrounds of the students they were teaching. Many African American mothers became teachers' aides and helped bridge the gap between the school and the community. During one of the teacher–parent meetings, a well-meaning middle-class white teacher commented on her students' inability to learn standard English: "I have tried everything under the sun. I have gone downtown to buy colorful books, I have bought crayons. I use overheads, and these students still don't seem to be able to learn the standard." She was interrupted by an African American mother who was serving as an aide in her classroom: "Ma'am, I'm sorry, but I have to disagree with you. When I take these students outside for recess and, when they play school, when they role play school, when they role play the teacher, they speak exactly like you do."

Here was a case in which students as young as seven or eight had, albeit un-consciously, begun to resist performing the academic discourse in the classroom although they were fully able to do so when the middle-class white teacher was absent. This example illustrates the fact that students whose language and culture are devaluated by schools generally develop resistance mechanisms to protect their already fractured culture from the symbolic and real violence perpetrated against it by the middle-class white school culture.

The blind imposition of the so-called de-contextualized academic discourse not only reproduces the false assumption that academic discourses are not context bound, it also functions as a measure against which linguistic-minority students' contextualization of their languages is devalued. This in turn may produce poten-tially serious psychological scars, even in students who fully master the academic discourses and go on to become highly successful professionals. For example, Jose Cardenas, former director of the Intercultural Development Research Association in San Antonio, Texas, noted that his school experience was linguistically trau-matic and left him identifiable psychological scars: "I still remember it, not as an uncomfortable, unpleasant, or challenging situation, but, rather, as a traumatic, disconcerting, terrorizing experience."

By not understanding the psychological ramifications of their pedagogy concerning the teaching of academic discourse to minority students, teachers more often than not blame the students for their failure. In the process, they fail to examine the erroneous assumptions that inform their pedagogy, which itself is predicated on the false dichotomy between context-bound and de-contextualized discourse. It is not true that minority students cannot learn standard academic discourses, as demonstrated by the young African Americans in the Boston public elementary schools and by Jose Cardenas. Instead, the problem often lies with the "traumatic, disconcerting, terrorizing experience" that generally leads minority students to find refuge in linguistic resistance to the imposition and promotion of what has been characterized by the dominant schools' culture as de-contextualized language.

As mentioned before, the tendency to label linguistically contextualized language as "de-contextualized" conjures up images of a mystical type of language, an entity in and of itself, which is touted as inherently superior to linguistic messages that may be entirely appropriate situationally but that rely on less academic ways of contextualizing. The theoretical framework that underlies my research effort is anchored in a critical sociology view of language and literacy. I find this approach useful for demystifying the notion of de-contextualizing language while objectively understanding the academic communicative benefits for producing this type of language separately from its socially ascribed value. In other words, all language is "contextualized" in some manner, and the ways in which individuals decide to contextualize their utterances reflect, in part, the ways in which they have been socialized to construct utterances in various social situations. In some instances, individuals contextualize their language by relying chiefly on linguistic cues. In others, individuals contextualize their utterances by relying on extra linguistic cues, or they co-construct the context by depending on active listener interaction and collaboration.

Despite the importance attributed to the ability to linguistically contextualize discourse in academic settings, I have found no studies that examine the real-life linguistic contextualizing demands placed on bilingual Mexican American students in classrooms where teachers take a culturally sensitive approach to working with students. Research conducted on working-class African American students suggest that these students, in contrast to their middle-class white peers, produce language that is contextualized prosodically and is perceived by their teachers as less explicit, logical, and precise than language characterized as de-contextualized. As a result, African American students (as is probably the case for other linguistic-minority students) are often misinterpreted and misassessed by their teachers. The few studies that have been conducted on bilingual students suggest that mainland working-class Puerto Rican students, like their African American peers, also rely chiefly on extralinguistic cues to contextualize their language.

Teaching Academic Language to Linguistic-Minority Students

Given the importance accorded linguistically contextualized language in the exhibition of academic knowledge, as well as the likelihood that working-class Latino students (similar to the other working-class students) may not-develop middle-class academic contextualizing skills in the home, teachers must assist their linguistic-minority students in developing these skills at school. Thus, the challenge is not merely acquiring the English language per se. The real issue is the creation of appropriate pedagogical spaces where students can appropriate the middle-class special English discourse in all of its dimensions. For this reason, I believe that it is important to determine whether teachers' instructional demands and their evaluations of students' contextualizing strategies correspond to their actual classroom practices regarding the teaching and use of academic discourse.

Mexican American Students and Linguistic-Contextualized Language

As discussed earlier one reason for the difference in academic performance among Mexican Americans may be linked to their varying ability to "appropriate" contextualized language (oral and written) in academic ways—that is, rely on linguistic cues to render their language overly explicit and precise. The important work that Catherine Snow and her associates conducted with upper-class bilingual elementary students indicates that those who possess the ability to linguistically contextualize language in their primary language are soon able to transfer this ability to the second language. This explanation lends support to the empirical work that shows that older immigrant students who are successful readers and writers in their first language are able to transfer and apply their literacy skills to the second language once they achieve some minimal level of English proficiency. I would argue that older working-class immigrant students not schooled in their primary language would not demonstrate the same ability to transfer discourse such as decontextualized correspondence does not apply to their linguistic reality. Class is usually a determining factor in the successful acquisition of English academic discourses.

It is interesting to note that it is precisely during the later elementary grades (fourth grade and beyond) when language (both oral and written) becomes more linguistically contextualized that Mexican American students begin to fall behind in school. As Snow and her associates suggested, "The reading and writing tasks expected of children in the later elementary, middle and high school grades cannot be accomplished without both productive and receptive skills [linguistic contextualizing language skills]." Despite these findings, little has been done to study the actual language demands placed on working-class Mexican American bilingual students to linguistically contextualize their language (in both English and Spanish).

Research in bilingual and linguistic-minority education has not thoroughly addressed the issue of linguistic conflict, although some efforts have been made to explain the resistance of linguistic-minority students to learning a second language and culture. Much of the literature continues to treat the phenomenon of acquiring English as a second language and acquiring standard dialects as apolitical undertakings that are relatively easy if students are cognitively capable language learners.

It is hoped that this chapter will serve to advance the present theoretical debate concerning what constitutes academic discourses and how they are (mis) taught in schools, particularly to working-class linguistic-minority students.

References

Anderson, Elaine S. (1990). *Speaking with Style: The Sociolinguistic Skills of Children.* New York: Routledge Press.

Arias, M. B. (1986). "The Context of Education for Hispanic Students: An Overview." *American Journal of Education,* 95(1): 25–57.

Baral, D. (1977). *Academic Level Among Foreign-Born and Native-Born Mexican-American Students.* San Francisco: R & E Associates.

Carrasquillo, A. L. (1991). *Hispanic Children and Youth in the United States.* New York: Garland Publishing.

Collins, J., and S. Michaels (1986). "Speaking and Writing: Discourse Strategies and the Acquisition of Literacy." In J. Cook-Gumperz (ed.), *The Social Construction of Literacy.* New York: Cambridge University Press.

Cook-Gumperz, J., and J. J. Gumperz. (1981). "From Oral to Written Culture: The Transition to Literacy." In M. F. Whiteman (ed.), *Writing: The Nature, Development and Teaching of Written Communication,* vol. 1. New York: Cambridge University Press.

Cummins, J. (1979). "Linguistic Interdependence and the Educational Development of Bilingual Children." *Review of Educational Research,* 49(2): 222–251.

Cummins, J. (1982) "The Role of Primary Language Development in Promoting Educational Success for Language Minority Students." In California State Department of Education (ed.), *Schooling and Language Minority Students: A Theoretical Framework.* Los Angeles: California State University Evaluation, Dissemination, and Assessment Center.

Cummins, J. (1984a) "Wanted: A Theoretical Framework for Relating Language Proficiency to Academic Achievement Among Bilingual Students." In C. Rivera (ed.), *Language Proficiency and Academic Achievement.* Avon, England: Multilingual Matters.

Cummins, J. (1984b). *Bilingualism and Special Education: Issues in Assessment and Pedagogy.* San Diego, Calif.: College Hill Press.

Cummins, J. (1989). *Empowering Minority Students.* Sacramento: California Association for Bilingual Education.

Donaldson, M. (1978). *Children's Minds.* London: Fontana.

Gee, J. P. (1990) *Sociolinguistics and Literacies: Ideology in Discourses.* London: Falmer Press.

Gee, J. P. (1991) "What Is Literacy?" In C. Mitchell and K. Weiler (eds.), *Rewriting Literacy: Culture and the Discourse of the Other.* New York. Bergin and Garvey.

Gee, J. P. (1992). "Reading." *Journal of Urban and Cultural Studies,* 2(2): 65–77.

Kimball, W. L. (1986) "Parent and Family Influences on Academic Achievement Among Mexican-American Students." Ph.D. diss., University of California at Los Angeles.

Lanauze, M., and C. E. Snow. (1989). "The Relation Between First- and Second-Language Writing Skills: Evidence from Puerto Rican Elementary School Children in Bilingual Programs." *Linguistics and Education,* 1, pp. 323–339.

Macedo, D. (1994). *Literacies of Power: What Americans Are Not Allowed to Know.* Boulder: Westview Press.

McCollum, P. (1994). "Language Use in Two-Way Bilingual Programs." *Intercultural Development Research Association Newsletter,* 21(2): 1, 9–11.

Michaels, S. (1986) "Narrative Presentations: An Oral Preparation for Literacy with First Graders." In J. Cook Gumperz (ed.), *The Social Construction of Literacy.* New York: Cambridge University Press.

Michaels, S., and J. Collins. (1984). "Oral Discourse Styles: Classroom Interaction and the Acquisition of Literacy." In D. Tannen (ed.), *Coherence in Spoken and Written Discourse,* Norwood, N.J.: Ablex.

National Commission on Secondary Education for Hispanics (1984). *"Make Something Happen": Hispanics and Urban High School Reform,* vol. 1, *Report of the National Commission on Secondary Education for Hispanics.* New York: Hispanic Policy Development Project.

Ochoa, A. M. (1980). *Issues in Language Proficiency Assessment.* San Diego: Institute for Cultural Pluralism, College of Education, San Diego State University.

Ogbu, J. (1991). "Immigrant and Involuntary Minorities in Comparative Perspective." In M. Gibson and J. Ogbu (eds.), *Minority Status and Schooling: A Comparative Study of Immigrant and Involuntary Minorities.* New York: Garland Publishing.

Olson, D. T. (1977). "From Utterance to Text: the Bias of Language in Speech and Writing." *Harvard Educational Review,* 47(3): 257–281.

Pelligrini, A. D. (1984). *The Development of Oral and Written Language in Social Contexts.* Norwood, N. J.: Ablex.

Ricard, R. J., and E.C. Snow (1990). "Language Use in and out of Context: Evidence from Children's Picture Descriptions." *Journal of Applied Developmental Psychology,* 11(3): 251–266.

Rodino, A. M. (1992). "'Y. . . no puedo decir más na': The Maintenance of Native Language Skills by Working-Class Puerto Rican Children in Mainland Schools." Qualifying paper, Harvard Graduate School of Education, Cambridge, Mass., pp. 10–11.

Shannon, S. M. (1995). "Hegemony of English: A Case Study of One Bilingual Classroom as a Site of Resistance." *Linguistics and Education,* 7(3): 175–200.

Simons, H. D., and S. Murphy (1986). "Spoken Language Strategies and Reading Acquisition." In J. Cook-Gumperz (ed.), *The Social Construction of Literacy.* New York: Cambridge University Press.

Snow, C. E. (1990). "The Development of Definitional Skill." *Journal of Child Language,* 17(3): 697–710.

Snow, C. E., H. Cancino, P. Gonzales, and E. Shribero (1989). "Giving Formal Definitions: An Oral Language Correlate of School Literacy." In D. Bloome (ed.), *Classrooms and Literacy.* Norwood, N. J.: Ablex.

Snow, C. F. (1987). "Beyond Conversation: Second Language Listener's Acquisition of Description and Explanation." In J. P. Lantolf and A. Labarca (eds.), *Research on Second Language Acquisition: Focus on the Classroom.* Norwood, N.J.: Ablex.

Suárez-Orozco, C. and M. Suárez-Orozco (1995). *Trans-Formations: Immigration, Family Life, and Achievement Motivation Among Latino Adolescents.* Stanford: Stanford University Press.

Valencia, Richard (1991). *Chicano School Failure and Success: Research and Policy Agendas for the 1990s.* New York: Falmer Press.

Wu, H.F., J.M. De Temple, J.A. Herman, and C.E. Snow (1994) "L'Animal qui fait oink! Oink!': Bilingual Children's Oral and Written Picture Descriptions in English and French Under Varying Instructions." *Discourse Processes,* 18(2): 141–164.

Relating Paulo Freire's Life to His Understanding of Education, Culture, and Democracy

Ana Maria Araújo Freire

Having been invited to an event in the motherland of Socrates, Plato, and Aristotle to speak about another pedagogue—a philosopher of Brazilian education, educator Paulo Freire, certainly the greatest in our history—is to me a never-before-enjoyed honor. This conference is also providing me extraordinary joy as it offers me this space where I will say who this man is that I met as a child and whom, from a very early age, I have had as the object of my studies and concerns as an educator, as his wife and collaborator, in the last twenty years, and now, as a result of the will left by him, as his legal successor. Such is not, therefore, an ordinary sort of joy; it is a profound, legitimate, childlike joy—one he always experienced and never tired of speaking about—and, I must proclaim, one I feel I have been strongly experiencing for years now.

This childlike joy of mine, however, extends onto the responsibility of being in the motherland of philosophy and among philosophers, educators, and sociologists of the highest caliber and, additionally, authentically Freirean ones, to say a few things about a man who, while known worldwide, would say of himself, "I did a few things." I am happy, yes, because I am among many true friends of his, but friends who will not demand from me loyalty to him or to that friendship, but rather loyalty to Paulo Freire's anthropological, philosophical, political, ethical, and epistemological principles.

This lecture was delivered by Nita Freire at the International Conference on critical pedagogy at the University of Thessaly, Greece with the theme: Democracy, Education, and Culture in 2007.

Further, you shall certainly demand that I speak about his capacity for being human. You shall demand that I speak of how much he knew about loving all beings because he was outraged by injustices, how much he knew about smiling and being in good spirits because he was serious and responsible in the things he did and thought, how much he knew about conducting himself with the same dignity and respect toward a peasant or a wise man. In sum, what I propose, about which demands are certainly being made here and now, is to speak about Paulo Freire's humanness by talking about what formed him, his work, and his praxis.

Speaking about Paulo's life, therefore, goes beyond the telling of a simple chronological story about his presence among us. I must speak about a man who has been serving as an example of a critical understanding of education and of culture as tactics that make possible the concretization of the greater strategy of which he dreamed and for which he fought so: authentic, plural, and universal democracy.

There are, in the bowels of Paulo's writings, stemming from how he made himself a man and an educator, two fundamental instances in the formation of his being, of concerns that made him allow and feel the emotions that mobilized him to his ethical actions and reflections about his *what-to-do* among us, *in* and *with* the world. The first was a concern for perfecting his virtues, which had the Greek paidea as inspiration and model. The second is his Recifeaness, his way of being human, his *humanness* deeply ingrained in the reality and the way of being of his people.

Contradictorily, Paulo had, thus, this radically Recifean behavior, stuck in Northeastern misery, and was, at the same time, driven by the search for the ideals of the Greek arête, of educating virtues, even though in ancient Greece it was geared toward educating the aristocracy. Both those influences "drench," to use his term, his entire behavior and the whole of his educational theory. Different as those realities are in space and time, they converge in a humanness of millennial ancestrality and in that more historically recent, experiential time, both of which left their mark on his body and his mind. They came to form into an unbreakable unity in the search for "making men and women better, for improving them, making them more virtuous." That was the path Paulo intentionally sought, with epistemological curiosity and with true emotions toward the concretization of *democracy* through *education* and *culture*.

Paulo understood that virtues are born *with* individuals—not simply tendencies or genetics—and they can be confirmed or negated by the type of education received and by the social context in which a person grows from childhood to adolescence and adulthood. Paulo was born with tendencies toward having the most important and noble virtues, which were gradually perfected, deliberately and intentionally so, by him in himself because the family environment where he grew up and the opportunities available socially made that possible. Among those, to my joy, were also the ones my parents opened up. On a humanist basis, they provided his schooling, without which Paulo would not have gotten to where he did. His life story forged within him a strong and magnanimous character.

Tolerance is, in Paulo, a virtue of human coexistence. "Genuine tolerance [. . .] does not require that I agree with this or that individual whom I tolerate, nor does it ask that I hold him or her in esteem. What authentic tolerance demands from me is that I *respect* the different, their dreams, their ideas, their choices, their tastes, and that I not negate them solely for being different. What legitimate tolerance winds up teaching is that, through experiencing the different, I learn from the different." He would later say, "I can learn even from my antagonist if I open myself up, with humility, to experiencing authentic tolerance."

Patience alone leads us to eternal waiting, a vain wait. Impatience alone leads us to despair and hasty actions. The dialectics between one and the other enables a balance between them that determines the possibility of acting with prudence and efficiency. The educative process, we know, does not take place in a small span of time, so we must be patient in the act of educating. But patience would not lead individuals to seek mastery of the knowledge and the behaviors that characterize us as human beings if we remained in eternal patience. We need impatience to mobilize us, side by side with patience as the limit of impatience. Lovingness has the following connotations in his educative theory: The educator must create an affective atmosphere of disquiet in the classroom, one that conduces students to the search for knowledge with joy, in cooperation, and without competition, one that encourages the adventure of creating and re-creating, with epistemological *curiosity* and scientific rigorousness; *educators* necessarily *have* to love the exercise of the educative act; and finally, they must like what they teach (the school's programmatic content). Lovingness does not mean, in Paulo's theory, the obligation to equally love all of our students but to respect them and to care for them equitably.

Authentic humility, which has nothing to do with humiliation, is the virtue that reinforces and reaffirms tolerance and lovingness. It is acceptance of the difficulties of life, as well as the successes one may attain, without whiningly pitying oneself and without making a fuss over one's victories. Authentic humility implies a gentle manner of being that negates pretentiousness and the belief that one is an all-knowing Being who, thus, learns from no one. The arrogance of the nonhumble educator would reduce, if that were possible, the learning-teaching exchange to the reductionism of only teaching, of only one knowing while assuming the ignorance of the other. Paulo treated his humility, especially after the publication of his book *Pedagogy of the Oppressed* around the world, when more and more people would come to him to say, "Professor, your work is genius, masterful. . . . It has changed my life." As he would tell me this, Paulo would comment, "If I had not treated my humility, I would have lost myself. . . . I would have lost my ontological address, the purpose toward which I had written that book."

The greatest example of Paulo's humility was his insistence that he not be repeated or followed but rather re-created. Should some wish to, they might take him as a reference, but he asked that they not "stop at" him, that they depart from him toward the fascinating world of creation and re-creation, as he never thought he had said or done it all.

Generosity: Paulo said little about it. He practiced it throughout his life. He was generous as he showed solidarity toward the pains, tribulations, and the trials of the dispossessed, the vilipended, without having ever shown hostility toward any person of a privileged social class. My husband always held an unshakable belief in the worth of men and women and, consequently, never used to point out others' flaws. He would simply *and generously* say, "A person who has more frailty than grandness." Although many had abused his generosity, he never did say, "I regret being this way!" Paulo was profoundly generous and humble in offering up both his possessions and his manuscripts—and with equal love and respect, everything he thought—to someone who wanted to put in practice his ideas or to re-create him.

Coherence was one of Paulo's greatest concerns with respect to his behavior. He sought to be coherent with what he observed, apprehended, understood, thought, systematized, and wrote in his works and what he practiced in day-to-day life. He would warn us, nonetheless, that there is no absolute coherence and that if it did exist, the world would be monotonous and bland; he would say so *in scientific truth*, but "*jokingly*" at the same time, so as to justify his own slips.

Paulo constantly believed in the act of listening. He always listened to everything, from everybody, all the way to the end, and only then would he *say his word*, oftentimes softly touching the other's shoulder in a welcoming gesture that encouraged the one speaking to continue his or her discourse. Paulo always listened, which to me is more than hearing: It is to let the other speak, to take what has been heard to reason and to the heart, to re-elaborate what is heard, systematize it, and give it back in a more elaborate manner to the speaker. Only the wise know how to do that!

The virtues which Paulo fought so hard to have and which he understood as necessary to the progressive educator—and to all people—include those described above as well as many others, which are requirements, I must emphasize, for the building of democracy, rather than simply for the act of educating and for being a conscious and engaged citizen.

Paulo and his theory of knowledge, which he himself preferred to humbly call "a certain critical understanding of education" is, thus, characterized by containing an attitude toward life aimed at respecting and dignifying all life, at the possibility of liberation and autonomy for historic beings. Created from the starting point of his feelings, his emotions, and his intuitions, informed by his attention to obviousness and to his Recifean experiences, and developed through reflections induced by his reading of countless philosophers, sociologists, educators, and anthropologists (ranging from Greek antiquity all the way to modernity and postmodernity), his theory has always been at the service of the oppressed and the excluded.

I mean to say that Paulo's theory is the fruit born from the realization of generalized poverty conditions and from the misery and trials caused by them, side by side with profound reflections elaborated in a genuine manner and engaged in favor of dispossessed men and women of all stripes, those exploited by the olden "lords of lands and of slaves," at the time, sugar producers. Today, the entire white elite of the country, equally discriminatory and authoritarian, has joined them.

When Paulo quit teaching secondary school in Recife and became an educator with Serviço Social da Indústria (SESI), he lived once again near the people—working people. It was a different relationship than the one he had experienced during his childhood and youth with the poor kids in Jaboatão. It was with those men and women, through "listening to them," that he profoundly understood differences of class and the injustices secularly committed by the Brazilian elite against the poor and black men and women, from whom it also robbed of the right to know how to read and write—*it made them illiterate.*

Without fears or trepidations about accusations of being "romantic" or a "third-world intellectual" because he started out from the obvious, from conventional wisdom, and *from intuition,* Paulo antagonized what was being done at that *historical* moment and created a philosophy of education originating from the real, the concrete, the day-to-day. He allowed his *conscious body*—the one that warns us that "here there is something to think through"—to lead him to reflexive thinking, the right thinking. That is, he allowed himself to think from the starting point of practice, to reflect upon that practice, and return to it in an uninterrupted practice-theory-practice movement—making science and fighting for democratic freedoms. His goal was to establish democracy in Brazil.

Hope is, in Paulo, more than a state of being or just a theological virtue. To him, hope surpasses those concepts; it is the result of our nonconclusion, of the incompleteness of human existence. It is, thus, part of our ontological nature. Human hope exists irrespective of whether the members of the human species so desire or not. Contradictorily, *hope* could not exist without those moments of despair, which when experienced in depth remake the previous phase of hope in a different manner. The possibility of education is born from our incompleteness. In other words, education is required in order that we may constitute ourselves into beings of a human existence, a means for overcoming simple animal life. Hope is, thus, an ontological human quality that warrants education. Despair is the moment contradictory to hope, which dialectically affirms hope as such.

Thusly understanding why we are capable of being educated, Paulo coupled his experiences and reflections with a praxis of solidarity, of complicity, and of engagement, one whose starting point was the relationship he maintained with rural workers and other laborers in Pernambuco, *always bearing in mind the virtues valued in ancient Greece and that he cultivated in himself.* He established, this way, the parameters for a new education and a new ethic.

Critical education: a problematizing, questioning, liberating education. *Life ethic:* one that negates the ethic of discourse and comes before the ethic of market. The former is the substratum and requirement of democracy, while the latter, a negation of the former, makes democracy unviable as it is rooted in disregard for life.

A market ethic is what provides support for neoliberal thinking and for economic globalization, both from which it dialectically emerges. Such "ethic" has, under the tutelage of the countries that created it for their own benefit, destroyed lives and pushed into misery a large portion of the population in Latin America, *some individuals* in rich countries, and almost the entire African population. It has fostered war and genocide, *plain-word* illiteracy, and diseases resulting from hunger and promiscuity. It has encouraged pedophilia, whether physical or virtual, child prostitution, and all sorts of conflict, making for unbridled exploitation of national resources and of the peoples considered weaker, all the while using competition, intolerance, and xenophobic egotism for its scale gauge. Meanness, Paulo used to call it. Therefore, neither such "ethic," nor a conservative education maintained at its service, can provide the political and ethical matrices needed for the building of democracy.

The intent to fight against such state of affairs has been terrorism, which, equally fundamentalist, has been disseminated throughout the world, especially since September 11, 2001, terrorizing and violently killing children, women, and men. The post-world-war dream of "golden years" and the fall of the Berlin Wall, unfortunately and against the ontological address of human beings, turned into the policy of those who dictate the orders as to what is to be done or not, whether there is food or not, whether there is rest or not, whether there is death from AIDS or not.

In short, a market ethic, in which money and disloyalty are the gods, in which death negates life, is one that promotes the following idea: The less that other men and women know, can, and have—whether in material possessions or utopian dreams—the better it is for those who *conquer*, invade, manipulate, order, domesticate, oppress, and exploit their brothers and sisters. Such market ethic can only benefit the imperialist countries and the men and women who forged it. It is the antithesis of what the rule of law in the democratic state requires.

It was against this order of things, certainly "softened," compared to today, in the second half of the last century under the power of the so-called "capitalist imperialism," that Paulo intuitively started to develop, still in adolescence, his ethical-political concerns. He asked himself, "What world is this?" He started to develop a particular certainty that the path to overcoming would be that of education through conscientization dialogue with those who "know nothing."

They were the rural laborers of the sugar industry and the factory workers of the Mocambos zone of Recife, with whom Paulo established such dialogue and from whom he learned, through their pains, joys, desires, and their frustrated dreams, from their condition as "dismissed from life." There, he created the strength and lucidity to fight in favor of the oppressed, the excluded, the marginalized, through an education in favor of humanization, of autonomy, and of liberation for all men and women without exception, irrespective of race, ethnicity, religion, age, gender, sexual orientation, or social class.

Paulo came to understand, from his experience with and analysis of that centennial situation of exploitation in Brazil, that in order to transform society, the only path to take was that of education. He started out from the principle that education is not the engine of social change, that education alone cannot change society, but that without it society cannot be transformed either. He had the conviction that he would have to start with the literacy education of those who had been forbidden from reading and writing, those "deserted by fate." And he wanted to make possible the educative process, for we are beings who know and who know that we can know more.

His adult literacy education practice in the '50s and '60s—initially in Recife and subsequently through the Northeast all the way to the National Literacy Program (Programa Nacional de Alfabetização; PNA)—started out by working through the *anthropological concept of culture*. The "Paulo Freire Literacy Method"—I want to emphasize this and make it very clear: The "method" starts out from his understanding of education and is made possible by it; it is a part of a whole—had as its origin and ultimate end the conscientization that would enable the emergence of the popular classes. Conscientization, thus, intended to get them to understand that they had been "living in the *shadows*"; that is, they could not read or write, not for any fault of their own but due to the historic construction of Brazil, which left them in the marginal situation in which they lived in society. They were forbidden from being, dehumanized as mere objects of manipulation. They were subjugated and subtracted from the ontological right to read and write the word. As a result of that "education as the practice of freedom," Paulo paid a price, after the coup d'état of April 1, 1964, and was exiled for almost 16 years.

Thusly, before teaching the reading and writing of the word, the Culture Circle facilitators, oriented by Paulo and his monitors, brought the literacy learners to an understanding, through conscientization, of the historical, political, economic, and social reality of Brazil, in order to help them out of their condition as *"dismissed from life"* and into becoming participants in society. Contrary to what they believed, they should have felt like builders of our national culture, which indeed they were.

At the Cultural Extension Service of the University of Recife, today the Federal University of Pernambuco, Paulo discussed *culture* as everything we do with what we were given, that is, nature. The initial and fundamental question was: If we change the nature God has given us as we turn mud into bricks to build our houses, then, why not change those things we, men and women, have invented? How about the level of knowing we are at now? By apprehending and realizing that we can change "what God has given us," the people who did not know how to read or write the word were encouraged to overcome the condition of being immersed in "the world of darkness" and to open up possibilities for realizing that they could make themselves literate and participate in the decisions of their private lives and of public life, as the artificers and producers of *culture* that they indeed were. They came to understand that things can, and many times must, be changed, transformed.

By dreaming the dreams possible and by realizing them, showing us always that "changing is difficult, but it is possible," doing as much as possible today to achieve tomorrow what is impossible today, Paulo made himself into an educator-political (as he viewed himself in the final years of his life), rather than a political educator (as he is viewed). He refused to understand education as a purely pedagogical act without emphasis on its political and ethical-aesthetic natures. For Paulo, politics, ethics, and aesthetics are intrinsic to education, and education is a cultural factor and a promoter of *culture.*

In closing, I would like to thank you for this opportunity, and I hope to have demonstrated the relationship between a "more egalitarian, beautiful, serious, and just society, that is, a democratic society" and my husband's understanding of liberating education, based on culture. I wish to end this talk by dedicating *one sole* paragraph to his profile: an extremely sensual, affable, cordial, and complicit man; a joyful, tender, and intelligent one; a lover of soccer, Brazilian music, and cachaça; a soft-spoken man of careful steps with his gray hair to the wind; a loyal companion; a man of dialogue rather than orders or prescriptions, devoid of macho chauvinisms; a generous, fascinating, small-bodied man. His eyes were the color of honey and projected a fascinating gaze that came from the very core of his being. He appreciated touching others with tenderness and being touched by them, without fear or guilt, but with energy and affection. He was jealous, very jealous of me. He liked the aroma of wet earth, of warm ocean waters, and the traditional foods from the Brazilian Northeast. He was a man who, above all, knew how to love without restrictions and who thoroughly enjoyed being and feeling loved.

This is my testimony about my husband, educator Paulo Freire. Thank you very much.

About the Authors

STANLEY ARONOWITZ is professor of sociology, cultural studies, and urban education at the CUNY Graduate Center. He is also a veteran political activist and cultural critic and an advocate for organized labor. He is the author of numerous books on class, culture, and sociology of science and politics.

ELEFTERIA BALOMENOS is an art historian and art teacher with a specialization in critical aesthetics. She is also an illustrator of children's books and has published in the area of cultural studies, visual arts, and critical pedagogy. She has taught in Canada and in Greece.

LILIA I. BARTOLOMÉ is associate professor at the Graduate College of Education at the University of Massachusetts Boston. She previously taught at the Harvard Graduate School of Education and San Diego State University. As a teacher educator, her research interests include the preparation of effective teachers of second-language learners in multicultural contexts. Her recent publications include "Critical Pedagogy and Teacher Education: Radicalizing Prospective Teachers" in the *Journal of Teacher Education* and "Democratizing Latino Education: A Perspective on Elementary Education" in *Latino Students in American Schools*. In addition, she has published *The Misteaching of Academic Discourses: The Politics of Language in the Classroom*; *Immigrant Voices: In Search of Pedagogical Equity* (co-editor and chapter co-author with Henry Trueba); and *Dancing with Bigotry* (co-author with Donaldo Macedo).

CORNELIUS CASTORIADIS (1922–1997) was a Greek philosopher, economist, psychoanalyst, author of *The Imaginary Institution of Society*, cofounder of the Socialisme ou Barbarie group, and philosopher of autonomy. His work is extensive, and he is regarded as one of the major thinkers of the twentieth century.

AVRAM NOAM CHOMSKY is an American linguist, philosopher, cognitive scientist, and political activist. He is an institute professor and professor emeritus of linguistics at the Massachusetts Institute of Technology. Chomsky is well known in the academic and scientific community as one of the fathers of modern linguistics and a major figure of analytic philosophy. Since the 1960s, he has become known more widely as a political dissident and an anarchist, referring to himself as a libertarian socialist. Chomsky is the author of more than 150 books and has received worldwide attention for his views, despite being typically absent from the mainstream media. He is also considered a prominent cultural figure, while his status as a leading critic of U.S. foreign policy has made him significant.

ANTÓNIA DARDER is an internationally recognized critical scholar and a distinguished professor of Education at the University of Illinois, Urbana Champaign. Dr. Darder is the author of *Culture and Power in the Classroom* and *Reinventing Paulo Freire: A Pedagogy of Love* and co-author with Rodolfo Torres of *After Race: Racism After Multiculturalism*. She is editor of *Culture and Difference* and co-editor of *Latinos and Education*, *The Latino Studies Reader: Culture, Economy and Society*, and *The Critical Pedagogy Reader* (Routledge, 2002/2008). As a former scholar of the Tomas Rivera Policy Institute, she authored the report *The Policies and the Promise: The Public Schooling of Latino Children* (1993).

TAKIS FOTOPOULOS is a political philosopher and editor, since 1992, of the international theoretical journal *Society & Nature* (now known as *Democracy and Nature: The International Journal of Inclusive Democracy*). He is also a columnist for the Athens Daily *Eleftherotypia*. He was previously (1969–1989) senior lecturer in Economics at the University of North London. He is the author of *Towards an Inclusive Democracy* (London & New York: Cassell/Continuum, 1997)—which has been translated into French, German, Spanish, Italian, Greek, and Chinese—and the books *The Multidimensional Crisis and Inclusive Democracy* (2005) and *The Pink Revolution in Iran and the "Left"* (2009), published by *The International Journal of Inclusive Democracy*. He has also contributed to several books in English, Italian, Chinese, Polish, and Greek. In addition, he is the author of numerous books in Greek on development; the Gulf War; the neoliberal consensus; the New World Order; the drug culture; the New Order in the Balkans; the new irrationalism; globalization and the Left; the war against "terrorism"; Chomsky's capitalism and Albert's metacapitalism; the present multidimensional crisis; inclusive democracy 10 years after; the present capitalist crisis and the antisystemic movement; and of a forthcoming book on Greece as a protectorate of the transnational elite (2010). He is also the author of more than 800 articles in British, American, and Greek theoretical journals, magazines and newspapers, several of which have been translated into more than 20 languages (see http://www.inclusivedemocracy.org/fotopoulos/).

ANA MARIA ARAÚJO FREIRE—Nita—was born on November 13, 1933. For decades, she had been dedicated to studying Brazilian Education History, focusing her research on the historical conditions linked to the production of illiteracy. She holds Master's and Doctoral degrees in education from the Catholic University of São Paulo. Nita and Paulo first met in 1937, when he started attending the school owned by her father. In 1942, he became a teacher of Portuguese at the same school. Both widowed they were married in 1988. Currently Nita is engaged in the creation of the "Living Paulo Freire Movement" and in deepening her studies about knowledge theory according to the great educator.

PAULO REGLUS NEVES FREIRE (1921–1997) is one of the 20th century's most heralded educators. Born in Recife, a city for which he continued to have a great passion throughout his life, Freire captured the imagination of many people in Brazil with his innovative approach to education. It was an approach that enabled people to "read the word and the world." His thinking is radical and postcolonial; his approach to education is one that stresses the politics of knowledge throughout. Despite his constant advocacy of democratic social relations of education, he always affirmed the directive nature of socially transformative education, centering around the notion of praxis, in which the educator has authority that, nevertheless, should not degenerate into authoritarianism. He has produced an extensive body of work on issues of education and social justice.

HENRY GIROUX, born September 18, 1943 in Providence, is a U.S. cultural critic. He is one of the founding theorists of critical pedagogy in the United States and is best known for his pioneering work in public pedagogy, cultural studies, youth studies, higher education, media studies, and critical theory. Giroux has published more than 35 books and 300 academic articles and is published widely throughout education and cultural studies literature. Routledge named Giroux in 2002 as one of the top 50 educational thinkers of the modern period.

JOE LYONS KINCHELOE (1950–2008) was a professor and Canada Research Chair at the Faculty of Education, McGill University in Montreal, Quebec, Canada. He wrote more than 45 books, numerous book chapters, and hundreds of journal articles on issues including critical pedagogy, educational research, urban studies, cognition, curriculum, and cultural studies. Kincheloe received three graduate degrees from the University of Tennessee. The father of four children, he worked closely for the last 19 years of his life with his partner, Shirley Steinberg.

VIVIAN GARCÍA LÓPEZ is a member of the Pascua Yaqui Tribe, originally from Tucson, Arizona, where her lived-realities along the U.S.-Mexico border as a multicultural *being* have made a difference in the unfolding of her identity and contribution to her teaching and service that fosters real educational alternatives, particularly for disenfranchised communities. Lopéz worked as an assistant professor in the Department of Bilingual Education at Boise State University before accepting the Director of Education position with the Pascua Yaqui Tribe. She earned a PhD in Curriculum and Instruction with a specialization in Literacy, Language and Culture and a minor in Bilingual Education from New Mexico State University in July 2008. Lopéz has more than 25 years of experience in education, which includes early childhood, K-12 education, special education, community college, and universities. She locates educational equity and social justice issues central to her cultural and interdisciplinary pedagogical approaches in education, which are influenced by indigenous notions of how individuals make meaning in their lives.

DONALDO MACEDO is a full professor of English and a Distinguished Professor of Liberal Arts and Education at the University of Massachusetts Boston. He is the Graduate Program Director of the Applied Linguistics Master's of Arts Program at the University of Massachusetts Boston. He has published extensively in the areas of linguistics, critical literacy, and bilingual and multicultural education. His publications include: *Literacy: Reading the Word and the World* (with Paulo Freire, 1987), *Literacies of Power: What Americans Are Not Allowed to Know* (1994), *Dancing with Bigotry* (with Lilia Bartolomé, 1999), *Critical Education in the New Information Age* (with Paulo Freire, Henry Giroux, and Paul Willis, 1999), *Chomsky on Miseducation* (with Noam Chomsky, 2000), and *Ideology Matters* (co-authored with Paulo Freire, 2002).

PETER MCLAREN, after earning his doctorate in 1983, served as special lecturer in Education at Brock University, where he specialized in inner-city education and language arts. McLaren left Canada in 1985 to teach at Miami University of Ohio's School of Education and Allied Professions, where he spent eight years working with colleague Henry Giroux during a time when the epistemology known as critical pedagogy was gaining traction in North American schools of education. McLaren also served as Director of the Center for Education and Cultural Studies and held the title of Renowned Scholar-in-Residence at Miami University before being recruited by the Graduate School of Education and Information Studies, University of California, Los Angeles, in 1993. McLaren is the author, co-author, editor, and co-editor of approximately 40 books and monographs. Several hundred of his articles, chapters, interviews, reviews, commentaries, and columns have appeared in dozens of scholarly journals and professional magazines worldwide.

MARIA NIKOLAKAKI is assistant professor of Pedagogy and Education at the University of Peloponnese. After she studied primary and preschool education, postgraduate studies on comparative education and earned a PhD in curriculum and teaching at the University of Athens, she was granted scholarships and completed a postdoctorate at the University of London and another at the University of Athens. She was honorary fellow at the University of Wisconsin, Madison. Nikolakaki has published extensively in the areas of neoliberalism and critical pedagogy, mathematics education, citizenship education, and lifelong learning. Her publications include the books: *The Modernization of Mathematics Education in Greek Primary Schools; The Myth and the Reality of Greek Education: Cross-curricularity and Collaborative Teaching in Schools; Critical perspectives in educational policy: The changing terrain of knowledge and power; Globalization, Technology and Paideia in the New Cosmpolis* (Ed.); *Towards a School for All: Cross-curricularity and Inclusion in Greek Primary Schools* (Ed); *Education of the Preschool Age.*

SHIRLEY R. STEINBERG is the Director and Chair of the Werklund Foundation Centre for Youth Leadership in Education, and Professor of Youth Studies at the University of Calgary. Her most recent books include: *Critical Qualitative Research Reader* (2012); *Kinderculture: The Corporate Construction of Childhood* (2011); *19 Urban Questions: Teaching in the City* (2010); *Christotainment: Selling Jesus Through Popular Culture* (2009); *Diversity and Multiculturalism: A Reader* (2009); *Media Literacy: A Reader* (2007); the award winning *Contemporary Youth Culture: An International Encyclopedia*; and *The Miseducation of the West: How Schools and Media Distort Our Understanding of the Islamic World* (2004). She is an Academic Affiliate of Chapman University's Paulo Freire Social Justice Project and was a research professor at the University of Barcelona in 2010. Originally a social/improvisational theatre creator, she has facilitated happenings and flashmobs globally. A regular contributor to CBC Radio One, CTV, *The Toronto Globe and Mail, The Montreal Gazette*, and the Canadian pPress, she is an internationally known speaker and teacher. She is also the founding editor of *Taboo: The Journal of Culture and Education, The International Journal of Youth Studies,* and the Managing Editor of *The International Journal of Critical Pedagogy.*

PETER TRIFONAS teaches in both preservice teacher education and graduate programs at the University of Toronto (OISE/UT). His graduate courses include "Foundation of Curriculum" (offered online) and "Technology and Education." His areas of interest and scholarly accomplishments extend to ethics, philosophy of education, literacy, media, technology, and curriculum. Professor Trifonas's most recent published works include: "The Ethics of Writing: Derrida, Deconstruction, and Pedagogy"; "Ethics, Institutions, and the Right to Philosophy" (with Jacques Derrida); "Barthes and the Empire of the Signs"; "Umberto Eco, and Football, Revolutionary Pedagogies" (edited); and "Pedagogies of Difference" (edited).

HOWARD ZINN (1922–2010) was an American historian, author, left-wing activist, playwright, intellectual, and professor of Political Science at Boston University from 1964 to 1988. He wrote more than 20 books, which included his bestselling and influential work *A People's History of the United States*. Zinn wrote extensively about civil rights, civil liberties, and antiwar movements. His memoir *You Can't Be Neutral on a Moving Train* was also the title of a 2004 documentary about Zinn's life and work.

SLAVOJ ŽIŽEK was born on March 21, 1949 in Ljubljana, Slovenia. He holds a Bachelor of Arts (philosophy and sociology, 1971), Master of Arts (philosophy, 1975), and Doctor of Arts (philosophy, 1981) from the Department of Philosophy, Faculty of Arts, Ljubljana; Doctor of Arts (psychoanalysis, 1985) from the Universite Paris-VIII; and Doctor Causa Honoris from the University of Cordoba, Argentina (2005). In 2002 he became senior researcher at the Department of Philosophy, University of Ljubljana. He was a researcher from 1979 to 2001 at the Institute for Sociology and Philosophy, University of Ljubljana and, from 1992, at the Institute for Social Sciences, Faculty for Social Sciences. In 2005, he became a codirector at the International Center for Humanities, Birkbeck College, University of London. Politically active in the alternative movement in Slovenia during the 1980s, Zizek ran for president of the Republic of Slovenia in the first multiparty elections in 1990 and served as Ambassador of Science of the Republic of Slovenia (1991). In the last 20 years, he has published 20 books in English, which were translated into all major world languages (Spanish, French, German, Portuguese, Italian, Japanese, Korean, Chinese, Russian). The main works are: *The Sublime Object of Ideology* (1989), *Tarrying with the Negative* (1993), *The Plague of Fantasies* (1997), *The Ticklish Subject* (1999), *The Fragile Absolute* (2000), *The Puppet and the Dwarf* (2004), *The Parallax View* (2006).

Studies in the Postmodern Theory of Education

General Editor
Shirley R. Steinberg

Counterpoints publishes the most compelling and imaginative books being written in education today. Grounded on the theoretical advances in criticalism, feminism, and postmodernism in the last two decades of the twentieth century, Counterpoints engages the meaning of these innovations in various forms of educational expression. Committed to the proposition that theoretical literature should be accessible to a variety of audiences, the series insists that its authors avoid esoteric and jargonistic languages that transform educational scholarship into an elite discourse for the initiated. Scholarly work matters only to the degree it affects consciousness and practice at multiple sites. Counterpoints' editorial policy is based on these principles and the ability of scholars to break new ground, to open new conversations, to go where educators have never gone before.

For additional information about this series or for the submission of manuscripts, please contact:

Shirley R. Steinberg
c/o Peter Lang Publishing, Inc.
29 Broadway, 18th floor
New York, New York 10006

To order other books in this series, please contact our Customer Service Department:

(800) 770-LANG (within the U.S.)
(212) 647-7706 (outside the U.S.)
(212) 647-7707 FAX

Or browse online by series:
www.peterlang.com